# Red Flags:
## A Lawyer's Handbook
## On Legal Ethics

# American Law Institute
# American Bar Association
## Committee on Continuing Professional Education

*Chair*
Michael Traynor   San Francisco   California
*President, The American Law Institute*

*Vice Chair*
Robert J. Grey, Jr.   Richmond   Virginia
*President, The American Bar Association*

| | | |
|---|---|---|
| Edward R. Becker | Philadelphia | Pennsylvania |
| Tom Bolt | St. Thomas | Virgin Islands |
| Bennett Boskey | Washington | District of Columbia |
| Timothy W. Bouch | Charleston | South Carolina |
| Paul J. Bschorr | New York | New York |
| Michael E. Flowers | Columbus | Ohio |
| Michael S. Greco | Boston | Massachusetts |
| Phoebe A. Haddon | Philadelphia | Pennsylvania |
| Allen K. Harris | Oklahoma City | Oklahoma |
| Kay H. Hodge | Boston | Massachusetts |
| Lynn A. Howell | St. Pete Beach | Florida |
| Theodore A. Kolb | San Francisco | California |
| Lance Liebman | New York | New York |
| Terence F. MacCarthy | Chicago | Illinois |
| Susan R. Martyn | Toledo | Ohio |
| Roderick B. Mathews | Richmond | Virginia |
| John J. McKetta, III | Austin | Texas |
| John H. Morrison | Evanston | Illinois |
| James R. Myers | Washington | District of Columbia |
| Joseph J. Ortego | Garden City | New York |
| Sherwin P. Simmons | Miami | Florida |
| Herbert S. Wander | Chicago | Illinois |
| Mervin M. Wilf | Philadelphia | Pennsylvania and |
| | Cambridge | Massachusetts |
| Stephen N. Zack | Miami | Florida |

*ABA Young Lawyers Division Liaison*
Tracie R. Porter   Chicago   Illinois

*ABA Law Student Division Liaison*
Shondra Longino   Ada   Ohio

---

As of April 2005

*Executive Director:* Richard E. Carter
  *Executive Assistant:* Donna K. Maropis
*Deputy Executive Director:* Lawrence F. Meehan
  *Administrative Assistant:* Norma Realphe

OFFICE OF COURSES OF STUDY
*Director:* Alexander Hart
  *Senior Assistant Director:* Kevin J. O'Connor
  *Assistant Directors:* Thomas M. Hennessey;
    William S. Stevens
  *Administrative Assistant:* Suzanne E. McCarthy
  *Course Assistants:* Jan McCarver;
    Pamela McC. DeLarge; Charlotte Rice

OFFICE OF ELECTRONIC AND PRINT PUBLICATIONS
*Director:* Mark T. Carroll
  *Assistant Directors:* Joseph L. DiPietro;
    John B. Spitzer
  *Editorial Assistant:* Susan Hader-Golden

OFFICE OF RESEARCH AND DEVELOPMENT
*Director:* Leslie A. Belasco
  *Senior Assistant Director:* Nancy A. Kane
  *Assistant Director:* Michelle H. Shapiro
  *Administrative Assistant:* Crystal Finch

OFFICE OF AUDIO AND VIDEO LAW REVIEWS
*Director:* Susan L. Tomita
  *Video Production Manager:* Matt Yaple
  *Audio Editor:* Mary Ann Robinson
  *Senior Administrative Assistant:* Linda Smith

AMERICAN LAW NETWORK
*Director:* Lawrence F. Meehan
  *Assistant Director:* Amy Danziger Shapiro
  *Administrative Assistant:* Ruth D. Johnson

ALI-ABA IN-HOUSE
*Director:* Howard B. Klein

OFFICE OF ADMINISTRATIVE SERVICES
*Director:* Joseph Mendicino
  *Assistant Directors:* Stephen Dushkowich;
    John J. Latch
  *Assistant Director, D2D Webmaster:* John V. Ceci
  *Webmaster:* Mark Ermel
  *Database Administrator:* Teri Y. Broadnax
  *PC Specialist:* Marykay Hamilton
  *Administrative Assistant:* Margaret Arndt

SERVICE DEPARTMENTS
*Accounting*
  *Director:* William J. McCormick
    *Accounting Supervisor:* Debra Foley
    *Accountant:* Hong Lu
  *Customer Service Director:* Patricia Hunt
    *Customer Service Supervisor:* John P. Delaney III
  *Human Resources Director:* Diane E. Schnitzer
    *Administrative Assistant:* Norma Realphe
  *Librarian:* Harry Kyriakodis
  *Meetings and Travel*
    *Director:* Kathleen C. Peters
  *Production and Design*
    *Director:* Herb Powell
    *Production Supervisor:* Linda J. Clemens
    *Designer:* Matthew Born
    *Design Assistants:* Catherine Lhulier;
      Rei Murakami
  *Professional Education Representative:*
    Frank Paul Tomasello
  *Professional Relations and Marketing*
    *Director:* Kathleen H. Lawner
    *Assistant Director:* Sarah R. Ausprich
    *Administrative Assistant:* Annette English

4025 Chestnut Street, Philadelphia, Pennsylvania 19104-3099 • www.ali-aba.org

# Related ALI-ABA Publications

**Achieving Excellence in the Practice of Law: The Lawyer's Guide, Second Edition** Paperbound; 496 pages (2000). $106.
www.ali-aba.org/aliaba/rbk01.htm

**Skills and Ethics in the Practice of Law: Law School Edition**
Paperbound, 168 pages (2000). $33.
www.ali-aba.org/aliaba/RBK04.htm

**From Law School To Law Practice: The New Associate's Guide, Second Edition**
*Suzanne B. O'Neill and Catherine Gerhauser Sparkman*
Softbound; 298 pages (1998). $51.
www.ali-aba.org/aliaba/B765.asp

To order any of these titles, or to find out more about ALI-ABA products, call 1-800-CLE-NEWS and ask for customer service, or visit our Web site at **www.ali-aba.org**.

# Red Flags:
# A Lawyer's Handbook
# On Legal Ethics

**Lawrence J. Fox**
Partner
Drinker Biddle & Reath, LLP

**Susan R. Martyn**
Stoepler Professor of Law and Values
University of Toledo College of Law

American Law Institute-American Bar Association
Committee on Continuing Professional Education
4025 Chestnut Street, Philadelphia, PA 19104-3099

www.ali-aba.org

Library of Congress Catalog Control Number: 2005924979

© 2005 by Lawrence J. Fox and Susan R. Martyn

All rights reserved

Printed in the United States of America

ISBN: 978-08318-0862-4

Mark T. Carroll of the ALI-ABA staff edited this book.

The views and conclusions expressed herein are those of the authors and not necessarily those of American Law Institute-American Bar Association Continuing Professional Education or its sponsors.

# Dedication

To Elainne Fox, who raised three lawyers and, though not a lawyer herself, still remains our family's most effective advocate.

To Peter, Angela, and Sarah, the ethics advisors in my life.

# Foreword

As Lawrence Fox and Susan Martyn point out in this book, much of a lawyer's ethical and professional responsibility can be reduced to the "4 C's": Communication, Competence, Confidentiality, and Conflicts of interest. If you think that sounds simple, you're right—it does *sound* simple. In practice, of course, it's much more complicated.

Complicated...but necessary for the busy practitioner to comprehend? Absolutely, and that is where *Red Flags: A Lawyer's Handbook On Legal Ethics* really shines. For rather than marching theoretically through the various rules of professional conduct, this book approaches ethics from the practitioner's perspective. Can I represent the husband and wife in a will or a divorce? What do I do with that mistakenly sent email that lays out the opposition's plans? Was I right to tell that guy at the cocktail party last night to forget a malpractice action against his doctor? Do I tell the sentencing judge about my client's prior convictions when they are missing from the judge's paperwork?

The authors begin by helping you to identify your client and establish your right to the proper fees for your hard work. They then spend a chapter each describing, in practical terms with numerous real-world examples, how to communicate with clients, how to represent them competently, how to retain their confidences, and how to avoid conflicts of interest while representing them. They follow up with those crucial situations in which you must say "no" (to clients, but also to others), as well as the remedies against violations of the rules. The last two chapters cover how to research ethics questions, and whom to turn to when you need help figuring out the tougher ethical dilemmas.

Mr. Fox and Professor Martyn have spent many years advising on, lecturing about, and living through the issues generated by the rules governing lawyers' professional responsibility and ethics. ALI-ABA thanks them for sharing their knowledge and experience with the bar at large.

MARK T. CARROLL
*Director, Office of Electronic and Print Publications*
ALI-ABA Continuing Professional Education

March 2005

# Preface

## The Book

This book is specifically designed to help the busy practicing lawyer. While we hope you will find it entertaining and informative enough to read straight through, we also hope you will find it accessible and short enough to sit close at hand to consult as a helpful guide anytime your gut tells you that you have come face to face with a professional responsibility issue.

Although we suspect that our book is unlike many you have so far encountered in practice, we trust its unique approach makes it more useful to those who need its guidance. Let us begin by introducing you to our rather unusual style as well as several distinctive features of the book you are about to use.

Larry wrote the Questions and Answers that appear in nearly every section of this book. These inquires are interspersed with short essays about relevant law written by Susan, complete with citations to the relevant Model Rule provisions and sections of the Restatement of the Law Governing Lawyers. We intend the Q & A's to engage you in interesting issues faced by modern lawyers, and we also see these problems as a means to motivate you to study the relevant provisions in various lawyer codes, the Restatement of the Law Governing Lawyers, and the cases and other materials that explain and construe them, which are explained in the short essays.

While we recognize that there are far more comprehensive publications addressing these issues, we do not believe there is any that covers as much material in such a relatively short and informal way. This means that this book's greatest asset is also its greatest liability. Without issuing *Miranda* warnings to our readers, suffice it to say that this book should be an excellent starting point for identifying issues and thinking through solutions, but that no slim volume can capture the full scope of this jurisprudence, as we point out in Chapter 9, where we advise our readers how to access the vast body of primary source material in this area.

We also hope that the relative brevity of each Q & A leads you to the correct conclusion that an exact answer depends upon specific law or additional facts that might change the outcome. We repeat: **DO NOT RELY ON THIS BOOK ALONE FOR LEGAL ADVICE.** Our guidance is premised upon national legal templates found in the ABA Model Rules and the Restatement from which an individual jurisdiction may have deviated. We also want the Q & A's to reflect the reality that legal ethics issues, like all legal issues, always require careful attention to facts as well as law. By articulating some of our assumptions, we invite you to do the same, and to anticipate how additional facts might change the appropriate response.

We have organized the material in this book to emphasize our general approach to the law governing lawyers. We begin in Part One by examining the commencement of the client-lawyer relationship. In Chapter 1, we address the red flags raised by the first issue of legal ethics: whether a client-lawyer relationship exists. Here, we identify a series of "accidental" clients, whom lawyers may be unaware they could be deemed to represent. In Chapter 2, we examine fee arrangements. In Part Two, we follow these initial issues with a lengthy consideration of the red flags raised by the "4 C" fiduciary duties lawyers owe clients: communication (Chapter 3), competence (Chapter 4), confidentiality (Chapter 5), and conflicts of interest resolution (Chapter 6). Here we explore the legal duties that automatically attach when a lawyer represents a client. In Part Three, we turn to the red flags raised by the limits of the law, or when you must say "no" to a client. We well know you would never bribe a judge, but we identify in Chapter 7 some less obvious limits that can ensnare unwary lawyers. In Part Four, we examine the extensive legal remedies that clients and third parties can pursue to prevent or rectify a violation of the law governing lawyers, from professional discipline to the inherent powers of tribunals (Chapter 8). We end with Part Five, where we look at how to avoid trouble. In Chapter 9, we detail how you can help yourself by describing the specialized resources at your disposal to research a legal ethics issue in your jurisdiction. In Chapter 10, we examine the ultimate red flags, situations when you should consult with another lawyer.

Throughout these materials, we offer you practical insights into how to avoid or mitigate unpleasant legal consequences. Overall, we intend this book to serve as a guide to identifying red flags, understanding the issues they raise, and avoiding the mistakes that the lawyers in these materials have confronted. We hope you enjoy this study as much as we have enjoyed preparing it.

## The Authors

It is altogether fitting that this endeavor is published by ALI-ABA. It was in the Advisors Room at the American Law Institute's headquarters in West Philadelphia that we first met while participating in endless discussions parsing dense text as the American Law Institute's Restatement of the Law Governing Lawyers project moved glacially from tentative drafts to final work product. From pursuing what is certainly an acquired taste, arose not only a wonderful friendship, but an opportunity for a longtime student of professional responsibility, Susan Martyn, to collaborate with a practicing lawyer, Larry Fox, who had quite a different perspective from Susan on issues relating to lawyer conduct.

Our first collaboration was a casebook for law students, *Traversing the Ethical Minefield: Problems, Law, and Professional Responsibility*, published in 2004 by Aspen. Our second collaboration, building on the first, is this handbook, which we hope will provide to practicing lawyers, judges and others a relatively brief, accessible and, we hope, somewhat entertaining guide to the very difficult topics we have addressed.

As with all such wonderful endeavors, this book would not be possible without the extraordinary assistance of so many others. The faculties and students at two law schools—the Universities of Pennsylvania and Toledo—contributed to these materials by consulting, arguing, and correcting many of our mistakes. Special thanks to Roger Andersen, Henry Bourguignon, Henry S. Bryans, James Caruso, Roger Cramton, Howard Friedman, David Harris, Geoffrey Hazard, Barbara and Charles Hicks, Nancy Moore, Deborah Mostaghel, Lee Pizzimenti, and Brad Wendel. We also received able research assistance from Michael Dockins, Anna Ficken, Jon Hanna, Liz McCuskey, Erika Mulich, Bryan Rannigan, Meredith Rubin, and Cory Taylor. Our ideas never would have taken shape without the capable, cheerful, and knowledgeable assistance of Bea Cucinotta. Susan thanks the University of Toledo and the assistance of the Eugene N. Balk Fund, which provided the funds to carry out most of the research. Larry never would have been able to develop all of the Q and A's if it were not for the invitation from Charles Wolfram to escape practice and teach at the Cornell Law School.

While we thank these selfless individuals for their guidance and support, we hasten to remind our general readers that any errors or omissions are the sole responsibility of the authors who welcome your comments as we look forward to publishing future editions of this volume.

Larry Fox & Susan Martyn

March 2005

# Contents

| | | |
|---|---|---|
| **Foreword** | | ix |
| **Preface** | | xii |
| **Part One: Recognizing Red Flags: Framing The Issue** | | 1 |
| **Chapter 1** | **Who Is Your Client?** | 3 |
| 1.01 | Why Identifying Your Client Matters | 5 |
| 1.02 | Court Appointments | 6 |
| | (a) The Involuntary Court Appointment? | 6 |
| | (b) Court-Mandated Client-Lawyer Relationships | 6 |
| 1.03 | Establishing Consensual Client-Lawyer Relationships | 7 |
| | (a) Engagement Or Retainer Letters? | 7 |
| | (b) Establishing A Consensual Client-Lawyer Relationship | 8 |
| 1.04 | The Engagement Letter | 9 |
| 1.05 | Prospective Clients | 9 |
| | (a) The Rejected Prospective Client? | 9 |
| | (b) The Non-Engagement Letter | 10 |
| | (c) The Beauty Contest? | 10 |
| | (d) Legal Duties To Prospective Clients | 11 |
| 1.06 | Prospective Clients: Public Speeches | 12 |
| 1.07 | Prospective Clients: Advertising | 13 |
| 1.08 | Prospective Clients: E-Lawyering | 13 |
| | (a) Website Advertising And Email | 13 |
| | (b) The Targeted Email? | 14 |
| 1.09 | Prospective Clients: Social Gatherings | 14 |
| 1.10 | Prospective Clients: Consulting Lawyers | 15 |

| | | | |
|---|---|---|---|
| 1.11 | | Prospective Clients: Referral Fees | 15 |
| 1.12 | | Prospective Clients: Unrepresented Parties | 16 |
| 1.13 | | Prospective Clients: Family Members | 16 |
| 1.14 | | Prospective Clients: Limited-Term Pro Bono Services | 17 |
| | (a) | The Legal Services Hotline? | 17 |
| | (b) | Volunteering For A Nonprofit Program | 17 |
| 1.15 | | Joint Clients | 18 |
| 1.16 | | Third-Person Direction | 18 |
| 1.17 | | Insurance Defense | 19 |
| | (a) | How Many Clients? | 19 |
| | (b) | Defending Insureds | 19 |
| 1.18 | | Organizations And Employees | 20 |
| | (a) | Defending Constituents? | 20 |
| | (b) | Organizational Clients | 21 |
| 1.19 | | Clients Who Morph | 22 |
| 1.20 | | Entities | 22 |
| | (a) | The Corporate Buyout? | 22 |
| | (b) | Entity Clients, Of Constituents And Parents | 23 |
| 1.21 | | Death Of A Client | 23 |
| | (a) | Settling A Pending Case? | 23 |
| | (b) | When A Client Dies | 24 |
| 1.22 | | Clients With Diminished Capacity | 24 |
| 1.23 | | Class Actions | 25 |
| | (a) | The Uncertified Class? | 25 |
| | (b) | Class Clients | 26 |
| 1.24 | | Ending A Representation | 27 |
| 1.25 | | The Disengagement Letter | 27 |
| 1.26 | | Quasi-Clients | 28 |
| 1.27 | | Third-Party Beneficiaries | 28 |
| | (a) | The Opinion Letter? | 28 |
| | (b) | Duty To Intended Beneficiaries | 29 |
| 1.28 | | Client-Fiduciaries | 30 |
| 1.29 | | "Accommodation" Clients | 31 |
| | (a) | The Accommodated CFO? | 31 |

|  |  |  |
|---|---|---|
| | (b)  Accommodating A Third Party | 32 |
| 1.30 | Imputed Clients: Law Firms And Shared Office Space | 32 |
| **Chapter 2** | **Fees: Contract Or Fiduciary Duty?** | **35** |
| 2.01 | Fee Contracts | 36 |
| 2.02 | Reasonable Fees And Expenses | 37 |
| | (a)  The Initial Agreement? | 37 |
| | (b)  Fiduciary Limitations On Contract | 37 |
| 2.03 | Chart: State Rules Requiring Written Fee Agreements | 39 |
| 2.04 | Fee Modifications | 41 |
| | (a)  The Unanticipated Bad Case? | 41 |
| | (b)  Fiduciary Limits On Fee Modifications | 42 |
| 2.05 | Statutory Fee Requirements | 43 |
| | (a)  Statutory Limitations On Contract | 43 |
| | (b)  The Statutory Windfall? | 44 |
| | (c)  Statutory Fee Shifting | 44 |
| 2.06 | Judicial Power To Limit Contractual Fees | 45 |
| 2.07 | Hourly Fees | 45 |
| | (a)  The Professional Hour? | 45 |
| | (b)  Reasonable Hourly Fees | 46 |
| 2.08 | Contingent Fees | 48 |
| | (a)  The Contingent Fee Windfall? | 48 |
| | (b)  Reasonable Contingent Fees | 49 |
| | (c)  Negative Contingent Fees? | 49 |
| | (d)  Contingent Fee Conflicts Of Interest | 49 |
| 2.09 | Fixed Or Flat Fees | 51 |
| | (a)  The Flat Fee Risk? | 51 |
| | (b)  Reasonable Flat Fees | 52 |
| 2.10 | Retainers | 52 |
| | (a)  The Nonrefundable Retainer? | 52 |
| | (b)  General And Special "Retainers" | 53 |
| 2.11 | Fees On Termination (Withdrawal Or Firing) | 54 |
| 2.12 | Fee Sharing | 55 |

|  |  |  |  |
|---|---|---|---|
|  | (a) | The Fee-Splitting Windfall? | 55 |
|  | (b) | Reasonable (And Proper) Fee Splits | 55 |
| 2.13 | Fee Collection | | 56 |
| 2.14 | Trust Accounts | | 57 |

**Part Two: Responding To Red Flags: Fiduciary Duty**    61

**Chapter 3    Communication: The Foundation Of The 4 C's**    63

|  |  |  |  |
|---|---|---|---|
| 3.01 | Communication: Disclosure And Conversation | | 63 |
| 3.02 | General Duty To Communicate | | 64 |
| 3.03 | Settlement Offers, Plea Bargains, And Comparable Decisions | | 65 |
|  | (a) | The Ridiculous Plea Bargain? | 65 |
|  | (b) | Avoiding The Unreasonable Client? | 65 |
|  | (c) | Specific Communication Mandates | 66 |
|  | (d) | The Settlement Conference? | 67 |
| 3.04 | Waivers: Confidentiality | | 67 |
| 3.05 | Waivers: Conflicts | | 68 |
|  | (a) | A Prospective Waiver? | 68 |
|  | (b) | Nonconsentable Conflicts? | 69 |
|  | (c) | Obtaining A Conflicts Waiver | 70 |
|  | (d) | Informed Consent? | 71 |
| 3.06 | Specific Requirements: Contingent Fees, Fee Sharing, Liability Insurance, And Client's Rights | | 72 |

**Chapter 4    Competence: Why You Were Hired In The First Place**    73

|  |  |  |  |
|---|---|---|---|
| 4.01 | Competence: Care And Diligence | | 73 |
| 4.02 | Care: Skill And Knowledge | | 74 |
| 4.03 | Care: Scope Of The Representation | | 75 |
|  | (a) | The Short Representation? | 75 |
|  | (b) | Reasonable Scope Limitations | 75 |
| 4.04 | Obedience | | 77 |
|  | (a) | Whose Tactics? | 77 |
|  | (b) | Objectives And Means | 78 |

| | | | |
|---|---|---|---|
| 4.05 | | Diligence | 79 |
| 4.06 | | Obvious Errors And Common Knowledge | 79 |
| | (a) | Timely Filings | 80 |
| | (b) | Legal And Factual Research | 80 |
| | (c) | Breach Of Fiduciary Duty | 81 |
| 4.07 | | What To Do If You Make A Mistake | 81 |
| | (a) | The Blown Statute? | 81 |
| | (b) | How To Avoid Even More Trouble | 82 |

**Chapter 5  Confidentiality: The Never-Ending Obligation**  85

| | | | |
|---|---|---|---|
| 5.01 | | The Scope Of Confidentiality | 87 |
| | (a) | A Rose By Any Other Name? | 87 |
| | (b) | Fiduciary Obligation And Privilege | 88 |
| | (c) | Client Confidentiality Chart: Fiduciary Obligation And Privilege | 89 |
| 5.02 | | The Extent Of Confidentiality | 90 |
| | (a) | The Juicy Tidbit? | 90 |
| | (b) | The Beginning And End Of Confidentiality | 90 |
| 5.03 | | Disclosure And Use Of Confidential Information | 91 |
| | (a) | Helping The Press? | 91 |
| | (b) | The Opportunity? | 92 |
| | (c) | Confidentiality: Scope Of The Protection | 92 |
| 5.04 | | Litigation Disclosures | 93 |
| | (a) | A Question Of Privilege? | 93 |
| | (b) | Attorney-Client Privilege: Scope Of The Protection | 94 |
| | (c) | Client Identity And Public Documents | 95 |
| | (d) | The Privilege Boilerplate? | 96 |
| | (e) | The Brilliant Gambit? | 96 |
| | (f) | The Organizational Privilege? | 97 |
| | (g) | The Corporate Gamble? | 97 |
| 5.05 | | Work-Product Privilege | 98 |
| | (a) | The Engineer's Report? | 98 |
| | (b) | Work Product Protection | 98 |
| | (c) | The Supervised Expert? | 99 |

| | | | |
|---|---|---|---|
| 5.06 | Confidentiality Exceptions | | 100 |
| | (a) Countervailing Policies | | 100 |
| | (b) Chart: State Lawyer Code Exceptions To Client Confidentiality | | 100 |
| 5.07 | Confidentiality Exceptions: Express Or Implied Authorization | | 108 |
| | (a) The New CEO? | | 108 |
| | (b) The Administrative Privilege? | | 108 |
| | (c) Company Agents? | | 109 |
| | (d) The Inadvertent Email? | | 109 |
| | (e) The Helpful Opponent? | | 110 |
| | (f) Express And Implied Confidentiality Waivers | | 110 |
| 5.08 | Confidentiality Exceptions: Threatened Serious Bodily Harm | | 112 |
| | (a) The Suicidal Client? | | 112 |
| | (b) The Undisclosed Aneurysm? | | 113 |
| | (c) Threatened Physical Harm | | 113 |
| 5.09 | Confidentiality Exceptions: Future Crime | | 114 |
| | (a) Blowing Off Steam? | | 114 |
| | (b) The Future Crime Exception | | 115 |
| 5.10 | Confidentiality Exceptions: Client Fraud | | 116 |
| | (a) Puffing? | | 116 |
| | (b) The Innocent Misrepresentation? | | 117 |
| | (c) Tax Compliance? | | 117 |
| | (d) The Prepared Witnesses? | | 118 |
| | (e) Client Fraud | | 118 |
| 5.11 | Confidentiality Exceptions: Lawyer Self-Defense | | 119 |
| | (a) The Ungrateful Client? | | 119 |
| | (b) Helping Successor Counsel? | | 119 |
| | (c) Defending Yourself | | 120 |
| 5.12 | Confidentiality Exceptions: Seeking Advice | | 121 |
| | (a) Help? | | 121 |
| | (b) Getting Advice | | 121 |

| | | |
|---|---|---|
| 5.13 | Confidentiality Exceptions: Law And Court Orders | 122 |
| | (a) The Deposition Lie? | 122 |
| | (b) The False Alibi? | 123 |
| | (c) Law And Court Orders That Require Disclosure | 123 |
| 5.14 | Jurisdiction-Specific Exceptions And Conflicts Of Law | 124 |
| | (a) The Heavy Burden? | 124 |
| | (b) Guaranteed Confidentiality? | 125 |
| | (c) The Dizzying Diversity? | 125 |
| | (d) Understanding Confidentiality Conflicts | 125 |
| **Chapter 6** | **Conflicts Of Interest: The Loyalty Obligation** | **129** |
| 6.01 | The Loyalty Obligation | 132 |
| 6.02 | The Unexpected Conflict? | 133 |
| 6.03 | Identifying And Resolving Conflicts | 133 |
| 6.04 | Basic Steps To Identifying And Resolving Conflicts Of Interest | 134 |
| 6.05 | Law Firm Imputation | 135 |
| 6.06 | Conflicts Control Systems | 136 |
| 6.07 | Building And Using A Conflicts Control System | 137 |
| | (a) Building A Database | 137 |
| |     (1) Personal Conflicts: Law Firm Lawyers | 137 |
| |     (2) Concurrent And Third-Person Conflicts: Current Clients | 137 |
| |     (3) Former-Client Conflicts: Former Clients | 138 |
| | (b) Using The Data Base | 138 |
| | (c) Identifying And Responding To Conflicts | 139 |
| 6.08 | Recognizing Conflicts | 139 |
| 6.09 | Nonconsentable Conflicts | 140 |
| | (a) The Friendly Divorce? | 140 |
| | (b) When Client Consent Is Not Enough | 141 |
| 6.10 | Conflicts Of Interest: Lawyer Personal Interests | 142 |
| 6.11 | Business Deals With Clients | 143 |
| | (a) A Share Of The Deal? | 143 |

|       |       |                                                              |      |
|-------|-------|--------------------------------------------------------------|------|
|       | (b)   | Legal Regulation                                             | 143  |
|       | (c)   | The Board Member?                                            | 145  |
| 6.12  |       | Client Gifts                                                 | 145  |
| 6.13  |       | Literary Or Media Rights                                     | 146  |
|       | (a)   | The Hollywood Story?                                         | 146  |
|       | (b)   | Literary Or Media Rights                                     | 147  |
| 6.14  |       | Proprietary Interests In The Subject Matter Of Litigation    | 147  |
| 6.15  |       | Financial Assistance To Clients                              | 148  |
|       | (a)   | The Client In Need?                                          | 148  |
|       | (b)   | Pending Litigation And Financial Assistance                  | 148  |
| 6.16  |       | Limitations On Lawyer Liability                              | 148  |
| 6.17  |       | Aggregate Settlements                                        | 149  |
|       | (a)   | The Policy Limit Bonanza?                                    | 149  |
|       | (b)   | Joint Decisions To Settle                                    | 149  |
| 6.18  |       | Sexual Relationships With Clients                            | 150  |
|       | (a)   | Dating The CFO?                                              | 150  |
|       | (b)   | Legal Implications Of Sexual Relationships With Clients      | 151  |
| 6.19  |       | Personal Relationships                                       | 152  |
| 6.20  |       | Imputation Of Personal Conflicts                             | 152  |
| 6.21  |       | Conflicts Of Interest: Joint Clients                         | 153  |
| 6.22  |       | Joint Client Confidentiality                                 | 154  |
|       | (a)   | The Boiler-Plate Joint Defense Agreement?                    | 154  |
|       | (b)   | Handling Confidentiality In Joint Client Representations     | 154  |
| 6.23  |       | Litigation Opponents                                         | 155  |
|       | (a)   | Divorce And Dissolution                                      | 155  |
|       | (b)   | The Family Accident?                                         | 156  |
| 6.24  |       | Simultaneous Representation Of Adversaries In Unrelated Cases| 156  |
| 6.25  |       | Co-Parties: Civil Litigation                                 | 157  |
| 6.26  |       | Joint Defendants In Criminal Cases                           | 158  |
|       | (a)   | Common Defense Among Friends?                                | 158  |
|       | (b)   | Co-Defendants: Criminal Defense                              | 158  |

| | | |
|---|---|---|
| 6.27 | Joint Representation In Transactions | 159 |
| | (a) The Simple Real Estate Transaction? | 159 |
| | (b) The New Business Venture? | 159 |
| | (c) Joint Wills? | 160 |
| | (d) Co-Parties: Transactions | 161 |
| 6.28 | Positional Or Issue Conflicts | 161 |
| | (a) Taking Different Legal Positions? | 161 |
| | (b) Legal Regulation Of Issue Conflicts | 162 |
| 6.29 | Representing Entities | 163 |
| | (a) The Corporate Transaction? | 163 |
| | (b) The Employee Deposition? | 164 |
| | (c) The Subsidiary Problem? | 164 |
| | (d) The Homeowner's Association? | 165 |
| | (e) Organizations And Employees | 166 |
| 6.30 | Imputation Of Current-Client Conflicts | 166 |
| | (a) Side-Switching? | 166 |
| | (b) Law Firm Imputation | 167 |
| 6.31 | Conflicts Of Interest: Third-Party Direction | 168 |
| | (a) Corporate Control? | 168 |
| | (b) Relative Matters? | 168 |
| | (c) Third-Person Payment | 169 |
| | (d) Third-Person Influence | 169 |
| 6.32 | Insurance Defense | 170 |
| | (a) Litigation Strategy? | 170 |
| | (b) The Confidential Policy Defense? | 170 |
| | (c) Settlement? | 171 |
| | (d) Understanding The Tripartite Relationship | 171 |
| 6.33 | Former-Client Conflicts Of Interest | 173 |
| | (a) The Hot Potato? | 173 |
| | (b) Firing A Client? | 174 |
| | (c) Keeping It In The Family? | 175 |
| | (d) The Substantial Relationship Test | 175 |
| | (e) The Substantially Related Transaction? | 176 |
| 6.34 | Screens And Imputation For Former-Client Conflicts | 178 |

|  |  |  |
|---|---|---|
|  | (a) Screens When? | 178 |
|  | (b) The Joy Of Screening? | 179 |
|  | (c) Chart: State Lawyer Code Rules That Allow Screens To Prevent Imputed Disqualification | 179 |
| 6.35 | Former Clients And Peripheral Representation | 185 |
|  | (a) The Lateral Hire? | 185 |
|  | (b) The Peripheral Representation Exception | 186 |
| 6.36 | Former Clients And Actual Receipt Of Confidential Information | 186 |
| 6.37 | Conflicts Of Interest: Former Government Lawyers | 187 |
|  | (a) A Typhoid Mary? | 187 |
|  | (b) Legal Regulation Of Former Government Lawyers | 188 |
| 6.38 | Conflicts Of Interest: Judges, Arbitrators, And Third-Party Neutrals | 188 |
|  | (a) The Mediator Lawyer? | 188 |
|  | (b) Subsequent Law Practice Of Adjudicative Officers And Mediators | 189 |

**Part Three: Responding To Red Flags: The Limits Of The Law** — **191**

**Chapter 7 The Limits Of Zealous Representation: When You Must Say "No"** — **193**

|  |  |  |
|---|---|---|
| 7.01 | Chart: Legal Sources Of Some Common Limits Of The Law | 195 |
| 7.02 | Withdrawal: Voluntary And Involuntary | 196 |
|  | (a) When You Really Want To Get Out? | 196 |
|  | (b) Do I Have A Lien? | 196 |
|  | (c) Legal Grounds For Withdrawal | 197 |
|  | (d) Wrongful Termination? | 198 |
| 7.03 | Crime: Lawyer And Client | 199 |
|  | (a) The Ponzi Scheme? | 199 |
|  | (b) The Criminal Law And Professional Obligation | 199 |
| 7.04 | Fraud: Lawyer And Client | 201 |

|       |      |                                                              |     |
|-------|------|--------------------------------------------------------------|-----|
|       | (a)  | The Client Who (Most Likely) Won't Be Caught?               | 201 |
|       | (b)  | The Tester?                                                  | 201 |
|       | (c)  | The Law Of Fraud And Professional Obligation                 | 202 |
|       | (d)  | The Lying Tax Auditee?                                       | 203 |
| 7.05  |      | Procedural Rules: Frivolous Lawsuits                         | 204 |
|       | (a)  | The Last-Minute Lawsuit?                                     | 204 |
|       | (b)  | Legal Regulation Of Frivolous Advocacy                       | 205 |
| 7.06  |      | Procedural Rules: Discovery Abuse                            | 206 |
|       | (a)  | The Damaging Documents?                                      | 206 |
|       | (b)  | Legal Regulation Of Discovery Abuse                          | 206 |
| 7.07  |      | Court Orders And Contempt                                    | 207 |
| 7.08  |      | Candor To The Tribunal                                       | 207 |
|       | (a)  | The Undiscovered Case?                                       | 207 |
|       | (b)  | The Undiscovered Conviction?                                 | 208 |
|       | (c)  | The Undiscovered Witness?                                    | 209 |
| 7.09  |      | Bias                                                         | 209 |
|       | (a)  | The Sexist Opponent?                                         | 209 |
| 7.10  |      | Contact With Represented And Unrepresented Persons           | 210 |
|       | (a)  | The Worthless Lawyer?                                        | 210 |
|       | (b)  | The Former CEO?                                              | 210 |
|       | (c)  | Employees?                                                   | 211 |
|       | (d)  | The Justice Department Badges?                               | 211 |
|       | (e)  | The Scared Defendant?                                        | 212 |
|       | (f)  | Legal Regulation Of Third-Person Contact                     | 213 |
| 7.11  |      | *Ex Parte* Communications With Judges And Jurors             | 214 |
|       | (a)  | Legal Regulation                                             | 214 |
|       | (b)  | The Misguided Expert?                                        | 214 |
| 7.12  |      | Restrictions On Law Practice                                 | 215 |
|       | (a)  | Make That Lawyer Go Away?                                    | 215 |
|       | (b)  | Business Development?                                        | 216 |

| 7.13 | Advertising And Solicitation | 216 |
| | (a) Chat Room Advertising? | 216 |
| | (b) Chart: Advertising, Solicitation, And The First Amendment | 217 |
| 7.14 | Trial Publicity | 222 |
| | (a) The Campaigning DA? | 222 |
| 7.15 | Lawyer As Witness | 222 |
| | (a) The Involuntary Witness? | 222 |
| 7.16 | Other Law: Federal And State Statutes And Regulations | 223 |
| | (a) The Curious IRS? | 223 |
| | (b) Sarbanes-Oxley Obligations Of Lawyers | 224 |

**Part Four: Red Flags You Cannot Ignore: Remedies** — 227

| Chapter 8 | So What Can Happen? Client And Third-Person Remedies | **229** |
| 8.01 | The Nervous Associate? | 230 |
| 8.02 | Professional Discipline | 231 |
| 8.03 | Criminal Accountability | 233 |
| | (a) The Client Fundraiser? | 233 |
| | (b) The Criminal Law | 234 |
| 8.04 | Misrepresentation | 235 |
| 8.05 | Lawyer Tort Liability To Non-Clients | 237 |
| | (a) The Estate Executor? | 237 |
| | (b) Legal Accountability To Non-Clients | 238 |
| 8.06 | Lawyer Tort Liability To Clients: Malpractice And Breach Of Fiduciary Duty | 241 |
| | (a) The Puny Settlement? | 241 |
| | (b) The Vast Scope Of Potential Liability | 242 |
| 8.07 | Ineffective Assistance Of Counsel | 244 |
| 8.08 | Disqualification And Other Court Orders | 247 |
| | (a) Dropping The Small Potato? | 247 |
| | (b) Losing A Client By Disqualification Or Injunction | 247 |

|  |  |  |
|---|---|---|
| 8.09 | Loss Of Contractual Rights | 251 |
|  | (a) The Client Gift? | 251 |
|  | (b) The Undue Influence Hurdle | 251 |
| 8.10 | Fee Forfeiture | 252 |
|  | (a) The Lost Fee? | 252 |
|  | (b) The Equity Of Fee Forfeiture | 253 |
| 8.11 | Procedural Sanctions | 255 |
| 8.12 | Avoiding Problems | 257 |

**Part Five: How To Get The Help You Really Need** — **259**

| **Chapter 9** | **How To Help Yourself:** **Researching The Law Governing Lawyers** | **261** |
|---|---|---|
| 9.01 | Why Research? | 262 |
|  | (a) The Imposition? | 262 |
|  | (b) Researching The Law Governing Lawyers | 263 |
| 9.02 | Issue Spotting | 264 |
|  | (a) Which Issues? | 264 |
|  | (b) Spotting All Of The Red Flags | 264 |
| 9.03 | Basic Resources | 265 |
|  | (a) Lawyer Codes | 265 |
|  | (b) The Restatement | 267 |
|  | (c) Treatises | 269 |
|  | (d) On-Line Resources | 271 |
| 9.04 | Finding Lawyer Code Provisions | 271 |
|  | (a) Which Rules? | 271 |
|  | (b) Finding All Relevant Rules | 272 |
| 9.05 | Recognizing Overlapping Remedies | 272 |
|  | (a) Which Remedies? | 272 |
|  | (b) Identifying All Of The Consequences | 273 |
| 9.06 | Judicial Opinions | 274 |
|  | (a) Which Cases? | 274 |
|  | (b) Uncovering All Of The Law | 275 |
| 9.07 | Ethics Opinions | 275 |
|  | (a) Which Ethics Opinions? | 275 |
|  | (b) Discovering Additional Guidance | 276 |

| | | |
|---|---|---:|
| 9.08 | Using Experts | 277 |
| | (a) Do We Need An Expert Witness? | 277 |
| | (b) Which Expert? | 278 |
| | (c) Relying On Expert Testimony | 278 |

### Chapter 10  When You Need To Seek Additional Advice And Perspective — 281

**Part One: Representing Clients — 282**

| | | |
|---|---|---:|
| 10.01 | Investing In A Client Business | 282 |
| | (a) The Business Opportunity? | 282 |
| | (b) The Directive Lawyer And Fiduciary Duty | 283 |
| 10.02 | The Expanding Enterprise | 285 |
| | (a) Too Good To Be True? | 285 |
| | (b) The Instrumental Lawyer And The Limits Of The Law | 285 |
| 10.03 | Successor Counsel | 289 |
| | (a) The New Client? | 289 |
| | (b) The Collaborative Lawyer Alternative | 290 |
| 10.04 | Clients With Diminished Capacity | 291 |
| | (a) The Misguided Will? | 291 |
| | (b) Understanding The Autonomy And Best Interests Of Impaired Clients | 292 |
| 10.05 | Joint Clients | 295 |
| | (a) The Cooperative Venture? | 295 |
| | (b) Dual Professional Difficulties | 296 |
| 10.06 | Triangular Relationships | 298 |
| | (a) Music To Your Ears? | 298 |
| | (b) Dual Difficulties Revisited | 299 |

**Part Two: Operating Your Law Practice — 301**

| | | |
|---|---|---:|
| 10.07 | Unpaid Fees | 301 |
| | (a) Pure Ingrates? | 301 |
| | (b) Collecting Fees | 302 |
| 10.08 | Expanding Beyond Law Practice | 304 |
| | (a) Doing Fine? | 304 |

|  |  | (b) Whose Rules? | 305 |
|---|---|---|---|
|  |  | (c) Ancillary Businesses And Multidisciplinary Practice | 305 |
|  | 10.09 | Supervisory And Subordinate Lawyers | 309 |
|  |  | (a) Supervising Discovery? | 309 |
|  |  | (b) When To Defer To Another Lawyer's Judgment | 309 |
|  | 10.10 | Helping Colleagues | 311 |
|  |  | (a) The Disconnect? | 311 |
|  |  | (b) Law And Life | 312 |

**Index Of Subjects** 315

# Part One

# Recognizing ►Red Flags►: Framing The Issue

It seems so simple. Lawyers earn fees by representing their clients. But is it? Your license to practice and your income rest upon your understanding of these legally defined and regulated concepts. Hidden traps await the unwary lawyer who too facilely assumes that clients are those whom the lawyer has explicitly agreed to represent for any fee the market will bear.

Chapter 1 begins by examining 10 ways—some unexpected—that the law governing lawyers frames the first issue [§9.02] of legal ethics: identifying your clients.

1. Court appointments.
2. Agreeing to represent someone.
3. Clients who reasonably rely on your advice.
4. Prospective clients, garnered from:
    a. A beauty contest;
    b. Your public speeches;
    c. Your advertising;
    d. Your website;
    e. Your conversations at social gatherings;
    f. Consulting lawyers;
    g. Referral fees;
    h. Reasonable reliance by an unrepresented party
    i. Family members;
    j. Pro bono services.

5. Joint clients.
6. Third-person payment.
7. Representing organizations.
8. Clients who change during the course of a representation:
   a. Entities and constituents of entities;
   b. Client deaths;
   c. Clients with diminished capacity;
   d. Class actions;
   e. Clients for whom you stopped working on a matter (by completing it, by withdrawing from the representation, or because you were fired).
9. Quasi-clients created by:
   a. Opinion letters;
   b. Representing a fiduciary;
   c. Accommodating another client.
10. Working in a law firm or sharing office space.

Chapter 2 examines another seemingly obvious topic with hidden issues [§9.02]: fees. Here, we hope to help you bargain for and collect reasonable fees by meeting all of the quasi-fiduciary obligations imposed beyond the terms of a fee agreement by the increasing regulation of fees found in lawyer codes [§9.04], court opinions [§9.06], and statutes.

# 1
# Who Is Your Client?

- §1.01 Why Identifying Your Client Matters
- §1.02 Court Appointments
    - §1.02(a) The Involuntary Court Appointment?
    - §1.02(b) Court-Mandated Client-Lawyer Relationships
- §1.03 Establishing Consensual Client-Lawyer Relationships
    - §1.03(a) Engagement Or Retainer Letters?
    - §1.03(b) Establishing A Consensual Client-Lawyer Relationship
- §1.04 The Engagement Letter
- §1.05 Prospective Clients
    - §1.05(a) The Rejected Prospective Client?
    - §1.05(b) The Non-Engagement Letter
    - §1.05(c) The Beauty Contest?
    - §1.05(d) Legal Duties To Prospective Clients
- §1.06 Prospective Clients: Public Speeches
- §1.07 Prospective Clients: Advertising
- §1.08 Prospective Clients: E-Lawyering
    - §1.08(a) Website Advertising And Email
    - §1.08(b) The Targeted Email?
- §1.09 Prospective Clients: Social Gatherings
- §1.10 Prospective Clients: Consulting Lawyers
- §1.11 Prospective Clients: Referral Fees

- §1.12 Prospective Clients: Unrepresented Parties
- §1.13 Prospective Clients: Family Members
- §1.14 Prospective Clients: Limited-Term Pro Bono Services
  - §1.14(a) The Legal Services Hotline?
  - §1.14(b) Volunteering For A Nonprofit Program
- §1.15 Joint Clients
- §1.16 Third-Person Direction
- §1.17 Insurance Defense
  - §1.17(a) How Many Clients?
  - §1.17(b) Defending Insureds
- §1.18 Organizations And Employees
  - §1.18(a) Defending Constituents?
  - §1.18(b) Organizational Clients
- §1.19 Clients Who Morph
- §1.20 Entities
  - §1.20(a) The Corporate Buyout?
  - §1.20(b) Entity Clients, Of Constituents And Parents
- §1.21 Death Of A Client
  - §1.21(a) Settling A Pending Case?
  - §1.21(b) When A Client Dies
- §1.22 Clients With Diminished Capacity
- §1.23 Class Actions
  - §1.23(a) The Uncertified Class?
  - §1.23(b) Class Clients
- §1.24 Ending A Representation
- §1.25 The Disengagement Letter
- §1.26 Quasi-Clients
- §1.27 Third-Party Beneficiaries
  - §1.27(a) The Opinion Letter?
  - §1.27(b) Duty To Intended Beneficiaries
- §1.28 Client-Fiduciaries

➤§1.29 "Accommodation" Clients

    ➤§1.29(a) The Accommodated CFO?

    ➤§1.29(b) Accommodating A Third Party

➤§1.30 Imputed Clients: Law Firms And Shared Office Space

### ➤§1.01 WHY IDENTIFYING YOUR CLIENT MATTERS

Your role as an officer of the legal system creates primary obligations to clients [Chapters 1-6], as well as responsibilities to courts and third parties [Chapter 7]. All of these obligations require you to identify your clients, an inquiry that can produce unanticipated results.

When you enter a client-lawyer relationship, the law governing lawyers recognizes that you have assumed four core fiduciary obligations (the 4 C's):

1. Competence,[1]
2. Communication,[2]
3. Confidentiality,[3]
4. Conflict of interest resolution.[4]

Legal remedies [§9.05][5] for breach of the 4 C's (think professional discipline [§8.02],[6] malpractice [§8.06],[7] breach of fiduciary duty [§8.06],[8] fee forfeiture [§8.10][9] and disqualification [§8.08][10] also belong primarily, but not exclusively, to "clients."

➤**Red Flag**➤ The situations we describe in this chapter create legally recognized client-lawyer relationships that sometimes may sur-

---

[1] ABA Model Rules of Professional Conduct 1.1 and 1.3 (2002). (Hereinafter "Model Rules".)

[2] Model Rule 1.4.

[3] Model Rules 1.6, 1.8(b), and 1.9.

[4] Model Rules 1.7, 1.8, 1.11, and 1.12.

[5] *Restatement of the Law Third, The Law Governing Lawyers*, §§5 and 6 (ALI 2000). (Hereinafter "RLGL".)

[6] RLGL §5.

[7] RLGL §§48, 50, 52-54.

[8] RLGL §49.

[9] RLGL §37.

[10] RLGL §6 comment i.

prise you. You will not be able to limit the scope of your 4 C fiduciary obligations to these "accidental" clients, unless you remain alert to the obvious as well as the subtle circumstances that can trigger a full blown client-lawyer relationship in your own law practice.

## ➤ §1.02 COURT APPOINTMENTS

### ➤ §1.02(a) The Involuntary Court Appointment?

We've gotten the damnedest problem. Judge Murphy called me up the other day and told me he was appointing me to represent some indigent wife-beating husband. He didn't ask me; he told me! The defendant is a Neanderthal. The case has been in the papers day after day. I don't want to be associated with him, and I have never done a criminal case.

It is the duty of the bar to accept court appointments.[11] Our monopoly on legal services certainly gives the courts authority to make such appointments. No involuntary servitude arguments will carry the day here. You could claim that you are not competent to undertake this matter, and Model Rule 1.16 permits you to withdraw from a representation if the client insists on taking action you consider to be personally repugnant. But that rule doesn't quite fit because what is repugnant to you is what the client is accused of doing at an earlier date. The client has done nothing repugnant about the representation itself. The same rule permits you to withdraw from the case when unreasonable financial hardship will result. With your wonderful practice that probably won't work. In any event, the best you can do is remonstrate with the court. After all, once you are appointed the only way you can withdraw from a litigation matter is with the permission of the court. Lawyers have gotten in real trouble practicing civil disobedience in this area. So if the judge orders you in, sit back and enjoy the learning experience. You might even be proud of the fact you are serving in a system that doesn't consign people to jail without due process.

### ➤ §1.02(b) Court-Mandated Client-Lawyer Relationships

Client-lawyer relationships can be established by private agreement or court order [§9.06]. Courts have inherent power to appoint counsel in criminal and civil cases to preserve access to public dispute

---

[11] Model Rule 6.2; RLGL §14(2).

§1.03(a)  Who Is Your Client? • 7

resolution for individual litigants and to maintain public respect for the courts as a politically legitimate arm of the justice system.[12] The Model Rules reflect this understanding by obligating a lawyer to serve when appointed by a court unless that lawyer convinces the judge that a particular appointment would violate some other provision of the lawyer code, such as a duty of competence [Chapter 4], confidentiality [Chapter 5], or loyalty [Chapter 6].[13]

## ➤ §1.03 ESTABLISHING CONSENSUAL CLIENT-LAWYER RELATIONSHIPS

### ➤ §1.03(a) Engagement Or Retainer Letters?

**If I take on the matter, do I need an engagement or retainer letter? It's such a pain!**

Except in a few jurisdictions, lawyer codes [§9.04]—for matters other than contingent fee agreements (a quite important exception)—do not require retainer or engagement letters. This does not mean the use of such letters is not a good idea. Indeed, taking the time to craft an effective engagement letter is the best insurance policy (even better than a good result for the client) for collecting your fee.

You are so delighted to have new business; translate that enthusiasm into a gracious epistle that actually states your hourly rate or other fee agreement and otherwise tells the client the terms of the engagement. That way there will be no dispute as to the scope of the representation, the basis for the fee, or the way in which disbursements and other expenses will be handled. You can add that one of the obligations of the client, the breach of which might provide a basis for withdrawal [§7.02], is that the client make timely payment of fee bills rendered. How much better is such a letter than something mumbled by the lawyer at that first interview regarding all of these matters, a conversation the client may well remember quite differently from the lawyer, if the client remembers it at all.

Although there are critical items that should be addressed in the engagement letter, there are others that should be avoided no matter how helpful the lawyer may think they might be. For example, an engagement letter is no place for business development, no place for

---

[12] *Bothwell v. Republic Tobacco Co.*, 912 F. Supp. 1221 (D. Neb. 1995).
[13] Model Rule 6.2; RLGL §14(2).

the lawyer to expand this assignment to handle one contract negotiation by using a scope description that sounds like the lawyer plans on serving as outside general counsel for the client. Similarly, no matter how expert or experienced you are in the matters to be undertaken, this is no time to translate your pride in your accomplishments into a higher standard of care [§4.02], or to brag about your special expertise or experience. For if you do, and your work should ever be challenged by a disgruntled former client (heaven forbid), some court may conclude that a higher standard should apply to your work because of the wording in your letter. Nor should the engagement letter promise the client any particular result. If the letter addresses this topic at all it should be to remind the client of the vagaries of legal engagements that lawyers and clients confront together in an uncertain if not treacherous world.

### ➤§1.03(b) Establishing A Consensual Client-Lawyer Relationship

Nearly all lawyer code provisions [§9.04] assume that a professional relationship has been established, but do not explain how that occurs. General legal principles found in contract and tort law fill this gap.

Courts [§9.06] find that a consensual client-lawyer relationship has been formed if a prospective client [§§1.05-1.14] requests legal assistance or advice (offer), a lawyer provides the service or agrees to provide it (acceptance), and the client pays for the service or agrees to pay for it (consideration). Courts [§9.06] hold that a prospective client's reasonable reliance on a lawyer's advice or assistance suffices as an alternative for consideration (promissory estoppel).[14] Some courts [§9.06] prefer a torts analysis, which leads to similar results: A lawyer who renders legal service or advice to a person under circumstances which make it reasonably foreseeable that harm will occur to that person if the services are rendered negligently will be accountable to that person, even in the absence of any overt agreement to provide services or promise to pay.

➤**Red Flag**➤ Courts [§9.06] impose a precontractual duty of good faith on lawyers by looking back on the matter from the perspective of a reasonable client. As a result, your memory of who said

---

[14] *Togstad v. Vesely, Otto, Miller & Keefe*, 291 N.W.2d 686 (Minn. 1980).

what when may not be the version that ultimately prevails. An engagement [§1.04] or nonengagement letter [§1.05(b)] will clarify the meaning of an initial consult, as well as plant the seeds of good will for future potential retainers.

### ➤ §1.04 THE ENGAGEMENT LETTER

Use engagement letters to prevent misunderstandings by clarifying the scope and basis for undertaking a client representation. They also can be used to address other issues that might arise during the course of the matter, such as:

- Identifying the client and related parties;
- Identifying the goals of the representation;
- Defining the scope of the engagement;
- Identifying proposed staffing as well as agents of client or lawyer;
- Identifying third-party neutrals;
- Identifying and providing consents to actual or potential conflicts of interest;
- Determining confidentiality ground rules in multiple representations;
- Describing responsibilities of lawyer and client;
- Describing the fee agreement and billing schedule;
- Describing law firm policy about file retention;
- Specifying methods of communication;
- Specifying grounds for withdrawal or termination;
- Specifying methods of dispute resolution between lawyer and client[15]

### ➤ §1.05 PROSPECTIVE CLIENTS

### ➤ §1.05(a) The Rejected Prospective Client?

**I just sent a prospective client packing, informing her that her claim was weak but that, if her symptoms should turn worse before the statute of limitations expires next year, she should give me a call. I think I was wrong about the statute. It expires next month.**

---

[15] 1 Ronald E. Mallen & Jeffrey M. Smith, *Legal Malpractice* §2.12 (West Group 5th Ed. 2000); Gary A. Munneke & Anthony E. Davis, *The Essential Formbook: Comprehensive Management Tools for Lawyers* 141-144 (ABA Law Practice Management Section, 2003).

Though this person may not have become a full-fledged client, she became your client to the extent that she reasonably relied on your legal advice, and you therefore had an obligation to advise her competently under Model Rule 1.18.[16] You had better contact her as soon as possible to correct the misinformation you supplied, and you should do so in writing. Prospective clients are entitled to sound advice. In fact, anytime you banish a prospective client from your office you are well advised, even in the absence of a possible mistake, to confirm the rejection of the client in writing, lest the client assert later she thought you agreed to handle her matter. Remember: in a battle between lawyer and former prospective client over a misunderstanding as to how things were left, unless the lawyer has engraved the lawyer's understanding on the lawyer's cushy letterhead in a polite missive to the client, the client's perception will be given great weight no matter how strenuously the lawyer protests. As long as you made clear they were rejected, prospective clients have no reason to rely on you.

### ➤§1.05(b) The Non-Engagement Letter

Just as engagement letters can help you clarify duties to a new client, a non-engagement letter can help you clarify the absence of any such duty to a prospective client. Use them to decline a specific request for representation, to clarify that you represent some, but not all of the parties to a matter, to prevent reliance by unrepresented third parties who may or may not be beneficiaries of your client, or to prevent a claim for negligent misrepresentation [§§8.04, 8.05].[17]

### ➤§1.05(c) The Beauty Contest?

**There's a big suit just been filed. Everyone's involved. The bank. Accountants. They even sued a local law firm. Yesterday one of my partners went to "try out" for representing the accounting firm. They said they'd get back to him next week. Today the law firm called me. No tryouts. They just want to hire us. I told my buddy a bird in the hand is worth more than a bird in the bush.**

Go slowly, friend. If your partner had no understanding with the accountants that meeting with them—regardless of what was said—

---

[16] Model Rule 1.18; RLGL §15.
[17] Munneke and Davis, *supra* note 15 at 280.

would not preclude an alternative representation, then the accounting firm will be able to conflict you out of representation of the lawyers if your buddy learned any confidential information. We know it's counterproductive to participate in a beauty contest by insisting on protection for other representations if you should not get selected for this one, but the fact is that's the only way to avoid the problem. What you need is a prospective waiver from the prospective client that anything said at the beauty contest will not be asserted as a basis for barring you from taking on another client if you should win the Miss Congeniality award here. And, as with all prospective waivers, this one will be subject to challenge on the ground that the client had no idea when it entered into it that the law firm would learn so much about the prospective client. You can grasp the irony here: The more you show off at the tryout, the more likely it is you will be conflicted out, even if you secured a prospective waiver.

The ABA Model Rules now include Rule 1.18 that parallels case law [§9.06] and reminds lawyers of their confidentiality obligations to their prospective clients. It also provides that learning confidential information from another party to the matter need not necessarily conflict a law firm out, as long as two conditions are met. First, the firm has to have gained no more than the minimum information required to learn if it can take on the matter (which is why this provision won't help you). Second, the lawyer or lawyers who learned the information have to be screened from working on the new matter.

▶**§1.05(d) Legal Duties To Prospective Clients**

Prospective clients are those who discuss with lawyers the possibility of obtaining legal advice or services.[18] To the extent a lawyer offers legal advice and gains information from such a person, two duties, however limited, attach to such an encounter: Competence in any advice you offer and confidentiality that cloaks anything you learn.

With respect to competence, be careful to say what you mean. "You have no case" is legal advice, and if offered to a prospective client it means that you have accepted that person's offer or request for legal services. Add consideration (any payment for the consult) or detrimental reliance and you have a client-lawyer relationship [§1.03(b)], complete with the 4 C's appropriate to the scope of the representation.

---

[18] Model Rule 1.18(a).

If you mean, "I don't want to waste my time determining whether you have a case," or "I don't ever handle matters like this one," or "I can't take your case because I currently represent the other side" make that clear, or run the risk that a prospective client will remember the conversation differently after the statute of limitations expires.[19]

Determining whether to retain a lawyer requires a prospective client to disclose some information. To facilitate this exchange, the law governing lawyers cloaks the initial prospective client consult with the same confidentiality protection [§5.01] clients receive. If you decide not to represent the prospective client, that person or entity becomes a "former client" for purposes of the confidentiality rules [§§1.23 and 6.33]. The result: Even if you never open a client file, you must enter the prospective client's identity in your conflicts database, and refrain from using or disclosing the information shared in the discussion.[20]

▶**Red Flags**▶ The nine circumstances described in §§1.06 to 1.14 below have trapped unwary lawyers in accidental client-lawyer relationships that they never intended to create. Be especially careful what you say and represent in these circumstances.

### ▶§1.06 PROSPECTIVE CLIENTS: PUBLIC SPEECHES

You should be proud of your role in educating the public about legal rights and obligations, and it doesn't hurt that such occasions present the opportunity to advertise your expertise and willingness to take on new clients. As long as you describe the law generally or explain its applications to general patterns of conduct, you are not by your conduct accepting any offer of any prospective client to take on a new matter. However, when a member of the audience asks you a question that depends upon an assumption of specific facts, be careful not to offer an answer that sounds like legal advice to that person. You can begin your answer with "I'm not here to offer specific legal advice" (and don't do so), or "A person facing that situation would be wise to hire a lawyer for further advice" (which constitutes legal advice, but reliance on that admonition is unlikely to get you in trouble).

---

[19] *Flatt v. Super. Ct. of Sonoma City*, 885 P.2d 950 (Cal. 1994) (lawyer who informed prospective client she could not represent her due to a conflict has no duty to warn prospective client about relevant statute of limitations).

[20] Model Rule 1.18(b); RLGL §15.

▶**Red Flag**▶ You are in especially dangerous territory if you begin your answer with "There's no case/redress/cause of action in that circumstance" because the listener could rely on that advice and fail to seek a lawyer for a full opinion before the statute of limitations expires.

### ▶§1.07 PROSPECTIVE CLIENTS: ADVERTISING

If you wouldn't say it in person to an audience [§1.06], don't say it in writing. It's great to educate the public about your services and the law that provides persons with legal rights and responsibilities, but don't state anything about the law applied to facts that might be detrimentally relied on by a person unfamiliar with the law and its application. To do so may not only create unrealistic or even false expectations in violation of the "do not lie or falsely suggest" advertising rules [§7.13],[21] but also could buy you a "client" whose name you do not know.

▶**Red Flag**▶ If you want to add a disclaimer to your advertising to prevent reliance, be sure that it clearly informs your readers why any reliance on your ad is not reasonable. "You should not rely on this message for legal advice" may not be sufficient if you have already given legal advice. Add a "because" (every case differs, or a lawyer must evaluate all the facts, or the law provides for various defenses, or whatever else explains the situation) to spell out why the prospective client needs you (not just your ad) and why reliance on your ad alone is unreasonable.

### ▶§1.08 PROSPECTIVE CLIENTS: E-LAWYERING
### ▶§1.08(a) Website Advertising And Email

If you wouldn't say it in person to an audience [§1.06], or write it in a newspaper [§1.07], why would you put it on your website? Feel free to use your website to advertise and educate the public, and to establish client-lawyer relationships with those who request your assistance after reading your informative communication. But remember that an unknown person can rely on website legal advice that applies to that person's individual situation. So, invite inquiries, not reliance. If you want to offer prospective clients legal advice, know who they are, do a conflicts check [§§6.06-6.07], and, if you like, charge for the consult. These overt steps should trigger your natural tendency to

---

[21] Model Rules 7.1-7.5.

remember that the 4 C's have attached. If you want to attract new clients only after you have spoken to them, make sure your disclaimer clearly informs them why [§1.07].

### ➤§1.08(b) The Targeted Email?

**We were talking the other night. We thought a great business development tool could be sending targeted emails to prospective clients. We're not talking spam, you know. Classy stuff. Information about taxes; real estate deals; that sort of thing.**

You are entering the murky divide. Targeted mailings—for example to the victims of an accident—are permissible.[22] In-person or telephone solicitations are not.[23] Although the Supreme Court has not yet weighed in on the issue [§7.13], the comments to Model Rule 7.3 permit targeted email solicitation but do not permit interactive email conversations. So the question is whether this is a solicitation or a conversation, and that depends on the role of the recipient. Is the approach more like an ad in the Yellow Pages or a telephone call designed to sign up new clients?

### ➤§1.09 PROSPECTIVE CLIENTS: SOCIAL GATHERINGS

Everyone loves to get free legal advice, even if it is worth what they are paying for it. Lawyers are easy targets, especially at social events, where you and that person may be loosened up a bit and ready to talk. Remember, when the person the host just introduced you to says: "So, you're a lawyer," think: *This may be a prospective client, so I should be careful about getting information and giving legal advice.* If you're too tired or otherwise under the weather, just say, "Not tonight, I'm off the clock."

➤**Red Flag**➤ Any response to a legal question could indicate your acceptance of the other person's offer or request for legal advice. If that person reasonably relies and is harmed, malpractice could result [§8.06]. Even if he or she doesn't rely on your advice, the information shared could be confidential if that person later is identified as a prospective client under Model Rule 1.18.

---

[22] *Fla. Bar v. Went For It, Inc.*, 515 U.S. 618 (1995); *Shapero v. Ky. Bar Ass'n.*, 486 U.S. 466 (1988).

[23] *Ohralik v. Ohio St. Bar Ass'n.*, 436 U.S. 447 (1978).

## ➤ §1.10 PROSPECTIVE CLIENTS: CONSULTING LAWYERS

An old law school friend calls and asks what to do about a difficult client who won't pay his bill and threatens a malpractice suit. Do you have a client? Yes, at least one. Your friend is asking you for legal advice and will become your client if you offer it. If your friend shares confidential information about his client [§5.12] for the purpose of furthering his representation of that client, then his client also might become your client. If you don't want either result, see if the entire conversation can be conducted in a hypothetical format. Even then, your friend can be considered your client insofar as you offer advice about the effect of the law governing lawyers on your lawyer-friend's conduct (whether he can withdraw from the representation [§ 7.02], collect his fee [§§ 2.13, 10.07], or avoid a malpractice suit [§§ 4.07, 8.06]). If you learn the identity of your friend's client, and especially if your friend obtained permission for the consult, his client may be your client. Do a conflicts check [§§6.06-6.07] and remember the rest of the 4 C's.[24]

## ➤ §1.11 PROSPECTIVE CLIENTS: REFERRAL FEES

You're too tired or busy or inexperienced to handle a matter, so you wisely refer the prospective client to the best lawyer in town, who has agreed to share her fee with you. Everybody wins. But, do you have a client? If you want part of the fee, yes. Model Rule 1.5(e) allows for referral fees as long as three conditions are met. The total fee must be reasonable, the client must agree in writing to the arrangement including the share each lawyer will receive, and the clincher: the fee must either reflect the proportion of services you provided to the client, or you must agree to "assume joint responsibility for the representation" [§2.13]. The latter condition makes you jointly and severally liable for the "representation as a whole,"[25] meaning that you have a client whether or not you agree to or actually perform any service beyond the referral.

Recognizing that you have a client should lead you to take a number of other steps. First, enter the client's name in your conflicts database [§6.06]. Second, if the client calls you for reassurance about advice or service received from the best lawyer in town, remember that

---

[24] ABA Formal Opinion 97-406.
[25] Model Rule 1.5, Comment [7].

you might want to follow up to avoid your own tort liability [§8.06]. Third, you should be sure that the best lawyer in town properly informed the client in writing about the nature of the agreement. Otherwise, you both have charged an illegal fee and may not be able to collect at all [§2.12].

➤**Red Flag**➤ If you refer a case to another lawyer because you or someone in your firm has a conflict of interest [Chapter 6], you cannot agree to or collect a referral fee, because it will be impossible for you to work on the matter or "assume joint responsibility for the representation."

### ➤§1.12 PROSPECTIVE CLIENTS: UNREPRESENTED PARTIES

You close the real estate transaction, and the unrepresented seller asks whether you will register the deed. If you agree, most courts [§9.06] will find that you have a new client, albeit for a limited purpose.[26] The unrepresented party asked you to perform a legal task, you agreed, and that person's detrimental reliance substitutes for consideration. If you failed to follow through and caused harm, you are liable [§8.05]. Ask yourself: From the seller's perspective, is it foreseeable that he could be harmed if you fail to register the deed? If you agree to perform a legal task for an unrepresented party, you should follow through or risk liability.

### ➤§1.13 PROSPECTIVE CLIENTS: FAMILY MEMBERS

Son asks you to draft Dad's will, or transfer Dad's assets to make Dad eligible for Medicaid in the nursing home. Your client? Dad, whose money and legal rights are at stake. Son is Dad's agent in requesting your services. But what if Son is the beneficiary of some of Dad's transactions? Is Son relying on you for legal advice for himself as well?

➤**Red Flag**➤ You bear the burden of clarifying which family members you represent, and if you intend to represent more than one, to identify and respond appropriately to joint client conflicts of interest [§§1.15, 6.31]. Written engagement agreements [§1.04] will force

---

[26] E.g., *Kremser v. Quarles & Brady, L.L.P.*, 36 P.3d 761 (Ariz. App. 2001) (corporation's lawyers undertook responsibility to perfect nonclient creditor's security interest); *Nelson v. Nationwide Mortgage Corp.*, 659 F. Supp. 611 (D.D.C. 1987) (lawyer volunteered to answer questions and explain document).

§1.14(b)          Who Is Your Client? • 17

you to think about the implications of any joint representation and clarify murky family situations.

## ➤ §1.14 PROSPECTIVE CLIENTS: LIMITED-TERM PRO BONO SERVICES

### ➤ §1.14(a) The Legal Services Hotline?

**The local legal services office has asked our firm to staff a hotline one night per month. We will either give quick advice over the telephone or make an appointment for the person with a staff lawyer for more difficult questions. How can we handle the conflict of interest issues?**

You (and the legal service program and its clients) are fortunate. You are making good on your *pro bono* commitment under Model Rule 6.1 and helping people who really need your services. Under new Model Rule 6.5, lawyers serving pro bono hotlines such as the one you describe will be free to take on any matter that does not involve an obvious conflict of interest without making the elaborate check that would so obviously destroy the very purpose the hot line was designed to fulfill. With that good news, maybe you will do it once a week.

### ➤ §1.14(b) Volunteering For A Nonprofit Program

You agree to staff a hotline or "Ask a Lawyer" night at a local television station or at the local courthouse kiosk once a month, where you answer questions about legal problems. Clients? Yes, for a limited time and purpose.[27] You have assumed the 4 C's, which mean that you must communicate adequately, give competent advice, keep the client's confidences, and resolve conflicts. But here, running a conflicts check [§§6.06-6.07] before you answered any question would make short-term legal services virtually impossible to provide. Yet without such a check, the potential exists for you to give a person legal advice against a current client of your law firm.

Model Rule 6.5 was drafted with these considerations in mind. It facilitates your pro bono service by making you responsible for conflicts only when you know about them on the spot. If your caller wants to sue your law firm's biggest client, Big Bank, you must excuse yourself from answering the question. But if you don't know the name of

---

[27] Model Rule 6.1; RLGL §38 comment c.

the caller or the name of the potential adversary, or if you do but do not know that the adversary is currently a client of your firm, then the rule protects you by suspending the need for conflicts checks in short-term pro bono representations. We hope this encourages you to assist nonprofit pro bono projects.

### ▶§1.15 JOINT CLIENTS

Whenever two or more prospective clients discuss a future representation with you, you must be clear whether you can represent one, some, all, or none. Some joint client conflicts are nonconsentable [§6.21], which means that you must tell the parties that you cannot represent any or all of them. Other joint client conflicts are consentable, but first must be recognized [§§6.21- 6.31] before they can be waived by adequate informed consent [§3.05], including attention to confidentiality as well as loyalty issues. Once again, you bear the burden of identifying the conflicts issues [§9.02] and obtaining informed consent. If you have identified more than one client, §6.21 will guide you through the loyalty maze.

▶**Red Flag**▶ If a prospective client seeks representation that will have a material adverse effect on another current client of your law firm, you have a potential joint or concurrent client conflict situation. You will rarely be able to respond to such a circumstance unless you know it exists. This is why every law firm, from solo practices to huge multi-office conglomerates, must have a conflicts system that allows each lawyer to search the file, as well as poll her colleagues, to determine whether a proposed client representation will conflict with the firm's representation of another current client [§§6.06 and 6.07]. The situations discussed below in §§1.16-1.18 also present the potential for joint client conflicts.

### ▶§1.16 THIRD-PERSON DIRECTION

In law practice, he who pays the piper does not always call the tune [§6.31]. If Son pays for Dad's legal advice or services, Dad, not Son, is your client. Parents who pay for the representation of minor children may want to know everything and control most aspects of the representation, but Child, not Parents, is your client. As a result, Child controls what Parents get to hear and ultimately, Child determines his or her own best interests. Model Rule 1.8(f) requires that you get a client's consent to any third-person payment, inform your client that you will keep client's confidences from all, including the third-party payer, and that you will exercise your independent professional judgment on behalf of the client. Model Rule 5.4(c) further mandates that you continue this single-minded devotion to your client's interests throughout the representation. Insurance defense, discussed below, presents one of the most common third-person payment conflicts.

## ➤ §1.17 INSURANCE DEFENSE

### ➤ §1.17(a) How Many Clients?

**When the insurance company hires me to represent its insured, do I have one client or two?**

It depends. In most states, the *insured* is the only client. In some, however, the insurance company is also deemed a client. This construct solves some problems and creates others. It gives the insurance company financing the engagement more clout with the lawyer; some would say too much clout. It also cements claims of privilege for communications with the insurance company. On the other hand, if it is a joint representation, the lawyer, from the beginning, has to worry about conflicts between the insurance company and the insured. As a result, some of these proposed joint representations will be non-starters because issues relating to coverage are already present. And if those conflict issues are not apparent in the beginning they can develop at any time. In addition, the joint representation model means that issues relating to the confidentiality of information must be addressed. When the lawyer could learn from the insured client confidential information that could provide a policy defense (such as intentional misconduct or lack of cooperation), the lawyer is barred from sharing that information with the co-client insurance company.

### ➤ §1.17(b) Defending Insureds

Typical liability policies promise to "defend" when a covered person is sued for a covered event, and to "indemnify" that person up to an insured amount. Defending a claim requires the insurer to provide a lawyer to represent the insured. The same policies provide that the insurer retains the right to control most aspects of the representation, including the right to select counsel and usually, when to settle the matter. This policy language grafts an additional layer of conflict on the client-lawyer relationship, which courts [§9.06] routinely resolve in favor of insureds [§6.32].

Policy language also creates an initial issue of whether you as defense counsel have one or two clients. All jurisdictions agree that you represent the insured. At this point, a split develops. Many characterize insurance defense as a one-client situation, with defense counsel paid by a third party, the insurer. Others prefer a joint client approach, meaning that you represent both the insured and the insurer.[28] In fact, it may not matter which of these characterizations exists in your jurisdiction, because two-client courts [§9.06] usually go on to assert that the insured is the "primary client" whenever a conflict develops. And third-party payment one-client jurisdictions often find that the insurer is the agent of the insured for purposes of the attorney-client privilege. So, be clear that your primary or only duty is to the insured, despite daily pressures to the contrary. The insured, not the insurer, controls the representation because neither Model Rule 1.8(f) nor 1.7(b) will let you behave any other way [§6.32].

## ➤§1.18 ORGANIZATIONS AND EMPLOYEES

### ➤§1.18(a) Defending Constituents?

**I don't know what it is but our prospective clients seem to come in groups. We represent this small public company. The SEC is investigating insider trading and alleges two employees bought ahead of some good news. General Counsel says it's a bogus claim. Wants us to represent company and the two employees. That way company won't incur too big of an expense since it's liable to advance the employees' legal fees.**

What a sweet deal. Unfortunately, we don't see how it'll work. Their interests are certainly not directly adverse. The real question, however, is whether as the broker's lawyer you will ever be free to give the individuals the advice they may need. Just think about the fact that they might want to take the Fifth Amendment. Or that they are worried about keeping their jobs. Or what you may do with the information that these employees share with you. We are not sure the company's lawyer could even give them advice on this issue. On the other hand, it could be that the interests of the employer and the employees are perfectly aligned. The problem is that at the time you take on the representation of the employees you may not know enough to make that determination, and there may be a substantial risk that material

---

[28] RLGL §134 comment f.

§1.18(b)  WHO IS YOUR CLIENT? • 21

limitations will arise later that your corporate client and you will deeply regret. Tell GC you sympathize with his interest in the corporate fisc but the economical route may prove quite a bit more costly.

### ▶§1.18(b) Organizational Clients

You are inside or outside counsel to a large publicly held corporation or a governmental unit. Or you occasionally provide legal advice to a partnership, a family business, or a non-profit organization. Who is your client? Model Rule 1.13 governs all of these representations and begins by instructing you that your client is the organization, not any constituent of the organization. It further requires that when any doubt clouds a given representation or occasion (from the client's point of view) you must clarify the identity of the client as well as your own role in the client's matters [§6.29]. If you frequently deal with one or a select group of officers or directors, be sure that they do not become clients as well. Remember, if that person asks you for personal legal advice and you give it, you are only that person's detrimental reliance away from another client-lawyer relationship [§1.03(b)]. Think, for example, of your membership on the client's board of directors. Do they rely on you for legal advice? If so, you should clarify when you are acting as a lawyer (and for whom) to ensure that the attorney-client privilege attaches to the conversation.[29] Similarly, accompanying employees to depositions does not necessarily mean that you represent them. But if the employee depends upon you for personal legal advice, be sure to clarify your role.[30]

This does not mean that you cannot represent both organization and employee.[31] If you decide to proceed with a joint representation, make clear to the employee that he or she is a client, owed the same fiduciary duties you afford to that person's employer. But joint representation depends upon a careful conflicts analysis [§6.21], as well as attention to confidentiality [§6.22]. Finally, if you undertake such a joint representation, make clear what events (conflicts) will require you to withdraw from the matter.

▶**Red Flag**▶ If you learn of misconduct from a constituent of your organizational client, and you do nothing about it, you may suf-

---

[29] Model Rule 1.7, Comment [35].
[30] Model Rules 1.13 and 1.7 Comment [34].
[31] Model Rule 1.13(g).

fer later liability to your organizational client for failing to protect it from the actions of a rogue employee. Your duty of care [§4.02] requires you to protect your client from harm, which is why you may be required to refer the matter to a higher authority in the organization.[32]

### ➤§1.19 CLIENTS WHO MORPH

A state of the art conflicts system [§§6.06, 6.07] is only as good as the information you put into the database. Lawyers have been inadvertently caught in conflicts,[33] accused of incompetence,[34] and even charged with fraud[35] because a client's name was misspelled, or because a lawyer forgot to recognize that client identity can change over time. The most obvious client metamorphoses occur because of a specific event, such as a change in a client name, brought about by marriage, merger, acquisition, or corporate reorganization. All these changes must be entered in your database. The situations discussed below are less obvious and have accordingly caught the most well-intentioned lawyers unaware. Remember that your client can morph on you, either because the client assumes or operates under a different identity from the one you initially encountered, or because natural events such as death or completion of a client representation cause legally required changes in identity. The situations discussed in §§1.20-1.24 below all involve clients who can morph into new "accidental" clients.

### ➤§1.20 ENTITIES

#### ➤§1.20(a) The Corporate Buyout?

**I'm in a real pickle. I've been suing this realtor on behalf of a disgruntled buyer. Suit's been ongoing for two years. Now I learn the realtor was just purchased by my client, the Title Company.**

That is called a "thrust upon" conflict. You didn't do anything to create it. Neither did your buyer client. It doesn't seem fair that you would have to stop representing buyer. On the other hand, if you proceed without consent this is a clear violation of the rules of profession-

---

[32] 1 Geoffrey C. Hazard & W. William Hodes, *The Law of Lawyering* §4.8 (Aspen 3d ed. 2005). (Hereinafter "Hazard & Hodes".)

[33] *A. v. B.*, 726 A. 2d 924 (N.J. 1999).

[34] *In re American Continental Corp./Lincoln Savings and Loan Securities Litigation*, 794 F. Supp. 1424 (D. Ariz. 1992).

[35] *In re Forrest*, 730 A.2d 340 (N.J. 1999).

al conduct [§6.24]. Maybe your title company client will give you a waiver. If not, you could proceed and, if the title company moves to disqualify you, you could urge the judge to use her discretion to let you continue. Some courts [§9.06] have done that. The ABA has promulgated a new comment to Model Rule 1.7 that would permit you to choose to continue to represent one client or the other.[36] If that comment were applied, you would still have to choose which of your clients you wish to abandon. Better than losing both, but hardly the kind of choice that is designed to generate warm and fuzzy feelings.

### ➤§1.20(b) Entity Clients, Of Constituents And Parents

Entity clients may or may not think and act like their legal structure. Some assume that every subsidiary, sibling, or even joint venture morphs into one unified profit center for purposes of shareholder success, employee pensions, or lawyer loyalty. Others operate subsidiaries independently. Family-owned businesses may treat the corporation as Dad's, and Dad may assume that you are his personal as well as his corporate lawyer. In identifying your entity clients, all of this matters. Generally, you can rely on the name of the entity in identifying the client. But if your client is a family business, a wholly owned sub, a sister company, or the parent of a wholly owned sub, you need to clarify which entities or constituents you represent [§6.29]. If you don't, then the CEO or affiliated company later may claim that you represent all of them, and seek your disqualification in any subsequent matter against the affiliates you did not think were clients.[37]

➤**Red Flag**➤ If you represent a family business, be clear that taking on personal matters for family members may create reasonable expectations by those individuals that you are their personal as well as their corporate lawyer.

### ➤§1.21 DEATH OF A CLIENT

### ➤§1.21(a) Settling A Pending Case?

What if my client died last week? Can I still settle her case? If the other side finds out first, they'll probably withdraw their latest offer.

---

[36] Model Rule 1.7 Comment [5]; RLGL §132 comment j.
[37] RLGL §121 comment d.

Don't even think about it. This one may appear to be difficult, but courts [§9.06] agree that it's simple. The truth is right now you have no client. Yet if you pursue the settlement you will be implicitly representing that you do. Under these circumstances you may not take any further steps until you are retained by a new client (e.g., the estate of your former client) and the other side is informed of the unfortunate untimely demise of your former client.

### ➤§1.21(b) When A Client Dies

If a client dies while a matter is pending, you have lost one client and probably gained another. Survivor statutes retain a cause of action for a deceased person, but transfer it to a legal representative, such as a personal executor or the estate. Wrongful death statutes create a new cause of action on behalf of new parties.

➤**Red Flag**➤ Continuing to assert even implicitly that you represent a living person who has died is a fraud [§8.04], both because the client ceases to exist for legal purposes and because the client's legal rights may change upon death.[38] So acknowledge the client's change of identity with opposing counsel, in court, and in your conflicts database [§§6.06, 6.07] as soon as this event occurs.[39] Entity clients also die, through bankruptcy, reorganization, or dissolution. Competence [Chapter 4] demands that you understand the nature of this legal metamorphosis and respond accordingly.

### ➤§1.22 CLIENTS WITH DIMINISHED CAPACITY

A client's diminished capacity to make decisions can cause a subtle or complete change in the client-lawyer relationship, creating one of the most difficult of legal ethics problems [§10.04]. Model Rule 1.14, the rule that addresses this issue, recognizes that capacity exists on a continuum and requires that lawyers "maintain a normal client-lawyer relationship" "as far as reasonably possible."[40]

➤**Red Flag**➤ When you represent a client with diminished capacity, be circumspect in relying on another person who purports to

---

[38] *Virzi v. Grand Trunk Warehouse & Cold Storage Co.*, 571 F. Supp. 507 (E. D. Mich. 1983).

[39] A.B.A. Formal Op. 95-397.

[40] Model Rule 1.14(a); RLGL §24.

§1.23(a)                 Who Is Your Client?   •   25

speak for your client, especially when that family member or friend stands to gain or lose from the communication. You have an obligation to clarify your client's intent, or to protect your client if you cannot discern it.

When you client's intent is not clear, the Restatement recommends that you should pursue your own "reasonable view of the client's objectives or interests of the client as the client would define them if able to make adequately considered decisions on the matter, even if the client expresses no wishes or gives contrary instructions."[41] When a client's diminished capacity threatens serious physical, financial, or other harm, you should take other protective measures, and you are impliedly authorized to breach confidentiality to consult with others to do so, such as client's family, or consulting with other individuals or entities that can act to protect the client.[42] In an extreme case of threatened harm, lawyers may seek the appointment of a guardian to protect the client. If that occurs, you may have a new client, the guardian, or, depending on the extent of the guardianship, you may have two clients: Your client with diminished capacity for all purposes not covered by the guardianship, and the guardian for all other purposes. Remember, however, that the guardian can choose another lawyer, which leaves you with either your client for matters outside the guardianship or, if a general guardianship has been established, with a former client but no current client at all.

➤**Ultimate Red Flag**➤ Representing a client with diminished capacity creates some of the most difficult dilemmas for lawyers because they can neither blindly follow such a client's instructions nor ignore them. We explore this clash between fiduciary duty and preventing client harm more thoroughly in §10.04.

### ➤§1.23 CLASS ACTIONS

### ➤§1.23(a) The Uncertified Class?

**The power of a class action! I have a client who has been terminated in clear violation of the age discrimination laws. From what he told me, there were dozens in his position. So I brought it as a class action just last week. Now the company's lawyer has**

---

[41] RLGL §24(2).
[42] Model Rule 1.14(b) and Comment [5].

called me up. Offered an extra $100,000 to my client if we settle now and the only condition is that I promise not to sue 'em again. When I asked whether they thought the court would approve this deal, they told me the best news of all: The settlement doesn't require court approval. Who knew?

It is true that recent changes to Rule 23 of the Federal Rules of Civil Procedure only require court approval of a settlement after the class is certified. Obviously your worthy opponent is relying on this change. The problem is, you may be sorry to learn, the rules of civil procedure do not have the ability to change the lawyer codes [§9.04]. You filed a lawsuit as a class action. When you did so you undertook to represent the class. At that moment you accepted a fiduciary duty to the class that you cannot so easily jettison simply because suddenly you wish to put the interests of your initial individual client or your own interests in the driver's seat.

Making the offer contingent on your agreeing never to sue the company again is another ethics violation. Lawyers are banned from offering or accepting as part of a settlement any restriction on their right to practice law. The rule, Model Rule 5.6, is designed to save lawyers from the trap that would be created by it being in the best interests of the present client to accept the limitation even though the lawyer, and more important the public, would want the lawyer experienced in these matters to be able to take on new representations against the company. If the company wants to prevent the lawyer from suing it again it may do so by hiring the lawyer to represent the company; any such engagement, however, must come after the first matter is settled and not even be hinted at as part of the settlement process.

### ➤§1.23(b) Class Clients

Identifying your client in a class action may not be easy. Initially, you represent the named class representatives, but not the unnamed class members, especially for the purposes of conflicts resolution.[43] Yet, a "fiduciary duty not to prejudice the interest that putative class members have in their class action litigation" may exist even before the class is certified, including the duty to notify and afford absent class members a chance to object to your actions that would

---

[43] Model Rule 1.7, Comment [25].

put their rights at risk.[44] After certification, the named plaintiffs represent a larger group, which means that you have assumed fiduciary duties to the entire class, not just the named plaintiffs.[45] As the representation continues, you have the obligation to "act for the benefit of the class as its members would reasonably define that benefit."[46] At this point your client can morph because conflicts between class representatives and class members may require that you recommend redefining the class or creating subclasses.

### ➤§1.24 ENDING A REPRESENTATION

When you complete a client matter, or voluntarily or involuntarily withdraw from a representation [§7.02], your current client becomes a former client. At this point, you lose all but one of the fiduciary duties you assumed when you took on the representation. You no longer owe duties of competence or communication, and your fiduciary obligation of loyalty only remains to the extent that you cannot undermine what you have accomplished. Confidentiality, on the other hand, lasts forever, even after the death of the client. The "substantial relationship" test protects former clients by requiring that you obtain their informed consent before you represent any subsequent clients whose interests are materially adverse to those of the former client in a substantially related matter [§6.33].[47] You can be disqualified or disciplined if you take on a new matter when you should not. To clarify this change in status and obligation, be sure to move the client's entry in your conflicts database from your current client conflicts file to your former client conflicts file [§6.07] whenever you complete a matter or your representation otherwise ends.

### ➤§1.25 THE DISENGAGEMENT LETTER

Disengagement letters are helpful when you complete a matter, decide to withdraw or are fired by the client, or when you leave a law firm and do not intend to continue work on a matter. The letter should make clear the reason the relationship has ended, and include appropriate

---

[44] *Schick v. Berg, Moriarity, & Leyendecker, P.C.*, 2004 U.S. Dist. Lexis 6842 (S.D.N.Y. Apr. 20, 2004).

[45] RLGL §14 comment f.

[46] *Id.*

[47] Model Rule 1.9; RLGL §132.

warnings about unfinished work and time deadlines.[48] You may want to address whether the client wants you to communicate with successor counsel, and how you intend to provide for the orderly transmission of client files and documents. You also can use this opportunity to convey a willingness to serve in additional matters in the future.

➤**Red Flag**➤ When you hope for future business in a disengagement letter, be careful to clarify your lack of continuing obligation in the matter for which you no longer assume any responsibility. Otherwise, the client may reasonably believe you stand ready to be his continuing counsel, and may rely on your lack of communication as legal advice that all is well, or that nothing else needs to be done.

### ➤§1.26 QUASI-CLIENTS

Most clients hire you to protect them against or to deal with some third party. Generally, you owe no fiduciary duties to those third parties.[49] But some situations create quasi-fiduciary duties to some third persons or entities. We call these third parties "quasi-clients" because they do not have all the legal rights clients possess, but they can impose legal obligations upon you, simply because you are another person's lawyer.

➤**Red Flag**➤ The situations described in §§1.27-1.29 below create legal minefields and may create additional "accidental" clients for lawyers unaware of their requirements. If you draft documents, represent fiduciaries, or agree to accommodate someone else on behalf of a client, be clear whether you have assumed obligations to someone you never intended to represent.[50]

### ➤§1.27 THIRD-PARTY BENEFICIARIES

### ➤§1.27(a) The Opinion Letter?

**My client wants me to issue an opinion to the bank that the client is duly incorporated and authorized to enter into this loan. What should I be worried about?**

---

[48] *Gilles v. Wiley, Malehorn & Sirota*, 783 A.2d 756 (N.J. Super. Ct. App. Div. 2001) (former client stated cause of action against lawyers who withdrew at the last minute without adequately warning her by certified mail that the statute of limitations was about to run on her medical malpractice case).

[49] *Connely v. McColloch*, 83 P.3d 457 (Wyo. 2004) (daughter not intended beneficiary of father's divorce).

[50] RLGL §51.

Plenty. You, of course, owe your client the duty to be sure your opinion is correct. Moreover, unlike the typical matter in which your only exposure is to the client, here you know that a third party—to whom you otherwise owe no duties and as to whom you may have been negotiating vigorously on behalf of your client—is relying on your opinion. Therefore, if it is negligently prepared, even though there is no privity between the bank and you, you may be held liable to the bank as well if it turns out your opinion is in error.

### ➤§1.27(b) Duty To Intended Beneficiaries

If a client asks you to benefit a specific third party, for example, by writing an opinion letter or by drafting a document like a will or trust, you only act competently by fulfilling the wishes of the client. The third-party beneficiary is not your client, but many courts [§9.06] grant certain classes of third-party beneficiaries duties of competence for malpractice purposes [§8.05].[51] If your client specifically names a third-party beneficiary in a document, you should assume that you owe coextensive duties to that person. If your drafting requires that you assert certain propositions to be true, make sure your boilerplate accurately conveys what you have done (conducted a UCC tax and judgment search) and found (the farm property is free and clear of all liens). Relying on your client for these assertions is risky at best, because inaccurate statements can make you liable for malpractice [§8.06] or misrepresentation [§§8.04, 8.05] to the third-party beneficiary.[52]

A different rule may apply if you draft a public offering that will be relied on by thousands. They are not third-party beneficiaries, even if they may be foreseeable plaintiffs. Here, absent fraud, many courts [§9.06] limit liability to those who are specifically identified or invited to rely on your work at the time of the service [§8.05].[53]

---

[51] *In re Guardianship of Karan*, 38 P.3d 396 (Wash. App. 2002) (minor child has cause of action against mother's lawyer who set up child's trust to allow pilfering of the estate); *Lucas v. Hamm*, 364 P.2d 685 (Cal. 1961), *cert. denied*, 368 U.S. 987 (1962) (intended beneficiaries of a will could recover from lawyer whose negligence in drafting document caused them to lose their testamentary rights).

[52] *Greycas, Inc. v. Proud*, 826 F.2d 1560 (7th Cir. 1987), *cert. denied*, 484 U.S. 1043 (1988).

[53] RLGL §51 comment e; *Conroy v. Andeck Resources '81 Year-End Ltd.*, 484 N.E.2d 525 (Ill. App. 1985).

What if, in drafting a document that third parties will rely upon, you discover confidential information that the third party would love to know, but your client does not want to share? Remember, you owe only one client the 4 C's. You must first be competent [Chapter 4], and second communicate [Chapter 3] your client's legal obligation to disclose. Third, confidentiality [Chapter 5] requires you to seek your client's permission to disclose the smoking gun. With respect to conflicts of interest [Chapter 6], if disclosure is just too much for your client to bear, then your client, not you, decides whether to forgo the whole deal (because law requires disclosure) or to disclose the information. Your loyalty obligation to your client comes first, and only when your client decides to provide information or benefit to a third party is your duty of competence to that third person triggered.[54] If your client insists that you write the letter without the legally required disclosures, you cannot proceed, because to do so would violate a legal limitation [Chapter 7].

### ➤ §1.28 CLIENT-FIDUCIARIES

If your client is a trustee, guardian, corporate director, or partner, you should be mindful of the beneficiaries of your client's fiduciary duties as well as your client to avoid later claims of malpractice by either [§8.05]. Some commentators call the beneficiaries of your client's fiduciary duties "derivative clients," because the beneficiary does not stand at arm's length with your client. Your legal advice to these clients, such as trustees, can impose a duty of competence to the beneficiaries.[55] If you suspect breach of fiduciary duty by a client, tell him or her so in no uncertain terms. If the conduct does not stop, withdraw to avoid counseling or assisting an illegal or fraudulent act [§7.02].[56]

You should not be held liable for later malpractice when your client's legal duties to another conflict with your client's own rights or responsibilities. For example, courts [§9.06] have refused to find that a lawyer who represented an estate executor had a duty to beneficiaries of the estate, whose interests may conflict with those of the estate's

---

[54] Model Rule 2.3.
[55] Hazard and Hodes, §2.7.
[56] *Fickett v. Superior Court*, 558 P.2d 988 (Ariz. App. 1976).

administration.[57] You should be free to advise about both, so your sole client is the executor.

## ▶ §1.29 "ACCOMMODATION" CLIENTS

### ▶ §1.29(a) The Accommodated CFO?

I've been representing a company. During discovery as a favor I represented the company's CFO at his deposition. Now the CFO has been named a defendant. When the company decided to file a cross claim against the CFO, the CFO's new lawyer moved to have me disqualified. Talk about no good deed goes unpunished.

When you went to the deposition with the CFO, he was either unrepresented or he was your client.

**Someone said the CFO was just an accommodation client.**

That term gets invoked from time to time. The problem is calling the CFO an accommodation client doesn't answer any question that will guide your conduct. The fact is you had two concurrent clients in the same matter. Even if your representation of the CFO is completed, the CFO is a former client. And if you are bringing a claim by the company against the CFO in the same matter in which you once represented the CFO, you violate Model Rule 1.9 in doing so. This matter is not just substantially related; it's the same matter. The CFO was a real client. The information the CFO shared with you must be kept confidential. And whether you were just doing her (or your company client) a favor, the CFO is entitled to the loyalty the rules provide for former clients.

By the way, your question does not tell us enough, but if facts came to your attention during your representation of the CFO that indicated any conflict between the CFO and her employer, you had an immediate obligation to withdraw from representing the CFO, not wait until the "accommodation" representation was over. Even after doing that, there is a chance the CFO can knock you out of representing the company as well. The lesson is clear: Being accommodating can get a lawyer in real trouble.

---

[57] *Trask v. Butler*, 872 P.2d 1080 (Wash. 1994).

▶**§1.29(b) Accommodating A Third Party**

The Restatement created the label "accommodation client" to describe agreements by lawyers to provide limited services to third parties as an accommodation to a current client (often for no additional charge), for example in a joint defense situation.[58] The courts [§9.06] have often rejected this concept, holding that an agreement to represent an accommodation client creates a real client-lawyer relationship. If you want to accommodate a client by taking on another representation, you are free to do so, but recognize that you are taking on a new client, and that the burden rests on your shoulders to clarify and justify the limited nature and scope of the service [§1.03], as well as any conflicts that may lurk in the representation [§6.21].[59]

▶**Red Flag**▶ Do not rely on your characterization of a favor to a client as "perfunctory" or "an accommodation," because a court, if later asked to address the matter, usually in the context of a disqualification motion or a malpractice claim, probably will disagree and find a client-lawyer relationship. If you want to accommodate a current client by providing service to a related party or entity, add that party to your current client database [§6.07] and assume all the obligations to the "accommodatee" you provide to all of your clients.

### ▶§1.30 IMPUTED CLIENTS: LAW FIRMS AND SHARED OFFICE SPACE

If you have a client, so does your entire law firm. Likewise, if any other lawyer in your firm has a client, so do you.[60] But even when you haven't set up your practice to share revenue and clients, you may in fact look or act like you have done so. Lawyers who share office space often also share secretarial or other office help, and may cover for each other, or share file space as well. Office-sharing lawyers also may interact informally as lawyers in law firms do, consulting each other on cases or becoming involved in informal office discussions about the matters of the day. If you use a common letterhead, or have a secretary answer a common phone with all of the lawyer's names in the same sentence, you are holding yourselves out as a firm even if you do not otherwise

---

[58] RLGL §132 comment i.

[59] *Universal City Studios, Inc. v. Reimerdes*, 98 F. Supp. 2d 449 (S.D.N.Y. 2000).

[60] Model Rule 1.10.

share revenue.[61] Similarly, if you allow other lawyers access to your client files, or discuss your cases with other lawyers in your office space, you are sharing client confidences and therefore treating your clients as if they were clients of the "firm."[62] This will impute all of your conflicts of interest to the other lawyers in your firm and vice versa [§6.05].

▶**Red Flag**▶ If you share office space, be clear about the legal implications created by your practices. Courts [§9.06] will treat your clients or those of your office-sharers as those of a law firm if you either hold yourself out or otherwise act like you are a "firm." If you want this flexibility and interaction, enjoy the benefits of the collaboration, but combine each lawyer's client files for purposes of conflicts checks [§§6.06-6.07]. If you don't want to be treated as a firm for conflicts purposes, don't act or look like one. Bar access to client files, keep client confidences, answer each phone individually, and use separate letterheads.

---

[61] *In re Sexson,* 613 N.E. 2d 841 (Ind. 1993).

[62] Model Rule 1.0(c) and Comment [2].

# 2

# Fees: Contract Or Fiduciary Duty?

➤ §2.01 Fee Contracts
➤ §2.02 Reasonable Fees And Expenses
　　➤ §2.02(a) The Initial Agreement?
　　➤ §2.02(b) Fiduciary Limitations On Contract
➤ §2.03 Chart: State Rules Requiring Written Fee Agreements
➤ §2.04 Fee Modifications
　　➤ §2.04(a) The Unanticipated Bad Case?
　　➤ §2.04(b) Fiduciary Limits On Fee Modifications
➤ §2.05 Statutory Fee Requirements
　　➤ §2.05(a) Statutory Limitations On Contract
　　➤ §2.05(b) The Statutory Windfall?
　　➤ §2.05(c) Statutory Fee Shifting
➤ §2.06 Judicial Power To Limit Contractual Fees
➤ §2.07 Hourly Fees
　　➤ §2.07(a) The Professional Hour?
　　➤ §2.07(b) Reasonable Hourly Fees
➤ §2.08 Contingent Fees
　　➤ §2.08(a) The Contingent Fee Windfall?
　　➤ §2.08(b) Reasonable Contingent Fees
　　➤ §2.08(c) Negative Contingent Fees?

▶ §2.08(d) Contingent Fee Conflicts Of Interest
▶ §2.09 Fixed Or Flat Fees
  ▶ §2.09(a) The Flat Fee Risk?
  ▶ §2.09(b) Reasonable Flat Fees
▶ §2.10 Retainers
  ▶ §2.10(a) The Nonrefundable Retainer?
  ▶ §2.10(b) General And Special "Retainers"
▶ §2.11 Fees On Termination (Withdrawal Or Firing)
▶ §2.12 Fee Sharing
  ▶ §2.12(a) The Fee-Splitting Windfall?
  ▶ §2.12(b) Reasonable (And Proper) Fee Splits
▶ §2.13 Fee Collection
▶ §2.14 Trust Accounts

### ▶ §2.01 FEE CONTRACTS

Generally (but not always) clients and lawyers are free to bargain for any kind of fee (hourly, flat, contingent, or a blend of any or all of these)[1], and for this reason, lawyers' fees are subject to contract law. But because clients repose trust in lawyers and because nearly every fee a lawyer charges involves some personal economic conflict of interest [§6.10], fees also are subject to quasi-fiduciary limitations imposed by lawyer codes [§9.04] and case law [§9.06]. These obligations impose an objective standard of reasonableness on every fee and expense you agree to or in fact collect.

▶**Red Flag**▶ Do not assume that you are free to contract for or collect any fee or reimbursement the market or your client will bear. Doing so can result in both the loss of your ability to collect all or part of the fee [§8.10, §10.07], as well as professional discipline [§8.02]. So be aware of the limitations imposed on lawyer fee contracts listed in §§2.02–2.13 below.

---

[1] Richard C. Reed, *Billing Innovations: New Win-Win Ways to End Hourly Billing* (ABA Law Practice Management 1996).

## ▶ §2.02 REASONABLE FEES AND EXPENSES

### ▶ §2.02(a) The Initial Agreement?

**Do my engagement letters really need to address fees and expenses? What a nuisance!**

If you want to collect your fee and you don't want to engage in elaborate cost accounting you should address expenses in your engagement letter. The ABA Ethics Committee issued a well-received opinion that requires lawyers to disclose the basis on which the client is to be billed for both professional time and any other charges. Even in jurisdictions where a written fee contract is not required [§9.04], in most representations it is difficult to imagine how you can convey this information without a writing. With respect to expenses, the ABA Opinion provided that lawyers had a choice. Either the client agrees to pay the lawyer X¢ for photocopying and $Y for incoming faxes or the lawyer is required to figure out the cost of these services to the lawyer and charge the client no more than that amount. In other words, without client agreement, the opinion concluded that expenses were not to become a profit center for the law firm. As a result, the best practice is to prepare a written expense disclosure statement that details for each new client the basis on which you will charge for these services. That statement can be an attachment to your engagement letter [§1.04], and can simply list the categories of anticipated expenses and disbursements and the basis on which you will charge for each.

### ▶ §2.02(b) Fiduciary Limitations On Contract

The fiduciary duty a lawyer assumes when agreeing to represent a client does not attach until the client-lawyer relationship is established. However, because clients often repose trust in lawyers before this official starting point (assuming that point is clear), lawyer codes [§9.04] and cases [§9.06] where judges set, supervise, or decide disputed fees impose four different obligations that limit a lawyer's ability to charge whatever he or she chooses.

First, every fee agreement and collection of fees and expenses is subject to an objective standard of reasonableness, measured by the range of reasonable fees other reasonable lawyers would charge for the same or similar representation.[2] Courts [§9.06] look to the same fac-

---

[2] ABA Model Rule of Professional Conduct 1.5(a) (2002) (hereinafter "Model Rules"); *Restatement of the Law Third, The Law Governing Lawyers*, §34 (ALI 2000). (Hereinafter "RLGL".)

tors lawyers do: The time, labor and skill involved, the fee customarily charged by similarly situated lawyers, the amount involved and results obtained, limitations put on a lawyer's time or acceptance of other employment, and the kind of fee, fixed or contingent. With respect to disbursements and expenses, it is perfectly proper to agree in advance on the fees that you will charge for such services (e.g., 15¢/page for photocopies; $200/hr. for electronic research). In the absence of such an explicit agreement, you may bill only the actual cost of these services.[3] If you bill more, you have turned the provision of these services into a "profit center" in violation of Model Rule 1.5's reasonableness requirement.[4]

▶**Red Flag**▶ If another lawyer would consider it unreasonable to charge the fee or expense you anticipate, that lawyer could be the source of expert testimony [§10.08] in a later disciplinary action or fee dispute should the client object. And client challenges to fee arrangements—whether warranted or not—are not an infrequent occurrence.

Second, statutes and lawyer codes [§9.04] require special and specific writing obligations for many fee agreements. All contingent fee arrangements, for example, require a written agreement,[5] and many jurisdictions regulate the amount of the contingency or require specific language in engagement agreements.[6] In a growing number of jurisdictions, as the chart in §2.03 indicates, *all* fee contracts must be reduced to a written format.[7]

Third, some fee contracts are not permitted at all in certain circumstances. For example, most jurisdictions do not allow contingent

---

[3] ABA Formal Opinion 00-420, Surcharge To Client for Use of Contract Lawyer (If contract lawyer is billed as an expense, in absence of contrary understanding, the client may be charged only the direct cost of the lawyer. If contract lawyer billed as legal services or fees, a surcharge may be added without client consent, as long as rate charged is reasonable).

[4] ABA Formal Opinion 93-379, Billing for Professional Fees, Disbursements and Other Expenses.

[5] Model Rule 1.5(c).

[6] Cal. Bus. & Prof. Code §6146 (2004) (Actions Against Health Care Providers); N.Y. Jud. Law §474-a (2004) (Contingent Fees in Medical, Dental and Podiatric Malpractice Actions).

[7] Ala., Colo., Conn., D.C., N.J., Pa., R.I., and Utah Rule 1.5(b), Cal. Bus. & Prof. Code §6148 (all fees over $1,000); N.Y. DR 2-106(c)(2)(ii) (all domestic relations fees); 22 N.Y. C.R.R. Part 1215 (2002) (all fees over $3,000).

§2.03    FEES: CONTRACT OR FIDUCIARY DUTY?    •    39

fees in divorce or dissolution matters or in criminal cases [§2.08]. Flat fees may not be allowed in insurance defense [§2.09].

Fourth, because clients can fire lawyers at any time for any reason, most courts [§9.06] hold that when this occurs, lawyers lose their right to a contract fee and can recover only in quantum meruit [§2.11]. If your client fires you "for cause," total or partial fee forfeiture also becomes a real possibility [§8.10].

▶**Red Flag**▶ You should reduce all fee agreements to a writing and keep track of billable hours in all representations. If you do not complete the matter, the burden of proof will be on you to establish the basis for quantum meruit, which a court may well decide should be measured by the "lodestar": Reasonable number of hours times a reasonable hourly rate.

### ▶§2.03 CHART: STATE RULES REQUIRING WRITTEN FEE AGREEMENTS

|  | **Contingent Fees:** | **Other Fees:** |
|---|---|---|
| **ABA Model Rules** | 1.5(c): Writing Required | 1.5(b): "The scope of representation and the basis or rate of the fee and expenses for which the client will be responsible shall be communicated to the client, preferably in writing, before or within a reasonable time after commencing the representation, except when the lawyer will charge a regularly represented client on the same basis or rate. Any changes in the basis or rate of the fee or expenses shall be communicated to the client." |
| **Alabama** | 1.5(c): Writing Required | 1.5(b): Writing Preferred |
| **Alaska** | 1.5(c): Writing Required | 1.5(b): Writing Required if fee >$500; writing must be consistent with Rule 1.4(c). |
| **Arizona** | 1.5(c): Writing Required | 1.5(b): Writing Required |
| **Arkansas** | 1.5(c): Writing Required | 1.5(b): Writing Preferred |
| **California** | Cal. Bus. & Prof. Code §6147: Writing Required | Cal. Bus. & Prof. Code §6148: Writing Required if fee > $1,000 and client not a corporation. |
| **Colorado** | 1.5(c): Writing Required | 1.5(b): Writing Required |

|  | **Contingent Fees:** | **Other Fees:** |
|---|---|---|
| **Connecticut** | 1.5(c): Writing Required | 1.5(b): Writing Required, except public defenders or when the lawyer will be paid by the court or a state agency. |
| **Delaware** | 1.5(c): Writing Required | 1.5(b): Writing Preferred |
| **District of Columbia** | 1.5(c): Writing Required | 1.5(b): Writing Required |
| **Florida** | 4-1.5(b): Writing Required | 4-1.5(e): Writing Preferred |
| **Georgia** | 1.5(c): Writing Required | 1.5(b): Writing Preferred |
| **Hawaii** | 1.5(c): Writing Required | 1.5(b): Writing Preferred |
| **Idaho** | 1.5(c): Writing Required | 1.5(b): Writing Preferred |
| **Illinois** | 1.5(c): Writing Required | 1.5(b): Writing Required |
| **Indiana** | 1.5(c): Writing Required | 1.5(b): Writing Preferred |
| **Iowa** | 32:15(c): Writing Required | 32:15(b): Writing Preferred |
| **Kansas** | 1.5(d): Writing Required | 1.5(b): Writing Preferred |
| **Kentucky** | 1.5(c): Writing Required | 1.5(b): Writing Preferred |
| **Louisiana** | 1.5(c): Writing Required | 1.5(b): Writing Preferred |
| **Maine** | Maine Bar Rule 8(d): Writing Required | 3.3(a): Factors to be considered as guides in determining the reasonableness of a fee include: (9) the informed written consent of the client. |
| **Maryland** | 1.5(c): Writing Required | 1.5(b): Writing Preferred |
| **Massachusetts** | 1.5(c): Writing Required | 1.5(b): Writing Preferred |
| **Michigan** | 1.5(c): Writing Required | 1.5(b): Writing Preferred |
| **Minnesota** | 1.5(c): Writing Required | 1.5(b): Writing Preferred |
| **Mississippi** | 1.5(c): Writing Required | 1.5(b): Writing Preferred |
| **Missouri** | R. 4-1.5(c),(d): Writing Required | R. 4-1.5(b): Writing Preferred |
| **Montana** | 1.5(c): Writing Required | 1.5(b): Writing Required if >$500. |
| **Nebraska** | EC 2-19: Writing Preferred | EC 2-19: Writing Preferred |
| **Nevada** | SCR 155(3): Writing Required | SCR 155(2): Writing Preferred |
| **New Hampshire** | 1.5(c): Writing Required | 1.5(b): Writing Preferred |
| **New Jersey** | RPC 1.5(c): Writing Required | RPC 1.5(b): Writing Required |
| **New Mexico** | R 16-105(C): Writing Required | R 16-105(B): Writing Preferred |

|  | **Contingent Fees:** | **Other Fees:** |
|---|---|---|
| **New York** | DR 2-106(d): Writing Required | DR 2-106(c)(2)(ii): Writing required in domestic relations matters, and 22 N.Y.C. R.R. Part 1215: all other fees >$3,000. |
| **North Carolina** | 1.5(c): Writing Required | 1.5(b): Writing Preferred |
| **North Dakota** | 1.5(c): Writing Required | 1.5(b): Writing Required |
| **Ohio** | ORC §4705.15(B): Writing required for tort claims | EC 2-18: Writing Preferred |
| **Oklahoma** | 1.5(c): Writing Required | 1.5(b) Writing Preferred |
| **Oregon** | ORS §20.340: Writing required for personal injury and property damage claims. | 1.5 No writing required |
| **Pennsylvania** | 1.5(c): Writing Required | 1.5(b): Writing Required |
| **Rhode Island** | 1.5(c): Writing Required | 1.5(b): Writing required for billings regarding the fees, costs, and on a quarterly basis or as otherwise provided in the agreement. |
| **South Carolina** | 1.5(c): Writing Required | 1.5(b): Writing Preferred |
| **South Dakota** | 1.5(c): Writing Required | 1.5(b): Writing Preferred |
| **Tennessee** | 1.5(c): Writing Required | 1.5(b): Writing Preferred |
| **Texas** | 1.04(d): Writing Required | 1.04(c): Writing Preferred |
| **Utah** | 1.5(c): Writing Required | 1.5(b): Writing Required if fee > $750. |
| **Vermont** | 1.5(c): Writing Required | 1.5(b): Writing Preferred |
| **Virginia** | 1.5(c): Writing Required | 1.5(b): Writing Preferred |
| **Washington** | 1.5(c)(1): Writing Required | 1.5(b): Writing preferred. Upon the request of the client in any matter, the lawyer shall communicate to the client in writing the basis or rate of the fee. |
| **West Virginia** | 1.5(c): Writing Required | 1.5(b): Writing Preferred |
| **Wisconsin** | 20:1.5(c): Writing Required | 20:1.5(b): Writing Preferred |
| **Wyoming** | 1.5(c): Writing Required | 1.5(b): Writing Required |

## ▶ §2.04 FEE MODIFICATIONS

### ▶ §2.04(a) The Unanticipated Bad Case?

The case has turned out to be a pain. I thought liability was clear. Now it turns out the hospital is defending the claim and has thrown my theory of liability into the waste can. I'm probably going to have to hire two more experts. And this is no million-dollar case. I think it's only fair that I up my contingent fee to 40 percent or maybe even 50 percent.

We feel your pain. But we wonder if you would be asking for permission to reduce your fee if the case turned out to be easier than you expected? If the case settled after one deposition? If the defendant admitted liability?

The rule is that, assuming the contingent fee set is reasonable in light of what is known at the outset, once you sign on to a contingent matter, you, but not the client, are bound to your "deal." There are a few notable exceptions when because of overwhelming hardship a lawyer has been permitted to withdraw from the matter (but not reset the fee), but in the garden variety case the client trades the risk that the lawyer will get a windfall if the case turns out far better or easier than expected for the certainty that the lawyer is committed to see the enterprise to conclusion, no matter how difficult it becomes.[8]

**And the client?**

Clients are free to fire their lawyers at any time for any reason or no reason at all. If that happens in a contingent fee case, the lawyer cannot collect under the agreement (because the contingency hasn't occurred), but the lawyer is entitled to seek a fee in quantum meruit if the client ultimately collects anything in the litigation represented by successor counsel [§2.11].

### ▶§2.04(b) Fiduciary Limits On Fee Modifications

You've taken on a client, provided a written fee agreement, and one or both of you want to modify the fee. At this point, you have assumed the 4 C's, so you have taken on special obligations to protect your client and you must be sure the agreement is fair and reasonable to your client if you want to be able to enforce the modification.[9] Courts [§9.06] presume undue influence [§8.09] if changes are made to fee agreements much beyond a reasonable time after the original

---

[8] *Haines v. Liggett Group Inc.*, 814 F. Supp. 414 (D.N.J. 1993) (lawyer assumes risk of unprofitability in contingent fee cigarette litigation); *Smith v. R. J. Reynolds Co.*, 630 A. 2d 820 (N.J. App. 1993) (lawyer in contingent fee tobacco litigation allowed to withdraw if trial court finds unreasonable financial burden).

[9] RLGL §18.

agreement was reached. You can rebut such a presumption only by showing a combination of these factors: Unanticipated circumstances arose that led to a change, the client asked for the change, the client benefited from the change, the client was aware (because you disclosed) the advantages and disadvantages of the change, and the client consulted an independent lawyer before deciding to accept the modification.

➤**Red Flag**➤ Courts [§9.06] carefully scrutinize fee modifications much like they carefully regulate business deals with clients [§6.11]. You should provide a writing to modify any fee agreement, and use it to articulate the factors that benefit your client. If you are unable to do so, you may have stepped into unreasonable territory, making the modified fee uncollectible and perhaps subjecting yourself to professional discipline [§8.02] as well.

### ➤§2.05 STATUTORY FEE REQUIREMENTS

### ➤§2.05(a) Statutory Limitations On Contract

State and federal statutes limit or shape all kinds of lawyers' fees. Limitations on contingent fees in certain classes of cases, e.g., worker's compensation and under tort reform statutes, are commonly found in state law. At the federal level, the size of a contingent fee in social security disability claims and appeals also is regulated by statute.[10] General provisions such as probate codes often grant or require review of attorney's fees by probate judges because they are expenses against an estate subject to the power of a court. Similar provisions grant judges the power to supervise fees when lawyers represent minors. Although a few courts [§9.06] have interpreted their state constitutional separation of power provisions to limit the legislative branch's ability to regulate fees,[11] most courts defer to legislative power reasonably exercised in this area.[12]

---

[10] *Gisbrecht v. Barnhart*, 535 U.S. 789 (2002).

[11] *Irwin v. Surdyk's Liquor*, 599 N.W.2d 132 (Minn. 1999) (declaring invalid statute that set a maximum permissible fee in worker's compensation cases).

[12] *Samuel v. Workers' Comp. Appeal Board*, 814 A.2d 274 (Pa. Commw. Ct. 2002) (upholding statutory provision that set standard for worker's compensation cases because statute did not limit a Worker's Compensation Judge in allowing a higher fee where appropriate).

### ►§2.05(b) The Statutory Windfall?

**I signed a contingent fee agreement in a Title VII case that provided for a 40 percent fee on any money received by the client. We won. The client is receiving $100,000 in back pay plus reinstatement. We also petitioned for statutory attorney fees and the court awarded the client $80,000. I say I'm entitled to 40 percent of $100,000, plus the $80,000, plus 40 percent of the client's future salary. The client says I get the $40,000 and that's it. What an ingrate.**

Let's dispose of your claim out of the client's future salary. Unless your fee agreement says you get a fee for reinstatement of the client, we are afraid you are out of luck on that one. One risk of any contingent fee case based on a client cash recovery is that the client won't receive any money, but will accept some kind of affirmative relief instead. Unless the fee agreement, which we are sure you crafted, provides for recovery on the client's receipt of something other than money, the courts [§9.06] will hold you to the terms of your agreement.

As for the fee on the back pay award and the statutory fee award, again the client and you will be held to the contingent fee agreement. Since statutory fee awards are almost invariably made to the client, the client here has received $180,000 in total. You, therefore, are entitled to 40 percent of that sum, or $72,000.

**But the fee award was $80,000. I should at least get that! Otherwise the client keeps my fee.**

Not so fast. Only if your fee agreement with the client contemplated that result and then only if the fee is considered reasonable.

### ►§2.05(c) Statutory Fee Shifting

Absent statute, the American (unlike the English) Rule does not provide for fee shifting to a prevailing party. But fee shifting statutes, often called private attorneys general provisions, can create a right to a "reasonable attorney's fee" to a "prevailing party."[13] Hundreds of

---

[13] *Buckhannon Bd. & Care Home, Inc., v. W. Va. Dep't of Health & Human Res.*, 532 U.S. 598 (2001) (parties who receive a judgment on the merits, or a court-ordered consent decree are "prevailing parties," but a party who recovers because of a defendant's voluntary change in conduct not caused by the underlying lawsuit is not); *Loggerhead Turtle v. County Council of Volusia County*, 307 F.3d 1318 (11th Cir. 2002) (*Buckhannon* applies only to "prevailing party" statutes, not to "whenever appropriate" fee award statutes such as the Clean Water and Clean Air Act).

§2.07(a)   FEES: CONTRACT OR FIDUCIARY DUTY? • 45

statutes, including environmental, securities, civil rights, and consumer provisions provide for fee shifting. When this occurs, the statute governs the entitlement.[14] Usually, these provisions pay your client (the prevailing party) not you. At the same time, you are free to contract for a reasonable fee, be it contingent, hourly or flat.[15] Many lawyers blend provisions, providing in the fee contract that any contingent fee will be offset by the statutory amount. So enjoy your newfound source of income. But remember competence: Carefully read the statute and the cases construing it to create a fee contract that benefits both you and your client.

### ➤§2.06 JUDICIAL POWER TO LIMIT CONTRACTUAL FEES

Judges increasingly exert control over fees. Statutory authority to award fees has become more common in the past few decades. Some general statutes, such as bankruptcy and probate codes, require judicial supervision of fees because they come out of the estate subject to court supervision. In class actions, court approval for fees occurs because relevant rules require court approval of all final settlements.[16] Apart from statute, judges have no inherent judicial power over fees, but they nevertheless exert control in a number of other ways. Courts [§9.06] are required to supervise fees because of other obligations, such as the *parens patriae* power of a court to protect a ward. If you sue a client for an unpaid fee, a court assumes jurisdiction over the dispute, including any counterclaims the client may interpose.

➤**Red Flag**➤ Counterclaims for malpractice are becoming increasingly common, so consider whether suing to recover an unpaid fee might trigger such a claim.

### ➤§2.07 HOURLY FEES

### ➤§2.07(a) The Professional Hour?

**Law Schools give a credit hour for students who sit in class 50 minutes. Psychiatrists charge an hourly rate for a similarly**

---

[14] *City of Burlington v. Dague*, 505 U.S. 557 (1992) (requires lodestar calculations under federal fee shifting statutes).

[15] *Gobert v. Williams*, 323 F.3d 1099 (5th Cir. 2003) (upholding validity of fee contract that provided for contingent fee in addition to any statutory fees awarded plaintiff).

[16] Fed. R. Civ. P. 23(e).

short time on the couch. Why can't I be equally creative? If a client turns out to need a memo that's basically the same as the memo we produced in 10 hours for another client, why can't we charge that second client for 11 hours—10 for the first memo and one hour to adapt it for this client's use?

Your creativity is stunning. Fortunately—for your clients—it won't work. Just as the ABA restated academic requirements in terms of minutes to avoid creative hour counting, the ABA has concluded that without full disclosure to the client about how it will be charged ("If we are lucky enough to reuse old work product, we can charge you the same number of hours we charged the first client"), clients who are told they will be billed by the hour are to be billed for actual time dedicated to the matter, not some qualitative measure of time that reflects your view of the value of the efforts. Thus, clients get the benefit of any time saved by the fact that the firm previously addressed the question for a previous client. Similarly, the ABA concluded that if you travel for client A, who has agreed to be charged for travel time, and you work for client B on the airplane, you cannot perform alchemy and turn a six-hour cross-country trip wedged in a middle seat into a 10-billable-hour event. Nor can you go to the courthouse for three clients and charge each for the total time you spent in court. That is, unless you have the temerity to disclose to your clients your creative way of calculating hours.[17]

## ➤ §2.07(b) Reasonable Hourly Fees

Hourly fees should provide the client with an itemized basis for evaluating your service, and mirror the way many lawyers work. But anyone who works at a law firm that depends on hourly fees knows there can be subtle and not so subtle pressures to bill hours. Like fee-for-service medicine of old, the more you do, the more you get paid. Although hourly fees certainly provide an incentive to cover all bases, exploitation of such an agreement also can lead to unnecessary professional services. Your agreement to bill implicitly includes an agreement to bill only for hours actually spent on the matter. As one federal judge recently put it: "Billing for hours not worked is fraud."[18]

---

[17] ABA Formal Opinion 93-379, Billing for Professional Fees, Disbursements.

[18] District Judge John Gleason in *Kelly v. Hunton & Williams*, 1999 U.S. Dist. Lexis 9139 (E.D.N.Y. June 17, 1999).

§2.07(b)     FEES: CONTRACT OR FIDUCIARY DUTY?   •   47

➤**Red Flag**➤ Though your engagement agreement provided the client would pay for every hour dedicated to the matter, your total bill as well as your initial agreement is subject to Model Rule 1.5's reasonableness requirement [§2.02].[19] The product of hours worked times hourly rate must yield a reasonable fee. So periodically check the entire bill and measure it against the reasonableness standard.

What happens if you actually spend the very same hours on two or more client matters at the same time? Can you bill client number one for your four hours of travel time, while billing client number two for the same time because you worked on that matter on the plane? Not unless both clients understand that you are double billing. Without such an explicit agreement, the practice of billing several clients for the same hours or work product results in charging or collecting an unreasonable fee. So, if you got an explicit agreement up front, you have a few more hours to yourself to relax this month. If not, you have actually earned only four hours and can only bill that total.[20]

To sum up: You need to keep track of billable hours for at least four reasons:

1. If you charge on the basis of hours worked, you must be able to document what you have done.

2. If your client becomes a prevailing party entitled to statutory fees [§2.05], judges often award a fee based upon your lodestar (reasonable hourly rate times reasonable number of hours actually worked).

3. If you win a sanctions motion, you must be able to document the time spent on the matter caused by the sanctionable conduct [§8.11].

4. If your client fires you [§2.11], you lose your contract rights and can recover only for quantum meruit, where you bear the burden of establishing the amount to which you are entitled, a task made far easier if you can identify the services you performed and know the number of hours you worked.

---

[19] *Matter of Fordham*, 668 N.E.2d 816 (Mass. 1996), *cert. denied*, 519 U.S. 1149 (1997) (lawyer disciplined for accurately charging client $50,000 for 227 hours of billed time in obtaining an acquittal on a drunk driving charge, based on expert testimony that a reasonable lawyer would charge no more than 40 billable hours).

[20] ABA Formal Opinion 93-379; Cal. Formal Opinion 1996-147.

## ▶ §2.08 CONTINGENT FEES

### ▶ §2.08(a) The Contingent Fee Windfall?

**We just got lucky. We signed a 40 percent contingent fee agreement with a client on a claim against Presbyterian Hospital. They never settle claims. In fact we discussed that with the client: How unlikely it was we could recover anything before trial. But there must be something about this case. Or that new GC they hired. They offered $3 million to settle and our client wants to take it. We've only got 50 hours in. Our fee would be $1.2 million. But we got the client a great result. The ingrate client, of course, now wants us to reduce the fee.**

We'll bet she wouldn't have offered to increase your fee, if the case had taken three years longer and required 20 extra depositions. If the fee agreement of 40 percent fairly reflected the risk of the case at the time the agreement was reached, the fact that something unexpected—like a great settlement—thereafter occurred should not affect the reasonableness of the fee. Tell the client to celebrate the splendid result.

**Even though our fee works out to $60,000 per hour?**

We didn't promise the client won't protest. The client will probably point out that Model Rule 1.5 requires that lawyers may not contract for or charge an unreasonable fee. It lists as one factor to take into account in determining the reasonableness of the fee the time dedicated to the matter. Your counter-argument is that each factor does not apply to every matter, that a contingent fee turns solely on results and that the only risk the client assumes in signing such an arrangement is that the fee may turn out to be higher than it would have been if the client paid you by the hour. But, of course, here the client did not guarantee you anything. You, of course, are free to follow the lead of some lawyers who voluntarily reduce their fee in this situation. An offer to compromise also may salve your conscience, burnish the image of the profession and may prevent protracted litigation about the fee. One last point: If you and your client can't agree on the fee, be sure to deposit the disputed amount in your trust account [§ 2.14] until you have arbitrated or otherwise come to some conclusion about the matter.[21]

---

[21] Model Rule 1.15(e); RLGL §44(2).

### ►§2.08(b) Reasonable Contingent Fees

Contingent fees offer clients risk-free access to the courthouse. They are allowed in a vast number of situations as long as the client has been advised of alternative fee options and there is some genuine risk of nonrecovery. Some contingent fee agreements are blended with other fees, such as an hourly fee up to a certain amount combined with a contingent fee above a specified recovery amount.

Generally, contingent fees align the interests of the lawyer with those of the client. As the client's recovery goes up, so does the lawyer's. Also, it is not unreasonable to charge a contingent fee when no real risk of nonrecovery exists, so long as the question of the *amount* of recovery is subject to a good faith dispute.[22]

### ►§2.08(c) Negative Contingent Fees?

**I've got a great idea. This client came to visit me yesterday. He's been sued for two million. The claim's bogus in my humble opinion. Guy says he's having a cash flow problem. How 'bout if I take it on a contingent fee? I'll charge him 25 percent of everything I save him from the two mill?**

Well, reverse contingent fees are ethical. The problem is setting the benchmark. If he's been sued for millions but the claim is only worth $100,000, charging the guy 25 percent of his real savings means that, if you are successful, you should only collect 25 percent of a much smaller number, say $100,000. But if you set the benchmark fairly—remember this number may be challenged later—the arrangement should pass ethical muster. But there is one more thing you should worry about.

**What's that?**

Unlike a straight contingent fee, the reverse contingent fee does not produce a pot o' gold from which to collect your fee. So if your new client's cash flow problems continue, there may be another big contingency at the very end.

### ►§2.08(d) Contingent Fee Conflicts Of Interest

Courts [§9.06] and lawyer codes [§9.04] have responded to conflicts inherent in contingent fees with several clear provisions. First,

---

[22] ABA Formal Opinion 94-389, Contingent Fees.

contingent fees are prohibited in several circumstances, essentially because the conflict is deemed uncontestable. In domestic relations matters, the clients must feel free to reconcile, so lawyers are not allowed to take on such matters on a contingency. On the other hand, once the divorce or dissolution occurs, some courts [§9.06] distinguish collection of past-due child support, and allow contingent fees in those matters. Contingent fees are prohibited in criminal matters for the reason that no res exists from which to determine the fee. Inventive lawyers who wish to charge negative contingent fees, such as $X for each year or month saved from a potential sentence, have been disciplined for violating this rule. The risk of overestimating the potential penalty to a client in desperate circumstances is simply too great. On the other hand, negative or reverse contingent fees outside of criminal practice, where client and lawyer reasonably base the fee on a realistic exposure to liability, are consistent with the Model Rules.[23]

Second, regardless of whether a jurisdiction generally requires that fee contracts be in writing, all jurisdictions require written contingent fee contracts to give clients information about the nature of the fee and its collection [§9.04]. Some jurisdictions require extensive disclaimers and regulate the percentage of the contingent fee as well. Agreeing to or charging more than this regulated amount violates the reasonableness standard of Model Rule 1.5.[24]

Third, issues regarding settlement also raise potential conflicts of interest. Sometimes the client will insist on going to trial when the lawyer believes that is imprudent; sometimes the client will want to snare an early low-ball settlement offer as a sure thing when the lawyer's best judgment is to take the matter to trial to achieve a fair recovery. Though there is no perfect remedy when such a conflict occurs, lawyers must be mindful that the decision to settle or go to trial is the client's, and therefore, although the lawyer owes the client her best advice, the lawyer must avoid overreaching. Thus, every settlement offer must be relayed to the client, and every settlement decision is the client's own [§3.03]. If you have a different point of view, especially

---

[23] ABA Formal Opinion 93-373, Reverse Contingent Fees.
[24] *See, e.g.*, Fla. R. Prof. Conduct 1.5(f), N.J. Ct. R. 1:21-7(2004), N.Y. Jud. L. §474-a (2004). Some states also require a closing statement that regulates the actual calculation of the contingent fee. *E.g,* Ohio Rev. Code Ann. §4705.15 (2004).

one colored by your need for a certain payoff now or later, you must explain that view to the client under the rubric of "conflict of interest." Failure to identify your conflicting interest could be grounds for an allegation of breach of fiduciary duty, which if found, could suffice to support total or partial forfeiture of your fee [§8.10].

Finally, before you collect your fee, be sure to provide an accounting at the end of the representation. Some jurisdictions require a specific form, or regulate how you calculate the contingency. The general rule requires that unless your contract specifies otherwise, you are not entitled to a percentage of items not generally considered damages, such as costs and attorney's fees, and the amount of the client's recovery should be computed "net of any offset, such as a recovery by an opposing party on a counterclaim."[25]

### ➤ §2.09 FIXED OR FLAT FEES

### ➤ §2.09(a) The Flat Fee Risk?

**How about taking a matter on at a fixed fee? Can I do that?**

It depends. A fixed fee can be an excellent way, much like a contingent fee, to put the client in a position where the client need not worry about the hours the lawyer is dedicating to the matter. On the other hand, the lawyer, under this arrangement, might quickly lose interest and incentive in a matter in which the last hours, particularly if there are many of them, go essentially uncompensated. If the matter's time requirements can be reasonably predicted and if the fixed fee reasonably compensates for the number of hours, a fixed fee is permissible. If not, the fixed fee alternative should be rejected. When the lawyer is being paid by a third party to represent the client, the use of a fixed fee may be viewed as particularly suspect because it is the real client who will suffer from the lawyer's lack of ardor if the fee amount is set unreasonably low. Experience suggests that as favorable as fixed-fee arrangements appear at the outset of a representation, too often matters require far more time than anticipated and the idea that, if one takes on 10 matters, the time commitment will "even out" too often turns out to be a very misguided notion.

---

[25] RLGL §35 comment d.

### ▶§2.09(b) Reasonable Flat Fees

Flat fees offer your client certainty about cost, but create a perverse incentive. Like managed care, you get more the less you do, subject only to the threat of malpractice. To make sure your flat fee is reasonable, think about the other lawyers in your jurisdiction. Would they charge that much? That little? If you estimate a flat fee on the basis of your experience with other similar cases, using it as a kind of average fee, you have the right idea. If you intend to undercut the competition, e.g., by offering the insurer a flat fee per case, you may risk a charge of incompetence or unreasonable interference with your professional judgment in violation of Model Rule 5.4(c) if the compensation is not adequate to ensure competent representation. To prevent such an abuse, some jurisdictions prohibit flat fees for insurance defense work.[26] Remember, you can blend a flat fee with another fee, such as an hourly rate. Many clients will be willing to pay an hourly fee, but want the assurance of a flat-fee ceiling.

▶**Red Flag**▶ There is no such thing as a nonrefundable flat fee. A client who decides to fire you the day after hiring you is entitled to a refund of the portion of the fee you have not yet earned. And if some unforeseen circumstance occurs, like the complaining witness in a criminal case retracts her testimony causing the charges to be dropped the next day, you also owe your client a refund, because the total fee you charged has now become unreasonable.[27]

### ▶§2.10 RETAINERS

### ▶§2.10(a) The Nonrefundable Retainer?

**This client retained me to draft a new supply contract. The company was a start-up so I insisted on a $25,000 retainer. Now they tell me they found a law firm that will do the work for shares in the client's company. They want me to return the $25,000. I don't think they are entitled to a refund from me. And besides I spent it.**

---

[26] *Am. Ins. Ass'n v. Ky. Bar Ass'n*, 917 S.W.2d 568 (Ky. 1996).

[27] *In re Kutner*, 399 N.E.2d 963 (Ill. 1979) (lawyer disciplined for charging $5,000 flat fee for defense of criminal battery case where complainant asked judge one week later to drop charges and case was dismissed).

Well, we have two different issues here. First, do you get to keep the $25,000? The answer is almost certainly no. You may seek a retainer from a client. Nothing wrong with that. But you have not earned the retainer unless you have either dedicated $25,000 worth of time to the matter or, if you were working on a fixed-fee agreement, you have completed the work. Thus the client is entitled to the refund. Not the whole $25,000, mind you. But the amount that is unearned. So if you put $10,000 in time in already, the client gets back $15,000. If you have done half the required work on a fixed fee arrangement, the client gets back $12,500.

It is possible to have an arrangement with a client where the lawyer receives a minimum fee or an engagement fee that is earned upon receipt. But agreements covering such arrangements have to be quite explicit about the ramifications of the client's deciding to go elsewhere. Garden-variety retainers, however, may not be kept unless earned.

**You said there were two issues?**

Yes, the second is your admission the money is gone. Absent some agreement by the client to the contrary, lawyers are obliged to keep retainers in a client trust account [§2.14] until they are earned. If you made it clear to the client in your engagement letter that you would not maintain the retainer in trust, you are in fine shape (though you still owe the client money). If not, you have probably run afoul of the applicable rules [§9.04].[28]

### ➤§2.10(b): General and Special "Retainers"

"Retainers" come in two distinct forms. You must know the difference to avoid professional discipline [§8.02] and to be able to collect your fee [§10.07]. Most common are "special" or "specific" retainers, designed to advance payments for fees and expenses. These funds must be placed in your client trust account [§2.14] until earned. They are never nonrefundable, because the retainer remains the client's property until you earn it.[29]

➤**Red Flag**➤ Do not call an advanced payment retainer "nonrefundable," because that is not a true statement and you will have deceived a client by doing so.[30]

---

[28] Model Rule 1.15(c); RLGL §44(1).

[29] Model Rule 1.15(c).

[30] *In re Sather*, 3 P.3d 403 (Colo. 2000).

The only retainer arguably earned when paid is a "general" or "availability" retainer, designed to compensate a lawyer for being available to perform legal services for a client for a specific time period. This retainer is a flat fee, which guarantees your attention—complete with the 4 C's—when the client needs you. You will know this retainer because it provides for additional compensation for actual legal work.[31] If this is what you and your client intend, use a written agreement that specifies "availability," includes a time period, details the basis for your other compensation, and indicates how the client benefits from the arrangement.[32] Here, some jurisdictions allow you to designate such a fee "nonrefundable," but others disagree, pointing out that all fees are subject to refund if unreasonable or unearned [§9.06].[33]

### ▶§2.11 FEES ON TERMINATION (WITHDRAWAL OR FIRING)

"You're fired." Words no lawyer wants to hear (unless you have been searching for a way to get rid of this client). If the client fires you, you lose the right to a contract fee, because courts [§9.06] imply a term in the contract that the client should be free to end the agency relationship at any time for any reason.[34] If the firing is without cause, you gain a fee based on quantum meruit, measured by a reasonable hourly rate times a reasonable number of hours expended on the matter. If you bargained badly and quantum meruit happens to be greater than your contract fee, most jurisdictions will allow you to recover quantum meruit or your contract fee, whichever is less.[35]

▶**Red Flag**▶ Always keep track of billable hours, whether you charge monthly retainers, flat, or contingent fees. Without this documentation, where will you be if you get fired? The burden will be on you to prove quantum meruit, which requires some proof of what you have done, usually an accounting of hours expended on the matter.

If the firing is for cause (a serious and clear breach of fiduciary duty) then you forfeit all or part of the fee. You have the burden to separate out the portion of the fee justified by loyal, competent, and confidential service. The rest is lost because of the breach [§8.10].

---

[31] RLGL §34 comment c.
[32] *Ryan v. Butera, Beausang, Cohen & Brennan, P.C.*, 193 F.3d 210 (3d Cir. 1999).
[33] *Id.*; *In re Cooperman*, 633 N.E.2d 1069 (N.Y. 1994).
[34] Model Rule 1.16(a) (3); RLGL §32(1).
[35] *Rosenberg v. Levin*, 409 So.2d 1016 (Fla. 1982).

► **Red Flag** ► If you fail to communicate material facts to a client, violate a conflicts rule, or breach confidentiality, you may be subject to fee forfeiture. To prevent this, know your 4 C fiduciary obligations [Chapters 3-6] and be prepared to respond immediately when a potential conflict or breach of confidentiality develops.

### ►§2.12 FEE SHARING

### ►§2.12(a) The Fee-Splitting Windfall?

Two years ago, we sent a client over to the best medical malpractice firm in town. The papers report a $3 million settlement but my congratulations and our request for the usual one-third referral fee were met with stony silence. What can I do?

If you crossed your T's and dotted your I's you may have a claim. First, was the client informed in writing of the division of the fee, including the percentage each lawyer was to receive? Second, did the client agree to the arrangement in writing? Third, did you retain joint responsibility for the matter? Fourth, is the overall fee reasonable? If you can answer yes to all these questions, then Model Rule 1.5(e) permits the referral fee. If not, since the burden was on you—the referring lawyer—to fulfill these requirements, your fee claim will not succeed. You should also recognize that some jurisdictions (perhaps yours) permit naked referral fees, i.e. the referring lawyer need not retain joint responsibility and the client only has to be informed of the fact that a referral fee is being paid without being informed of the amount [§§9.04, 9.06].

### ►§2.12(b) Reasonable (And Proper) Fee Splits

Model Rule 1.5 allows for fee splitting between lawyers in different firms[36] as long as three conditions are met:

- First, the fee must either reflect the proportion of services you provided to the client, or you must agree to "assume joint responsibility for the representation";
- Second, the client must agree in writing to the arrangement, including the share each lawyer will receive; and
- Third, the total fee must be reasonable.

---

[36] *Shimko v. Lobe*, 813 N.E. 2d 669 (Ohio 2004) (upholding constitutionality of lawyer code provision that requires arbitration of disputes regarding fee splits between lawyers).

These requirements create several issues. We have already discussed the joint responsibility requirement, which endows both lawyers with a client-lawyer relationship [§1.11]. Since the client must agree in writing to the fee split, you must clarify whether the referring or referred lawyer will take on the obligation to provide the client with the requisite writing.

▶**Red Flag**▶ Do not rely on the other lawyer to provide the writing. Remember, you have assumed joint fiduciary duties in this representation, including the obligation to provide a written clarification of the nature and division of the fee. If you fail to provide the written documentation, you share responsibility under Model Rule 5.1 for the violation of this rule, and will be attempting later to rely on an illegal fee arrangement, which in some jurisdictions is void or voidable [§9.06]. Reasonableness of the total fee is determined by the general requirements of Model Rule 1.5(a) and the specific requirements of contingent fees in your jurisdiction under Model Rule 1.5(c) [§2.08].

### ▶§2.13 FEE COLLECTION

If your client refuses to pay, you should have a fee contract on which to rely. A written agreement greatly increases your chance of success in proving the terms of the engagement. But before you decide to litigate, you might want to think about the full nature of the dispute. If you decide to litigate the matter, remember that a lawsuit always provides the opportunity for a counterclaim, and claims for malpractice or breach of fiduciary duty are not uncommon in fee disputes.[37] Recall also that the reasonableness requirement of Model Rule 1.5 applies not only to the agreement but also to the collection of the fee [§2.02(b)]. If you agreed to an hourly rate and charged the client what you actually spent,

---

[37] *Tabner v. Drake*, 780 N.Y.S.2d 85 (N.Y. App. Div. 2004) (client's counterclaim for breach of contract and malpractice due to business transaction with client, which might constitute a bona fide defense to lawyer's suit for legal fees, upheld); *Hatfield v. Van Epps*, 594 S.E.2d 526 (S.C. App. 2004) (client's counterclaim in fee suit that lawyer's malpractice caused her to lose custody of her children created jury issue); *Lloyd v. Hardman*, 583 S.E.2d 925 (Ga. App. 2003) (client unsuccessful in proving malpractice counterclaim; lawyer properly granted judgment for fees); *Barbara A. v. John G.*, 193 Cal. Rptr. 422 (Cal. App. 1983) (client successfully cross claimed for battery and deceit due to sexual relationship with lawyer); *McDaniel v. Gile*, 281 Cal. Rptr. 242 (Cal. App. 1991) (client's complaints for sexual harassment and legal malpractice upheld in lawyer's fee suit).

§2.14    FEES: CONTRACT OR FIDUCIARY DUTY?  •  57

but that turns out to constitute an unreasonable number of hours, you have violated the rule. And don't forget that any effort to amend a fee contract after the client-lawyer relationship has been established subjects the lawyer to a presumption of undue influence [§2.04].

In short, if you clarify why the client refuses to pay, you may be able to resolve the matter. If not, many jurisdictions offer voluntary or mandatory fee arbitration to resolve fee disputes, which may provide both your client and you more efficient and less adversarial results. If a fee dispute occurs, be sure to identify the disputed amount. If you hold some or all of that amount in a trust account [§2.14], Model Rule 1.15(d) requires that you keep the disputed amount in the trust account until the dispute is settled. So if you think the client owes you a $50,000 contingent fee, and the client thinks you are entitled to only $30,000, you can write yourself a check for the undisputed $30,000, but you must keep the disputed $20,000 in the trust account [§2.14] until the matter is resolved.

To sum up: You can avoid fee disputes by bargaining clearly up front, putting the agreement in writing, minding your 4 C's during the representation, and finishing the matter competently. If the client is a bum who just won't pay the bill, then you have created the basis for a successful recovery.

►**Ultimate Red Flag**► Fee disputes create more headaches for lawyers than almost any other issue. We explore the law and psychology of fee collection a bit further in §10.07.

### ►§2.14 TRUST ACCOUNTS

Model Rule 1.15 mandates separation of client and lawyer funds, identification and safeguarding of other client property, and complete record keeping. It is obviously intended to protect client funds and property, and it also serves to prohibit lawyers from using the fund to shield their own money from personal or business creditors.[38]

For these reasons, you may not deposit your funds in a client trust account, except to cover bank charges, and you may not deposit client funds, such as advance payments of legal fees and retainers [§2.10], in your own account. If you receive funds or property in

---

[38] *In re Velasquez*, 507 A. 2d 145(D.C. 1986) (lawyer who deposited personal and business funds in client trust account to avoid creditors disbarred in two jurisdictions).

which your client or a third person has an interest, you must notify both, promptly deliver the funds the client or third party is entitled to receive, and provide an accounting of the funds upon request.[39] If any portion of these funds is disputed, you must retain the disputed funds in the trust account. Rule 1.15(e) further requires that the lawyer must "promptly distribute all portions of the property as to which the interests are not in dispute."

Violating these obligations creates strict liability. Nearly every jurisdiction holds that knowing violations will result in severe discipline, even when client interests are not otherwise compromised.[40] They further agree that inadvertent commingling, even if temporary and without harm to the client, violates the rule.[41]

Yet, in spite of these requirements, so many clients have been the victims of lawyers who have "borrowed" or stolen client funds that many jurisdictions have adopted additional specific rules that govern trust account management. By 1976, nearly every jurisdiction had created a client protection fund, financed by assessments on all lawyers, which reimburses clients who have been the victims of lawyer

---

[39] *State ex rel. Okla. Bar Assn. v. Taylor*, 71 P.3d 18(Okla. 2003) (lawyer who failed to understand applicable law regarding the distribution of client funds to third-party medical providers publicly reprimanded); *Att'y Grievance Comm'n. v. Clark*, 767 A.2d 865 (Md. 2001) (lawyer who repeatedly failed to pay state income withholding taxes violated Rule 1.15 by failing to remit money that belonged to the state); *In re Haar*, 698 A.2d 412 (D.C. 1997) (lawyer who withdrew disputed legal fee from client's trust account negligently misappropriated funds despite lawyer's legal entitlement to the amount because client did not agree to the withdrawal).

[40] See, e.g., *Douglas' Case*, 809 A. 2d 755 (N.H. 2002) (lawyer who improperly withdrew funds from client trust account in the "startlingly erroneous" belief that withdrawal was proper suspended from practice for six months); *Att'y Grievance Comm'n. v. Hayes*, 789 A.2d 119 (Md. 2002) (lawyer who operated practice for 30 years using only a trust account suspended for 90 days for commingling and misusing funds despite otherwise spotless record); *In re Reynolds*, 39 P.3d 136 (N.M. 2002) (neither lawyer's consent to discipline for misappropriating checks nor his cooperation with disciplinary authorities were sufficient to show that he was fit to be automatically reinstated).

[41] *Atty. Grievance Comm'n. v. Jeter*, 778 A. 2d 390 (Md. 2001) (inexperienced lawyer who failed to deposit client personal injury funds in trust account suspended for six months despite lawyer's remorse and lack of intent to defraud); *In re Anonymous*, 698 N.E.2d 808(Ind. 1998) (lawyer who deposited earned fees and rent checks into client trust account and paid himself out of those funds privately reprimanded for violating anti-commingling rule despite no improper use of client funds and no improper motive).

## §2.14    Fees: Contract Or Fiduciary Duty? • 59

theft. In addition, some jurisdictions require that lawyers keep specific records. Others require that banks notify disciplinary authorities of any overdrafts in a trust account. A few even require random audits of trust accounts.[42]

To meet the requirement of a separate account for client funds, most lawyers today establish one IOLTA or Interest on Lawyer Trust Account with a local bank. All client funds that cannot earn net interest are kept in this account, and the interest is paid to a central fund that is used to fund legal services for those unable to pay.[43] Some client funds, such as those that are significant in size, held for a long period of time, or belong to trusts or estates, should be kept in another separate account where the interest accrues to that client.

How do lawyers avoid inadvertent breach of these trust account obligations? First, just as law firms should not allow any one lawyer carte blanche in billing clients, law firms also should make at least two lawyers responsible for administration of law firm trust accounts.[44] Second, all trust accounts should adhere to certain fundamental rules designed to prevent inadvertent breaches, such as those advocated by Jay Foonberg in what he calls "The Ten Commandments of Good Trust Accounts."[45]

Rule 1:    Have a trust account.

Rule 2:    Never let anyone else sign your trust account.

Rule 3:    Obtain and understand your IOLTA (Interest on Lawyers' Trust Account) rules.

Rule 4:    Immediately notify the client every time something is added to the client's account balance and every time something is taken from the account balance.

---

[42] For a compilation of the ABA Model Rules governing these subjects, see American Bar Association, Model Rules for Client Protection (2002).

[43] In *Brown v. Legal Found. of Wash.*, 538 U.S. 216 (2003), the Supreme Court upheld the constitutionality of state IOLTA programs as long as client funds held in the accounts do not earn net interest for the client.

[44] *See, Reynolds, supra* note 40 at 142, where the court recommends allocation of responsibility to at least two lawyers within a law firm. *See also, In re Bailey*, 821 A.2d 851 (Del. 2003) (managing partner of a law firm has enhanced duties to ensure the firm's obligation to comply with its recordkeeping obligations under the Rules of Prof. Conduct).

[45] Jay G. Foonberg, *The ABA Guide to Lawyer Trust Accounts*, 97-100 (1996).

Rule 5: Unearned fees and unexpended costs belong in the trust account until earned or spent.

Rule 6: Do not commingle your funds with the client funds in the trust account.

Rule 7: Be sure you understand the exact nature of the item deposited or credited to the trust account.

Rule 8: Reconcile the bank trust account monthly.

Rule 9: Reconcile and examine the individual client trust account balances monthly, and do not delay giving the clients their money.

Rule 10: Be alert to third-party claims.

In addition, to meet recordkeeping requirements, Foonberg recommends that lawyers maintain a journal, which records all deposits, checks, dates, and amounts and explains each item; and a client ledger, or running balance by client of all checks, disbursements, dates, amounts, and explanations.

➤**Red Flag**➤ Easy access to client funds continues to tempt lawyers. If history is any guide, you should remain alert to specific regulation by your jurisdiction of your bookkeeping practices.

# Part Two

# Responding To ▶Red Flags▶: Fiduciary Duty

---

**THE 4 C'S**

Lawyers automatically assume four key fiduciary duties —the 4 C's—when they agree to represent clients:

1. Communication;
2. Competence;
3. Confidentiality;
4. Conflict of interest resolution.

These fiduciary duties originated in agency law and are now restated in lawyer codes [§9.04]. They rest on a key agency insight about the client-lawyer relationship: Client-principals empower lawyer-agents, whose superior knowledge and skill enable them to control or manipulate a client representation for the benefit of themselves or others. To ensure that the client maintains control of the representation, fiduciary duty imposes affirmative obligations of competence, communication, confidentiality, and conflict of interest resolution on lawyers. When these duties are met, clients determine their own best interests within the bounds of the law. When they are breached, the law affords clients a myriad of remedies [Chapter 8], including civil liability, fee forfeiture, disqualification, injunctive relief, constructive trusts, and professional discipline [§9.05].[1]

---

[1] *Restatement of the Law Third, The Law Governing Lawyers*, §6 (ALI 2000).

# 3

# Communication: The Foundation of the 4 C's

➤ §3.01 Communication: Disclosure And Conversation
➤ §3.02 General Duty To Communicate
➤ §3.03 Settlement Offers, Plea Bargains, And Comparable Decisions
  ➤ §3.03(a) The Ridiculous Plea Bargain?
  ➤ §3.03(b) Avoiding The Unreasonable Client?
  ➤ §3.03(c) Specific Communication Mandates
  ➤ §3.03(d) The Settlement Conference?
➤ §3.04 Waivers: Confidentiality
➤ §3.05 Waivers: Conflicts
  ➤ §3.05(a) A Prospective Waiver?
  ➤ §3.05(b) Nonconsentable Conflicts?
  ➤ §3.05(c) Obtaining A Conflicts Waiver
  ➤ §3.05(d) Informed Consent?
➤ §3.06 Specific Requirements: Contingent Fees, Fee Sharing, Liability Insurance, And Client's Rights

## ➤ §3.01 COMMUNICATION: DISCLOSURE AND CONVERSATION

Communication is essential to every aspect of the client-lawyer relationship. It defines the initial terms of the relationship, and is required to make each of the 4 C's work properly. Disclosure triggers further conversations with clients, which allow them to assist you in defining the scope [§4.03], fee structure [Chapter 2], and purpose of the representation, deciding when to disclose information and what to do about potential conflicts of interest [Chapter 6]. Conversation also provides you with the opportunity to educate clients about the limits of the law [Chapter 7].

The key to understanding this foundational fiduciary duty is to remember that you must initiate the conversation. When you do, you may be in a position to know what your client wants and expects, when your client is willing to disclose confidences, and whether your client understands and waives conflicts of interest. When you do not, you may breach a basic fiduciary duty designed to protect the client-principal whose interests you have signed on to further. Because the duty to communicate is so fundamental, it is formulated broadly.

▶**Ultimate Red Flag**▶ Communication is essential to becoming a collaborative lawyer, that is, a lawyer who avoids the dangers of both under- and over-identification with clients. We explore this link further in §10.03.

### ▶§3.02 GENERAL DUTY TO COMMUNICATE

Both Model Rule 1.4 and the Restatement require lawyers to keep clients "reasonably informed about the status of the matter," "promptly comply with reasonable requests for information," and generally to consult with the client and "explain a matter to the extent reasonably necessary to permit the client to make informed decisions regarding the representation."[1]

▶**Red Flags**▶ Seven events trigger your duty to communicate with your clients:

1. Initially, to agree on a fee arrangement [§§2.01-2.03], and to define the scope of the representation [§4.03], both of which should be explained in an engagement letter [§1.04].

2. Initially and throughout the representation, to explain the matter to enable the client to determine the objectives of the representation [§4.04].

---

[1] ABA Model Rule of Professional Conduct 1.4 (2002) (hereinafter "Model Rules"); *Restatement of the Law Third, The Law Governing Lawyers*, §20 (ALI 2000). (Hereinafter "RLGL".)

3. Throughout the representation, to keep the client reasonably informed about the status of the matter.

4. When you make a mistake in the matter [§4.07].

5. When a client requests information.

6. When the law imposes limits on conduct that a client expects you to undertake [§§7.01-7.17].

7. When you must obtain the client's informed consent [§§3.04-3.07].

## ➤§3.03 SETTLEMENT OFFERS, PLEA BARGAINS, AND COMPARABLE DECISIONS

### ➤§3.03(a) The Ridiculous Plea Bargain?

**The AUSA called with a ridiculous plea bargain. Telling my client will just unleash another tirade. Do I really have to communicate the offer?**

Yes. Settlements, including plea bargains, are the exclusive domain of the client. And you must communicate this all-important information to your client. Thus, if there is any chance that, should your client lose the matter, this settlement offer—with the benefit of hindsight—will suddenly look reasonable, the better course is to call the client, communicate the offer, and endure the harangue. You could, of course, have a conversation with the client about minimally acceptable offers. And agree that ridiculous offers need not be passed on. The question is whether those instructions will remain effective for a long period of time. Which of us who has practiced for a few years hasn't observed clients gleefully accept offers they had contemptuously rejected at an earlier date? As a result, the very best practice is to tell the client, suffer through the diatribe and sleep well, knowing that you won't be second-guessed later.

### ➤§3.03(b) Avoiding The Unreasonable Client?

**So many clients have unrealistic views of the value of their cases. We get a great settlement offer and the client rejects it. Then you go to trial, get a verdict lower than the last offer, have a disgruntled client who quickly forgets your earlier recommendation, and you end up making peanuts. What if we add to our standard agreement delegation by the client to us of complete discretion to**

settle? Since we're on a contingency our interests and the client's are perfectly aligned.

Some days we definitely can conclude it would be great to eliminate clients altogether. They are such a pain. But the rules are clear. On settlement the client gets to decide. And that power to decide cannot be prospectively waived. Even if the client is totally comfortable delegating that kind of authority now, when a real offer is made the client cannot know his or her circumstances then and how he or she would react. Sorry. We guess this really proves that "perfectly aligned" may be a bit, just a bit, of an overstatement.

### ►§3.03(c) Specific Communication Mandates

In addition to the general events that trigger a lawyer's duty to communicate with a client, three specific events absolutely require it because of their finality in determining a client's rights: settlement and plea bargain offers; constitutionally recognized client choices in criminal cases; and whether to appeal a matter. In civil cases, all settlement offers must be communicated to your client. Although your client generally can delegate settlement authority, such a delegation is always revocable. If you do not disclose a specific offer, you run the risk of making or rejecting a settlement without the client's actual authority, subjecting you to liability to your client,[2] as well as to the third party (if the third party reasonably relies on your tortious misrepresentation of authority).[3] In criminal cases, the client has a constitutional right to decide what plea to enter,[4] whether to waive a jury trial, and whether to testify. In both civil and criminal cases, clients decide after lawyers fulfill their obligation to communicate relevant information about whether to appeal a matter.[5]

►**Red Flag**► Any decision that disposes of a client's rights also remains with the client and is subject to revocable delegation. If you contemplate a stipulation, consent judgment, waiver of a

---

[2] RLGL §22; *Moores v. Greenberg*, 834 F.2d 1105 (1st Cir. 1987) (lawyer who failed to relay a $90,000 settlement offer because it was "too niggardly to be relayed" liable for the difference between offer and eventual jury verdict).

[3] RLGL §30.

[4] *Arredondo v. United States*, 178 F.3d 778 (6th Cir. 1999), *rev'd in part, aff'd in part*, 349 F.3d 310 (6th Cir. 2003).

[5] RLGL §22; *Roe v. Flores-Ortega*, 528 U.S. 470 (2000).

§3.04                              COMMUNICATION   •   67

cause of action or defense, or any other action that will foreclose or limit a client's rights, be sure to seek and obtain specific authorization before acting.

### ▶§3.03(d) The Settlement Conference?

**We had a settlement conference coming up—mean judge. My client and I agreed we would offer $200,000 to settle, and our final offer would be $500,000. I get to the conference, and in response to a demand for my client's bottom line I tell the judge $200,000; he looks me in the eye and proclaims that $200,000 is a bargaining ploy. He wants to know my client's last final offer. I repeat $200,000, and the judge calls my client in. The judge throws the fear of God into my client, asks the same question, and the client blurts out $500,000. Now the judge wants me disbarred.**

One thing every lawyer must remember is that your client's settlement authority is confidential. You may only share that information with the client's consent. The judge had no business overreaching that way, but that does not justify your big white lie. Moreover, the judge had no basis for taking advantage of your client that way.[6] When a client hires a lawyer she is entitled to the protection of the lawyer. Let's hope the judge recognized that she overreached. Of course, another solution to the problem the next time you deal with a judge at settlement talks is to make sure your "authority" is limited to your client's first offer, or if it isn't, to decline to answer the judge's request.

### ▶§3.04 WAIVERS: CONFIDENTIALITY

Lawyers may not use or disclose any information gained in the course of representing a client without express or implied client consent [§5.01].[7] This duty extends forever, even after the representation ends, or the client dies.[8] Express waivers of confidentiality, the gold standard,

---

[6] ABA Formal Op. 93-370 (judge may inquire into settlement authority but a lawyer's deliberate lie in response to the questions violates Model Rule 4.1. If the lawyer expresses reluctance to disclose on ethical grounds, the judge should not require a lawyer to make such a disclosure because the Code of Judicial Conduct 3B(7)(d) conditions the judge's ability to conduct *ex parte* settlement conversations on the consent of the parties.

[7] Model Rules 1.6(a), 1.8(b); RLGL §§59-62.

[8] Model Rule 1.9; RLGL §132.

require "informed consent," or consent of the client after you have communicated "adequate information and explanation about the material risks of disclosure" (what you wish to disclose, to whom, and the probable consequences) and the "reasonably available alternatives to the proposed course of conduct" (not disclosing or forgoing an opportunity where disclosure is required by law).[9] In joint representations, explicit disclosure of confidentiality options is essential to an adequate waiver [§6.22].

Implied confidentiality waivers are more common, but determining whether a particular disclosure is impliedly authorized can be tricky. If a disclosure will harm a client's interests or if the client has instructed you to keep quiet, then you are not impliedly authorized to disclose or use the information.[10] Otherwise, you are impliedly authorized to make appropriate disclosures to carry out the representation. Whether a given disclosure might adversely affect a client is judged from the specific context of the client matter, taking into account the client's objectives and interest. When in doubt, do not rely on an implied waiver, and seek explicit informed consent.

▶ **Red Flag** ▶ Be especially cautious about relying on implied consent if you might gain personally or financially from a disclosure, or if disclosure might facilitate the representation of another client. If you have trouble imagining how to obtain explicit informed consent, remember that this is the time you most need to get it.

## ▶ §3.05 WAIVERS: CONFLICTS

### ▶ §3.05(a) A Prospective Waiver?

**Big Bank just called asking us if we would represent the bank in leasing space for an ATM at a 7-11. I don't mind helping Big Bank but I've made a lot of money representing folks on the other side of Big Bank. I don't want to lose that business either.**

What you are considering is a prospective waiver. In your engagement letter you want to make sure this engagement will not preclude you from taking on matters adverse to Big Bank in the future.

---

[9] Model Rule 1.0(e).

[10] *In re Pressly*, 628 A.2d 927 (Vt. 1993) (lawyer who revealed client's suspicion of child abuse to opposing counsel despite client's request not to disclose her suspicion violated Model Rule 1.6(a), even though he thought that disclosure was in client's best interests).

The problem is that conflicts waivers have to be based on informed consent. And right now neither Big Bank nor you know (a) what other work beyond the ATM you will take on for Big Bank; (b) what confidential information you will learn from Big Bank; or (c) the nature of the matter you will take on adverse to Big Bank. The closer you can get to defining all of these the more likely it is that, if Big Bank changes its corporate mind and decides to claim that the prospective waiver is now unenforceable, the courts [§9.06] will uphold the waiver. Indeed, representing borrowers on loans from a bank client is the classic example of an enforceable prospective waiver, that is, so long as you don't bring a lender liability claim!

▶**Red Flag**▶ If you seek an advance or prospective waiver of confidentiality or conflicts [§§6.08, 6.22]] from a client or prospective client be sure to think "express consent." Courts [§9.06] uphold advance waivers only when the client reasonably understood the material risks of the waiver at the time it was given.[11] So put as much detail in your written advance waiver as you can.

### ▶§3.05(b) Nonconsentable Conflicts?

**We've got a potential conflict of interest; how do I know if I am allowed to seek a waiver of the conflict?**

Business considerations aside (a not unimportant issue, but one that has no ethical dimension other than how one wants to be viewed in the world), a lawyer who identifies a potential conflict of interest, before seeking a waiver, must determine whether this is a nonconsentable conflict. The rules identify three categories of non-waivable conflicts. The first is if law prohibits the representation. For example, in some states government entities may not consent to a conflict and in other jurisdictions each capital defendant must have separate counsel regardless of consent [§9.06]. The second is the general prohibition on the same lawyers or law firm representing opposite interests in litigation. Third, a lawyer may not seek consent under circumstances in which a reasonable lawyer could not conclude that the lawyer would be able to provide competent and diligent representation. Many lawyers would include in this last category seeking consent to sue one's own client [§6.09].

---

[11] Model Rule 1.7, Comment [22].

In any event, the conscientious lawyer will not have as a defense the fact that consent was secured if, in the harsh light of day, a court concludes it was unreasonable in undertaking a conflicted representation to seek any consent in the first place.

### ▶ §3.05(c) Obtaining A Conflicts Waiver

Just as client informed consent is needed to permit disclosure of confidential information, in many (but not all) cases [§6.09], clients may choose to consent to potential or actual conflicts of interest created by your own interests, those of another current or former client, or those created by third-party influence.[12] Once again, informed consent requires that the client understand the material risks created by the conflict. In other words, you must describe the legal and factual basis of the conflict, how it might affect your representation, and how subsequent events might modify the circumstances. And, in a growing number of jurisdictions [§9.04], you must do so in writing.[13] Model Rules 1.7-1.12 similarly require that the client's informed consent be "confirmed in writing," that is, that either the client signs a document indicating her informed consent or a document memorializes a previously granted oral informed consent.[14] Even if a jurisdiction does not require a writing for all conflicts waivers, most require extensive written disclosures for specific conflicts like business transactions with clients.

The move to written conflicts waivers reflects repeated problems with their oral equivalents, which did not offer clients enough information, did not give them a continual reminder about the nature of the conflict, and did not protect the lawyer who properly obtained the client's oral informed consent from later client changes of heart. Although many lawyers routinely provide written conflicts waivers, others balk at the prospect. Most who have made the switch understand that they are protecting themselves as much as their clients. Clients benefit because they obtain a continual specific reminder about the nature of the conflict, which allows them to monitor and control the ongoing course of the representation. Lawyers benefit because drafting a waiver prods them into recognizing and articulating the nature of the

---

[12] Model Rules 1.7-1.12, 2.3; RLGL §122.

[13] Model Rule 1.7(b)(4), Cal. R. Prof'l Conduct 3-310(A)(2), Wash. R. Prof'l Conduct 1.7, Wis. SCR 20:1.7.

[14] Model Rule 1.0(b).

§3.05(d)        COMMUNICATION    •    71

conflict, and protects them against later allegations that no waiver was received or that insufficient disclosure was provided.

▶**Red Flag**▶ Be clear about which conflicts require a written waiver in your jurisdiction [§9.04].[15] You are always safe if you routinely reduce all waivers to a written format. If you have trouble drafting a conflicts waiver, or think that a client would be unwise to sign it, the conflict may well be nonconsentable [§6.09].[16]

### ▶ §3.05(d) Informed Consent?

#### What is required to get consent?

The Model Rules require "informed consent."[17] This means that you should communicate information and explanation sufficient so that all parties from whom consent is sought fully appreciate the significance of the decision each is being asked to make.[18] To do so, they also must understand the alternatives to the course of conduct you propose. For example, if your clients seek joint representation from you, you should disclose that they are entitled to consider separate lawyers, and explain the benefits of that alternative. And every joint client conflicts waiver must include information about the impact of the decision on the confidential communications of the parties involved [§6.22].

The new Model Rules also require that the informed consent be "confirmed in writing,"[19] which means that you can either provide a written document complete with disclosures for the client to sign, or confirm a previously given oral consent in a later document. Many jurisdictions also require a writing with specific disclosures for certain kinds of conflicts, such as business transactions with clients [§6.11].[20] Whether required or not, a writing confirming the discussion and the client's consent, preferably countersigned by the client, is the very best way of protecting not only the client, but also the lawyer who might

---

[15] *In re Halverson*, 998 P.2d 833 (Wash. 2000) (conflicts regarding sexual relationship with client must be waived in writing).

[16] Model Rule 1.8(j) prohibits sexual relationships with clients unless they predate the client-lawyer relationship.

[17] Model Rule 1.0(e).

[18] Model Rule 1.0, Comment [6].

[19] Model Rule 1.0(b).

[20] Model Rule 1.8(a).

find that the lengthy and quite informative conversation regarding this topic is remembered quite differently (if at all) by the now disgruntled client.

### ▶§3.06: SPECIFIC REQUIREMENTS: CONTINGENT FEES, FEE SHARING, LIABILITY INSURANCE, AND CLIENT'S RIGHTS

Lawyer codes [§9.04] may require a written document that discloses specific information about other recurring conflicts of interest. Two common provisions require written fee agreements for contingent fees [§§2.03 and 2.08] and to authorize a fee-sharing arrangement [§2.12]. Less common but growing in popularity are specific boilerplate disclosures, such as Ohio's rule that requires written disclosure to clients of lack of minimal liability insurance coverage,[21] or Florida's two-and-one-half page required document that must be provided by lawyers who provide insurance defense without additional cost to the insured. The "Statement of Insured Client's Rights" is intended to explain the conflicts of interest inherent in the three-way relationship among the insurer, lawyer, and policyholder [§6.33].[22] New York requires a similar "Statement of Client's Rights and Responsibilities" in domestic relations matters that must be provided before the signing of a written engagement agreement.[23]

---

[21] Ohio Code of Prof'l Responsibility DR 1-104 (2004).

[22] *Amendments to the Rules Regulating the Florida Bar*, 820 So.2d 210 (Fla. 2002).

[23] New York DR 2-106(f) (2004).

# 4

# Competence: Why You Were Hired In The First Place

➤ §4.01 Competence: Care And Diligence
➤ §4.02 Care: Skill And Knowledge
➤ §4.03 Care: Scope Of The Representation
　　➤ §4.03(a) The Short Representation?
　　➤ §4.03(b) Reasonable Scope Limitations
➤ §4.04 Obedience
　　➤ §4.04(a) Whose Tactics?
　　➤ §4.04(b) Objectives And Means
➤ §4.05 Diligence
➤ §4.06 Obvious Errors And Common Knowledge
　　➤ §4.06(a) Timely Filings
　　➤ §4.06(b) Legal And Factual Research
　　➤ §4.06(c) Breach Of Fiduciary Duty
➤ §4.07 What To Do If You Make A Mistake
　　➤ §4.07(a) The Blown Statute?
　　➤ §4.07(b) How To Avoid Even More Trouble

## ➤ §4.01 COMPETENCE: CARE AND DILIGENCE

Clients hire lawyers for competent service precisely because they are not able to navigate a complex legal system themselves. Lawyers know that the nature of law and the legal system means that not every client can be satisfied by the services the client receives or the result the lawyer achieves. Model Rules 1.1 and 1.3 codify the malpractice standard of care by requiring "reasonable" competence and diligence. This means you don't have to be perfect, but you do have to meet or exceed the standard of practice in your jurisdiction. Reasonable competence and diligence can be established by expert testimony [§9.08] in a malpractice case [§8.06], and also can provide the basis for discipline [§8.02], although disciplinary agencies typically do not proceed against lawyers for isolated instances of incompetence or lack of diligence.

## ▶§4.02 CARE: SKILL AND KNOWLEDGE

Reasonable care usually depends upon evidence of professional custom or expert testimony [§ 9.08] about what a reasonably prudent lawyer in your jurisdiction would know and do in the same or similar circumstances. Specifically, lawyers must know relevant law and facts, must possess the requisite skill to be able to use this information throughout a representation, and must take the time to prepare diligently for the matter. If you do not know enough or have enough experience to handle a matter, you can become competent by studying or associating with another lawyer with more experience. If you wonder whether you know enough, but aren't sure, you are well advised to find out. There is no such thing as an ignorant, inexperienced, or unaware lawyer defense to a claim of malpractice supported by expert testimony [§9.08].[1] Your license to practice holds out to clients and to courts that your agreement to handle a matter means you possess the skill and ability to do so. And don't forget specialization. Just as a family practice physician who delivers babies is held to the standard of an expert Ob-Gyn, so also will you be held to the expert standard of care if you dabble in an area of practice that your jurisdiction deems specialized [§9.04].[2]

---

[1] *In re Johnson*, 32 P.3d 1132 (Kan. 2001)(lawyer's inexperience in the practice of law and lack of a mentor, which may have led to his failure to pursue discovery and to appropriately respond to a summary judgment motion, as well as to his filing a frivolous appeal to avoid malpractice created no defense to professional discipline for lack of competence and diligence).

[2] *Battle v. Thornton*, 646 A.2d 315 (D.C. 1994)(absent proof that the defendants held themselves out as specialists in Medicaid fraud defense, or that jurisdiction or profession recognizes such a specialty, lawyer is required to exercise skill and care of lawyers acting under similar circumstances); *Horne v. Peckham*, 158 Cal. Rptr. 714 (Cal. App. 1979)(lawyer who acknowledged the need for expertise in tax had duty to refer client to an expert practitioner or to comply with the specialty standard of care).

▶**Red Flag**▶ If you aren't sure what similarly situated lawyers know or do in providing a specific legal service, you are risking an after-the-fact judgment that you have not met the requisite standard of care. Remember that any lawyer in your jurisdiction can testify to what you should have done later if your client suffers harm.

### ▶§4.03 CARE: SCOPE OF THE REPRESENTATION

### ▶§4.03(a) The Short Representation?

**Some guy contacted me through the firm's web site. Wants to hire me for an hour. What should I do?**

Model Rule 1.2(c) teaches us that lawyer and client should agree to the scope of the representation. But the admonition carries with it a warning. Just as a lawyer can get in trouble for stating the scope too broadly, a lawyer may not accept an unreasonable scope limitation that is too narrow. If the lawyer cannot provide helpful advice on that basis (no more than one hour) the lawyer should decline the representation.

On the other hand, there are times when it makes sense for a lawyer to provide partial or unbundled services so long as lawyer and client agree on the scope of the lawyer's responsibility. If you want to accept a scope limitation because you think something helpful can come from spending an hour (say a review of a proposed divorce agreement or property transaction), then you should make the scope limitation clear in the engagement letter [§1.04] (which one hopes won't take longer to draft than the engagement) so that there is no misunderstanding about the quality of the work you will be able to provide. While lawyers cannot ask clients to waive the lawyers' malpractice liability [§6.16], work performed under a scope limitation should be judged with that fact in view.

### ▶§4.03(b) Reasonable Scope Limitations

Clients usually hire lawyers to handle specific cases or matters. Lawyers generally, but not always, prefer the client who wants that lawyer to handle all legal matters. Increasingly common is the client who seeks or the lawyer who offers the opposite: "Unbundled" legal services which limit the scope of the representation, by breaking down legal services into discrete tasks such as drafting, negotiation, or court representation, or by providing service only for a particular legal issue, such as custody or property valuation.[3]

Model Rule 1.2(c) and the Restatement both approve of these contractual bargains, but only if the limitation is reasonable and the client gives informed consent [§3.05(d)].[4] Here, the reasonableness standard is determined from the viewpoint of the client, not the professional, so consider whether the benefits of the limitation to your client (reduced fee, able lawyer) would outweigh the risks (inadequate or incomplete legal advice).

The bookends are clear: You cannot agree to limit your client's right to settle a matter or plead guilty in a criminal case.[5] Nor can you agree to conduct a "preliminary" investigation that does not provide an opinion upon which the client can rely.[6] Be especially aware of specialty areas of practice: A bankruptcy court has held that a lawyer representing a Chapter 7 debtor may not limit the scope of representation and must represent the debtor in all aspects of the bankruptcy case.[7] And don't forget lesson number one: Identify your client. If you provide insurance defense, duties to your primary client (the insured) [§1.17] mean that the insurer may not interfere with your obligation to the insured, for example, by requiring prior approval of depositions, research, and motions [§6.32].[8]

On the other hand, agreeing to offer short-term legal services via a legal services hotline [1.14],[9] to handle a trial but not an appeal,[10] to

---

[3] Forrest S. Mosten, *Unbundling Legal Services: A Guide to Delivering Legal Services a la Carte* (ABA Law Practice Management Section 2000).

[4] *Restatement of the Law Third, The Law Governing Lawyers,* §19 (ALI 2000). (Hereinafter "RLGL".)

[5] *Jones v. Barnes,* 463 U.S. 745 (1983)(fundamental decisions to plead guilty, waive jury, testify or appeal are for defendant); *In re Lansky,* 678 N.E.2d 1114 (Ind. 1997)(fee agreement provision which gave up client's right to settle civil matter violated Rule 1.2(a)).

[6] ABA Model Rule of Professional Conduct 1.2, Comment [7]. (2002). (Hereinafter "Model Rules".)

[7] *In re Egwim,* 291 B.R. 559 (Bankr. N.D. Ga. 2003).

[8] *In re Rules of Professional Conduct,* 2 P.3d 806 (Mont. 2000)(insurance defense counsel may not abide by agreements to limit the scope of representation that interfere with their duty to insured client).

[9] *See* §1.04(i); Model Rule 6.4.

[10] *Young v. Bridwell,* 437 P.2d 686 (Utah 1968).

advise about one transaction or claim but not others,[11] or to provide a quick legal opinion about a proposed mediated settlement without additional factual investigation[12] all are reasonable as long as your client gives informed consent [§3.05(d)]. Informed consent requires that the client understands the alternatives, especially those that other lawyers might include in the same representation. So, for example, a lawyer may be reasonable in limiting a representation to worker's compensation alone, but only if the client understands that other lawyers might be retained who would be free to identify and pursue additional tort actions against third parties.[13]

▶**Red Flag**◀ The more complex the legal matter, the greater the need for explicit informed consent from your client to limit your representation. A good engagement letter [§1.04] provides you with an opportunity to clarify which legal services you do and do not intend to provide. Be sure to specify alternatives that you will not pursue to make it clear that a client should seek those services elsewhere.

### ▶§4.04 OBEDIENCE

#### ▶§4.04(a) Whose Tactics?

*I've always been a mensch. You need an extension; unless my client's cherry tree is going to be chopped down, I grant it. I do it for two reasons. I'm a nice guy. And I figure someday I will need more time. But this new client wants Rambo. I've been instructed by the client to grant no extensions. Ever. What can I do?*

Model Rule 1.2(a) says that clients define the objectives of the representation, but lawyers determine the means in consultation with the client. You can tell the client there is a limit to the extent to which the client will define how you conduct the matter, and that if the client wants a lawyer who will conduct himself that way, the client is free to switch lawyers. If the client does not relent and refuses to accept your invitation to look elsewhere, you would then be free to withdraw on the ground that the client wishes you to pursue a course

---

[11] *Delta Equip. & Constr. Co. v. Royal Indem. Co.*, 186 So.2d 454 (La. App. 1966).

[12] *Lerner v. Laufer*, 819 A.2d 471 (N.J. Super. Ct. App. Div. 2003).

[13] *Greenwich v. Markhoff*, 650 N.Y.S.2d 704 (N.Y. App. Div. 1996).

of conduct that you consider repugnant or with which you have a fundamental disagreement.[14]

### ▶§4.04(b) Objectives And Means

Lawyer-agents are empowered by clients and obligated by fiduciary duty to obey a client-principal's lawful instructions regarding the objectives of the representation.[15] Because clients may not know or understand the range of available legal alternatives, lawyers have an affirmative obligation to explain legal options sufficiently so that clients are able to make informed choices about their objectives. In addition to the client's right to determine the purposes of the representation, both Model Rule 1.2(a) and the Restatement identify several specific client decisions that may not be irrevocably delegated to a lawyer, including the right to decide whether to settle a civil matter and, in criminal cases, how to plead, whether to waive a jury trial, and whether the client will testify.[16]

Once the client has decided on an objective, the lawyer must act to implement it.[17] Lawyers are impliedly authorized [§5.07] to take such action but also must consult with the client as to the means by which the objective is to be accomplished.[18] Clients and lawyers are free to bargain about any lawful means that will be used to pursue the client's objectives. If you do not want to engage in the scorched-earth tactics your client insists upon, you may withdraw from the representation,[19] just as the client may discharge you if the client is unhappy with your approach to the matter [§2.11].

▶**Red Flag**▶ Your ability to bargain with your client about the objectives and means of the representation ends when either your client or you are about to embark on illegal or fraudulent activity. If

---

[14] Model Rule 1.16(b)(4).

[15] Model Rule 1.2(a); RLGL §16(1).

[16] RLGL §22.

[17] *Vandermay v. Clayton*, 984 P.2d 272 (Or. 1999)(lawyer liable for breach of fiduciary duty without expert testimony for drafting ambiguous indemnity agreement that did not include the protections client insisted upon); *Olfe v. Gordon*, 286 N.W.2d 573 (Wis. 1980)(lawyer liable without expert testimony for failure to effectuate client's instruction to secure a first mortgage in sale of her home).

[18] Model Rule 1.4(a)(2).

[19] Model Rules 1.2, Comment [2], l.16(b)(4).

your client insists on criminal or fraudulent action, you *must* withdraw [§§7.02, 7.04 and 7.05].

### ➤§4.05 DILIGENCE

Model Rule 1.3 requires that lawyers act with reasonable diligence and promptness. Diligence requires commitment and dedication to the client's interests, something called zealous representation in the ABA's earlier Model Code of Professional Responsibility. Promptness should speak for itself: You must manage the workload imposed by the rest of your practice so that you can give reasonable and timely attention to each client matter. If you have supervisory authority in a law firm, you have the same obligation to watch the workload of those you supervise. Simple procrastination in a matter may or may not be serious, depending on the time deadlines imposed and the exigencies of the situation. But anytime "being behind" causes harm to your client, you may face malpractice or disciplinary consequences.

➤**Red Flag**➤ The client or client matter you most dislike or least understand is the very one you are most likely to ignore. If you find yourself avoiding a matter, ask why. Do you lack the ability to handle it? Do you dislike the client? When you understand the problem, you can respond now and avoid trouble later, either by setting aside the time to tackle the matter, or by having a heart to heart with your client and perhaps suggesting replacement counsel. If you seek to withdraw, remember that you cannot prejudice your client's interests by doing so, and you must obtain the permission of the relevant tribunal if the matter is before a court [§7.02].

### ➤§4.06 OBVIOUS ERRORS AND COMMON KNOWLEDGE

In malpractice cases [§8.06], some errors are so obvious that they trigger the "common knowledge" exception to the expert testimony [§9.08] requirement, which deems some breaches of duty clear enough that a lay juror can recognize them without the aid of an expert witness.[20] In the same way that physicians can be found liable for leaving surgical instruments in a person's body or operating on the wrong wrist, lawyers can be found liable without expert testimony for three obvious errors:

• Failing to file within a mandatory time period;

---

[20] RLGL §§16, 49.

- Failing to do legal or factual research; and
- Failing to observe core fiduciary duties such as communication [Chapter 3], obedience [§4.04], or confidentiality [Chapter 5].

### ▶ §4.06(a) Timely Filings

If you miss a time period and cannot secure an extension, you always face a potential malpractice claim [§8.06], though disciplinary agencies will seldom impose sanctions unless you exhibit a pattern of such behavior. Model Rule 1.3 provides that lawyers must act with reasonable diligence and promptness in representing clients. In malpractice cases, diligence and promptness roughly correlate with the "common knowledge" exception to the expert testimony requirement [§9.08], because deadlines are obvious and lawyers should know and comply with them on behalf of clients. Juries don't need an expert to know that promptness requires you to file a case or appeal on a timely basis,[21] which translates into your need for an appropriate tickler system to remind you about dates.

### ▶ §4.06(b) Legal And Factual Research

Similarly, the failure to do any legal research or investigate relevant facts constitutes a breach of your diligence obligation [§4.05] to make sure both have been completed.[22] In criminal cases, these failures can amount to constitutionally deficient ineffective assistance of counsel [§8.07].[23]

---

[21] *George v. Caton*, 600 P.2d 822 (N.M. App. 1979).

[22] *Smith v. Lewis*, 107 Cal. Rptr. 95 (Cal. App. 1973), *opinion superseded by* 530 P.2d 589 (Cal. 1975)(expert testimony not required to prove lawyer's failure to research applicable law); *Schmitz v. Crotty*, 528 N.W.2d 112 (Iowa 1995)(expert testimony not required to prove lawyer's failure to research facts about property descriptions in valuing estate taxes after lawyer was put on notice of their inaccuracy).

[23] Regarding law: *E.g., People v. Hayes*, 593 N.E.2d 739 (Ill. App. 1992)(mistake as to the burden of proof of insanity defense); *Stanford v. Stewart*, 554 S.E.2d 480 (Ga. 2001)(appellate counsel failed to recognize the significance of an error in jury instructions); *Pena-Mota v. State*, 986 S.W.2d 341 (Tex. App. 1999)(failure to object to jury instruction resulted in a double jeopardy violation). Regarding facts: *Wiggins v. Smith*, 539 U.S. 510 (2003)(failure to investigate and present mitigating evidence in death penalty sentencing); *Wesley v. State*, 753 N.E.2d 686 (Ind. App. 2001)(failure to obtain psychiatric record of victim who had a history of false accusations); *In re K.J.O.*, 27 S.W.3d 340 (Tex. App. 2000)(failure to conduct investigation into juvenile's defense); *People v. Truly*, 595 N.E.2d 1230 (Ill. App. 1992)(failure to investigate and present alibi).

### ➤ §4.06(c) Breach of Fiduciary Duty

Finally, many courts [§9.06] have held that juries do not need expert testimony [§9.08] to understand basic breaches of fiduciary duty, including the failure of a lawyer to obey a client's instructions [§4.04], to communicate relevant legal advice and options,[24] and to maintain client confidentiality [Chapter 5]. If you are not sure what your client wants, you must clarify your client's objectives so that you can implement them. So if your client instructs you to draft an employment agreement or an estate plan, make sure that the client understands all of the relevant legal options, and make sure that you understand which options the client selects. Then draft the document competently to effectuate the client's wishes. And don't tell anyone else outside your firm what you have done, unless the client consents.

### ➤ §4.07 WHAT TO DO IF YOU MAKE A MISTAKE
### ➤ §4.07(a) The Blown Statute?

**I think I missed a statute of limitations. Sure hope I don't have to tell the client.**

Physicians may bury their mistakes. Lawyers are not so lucky. Ours live to play another day. And it is our duty as fiduciaries to communicate with our clients about important developments in the matter, even when those developments do not exactly represent good news, even when the bad news is that we screwed up.

This does not mean the lawyer must admit liability or write a large check on the spot. Not all mistakes give rise to valid claims. If you blow the statute on a losing claim you are still free to defend on the latter basis. Your duty, however, is to tell the client the facts, explain that, as to this issue, you have an impossible conflict of interest and that the client would be well advised to seek other counsel who can provide objective advice.

---

[24] *dePape v. Trinity Health Systems, Inc.*, 242 F.Supp.2d 585, 609 (N.D. Iowa 2003) (expert testimony not required to prove lawyers liable for failing to give immigration client any information about visa options, which caused a failed fraudulent entry attempt and lost wages); *Lane v. Oustalet*, 873 So.2d 92 (Miss. 2004)(expert testimony not required to prove closing lawyer had a duty to provide buyers with copy of termite inspection report at closing).

## ▶§4.07(b) How To Avoid Even More Trouble

If you discover that you have missed a deadline, or that you forgot to include a clause in a contract as the client instructed, or that your failure to investigate mitigation evidence resulted in your client's death penalty conviction, you need to respond. But you can get into even more trouble than your initial mistake has caused if you react with your first instinct (which may be to avoid the client or to settle the matter yourself). Because your mistake may have caused harm to a client, your error clearly affects "the status of the matter" under Model Rule 1.4 and therefore must be disclosed to your client (if you were the client, would you want to know?). Further, you now face an obvious personal conflict of interest and after fulfilling your communication obligation [§6.10], you probably should withdraw.

▶**Red Flag**▶ Disobey any thought of concealing or destroying evidence of your mistake or worse, creating evidence that someone else is responsible. All of these acts constitute dishonesty, deceit, or misrepresentation and will trigger disciplinary action that may not otherwise have occurred, or make the eventual disciplinary or monetary sanctions much more severe.[25]

First, you should inform your client of the relevant facts that led to your error,[26] explain the nature of your conflict of interest (that you probably should withdraw because your client may have a claim against you),[27] and advise your now former client in writing of the desirability of seeking the advice of independent legal counsel.[28]

Second, remember that you are subject to discipline if you settle the case with your former client unless that person or entity either has received disinterested legal advice from another lawyer not in your firm, or you have notified your former client in writing of the need for

---

[25] *In re Morrissey*, 305 F.3d 211 (4th Cir. 2002)(lawyer who, while suspended from practice, tried to bribe a Habitat for Humanity official in order to evade his community service obligations required by his criminal sentence, disbarred for engaging in criminal and dishonest conduct); *Fla. Bar v. Miller*, 863 So.2d 231 (Fla. 2003)(lawyer who disputed his failure to timely file suit when he knew he had failed to do so suspended from practice for one year); *In re Chovanec*, 640 N.E.2d 1052 (Ind. 1994)(lawyer who was not prepared and who falsely told court he was too sick to proceed subject to professional discipline).

[26] Model Rule 1.4; RLGL §20.

[27] Model Rule 1.7 (b); RLGL §122 comment g.

[28] Model Rule 1.8(h)(2); RLGL §54.

independent counsel and given that person or entity a reasonable opportunity to seek such advice [§6.16].[29] Even then, if your former client was not independently represented, the law of agency will presume undue influence [§8.09], putting the burden of proof on you to prove that the settlement was fair and reasonable to the client.[30] So send the client a disengagement letter [§1.25] complete with the disclosures listed in the last paragraph, and if a claim is made, call your liability carrier and turn the matter over to it. If you don't have malpractice insurance, retain other counsel or call yourself a fool.

Your fiduciary obligation of competence and communication, which requires you to provide this information, actually may help you reduce the chance of a lawsuit or disciplinary complaint, or if either occurs, can reduce the severity of the outcome, because your client understands that you did the right thing once a mistake was uncovered. If you fail to inform the client, he or she reasonably may suspect that you have more to hide, and many jurisdictions toll the statute of limitations on your client's malpractice claim until the time that person or entity reasonably should have known about the problem [§9.06]. So admit your error, start the clock ticking, and get on with your practice.

▶**Ultimate Red Flag**◀ Lawyers more than occasionally get into trouble with clients because they face some real trouble in their own lives. We explore these difficulties further in §10.10.

---

[29] Model Rule 1.8(h)(2); RLGL §54.
[30] RLGL §54 comment c.

# 5

# Confidentiality: The Never-Ending Obligation

➤ §5.01 The Scope Of Confidentiality
　　➤ §5.01(a) A Rose By Any Other Name?
　　➤ §5.01(b) Fiduciary Obligation And Privilege
　　➤ §5.01(c) Client Confidentiality Chart: Fiduciary Obligation And Privilege
➤ §5.02 The Extent Of Confidentiality
　　➤ §5.02(a) The Juicy Tidbit?
　　➤ §5.02(b) The Beginning And End Of Confidentiality
➤ §5.03 Disclosure And Use Of Confidential Information
　　➤ §5.03(a) Helping The Press?
　　➤ §5.03(b) The Opportunity?
　　➤ §5.03(c) Confidentiality: Scope Of The Protection
➤ §5.04 Litigation Disclosures
　　➤ §5.04(a) A Question Of Privilege?
　　➤ §5.04(b) Attorney-Client Privilege: Scope Of The Protection
　　➤ §5.04(c) Client Identity And Public Documents
　　➤ §5.04(d) The Privilege Boilerplate?
　　➤ §5.04(e) The Brilliant Gambit?

- §5.04(f) The Organizational Privilege?
- §5.04(g) The Corporate Gamble?

- §5.05 Work-Product Privilege
  - §5.05(a) The Engineer's Report?
  - §5.05(b) Work-Product Protection
  - §5.05(c) The Supervised Expert?
- §5.06 Confidentiality Exceptions
  - §5.06(a) Countervailing Policies
  - §5.06(b) Chart: State Lawyer Code Exceptions To Client Confidentiality
- §5.07 Confidentiality Exceptions: Express Or Implied Authorization
  - §5.07(a) The New CEO?
  - §5.07(b) The Administrative Privilege?
  - §5.07(c) Company Agents?
  - §5.07(d) The Inadvertent Email?
  - §5.07(e) The Helpful Opponent?
  - §5.07(f) Express And Implied Confidentiality Waivers
- §5.08 Confidentiality Exceptions: Threatened Serious Bodily Harm
  - §5.08(a) The Suicidal Client?
  - §5.08(b) The Undisclosed Aneurysm?
  - §5.08(c) Threatened Physical Harm
- §5.09 Confidentiality Exceptions: Future Crime
  - §5.09(a) Blowing Off Steam?
  - §5.09(b) The Future Crime Exception
- §5.10 Confidentiality Exceptions: Client Fraud
  - §5.10(a) Puffing?
  - §5.10(b) The Innocent Misrepresentation?
  - §5.10(c) Tax Compliance?
  - §5.10(d) The Prepared Witnesses?

§5.01(a)  CONFIDENTIALITY • 87

➤§5.10(e) Client Fraud

➤§5.11 Confidentiality Exceptions: Lawyer Self-Defense

    ➤§5.11(a) The Ungrateful Client?

    ➤§5.11(b) Helping Successor Counsel?

    ➤§5.11(c) Defending Yourself

➤§5.12 Confidentiality Exceptions: Seeking Advice

    ➤§5.12(a) Help?

    ➤§5.12(b) Getting Advice

➤§5.13 Confidentiality Exceptions: Law And Court Orders

    ➤§5.13(a) The Deposition Lie?

    ➤§5.13(b) The False Alibi?

    ➤§5.13(c) Law And Court Orders That Require Disclosure

➤§5.14 Jurisdiction-Specific Exceptions And Conflicts Of Law

    ➤§5.14(a) The Heavy Burden?

    ➤§5.14(b) Guaranteed Confidentiality?

    ➤§5.14(c) The Dizzying Diversity?

    ➤§5.14(d) Understanding Confidentiality Conflicts

## ➤§5.01 THE SCOPE OF CONFIDENTIALITY

### ➤§5.01(a) A Rose By Any Other Name?

**Confidentiality. Privilege. We use these words all the time. It's the same thing, right?**

Not at all. Though lawyers often use these words interchangeably, they are in fact quite different concepts.

Your duty of confidentiality is a fiduciary obligation that arises from agency law and the lawyer codes [§9.04]. Those rules require you to keep confidential all information learned in the course of a representation, with a few narrow exceptions as to which, depending on which state you are in, you may or must disclose what would otherwise be confidential. Your obligation of confidentiality governs what you may voluntarily disclose in any situation and basically provides that a lawyer should not voluntarily disclose any confidential information, unless the information falls within an exception.

The privilege, on the other hand, is a rule of evidence that, if you are called to testify, governs what you may be forced to disclose. Privileged information is a subset of the category of confidential information. When a lawyer is forced to testify, a lawyer can be required to disclose all confidential information unless that confidential information is also privileged. And in order to be privileged the conversation must have occurred between privileged persons, been intended to remain confidential, and been provided for the purpose of securing legal advice.

### ▶ §5.01(b) Fiduciary Obligation And Privilege

The fiduciary duty of confidentiality, which is found in both the law of agency and the lawyer codes, applies to all client confidential information in all representations, from prospective clients [§1.05] to long-term retainers. It can be traced historically to the development in evidence law of the attorney-client and work-product privileges, both rules of evidence that block disclosure of some client confidences in litigation. In the past century, these two bodies of law developed in parallel, creating overlapping yet distinct client protections and exceptions. The evidentiary privilege has never protected all client confidences, and has developed a number of widely accepted exceptions. The fiduciary duty, on the other hand, has always protected nearly all client information. Exceptions have developed less rapidly, and are less uniform, but tend to parallel those in the law of evidence.

Confidentiality encourages clients to communicate fully with lawyers so that they can be effectively represented. Without all the facts, lawyers will not be able to give competent and complete legal advice, which will in turn disserve clients seeking to follow the law and undermine the ability of lawyers to promote compliance with the rule of law. Confidentiality also promotes a primary value of the legal system, respect for human rights, by promoting trust and privacy in the client-lawyer relationship. The lawyer's obligation to protect this private sphere becomes especially important when the government seeks to invade it through compulsion. The chart in §5.01(c) below compares these two bodies of law.

## ▶ §5.01(c) Client Confidentiality Chart: Fiduciary Obligation And Privilege

| | Client Confidentiality | |
|---|---|---|
| | **Attorney-Client Privilege** | **Ethical/Fiduciary Obligation** |
| Source of Law: | Statute; Common Law of Evidence | Agency Law; MR 1.6 and CPR Canon 4 |
| Definition: | A communication made between privileged persons in confidence for the purpose of obtaining or providing legal assistance. RLGL §68 | MR 1.6(a): Information relating to the representation of a client; DR 4-101(A): Confidences and Secrets. |
| **Exceptions** | | |
| Client Consent | Waiver. RLGL §§78-80 (Implied by disclosure to any non-privileged third person) | Client consent, express or implied. MR 1.6(a) |
| Physical Harm | Future and continuing crime or fraud. RLGL §82 | Future (continuing) crime. MR 1.6(b)(2) |
| Lawyer Self-Defense | Lawyer self-protection. RLGL §83 | Lawyer self-defense. MR 1.6(b)(5) |
| Seeking Advice | | MR 1.6(b)(4) |
| Financial Harm | Future and continuing crime or fraud. RLGL §82 | Future crime, prevent, rectify, mitigate substantial financial loss. MR 1.6(b)(2),(3) |
| Required by Law or Court Order | Invoking the privilege. RLGL §86 | Required by law or court order. MR 1.6(b)(6) Comments 12,13 |

## ▶ §5.02 THE EXTENT OF CONFIDENTIALITY

### ▶ §5.02(a) The Juicy Tidbit?

**I hear you about this confidentiality noose, but what if I learn information another client must know? Just today we were asked to bring a big antitrust case against Excelsior Corporation. Our firm is representing Big Bank on a loan to Excelsior. The bank certainly will want to know about the suit. And guess what? Excelsior doesn't know about it.**

Uh oh. We won't ask if you took on the antitrust case, though that is an interesting question. But even if the folks suing Excelsior were only prospective clients, they are entitled to the same confidentiality as any client of your firm. If they consent, you can tell Big Bank. But something tells us they will not consent. So your duty of confidentiality to a prospective client trumps your duty to a present client of the firm. The truth is lawyers regularly possess information of one client that other clients of the law firm would like to know; no matter how material that information might be, the rules of confidentiality prohibit its being shared. This is simply an application of that principle to prospective clients.

The real open question here is whether you can continue representing Big Bank now that you know about the antitrust claim against Excelsior. Isn't Big Bank entitled to lawyers who are not limited in their ability to advise Big Bank regarding contingent liabilities of Excelsior? Think about it. We think you will conclude that learning the juicy little tidbit may require your firm's withdrawal from representing Big Bank.

### ▶ §5.02(b) The Beginning And End Of Confidentiality

Whether fiduciary duty or privilege, the lawyer's confidentiality obligation extends to information obtained in seeking and receiving legal assistance, and continues after the representation.

Prospective clients [§§1.05-1.14] repose some trust in and must disclose some information to determine whether to retain a lawyer. To facilitate this exchange, the law governing lawyers cloaks the initial prospective client consult with the same confidentiality protection clients receive.[1] Of course, any information you have received in the

---

[1] ABA Model Rule of Professional Conduct 1.18 (2002) (hereinafter "Model Rules"); *Restatement of the Law Third, The Law Governing Lawyers*, §15 (ALI 2000). (Hereinafter "RLGL").

§5.03(a)　　　　　　　　Confidentiality　•　91

course of representing a client becomes confidential when you receive it.[2] The same protection extends post representation to former clients [§1.24], and continues beyond the client's death.[3] If you decide not to represent a prospective client (or the prospective client decides not to hire you), that person or entity becomes a "former client" for purposes of the confidentiality rules, a change that does *not* diminish your confidentiality obligations.

▶**Red Flag**▶ Make sure that everyone in your firm (lawyers and staff) understands that confidentiality begins before and outlasts the client-lawyer relationship, continuing even past the client's death. If any of you disclose or use information learned about a prospective or former client, you have breached the same fiduciary duty you owe current clients. Educating and reminding all law firm personnel about the breadth and extent of this obligation will protect your clients and satisfy your supervisory obligations.[4]

▶**Ultimate Red Flag**▶ Do not assume that your confidentiality obligation to a client extends to successor counsel. We explore this dilemma further in §10.03.

### ▶§5.03 DISCLOSURE AND USE OF CONFIDENTIAL INFORMATION

### ▶§5.03(a) Helping The Press?

**I've got a highly publicized case. Reporters keep calling. I like being helpful. The truth is it's not bad for business to have my name in the local paper. Can I tell the reporter where to look in the deposition transcripts filed at the courthouse to find a juicy quote?**

Not if you want to comply with your duty of confidentiality to your client. Confidential information is not just secrets or stuff that is embarrassing. It's everything learned in the course of a representation. And unless your client consents to the disclosure (is it really in your client's best interests to disclose?) or it is generally known because it has already appeared on Fox News at 10, you may not disclose this infor-

---

[2] Model Rule 1.6; RLGL §60.

[3] RLGL 77; *Swidler & Berlin v. United States*, 524 U.S. 399 (1998).

[4] 4 Model Rule 5.1; RLGL §60(1)(b).

mation even though anyone could "look it up."[5] And even then, you should consult with the client before sharing the information. Again, erring on the side of caution is the best policy. There is no good reason for any lawyer at any time to test the limits of what should be considered confidential information.

### ▶ §5.03(b) The Opportunity?

**My client just told me about his plans to build a shopping center where I-80 meets the Parkway. Maybe I can cash in by buying the Franklin Inn across the way. I heard the owners are thinking of retiring.**

This is as good a place as any to remind all lawyers that, as much as we love our work (ok, sometimes) and as fascinating as we think it is (ok, sometimes) and as much as we think we might be the life of the party by sharing juicy tidbits of our latest "big suit" or "big deal" (always), the sharing of such information in the country club locker room or at the 19th hole is forbidden by rules governing confidentiality. Even your clumsy attempts to disguise the identity of the client and others do not cure the fact that the information you are sharing is undoubtedly confidential.

Just as you cannot disclose client confidential information, you may not use it.[6] In fact your client is entitled to know about the possible availability of the Franklin Inn. If the client then indicates no interest, you may proceed with your plan if nothing else about the purchase will create a conflict with the client. But the confidentiality of the client's information and the client's interest must come first. This is why, if you buy, you may be purchasing for your client's account. Which means, alas, you may never trade on your public company's inside information, but that's another story.

### ▶ §5.03(c) Confidentiality: Scope Of The Protection

In short, everything the lawyer learns during the course of a representation is protected by confidentiality. The fiduciary obligation of

---

[5] MR 1.6(a); RLGL §59.
[6] Model Rule 1.8(b), RLGL §60.

§5.04(b)  CONFIDENTIALITY • 93

lawyers that attaches to all client representations protects all "information relating to the representation" regardless of its source; it is not limited to matters the client requests you keep confidential.[7] Lawyers may not disclose or use such information without the informed consent of the client [§3.04] or pursuant to some other clear exception to the protection [§§5.06-5.14]. Information relating to the representation includes your client's identity, and any oral, written, electronic, or other information obtained from any source, whether client, witness, public record, document, or the like. Confidentiality attaches whether or not the communication is privileged [§§5.04 and 5.05], whether the client pays a fee, whether the information was obtained by the lawyer or an agent of the lawyer, and whether others know about or can uncover the information.[8] Even if publicly available, if you came across the information because of the client representation, the information and its location are protected. Lawyers may use hypotheticals to discuss issues relating to client representations, as long as the facts shared present "no reasonable likelihood that the listener will be able to ascertain the identity of the client or the situation involved."[9]

### ▶§5.04 LITIGATION DISCLOSURES

### ▶§5.04(a) A Question Of Privilege?

**We were representing a client in the purchase of some land. Now the client discovered there are some environmental problems, there's a lawsuit against seller and seller's lawyer deposed me and wanted to know about my conversation with an environmental engineer before the purchase. That's confidential, so I refused to answer. I'm right, right?**

Well, not exactly. If it's only confidential (which it is) that doesn't mean you can refuse to testify. The question is whether it is privileged in some way. You can't argue it's work-product since we assume no litigation was *then* contemplated. And the conversation was for the purpose of giving legal advice, but it was not between privileged persons. The environmental engineer was not your client. You could argue the

---

[7] Model Rule 1.6(a) and Comment [1].
[8] RLGL §59, comment d.
[9] Model Rule 1.6, Comment [4].

environmental engineer was your client's agent for these purposes, but there is no guarantee the judge will buy it. Sure is worth a try, however.

### ▶ §5.04(b) Attorney-Client Privilege: Scope Of The Protection

The attorney-client privilege recognizes a more limited version of confidentiality designed to address the admissibility of evidence in litigation. Because the adversary process requires access to facts to adjudicate disputes, an absolute privilege could destroy the value of fact-based adjudication. On the other hand, some confidentiality protection is necessary to encourage clients to disclose even embarrassing facts to lawyers, the disclosure of which in turn facilitates adequate representation. Although the privilege creates tension with the search for truth, it promotes client trust by preventing lawyers from being forced to testify against clients and also enables lawyers to candidly advise clients about relevant legal limits related to a client's past or future conduct.

Given this delicate balance, courts [§9.06] apply the privilege only when a communication occurs between privileged persons, in confidence, for the purpose of obtaining legal assistance.[10] Unlike fiduciary duty, which automatically attaches to all information learned in the course of representing a client, client or lawyer must claim the protection of the privilege when the evidence is sought or the client will lose the protection.[11]

Further, not all information is protected. The limitation to "communications" protects some but not all documents, and does not protect the facts contained in the communication. If the client is otherwise subject to the court's jurisdiction, the knowledge of the client can be probed during testimony.[12] "What happened on March 31?" is a proper question. "What did you tell your lawyer about what happened on March 31?" is the objectionable question. The requirement that the communication occur only between "privileged persons" includes only the client, the lawyer, or their agents.[13] For organizations,

---

[10] RLGL §68.
[11] RLGL §86.
[12] RLGL §69.
[13] RLGL §70.

this includes employees, officers, and directors acting within the scope of their employment.[14] The limitation to communications made "in confidence" means that no one other than client and lawyer and their agents can overhear the communication. Disclosure to an unprivileged person before or after disclosure to the lawyer can waive the privilege.[15] Finally, the communication must be for the purpose of obtaining legal assistance. If a lawyer works in a dual capacity, say board member and lawyer, or lover and lawyer, the privilege may not attach, unless it can be established that legal assistance was the purpose of the communication.[16] Exceptions to the privilege parallel but do not exactly mimic those of the fiduciary obligation of confidentiality [§5.01(c)].

### ►§5.04(c) Client Identity And Public Documents

Client identity and public documents you come across in representing a client are protected by confidentiality [§5.03(c)], which means you cannot disclose them without client consent. In the context of creating exceptions to the attorney-client or work-product privileges, however, some courts [§9.06] force disclosure of these bits of information. Client identity generally is not privileged because it does not constitute a "communication." The fact that a particular client retained a particular lawyer usually does not communicate anything about the content of the client's communication. In a few circumstances where disclosing client identity might not just prejudice the client, but will actually disclose the underlying client's confidential communication, courts [§9.06] are willing to extend the privilege.[17] Similarly, public documents by definition do not constitute limited or "confidential" disclosures solely between privileged persons.

►**Red Flag**► Remember that the privilege is not the sole definition of the scope of your obligation of confidentiality to clients [§9.02]. Finding a public document in the course of representing a client is subject to fiduciary duty. So is your client's identity, and the

---

[14] RLGL §73; *Upjohn Co. v. United States*, 449 U.S. 383 (1981). Governmental organizations and their employees also are protected. RLGL §74; *In re Lindsey*, 158 F.3d 1263 (D.C. Cir.), *cert. denied*, 525 U.S. 996 (1998).

[15] RLGL §§71, 79.

[16] RLGL §72.

[17] RLGL §69, comment g.

fact she retained you. If you *don't* disclose what clients tell you, what you learn about them, or the advice you give, and you *do* claim the appropriate privilege if the information is sought in litigation, you will be in great shape. Of course, you also should be aware of relevant exceptions to confidentiality, which can allow or on occasion mandate disclosure [§§5.06 - 5.14].

### ➤§5.04(d) The Privilege Boilerplate?

**Speaking of protecting the privilege, I am quite proud of the fact that at our firm all outgoing faxes and e-mails now have a legend on them that they are privileged and confidential. Pretty careful, don't you think?**

We are impressed. Every time the deli gets your firm's order for three corned beef sandwiches it is informed that this information is privileged and confidential with that ominous warning. We are sure they won't tell anyone how many of the sandwiches were on rye bread.

You see, putting the legend on everything is worthless. If everything is labeled privileged and confidential then nothing will be considered worthy of that status. Keep the legend if it makes you feel good, but instruct all your lawyers that if something is really privileged and confidential then the text of the document should specifically so state. Labeling privileged something that is not privileged does not make it so; labeling something privileged that should be privileged will help accomplish your goal.

### ➤§5.04(e) The Brilliant Gambit?

**Okay, now I get it. The good news is that I can tell my clients to tell me everything they know, and then we'll be able to block the other side from deposing them. Brilliant!**

It would be brilliant if such a gambit were to work. But, alas, what is protected is what these people told you. So these individuals cannot be asked whether they told *you* they were meeting in secret with their prime competitor to allocate market share. But they can be asked whether they met with anyone from their prime competitor, when, where and what was said. The work-product and attorney-client privileges protect the fact or content of the conversations with the lawyer; they do not bar inquiry into the underlying facts.

### ▶ §5.04(f) The Organizational Privilege?

**So if I conduct interviews of my client's employees, then they are privileged?**

Not precisely. It is critical to sort out several different concepts. Not all interviews of corporate employees fall within the attorney-client privilege. The interviews have to be in connection with providing advice to the client. Thus, if you have been retained on a matter and, in order to give wise counsel you need to gather information from corporate employees, that information should be deemed privileged.

In addition, if the work you are doing is in anticipation of litigation (as opposed to representation on a transaction or tax matters, just by way of example) then those conversations are subject to the attorney work-product privilege as well. You have a second arrow in your quiver to defend turning over your notes. One more thing. The more your notes not only reflect what people told you but also your thought process, the greater the likelihood that the notes will be deemed opinion or core work product not available to the other side even if the other side claims necessity. Although the necessity exception rarely arises, when it does—for example when the individual or individuals from whom the information was gathered are no longer available—then the courts [§9.06] may force you to turn over ordinary work product, i.e. work product that does not include your thinking.

### ▶ §5.04(g) The Corporate Gamble?

**I cannot wait to conduct these interviews. Once I tell them I'm the company's lawyer and the conversations are privileged, I am certain I will get to the bottom of the problem.**

You are about to enter an ethical minefield, so please proceed with caution. On the one hand, you want to learn as much as you can from your client's employees; on the other, you want to be scrupulous in your dealings with these corporate employees. Some are people you may have referred to as "my client." Others might otherwise think that you represent them. Telling them that what you learn from them will be kept confidential or privileged might lead them to conclude that what they tell you will not be shared with the company. So although there is no need to read these individuals *Miranda* warnings, you certainly want to make it perfectly clear that you only represent the company and that you are gathering the information to be shared with the company for the company's use. You also want to keep in mind that from an ethics rule perspective these are unrepresented persons, as to whom you should be providing no legal advice except, if appropriate, the advice to seek their own counsel. Good luck!

## ➤§5.05 WORK-PRODUCT PRIVILEGE

### ➤§5.05(a) The Engineer's Report?

**My client had a terrible explosion at a paper mill it operates. Weeks ago client sent me an engineer's report on the cause of the explosion. Now the plaintiffs are seeking any reports regarding the accident. Isn't this report work product? I'm going to bury it in my files.**

No you are not. Work product is material prepared in anticipation of litigation for sure. And this report probably meets that part of the work-product test. But the report has to be prepared under the direction and control of the lawyer. As you describe this report, the first you learned of it was when it was sent to you. If you had intervened in the expert's work some time before the final report was written, you might have had an argument, but not under these circumstances. Sometimes we just have to wonder why our clients don't consult us about such brilliant ideas before they spring into action. Next time, when a client faces such a crisis, you might immediately inform the client to conduct such investigations supervised by counsel. Although the client will think this is part of your business development plan, in fact it is wise advice designed to protect the client. How many times have lawyers despaired not of the underlying events, but the ham-handed way they were handled in the frenzy that immediately followed?

### ➤§5.05(b) Work-Product Protection

The work-product doctrine protects the lawyer's response to the client and encourages lawyers to prepare adequately for litigation. Like the attorney-client privilege, it will be lost if not timely asserted.[18] Work product protects everything lawyers prepare for clients in anticipation of litigation other than underlying facts.[19] It is broader than the privilege, because it includes materials obtained from persons other than the client, but also is narrower because it applies only to materials prepared in anticipation of litigation, not to all legal representations. Although the privilege absolutely bars the admission of evidence, work product creates an "immunity" that can be overcome with a proper showing of necessity. Your mental impressions, notes, legal theories, and opinions form the core of "opinion" work product, which is immune from discovery absent some clear exception.[20] Statements of witnesses prepared from lawyer interviews also are protected as "ordinary" work product, which may be a bit easier to obtain if substantial equivalent testimony is unavailable.[21]

### ➤ §5.05(c) The Supervised Expert?

**So if I supervise an expert's investigation into the cause of my client's paper mill explosion then my notes will be privileged forever, right?**

Not so fast. No matter how well we maintain all of the indicia of the privilege, there is one wild card we can never control.

**What's that?**

The client can always decide that it is in its best interest to waive the privilege, to disclose your notes, memoranda, and other privileged materials. Think about a company that changes management. Or one that decides to cooperate with the SEC. Or a corporate client that wants to cut a deal with an aggressive unrelenting prosecutor.

The lesson from all of this is never let down your guard in what you write simply because it has the words privileged and confidential emblazoned in red ink on each page. In fact, assume that everything you write may someday appear on the front page of the Wall Street

---

[18] RLGL §90.

[19] RLGL §87; *Hickman v. Taylor*, 329 U.S. 495 (1947).

[20] RLGL §89.

[21] 21 RLGL §88.

Journal. Then you may be dismayed that others are reading your work product. But you won't be embarrassed. The truth is lawyers too often put in writing matters that are best left unstated, and if they must be stated at all can be just as effectively stated orally. The proliferation of emails has only aggravated this problem.

## ➤ §5.06 CONFIDENTIALITY EXCEPTIONS

### ➤ §5.06(a) Countervailing Policies

The fiduciary duty of confidentiality and the evidentiary attorney-client and work-product privileges both recognize countervailing policies that justify exceptions. Once such an exception exists, lawyers are usually allowed, and occasionally required, to disclose client confidential information that falls within the exception, and they may be forced to testify to what otherwise might be considered privileged or work-product information. The exceptions discussed in §§5.07 to 5.14 often differ significantly in different jurisdictions. The chart below details these differing lawyer code provisions. Be sure to know the nuances of your state's rules [§9.04].

➤**Red Flag**➤ Do not assume that an exception gives you the right to share every juicy tidbit of related client information. Each exception allows disclosure only "to the extent reasonably necessary" to promote the countervailing policy.[22] Disclosures beyond this point violate your general fiduciary duty. Remembering that these exceptions are exceptions, not the general rule, should facilitate an appropriate response.

### ➤ §5.06(b) Chart: State Lawyer Code Exceptions To Client Confidentiality

---

[22] Model Rule 1.6(b); RLGL §§61-67, Title C Introductory Note.

§5.06(b)    CONFIDENTIALITY • 101

| Juris. | Express Author-ity | Implied Authority Entities (E) Clients with Diminished Capacity | To Prevent Future Crime (CR), Fraud (FR), Death/Subs. Bodily Harm (D/SBH), or Subs. Financial Harm (SFH) | To Secure Legal Advice | Lawyer Self-Defense | To Comply With Law Or Court Order Fraud On Tribunal Assisting Client Fraud |
|---|---|---|---|---|---|---|
| ABA Model Rules | 1.6(a) May | 1.6(a) May 1.13(c)(2)-(d) May (E) 1.14(c) May (DC) | 1.6(b)(1) May (D/SBH) 1.6(b)(2) May (CR or FR & SFH) | 1.6(b)(4) May | 1.6(b)(5) May | 1.6(b)(6) May 3.3 Must 4.1(b), Must if 1.6(b)(3) |
| AL | 1.6(a) May | 1.6(a) May | 1.6(b)(1) May (CR & D/SBH) | None | 1.6(b)(2) May | 1.6 comment 3.3 Must 4.1(b) Must not |
| AK | 1.6(a) May | 1.6(a) May | 1.6(b)(1) May (CR/FR & D/SBH/SFH) | None | 1.6(b)(2) May | 1.6 comment 3.3 Must 4.1(b), Must if 1.6(b)(1) |
| AZ | 1.6(a) May | 1.6(a) May 1.14(c) May (DC) | 1.6(b) Must (CR & D/SBH) 1.6(c) May (CR) 1.6(d)(1) May (CR/FR & SFH) | 1.6(d)(3) May | 1.6(d)(4) May | 1.6(d)(5) May 3.3 Must 4.1(b), Must if 1.6(d)(2) |
| AR | 1.6(a) May | 1.6(a) May 1.13(c)(2)-(d) May (E) 1.14(c) May (DC) | 1.6(b)(1) May (D/SBH) 1.6(b)(2) May (CR or FR & SFH) | 1.6(b)(4) May | 1.6(b)(5) May | 1.6(b)(6) May 3.3 Must 4.1(b), Must if 1.6(b)(3) |
| CA | None | None | Cal. Bus. & Prof. Code §6068(e)(2) May (CR & D/SBH) | None | None | None None None |

| Juris. | Expr. Auth. | Implied Auth. (E) (DC) | (CR), (FR), (D/SBH), (SFH) | To Secure Legal Adv. | Lawyer Self-Def. | Law Or Court Order Fraud On Tribunal Assist. Client Fraud |
|---|---|---|---|---|---|---|
| CO | 1.6(a) May | 1.6(a) May | 1.6(b) May (CR) | None | 1.6(c) May | 1.6 comment 3.3 Must 4.1(2) Must not |
| CT | 1.6(a) May | 1.6(a) May | 1.6(b) Must (CR & D/SBH) 1.6(c)(1) May (CR & SFH) | None | 1.6(d) May | 1.6 comment 3.3 Must 4.1(b), Must if 1.6(c)(2) |
| DE | 1.6(a) May | 1.6(a) May 1.14(c) May (DC) | 1.6(b)(1) May (D/SBH) 1.6(b)(2) May (CR/FR & SFH) | 1.6(b)(4) May | 1.6(b)(5) May | 1.6(b)(6) May 3.3 Must 4.1(b), Must if 1.6(b)(3) |
| FL | 4-1.6(a) May | 4-1.6 comment | 4-1.6(b)(1) Must (CR) 4-1.6(b)(2) Must (D/SBH) | None | 4-1.6(c)(2) May 4-1.6(c)(3) May 4-1.6(c)(4) May | 4-1.6 comment 4-3.3 Must 4-4.1(b), Must if 4-1.6(c)(5) |
| GA | 1.6(a) May | 1.6(a) May | 1.6(b)(1)(i) May (CR & SFH) 1.6(b)(1)(ii) May (D/SBH) | None | 1.6(b)(1)(iii) May | 1.6(a) May 3.3 Must 4.1(b), must if 1.6(b) |
| HI | 1.6(a) May | 1.6(a) May | 1.6(c)(1) May (CR/FR & D/SBH/ SFH) | None | 1.6(c)(3) May | 1.6(c)(6) May 3.3 Must 4.1(b), 1.6(b) Must |
| ID | 1.6(a) May | 1.6(a) May 1.13(c), (d) May (E) 1.14(c) May (DC) | 1.6(b)(1) May (CR) 1.6(b)(2) May (D/SBH) | 1.6(b)(4) May | 1.6(b)(5) May | 1.6(b)(6) May 3.3 Must 4.1(b), Must if 1.6(b)(3) |

§5.06(b)     CONFIDENTIALITY • 103

| Juris. | Expr. Auth. | Implied Auth. (E) (DC) | (CR), (FR), (D/SBH), (SFH) | To Secure Legal Adv. | Lawyer Self-Def. | Law Or Court Order Fraud On Tribunal Assist. Client Fraud |
|---|---|---|---|---|---|---|
| IL | 1.6(a) May | None | 1.6(b) Must (D/SBH) 1.6(c)(2) May (CR) | None | 1.6(c)(3) May | 1.6(c)(1) May 3.3 Must 4.1(b), Must if 1.6(c) |
| IN | 1.6(a) May | 1.6(a) May 1.13(c)(d) May (E) 1.14(c) May (DC) | 1.6(b)(1) May (D/SBH) 1.6(b)(2) May (CR/FR & SFH) | 1.6(b)(4) May | 1.6(b)(5) May | 1.6(b)(6) May 3.3 Must 4.1(b), Must if 1.6(b)(3) |
| IA | 32:1.6(a) May | 32:1.6(a) May 32:1.13(c)(d) May (E) 32:1.14(c) May (DC) | 32:1.6(b)(1) May (D/SBH) 32:1.6(c) Must if imminent 32:1.6(b)(2) May (CR/FR & SFH) | 32:1.6(b)(4) May | 32:1.6(b)(5) May | 32:1.6(b)(6) May 32:3.3 Must 32:4.1(b), Must if 32:1.6(b)(3) |
| KS | 1.6(a) May | 1.6(a) May | 1.6(b)(1) May (CR) | None | 1.6(b)(3) May | 1.6(b)(2) May 3.3 Must 4.1 Must not |
| KY | 1.6(a) May | 1.6(a) May | 1.6(b)(1) May (CR & D/SBH) | None | 1.6(b)(2) May | 1.6(b)(3) May 3.3 Must Must not |
| LA | 1.6(a) May | 1.6(a) May 1.13(c), (d) May (E) 1.14(c) May (DC) | 1.6(b)(1) May (D/SBH) 1.6(b)(2) May (CR/FR & SFH) | 1.6(b)(4) May | 1.6(b)(5) May | 1.6(b)(6) May 3.3 Must 4.1, Must if 1.6(b) |
| ME | 3.6(h)(1) May | 3.6(j) May (DC) | 3.6(h)(4) May (CR) | None | 3.6(h)(3) May | 3.6(b)(all fraud): Must if client and not privileged Must if non-client |

| Juris. | Expr. Auth. | Implied Auth. (E) (DC) | (CR), (FR), (D/SBH), (SFH) | To Secure Legal Adv. | Lawyer Self-Def. | Law Or Court Order Fraud On Tribunal Assist. Client Fraud |
|---|---|---|---|---|---|---|
| MD | 1.6(a) May | 1.6(a) May 1.13(c) May (E) 1.14(c) May (DC) | 1.6(b)(1) May (D/SBH) 1.6(b)(2) May (CR/FR & SFH) | 1.6(b)(4) | 1.6(b)(5) May | 1.6(b)(6) May 3.3 Must 4.1 Must |
| MA | 1.6(a) May | 1.6(a) May 1.14(b) May (DC) | 1.6(b)(1) May (CR/FR & (D/SBH/ SFH) | None | 1.6(b)(2) May | 1.6(b)(4) May 3.3, 1.6(b) Must, 3.3 (e) (criminal defense) 4.1(b), Must if 1.6(b)(2) |
| MI | 1.6(c)(1) May | 1.6 comment 1.13(c) May (E) | 1.6(c)(4) May (CR) | None | 1.6(c)(5) May | 1.6(c)(2) May 3.3 Must 1.6(c)(3) May |
| MN | 1.6(b)(1) May | 1.6 comment | 1.6(b)(3) May (CR) | None | 1.6(b)(5) May | 1.6(b)(2) May 3.3 Must 1.6(b)(4) May |
| MS | 1.6(a) May | 1.6 comment | 1.6(b)(1) May (CR) | None | 1.6(b)(2) May | 1.6(e) May 3.3 Must 4.1 Must |
| MO | 4-1.6(a) May | 4-1.6(a) May | 4-1.6(b)(1) May (CR & D/SBH) | None | 4-1.6(b)(2) May | 4-1.6 comment 4-3.3 Must 4-4.1 Must |
| MT | 1.6(a) May | 1.6(a) May 1.14(c) May (DC) | 1.6(b)(1) May (D/SBH) | 1.6(b)(2) May | 1.6(b)(3) May | 1.6(b)(4) May 3.3 Must 4.1 Must |
| NE | 4-101-(C)(1) May | None | 4-101(C)(3) May (CR) | None | 4-101-(C)(4) May | 4-101(C)(2) May 7-102(B) (all fraud): Must not (client); Must (non-client) |

## §5.06(b)     CONFIDENTIALITY • 105

| Juris. | Expr. Auth. | Implied Auth. (E) (DC) | (CR), (FR), (D/SBH), (SFH) | To Secure Legal Adv. | Lawyer Self-Def. | Law Or <u>Court Order</u> Fraud On <u>Tribunal</u> Assist. Client Fraud |
|---|---|---|---|---|---|---|
| NV | 156(1) May | 156(1) May | 156(2) Must (CR & D/SBH) | None | 156(3)(b) May | <u>None</u> <u>172 Must</u> 156(3)(a) May |
| NH | 1.6(a) May | <u>1.6(a) May</u> 1.13(c) May (E) | 1.6(b)(1) May (CR & D/SBH/ SFH) | None | 1.6(b)(2) May | <u>None</u> <u>3.3 Must</u> 4.1, Must if 1.6(b)(1) |
| NJ | 1.6(a) May | <u>1.6(a) May</u> 1.13(c) <u>May (E)</u> 1.14(c) May (DC) | 1.6(b)(1) Must (CR/FR & D/SBH/ SFH) | None | 1.6(d)(2) May | <u>1.6(d)(3) May</u> <u>3.3 Must</u> 4.1(b) Must |
| NM | 16-106(A) May | 16-106(A) May | 16-106(B) Should (CR & D/SBH) 16-106(C) May (CR & SFH) | None | 16-106(D) May | 16-106 <u>comment</u> <u>16-303 Must</u> 16-401, Must if 16-106(C) |
| NY | 4-101(C)(1) May | None | 4-101(C)(3) May (CR) | None | 4-101(C)-(4) May | 4-101(C)(2) <u>May 7-102(B)</u> (all fraud): Must not (client); Must (non-client); 4-101(C)(5) may if reliance on opinion |
| NC | 1.6(a) May | <u>1.6(a) May</u> 1.14(c) May (DC) | 1.6(b)(2) May (CR) 1.6(b)(3) May (D/SBH) | 1.6(b)(5) May | 1.6(b)(6) May | <u>1.6(b)(1) May</u> <u>3.3 Must</u> 1.6(b)(4) May |
| ND | 1.6(b) May | 1.6(c) May | 1.6(a) Must (Imminent D/SBH) 1.6(d) May (CR/FR & Non-imminent D/SBH/ SFH) | None | 1.6(e) May | <u>1.6(g) May</u> 3.3 must not (client) Must <u>(non-client)</u> 1.6(f) May |

| Juris. | Expr. Auth. | Implied Auth. (E) (DC) | (CR), (FR), (D/SBH), (SFH) | To Secure Legal Adv. | Lawyer Self-Def. | Law Or Court Order Fraud On Tribunal Assist. Client Fraud |
|---|---|---|---|---|---|---|
| OH | 4-101(C)(1) May | None | 4-101(C)(3) May (CR) | None | 4-101(C)-(4) May | 4-101(C)(2) May 7-102(B) (all fraud): Must |
| OK | 1.6(a) May | 1.6(a) May | 1.6(b)(1) May (CR) | None | 1.6(b)(3) May | 1.6(c) Must 3.3 Must 4.1(b), Must if 1.6(b)(2) |
| OR | 1.6(a) May | 1.6(a) May 1.13(c), (d) May (E) 1.14(c) May (DC) | 1.6(b)(1) May (CR) 1.6(b)(2) May (D/SBH) | 1.6(b)(3) May | 1.6(b)(4) May | 1.6(b)(5) May 3.3 Must 4.1(b), Must if 1.6(b)(5) |
| PA | 1.6(a) May | 1.6(a) May 1.14(c) May (DC) | 1.6(c)(1) May (D/SBH) 1.6(c)(2) May (CR & SFH) | 1.6(c)(5) May | 1.6(c)(4) May | 1.6 Comments [18], [19] 3.3 Must 4.1(b), Must if 1.6(c)(3) |
| RI | 1.6(a) May | 1.6(a) May | 1.6(b)(1) May (CR & D/SBH) | None | 1.6(b)(2) May | None 3.3 Must 4.1(b) Must not |
| SC | 1.6(a) May | 1.6(a) May | 1.6(b)(1) May (CR) | None | 1.6(b)(2) May | 1.6 comment 3.3 Must 4.1(b) Must not |
| SD | 1.6(a) May | 1.6(a) May 1.14(c) May (DC) | 1.6(b)(1) May (CR & D/SBH) | 1.6(b)(2) May | 1.6(b)(3) May | 1.6(b)(5) May 3.3 Must 4.1(b), Must if 1.6(b)(4) |
| TN | 1.6(a) May | 1.6(a) May | 1.6(b)(1) May (CR) 1.6(c)(1) Must (D/SBH) | 1.6(b)(2) May | 1.6(b)(3) May | 1.6(c) Must 3.3 Must 4.1(b)(c) Must |

§5.06(b)　　　　　　　　　　　　　　　Confidentiality • 107

| Juris. | Expr. Auth. | Implied Auth. (E) (DC) | (CR), (FR), (D/SBH), (SFH) | To Secure Legal Adv. | Lawyer Self-Def. | Law Or Court Order Fraud On Tribunal Assist. Client Fraud |
|---|---|---|---|---|---|---|
| TX | 1.05(c)(1) May 1.05(c)(2) May | 1.05(d)(1) May | 1.05(c)(7) May (CR/FR) 1.05(e) Must (CR & D/SBH) | None | 1.05(c)(5) May 1.05(c)(6) May 1.05(d)(2) May | 1.05(c)(4) May 3.03 Must 4.01(b) Must |
| UT | 1.6(a) May | 1.6 comment | 1.6(b)(1) May (CR/FR & D/SBH/ SFH) | None | 1.6(b)(3) May | 1.6(b)(4) May 1.6 and 3.3 Must 4.1(b) Must if 1.6(b)(2) |
| VT | 1.6(a) May | 1.6(a) May | 1.6(b)(1) Must (CR & D/SBH) 1.6(c)(1) May (CR) | None | 1.6(c)(2) May | 1.6 comment 3.3 Must 1.6(b)(2) Must |
| VA | 1.6(a) May | 1.6(a) May 1.14(c) May (DC) | 1.6(c)(1) Must (CR) | None | 1.6(b)(2) May | 1.6(b)(1) May 1.6(c)(2) 3.3 Must 4.1(b) Must |
| WA | 1.6(a) May | 1.6(a) May | 1.6(b)(1) May (CR) | None | 1.6(b)(2) May | 1.6(b)(2) May 3.3 Must 4.1(b), Must if 1.6(b)(1) |
| WV | 1.6(a) May | 1.6(a) May | 1.6(b)(1) May (CR) | None | 1.6(b)(2) May | None 3.3 Must 4.1 Must not |
| WI | 20:1.6(a) May | 20:1.6(a) May | 20:1.6(b) Must (CR/FR & D/SBH/SFH) | None | 20:1.6(c)(2) May | 20:1.6 comment 20:3.3 Must 20:4.1, Must if 20:1.6(c)(1); 20:1.6(b) Must |
| WY | 1.6(a) May | 1.6(a) May 1.6(b)(3) May (DC) | 1.6(b)(1) May (CR) | None | 1.6(b)(2) May | 1.6 comment 3.3 Must 4.1 Must |

## ▶ §5.07 CONFIDENTIALITY EXCEPTIONS: EXPRESS OR IMPLIED AUTHORIZATION

### ▶ §5.07(a) The New CEO?

**I had privileged conversations with old CEO two years ago relating to a big merger. New CEO now tells me he wants me to testify about those conversations. Can he do that?**

If you were talking to old CEO in his role as an officer of the company then the conversation was privileged as to the company. New CEO certainly has the authority to waive the privilege as to the company. Thus, the only question left unresolved is whether old CEO believes you were also representing him at the time of conversations. If so, then only if both clients in the joint representation waive the privilege may you disclose the contents of those conversations.

If you have any doubt how old CEO viewed these conversations, you should notify old CEO that you have been asked to testify regarding these conversations to permit him to raise any personal objections he might have. Lawyers are required to take all steps necessary to protect privileged information and the last thing you want to occur is for old CEO to learn after the fact that you testified to conversations old CEO thought were privileged not as to the company but personally as to him.

### ▶ §5.07(b) The Administrative Privilege?

**A lawyer from the SEC's enforcement division told us we should share our preliminary report to the Company with the agency. Things will go a lot better for our client, she said. I raised the privilege issue and she assured me that the SEC would not share the document with any of those damn plaintiffs' lawyers.**

We're certain her comforting assurance didn't give you any pause. How sweet of her. But the fact is the SEC cannot throw holy water on the privileged document you have been asked to produce. Only the courts can determine the effect of a selective waiver such as the one you are trying to accomplish here. And be warned; courts [§9.06] look with disfavor upon selective waiver. If you share it with the SEC, you may be deemed to have waived it as to anyone who claims they are otherwise entitled to see the document.

**Actually the SEC is only interested in a part of the report. How about if I give the agency just those pages?**

That may not cure the problem. You may not selectively waive the privilege as to only some documents relating to a particular subject matter. Once you waive the privilege as to one document that addresses that subject matter, you will be deemed to have waived it as to every privileged document relating to that same subject matter. Only you can judge how strong the argument will be that the rest of the report addresses an unrelated topic.

### ▶ §5.07(c) Company Agents?

**The Company thinks it would be great if I bring their outside public relations guy along on one of these interviews to assess how big a problem the Company really has.**

What a great idea! Why didn't you bring your mother along too so she can learn firsthand what a fine lawyer you are? Although you can bring along a paralegal or other firm employee to help you, adding outsiders to the interview could easily destroy the privilege. You must remember that the courts generally disfavor the privilege. If you seek to maintain it you must be scrupulous in observing all of the detailed requirements the case law [§9.06] establishes. The presence of a third party, unless you can establish that the third party was the agent of the client or lawyer and essential to the provision of the legal services, will be pointed to as an indication that the conversation was not between privileged persons, was not intended to be kept confidential and, therefore, is subject to inquiry. And the truly scary part is that you won't know until way after the fact—when someone seeks disclosure of the conversation—whether the presence of the third person destroyed the privilege.

### ▶ §5.07(d) The Inadvertent Email?

**Boy did I get lucky. I just got an email with an attachment that details the other side's jury consultant's report. What a help that will be.**

Slow down. The document is certainly attorney work product. We are sure the other side had no intent of sharing that with you. And we'll bet they have no idea you now possess it. Unless you can make some good faith argument that this document has been otherwise wrongfully withheld from you, you should read no further than you have, call the other side, notify them that it was inadvertently sent to you and abide by the other side's instructions as to what to do with it.

### ▶§5.07(e) The Helpful Opponent?

**What if I get a call from some guy who wants to share some sensitive documents with me? Can I meet with him?**

This one is no better and it could be a lot worse. Who is this person? Does the person have authority to possess these documents? Even if he does, are they privileged? And who has authority to waive the privilege? Two things you do not want to do: Receive stolen goods or invade the privilege of the other side. The former may be a crime [§7.03] and the latter will get you disqualified [§8.08]. No matter how tempting it may be to learn information that is this potentially useful to your client's cause, our obligation of zealous advocacy ends at the point where we might violate the law or unfairly invade the other side's privileged terrain. After you learn more about this person, it may be perfectly okay to meet him to inform yourself further. But you do want to proceed with caution.

### ▶§5.07(f) Express And Implied Confidentiality Waivers

We have described express informed consent as the "gold standard" of confidentiality exceptions [§3.04] because the agency law origin of fiduciary duty rests on a consensual foundation.[23] Conduct evidencing implied authorization can be far more ambiguous than express words, so lawyers bear the burden of clarifying any uncertainty. Generally, using client confidential information to advance a client's interests is impliedly authorized because it furthers the client's objectives.[24] But lawyers remain subject to their clients' definition of interests, and must remain aware of the clients' ultimate authority to limit their lawyers' ability to disclose or use the information [§10.03].

When lawyer and client differ about the client's best interests, the Model Rules specify that disclosures in two narrow circumstances are impliedly authorized because the client may not be fully able to determine his, her, or its own interests: (1) Protective disclosures necessary to prevent substantial physical or financial harm to clients with diminished capacity;[25] and (2) Disclosures reasonably necessary to prevent clear violations of law by an organization that will result in substantial

---

[23] Model Rule 1.6(a); RLGL §62.

[24] RLGL §61.

[25] Model Rule 1.14(b).

injury to the organization.[26] Once again, disclosure must be intended to facilitate the organization's best interests.

When facing these or any other circumstances where you wish to rely on implied authority, three situations should cause you to pause and seriously reflect before doing so: First, client inculpatory statements or acts can have a significant effect on the client's rights. Although you might deem it best to disclose, informed consent requires that your client first understand the consequences of and alternatives to disclosure. Second, the interests of another client have caused some lawyers, relying on some notion of implied consent, to disclose inculpatory statements of one client to another.[27] Remember that confidentiality is personal to each client it protects. When disclosing one client's information to another, seek explicit informed consent [§3.04], or clarify another express exception to confidentiality [§§5.08—5.14]. Third, your own interest or personal benefit from disclosure or use of client information never justifies your relying upon implicit client authority as a basis for acting. Likewise, without full and explicit informed consent, do not invest in a hot opportunity you learned about in handling a client matter. Your client has every right to the first opportunity at the bargain, and well might see such self-dealing as a use of confidential information that disadvantages the client's interests.[28] Finally, we trust you would not trade on your public company's inside information for the same reasons, not to mention the problem of securities fraud.[29]

The attorney-client and work-product privileges also recognize express and implied authorization as an exception under the rubric of "waiver."[30] Here, unlike the similar exception to confidentiality, the

---

[26] Model Rule 1.13(c).

[27] *Perez v. Kirk & Carrigan*, 822 S.W.2d 261 (Tex. App. 1991)(lawyers gave client's inculpatory statement to prosecutor without client's consent or knowledge, causing criminal indictments for 21 counts of involuntary manslaughter, for which client was acquitted, but not until three years later).

[28] Model Rule 1.8(b); RLGL §60(2); *Meinhard v. Salmon*, 164 N.E. 545 (N.Y. 1928)(agent who failed to disclose property purchase opportunity learned of in the course of representing principal held to have purchased property in constructive trust for principal).

[29] *United States v. O'Hagan*, 521 U.S. 642 (1997)(criminal liability of company's lawyer under §10b of the Securities Exchange Act of 1934 may be predicated on the misappropriation theory).

[30] RLGL §§78, 79, 91, 92.

interests of judicial administration make it much easier to imply consent to disclosure or waiver. Thus, failure to object to the introduction of privileged evidence constitutes implied waiver,[31] as does subsequent disclosure to a non-privileged person.[32] These exceptions mean that lawyer and client must take reasonable precautions to prevent subsequent disclosure, because even inadvertent disclosures, such as a missent email or fax, can be found to constitute a waiver.[33] A client who seeks to rely on a privileged communication, such as a document, in testifying, or in establishing an advice of counsel defense, also waives the privilege.[34]

## ▶ §5.08 CONFIDENTIALITY EXCEPTIONS: THREATENED SERIOUS BODILY HARM

### ▶ §5.08(a) The Suicidal Client?

**My client has a terminal illness and is threatening suicide. When I told my client I was going to warn her son about her plans, she reminded me that I had told her at the beginning of the representation that I would keep everything learned confidential. "Besides I didn't mean it," she said.**

One exception to the confidentiality obligation occurs when the lawyer knows confidential information that may result in reasonably certain death or serious bodily harm. The first question then is what do you know? And then, how certain is it? If your state has adopted new Model Rule 1.6 at least you don't have to worry whether suicide is "criminal" since the recent Model Rule amendments dropped that requirement. In addition, under Model Rule 1.14 you are permitted to disclose this information to others to protect a client who is suffering from such serious depression that the client has diminished capacity.

On the one hand, you certainly would like to prevent suicide. On the other, lawyers must respect authentic client autonomy. The one thing we can say is that lawyers' attempts to intervene in situations like this by and large have met with favor in the courts [§9.06].

---

[31] RLGL §78.
[32] RLGL §79.
[33] RLGL §79 comment h.
[34] RLGL §80.

§5.08(c)

▶**Ultimate Red Flag**▶ The potential suicide of a client obviously raises difficult and sensitive questions, which we discuss further in §10.04.

### ▶§5.08(b) The Undisclosed Aneurysm?

**Damnedest thing. I'm handling this auto accident case for the insurer. I send the plaintiff for a physical to our doc. Our doc tells us the plaintiff's expert has it all wrong. The plaintiff's injuries are much worse. The young kid has an aneurysm—a dangerous weakening of an artery. It might've been caused by the accident. So I call the insurance company. They say, whatever we do, we should not tell the kid's lawyer about the problem. It would turn a $10,000 case into a damage disaster. I gotta tell you, I'm worried about that kid.**

For good reason. And adding to your humanitarian instinct, consider that if the aneurysm ever ruptures, your insurance company may end up owing millions—or punitives. So maybe you want to appeal to their pocketbook as well as to their humanity.

Filthy lucre aside, maybe the call to the insurance company was the wrong call to make. Your client is the defendant driver [§1.17]. Maybe she'll have a different view about telling the kid's lawyer. The defense lawyer in *Spaulding v. Zimmerman* made the same mistake.[35]

If no one will give you permission to disclose, you probably can anyway. The rules everywhere permit disclosure of confidential information to prevent reasonably certain death or serious bodily harm. We don't know how certain it is, but aneurysms are not the kind of thing people trifle with. We cannot imagine anyone would second-guess your decision to disclose on these facts.

### ▶§5.08(c) Threatened Physical Harm

Confidentiality encourages clients to blow off steam and affords lawyers the opportunity to counsel clients to abstain from vigilante justice. Occasionally, you may worry that your efforts have failed, either because you cannot dissuade the client, or you learn about the pro-

---

[35] 116 N.W. 2d 704 (Minn.1962). *See also,* Roger C. Cramton & Lori P. Knowles, *Professional Secrecy and its Exceptions:* Spaulding v. Zimmerman *Revisited,* 83 Minn. L. Rev. 63 (1998).

posed conduct of someone else through a client. Here, your instinct to prevent serious harm to others is recognized by an explicit exception to confidentiality that allows you to respond, as long as you reasonably believe it necessary to warn to prevent reasonably certain death or serious bodily harm.[36] If the threatened person already knows about the danger, your action is not reasonably necessary. If the threat of bodily harm is imminent or is reasonably certain to occur at a later date if you take no action, a warning is reasonably necessary. Some jurisdictions tie this exception to a threatened future crime [§5.09], some to "imminent" harm, some allow disclosure only if the client threatens harm, and some make disclosure mandatory rather than discretionary. Others follow the Model Rules and the Restatement, which do not require any connection to client conduct or criminal intent, but rather focus on the likely outcome of the proposed threat [§9.04].

If you have disclosed to prevent harm, your client may be arrested, and the prosecution may seek your testimony in the criminal proceeding. Here, the future crime-fraud exception to the privileges may apply [§5.09], but only if the client sought your legal advice or used it to obtain assistance in a crime or fraud.[37] If you told the client he was a damn fool, should stop and why, but he did not, the conversation should remain privileged.[38]

➤**Red Flag**➤ Do not assume that disclosure to prevent serious bodily harm automatically waives the privilege. You should be encouraged to make disclosure to avoid such harm without worrying about the later legal effect on your client.[39]

## ➤§5.09 CONFIDENTIALITY EXCEPTIONS: FUTURE CRIME
### ➤§5.09(a) Blowing Off Steam?

**"I'm going to kill her" were my clients final words as he rushed out of my office, insisting he would never pay one dime in alimony to his very rich estranged wife. Now what do I do?**

This threat certainly qualifies as harm to a third person so no countervailing concerns there. But if every time one spouse said, "I'm

---

[36] Model Rule 1.6(b)(1); RLGL §66.

[37] RLGL §§82 and 93.

[38] *United States v. Bauer*, 132 F.3d 504 (9th Cir. 1997).

[39] *Purcell v. District Attorney for the Suffolk District*, 676 N.E.2d 436 (Mass. 1997).

going to kill my wife (or husband)" he or she meant it, there would be an epidemic of spousal murder in America. You have to make a judgment whether the guy was blowing off steam or really plans to commit mayhem. If the latter, then you are free to disclose the confidential information. Although we don't want to skew your analysis, you should remember that lurking in the background may be later claims that you had some obligation to disclose, not under the rules, but under common law doctrines of civil liability.

**What if I am wrong?**

As long as you acted reasonably, you cannot be faulted, even though you will have violated your client's right to confidentiality. The good news is that it is highly unlikely you can be forced to testify about the conversation. The courts [§9.06] have been quite solicitous of the notion that lawyers should not be discouraged from breaching confidentiality under troubling circumstances like this, so the courts won't compound the problem by requiring the lawyer to assist the prosecutor in developing a case of attempted assault or murder.

You should also note that the old model rule limited the right to disclose threatened bodily harm to that involving client conduct. New Model Rule 1.6 would permit disclosure even if what the husband disclosed was that his son planned to kill his mother.

### ▶ §5.09(b) The Future Crime Exception

The exception that recognizes the importance of preventing serious bodily harm originated as a future crime exception in both the lawyer codes [§9.04] and the crime-fraud exception to the attorney-client and work-product privileges. Many jurisdictions continue to hinge disclosure on such a requirement, and some allow disclosure to prevent any future crime [§9.04].

A future crime exception tracks the legislative classification of illegal acts as crimes, but may be both narrower, because it does not allow for disclosure to prevent tortious conduct which is not a crime, and broader, because it allows for warning about any criminal conduct, including misdemeanors. The fiduciary duty found in lawyer codes [§9.04] tends to recognize the countervailing value of human life regardless of the characterization of the threatened conduct [§5.08(c)]. The crime-fraud exception to the privileges, on the other hand, remains tied to the classification of the conduct as criminal or fraudulent.[40] Further, unauthorized disclosure that thwarts rather than furthers a client's interests under this exception does not constitute a waiver of the evidentiary privileges.[41]

## ▶§5.10 CONFIDENTIALITY EXCEPTIONS: CLIENT FRAUD
### ▶§5.10(a) Puffing?

**I read all this stuff about lawyers telling the truth. But it doesn't seem fair. I know my client will settle this case for $50,000 but I want to tell the other side we'll pay no more than ten grand.**

You are right that lawyers are burdened with an obligation to be truthful. We're sure you think that's a good thing too. But the comments to Rule 4.1 do permit a certain level of puffing, particularly in connection with negotiations. So comments such as "your case is worthless" or "my client's bottom line is $150,000" are perfectly okay, even if you know they really are not true. But the line between legitimate puffing and misrepresentation can be crossed very quickly. For example, the statement "we've lined up an expert who will put $3 million in damages on the blackboard" better not be uttered if your attempts to find an expert have proved unavailing.

How puffing plays out in front of a member of the judiciary may be another story. A lawyer's duty of candor to the tribunal may be triggered in questioning from the judge. Yet bottom line numbers are confidential. And the moment the judge suggests you are posturing and insists on your bottom line may not be the time the lawyer (or client) is prepared to go that far. Which means that, particularly in negotiations being supervised by a judge or magistrate judge, the lawyer would be well served to have limited authority, so she can answer all potentially embarrassing questions truthfully.

---

[40] RLGL §§82 and 93; *In re Grand Jury Investigation,* 772 N.E.2d 9 (Mass. 2002)(private school's investigation into abuse of students under age 18 falls within crime-fraud exception if school used lawyer's services to evade mandatory reporting requirement with criminal penalties, but does not apply to similar conduct directed at students over age 18 because not a crime to fail to report such conduct); *Am. Tobacco Co. v. State,* 697 So.2d 1249 (Fla. Dist. Ct. App. 1997)(tobacco company's use of lawyers to misrepresent health effects of smoking to the public constituted a fraud, triggering crime-fraud exception).

[41] RLGL §79, comment c.

### ▶ §5.10(b) The Innocent Misrepresentation?

**We were at a negotiation session. The other side asked how the property was zoned. My client told me it was C-2, Commercial-Warehouse, so that's what I told them. Now I find out my client was wrong. I told my client we should correct the record. Client says it might screw up a good deal and besides, who does a deal like this without checking zoning for himself? Its not like it was a representation in an agreement of sale.**

It depends. You certainly did not violate Model Rule 4.1(a) when you made the statement. You thought you were correct. Now because of Model Rule 4.1(b) you must determine whether failure to disclose your error is necessary to avoid assisting a criminal or fraudulent act of your client. If your client used you as an instrumentality of an intentionally misleading statement you have to decide if the representation was material. Can an error about zoning rise to that level? What buyer wouldn't independently check what the zoning is before making a real estate purchase? Was this buyer represented by counsel? Is the other side really relying on what you said? In any event you may want to persuade your client to correct the misstatement now to avoid trouble later should buyer try to undo the transaction on the ground of fraud.

If you conclude, however, that your statement was assisting a client fraud, then, unless Model Rule 1.6 in your jurisdiction [§9.04] prohibits disclosures relating to client fraud, you must disclose the mistake to the other side. Note well that in this instance the disclosure by the lawyer is not just permitted, it is required.

### ▶ §5.10(c) Tax Compliance?

**I counseled a tax client two years ago. He had this idea that if he invested in a limited partnership that bought both puts and calls, he could use the loss from the failed side of the hedged transaction to shelter his income. I told him it wouldn't fly and sent him on his way. Now he's been indicted for tax fraud and the IRS has subpoenaed me to testify about the conversation way back when. I said it's privileged; the IRS says crime-fraud. Who's right?**

As you describe it, the crime-fraud exception would not apply. A client is totally privileged to consult a lawyer on legal matters and receive the lawyer's best advice. What is not privileged is advice that goes further to facilitate a client crime or fraud. Your characterization of the conversation did nothing of the kind. Your obligation is to stand on the privilege and continue to do so until the client has exhausted all reasonable opportunities to convince the courts [§9.06] that you should not be forced to testify about those discussions.

### ▶§5.10(d) The Prepared Witnesses?

I think we're in trouble. We had a bunch of asbestos cases. To facilitate preparation of our clients' depositions, one of our paralegals prepared this little questionnaire. In the harsh light of day, one could argue the questionnaire was a little aggressive in suggesting what the client should "remember" about which company's asbestos products were used at the Red Hook facility. Now the defense wants to subpoena all of our questionnaires. We think they're privileged. The other side screams crime-fraud. I sure don't want our clients' claims disparaged by these questionnaires.

The documents start off privileged even though they reflect conversations between a paralegal and your clients; since the paralegal is your agent for purposes of delivering legal services, the attorney-client and work-product privileges should attach. The question then becomes whether the crime-fraud exception applies. The good news for your clients is that the crime-fraud exception only applies to the client's crime or fraud. Here, you'll pardon one for saying so, but if anyone engaged in a crime or fraud, it was the paralegal. The clients are innocent and should not be injured by the law firm's misconduct…we mean alleged misconduct.

### ▶§5.10(e) Client Fraud

No one disputes that lawyers may not commit crimes or frauds, or counsel or assist client crimes or frauds [§7.04], but specific confidentiality exceptions that allow disclosure to prevent, rectify, or mitigate such harm continue to generate substantial disagreement among lawyers and courts [§§9.04, 9.06]. Obviously, if everyone were free to use lawyers to promote their fraudulent schemes, the honesty that makes many aspects of our market system function would be compromised. The attorney-client privilege has long recognized the future crime-fraud exception, which hinges on the client's purpose to use the lawyer's services to assist the client's fraud. Clients who lie to lawyers about their nefarious purposes and use lawyers to further it find themselves without protection of either the attorney-client or work-product privilege.[42] Lawyers hired to ferret out or defend past frauds can assure their clients of the privileges, but if the client's activity continues with the lawyer's help, the various client fraud exceptions may be triggered [§7.04].

Exceptions to the fiduciary duty of confidentiality to prevent client fraud are much more varied. Some depend entirely on the finding of a future crime [§5.09(b)]. Others follow Model Rule 1.6(b)(2) and (3) and the Restatement, allowing discretion where necessary to disclose to prevent, rectify, or mitigate substantial financial loss, whether criminal or fraudulent.[43] Once again, disclosure under these exceptions may or may not trigger the crime-fraud exception to the privilege.

### ▶§5.11 CONFIDENTIALITY EXCEPTIONS: LAWYER SELF-DEFENSE

### ▶§5.11(a) The Ungrateful Client?

**Some ungrateful client. I killed myself in that transaction and now the client won't pay. Maybe I'll threaten to disclose his illegitimate son. That would serve him right.**

Now, now, calm down. You're not the first lawyer to get stiffed. It is true you can disclose client confidential information in connection with a claim against a client. Or to defend a malpractice claim brought against you. But this exception is narrow. You can only disclose confidential information essential to the claim or defense. We don't think the illegitimate son has much to do with that. Equally important, you have to take steps to disclose the confidential information only to the extent absolutely necessary. Thus you might be required to file your action, motions and depositions under seal and, even if something is disclosed, for example, in depositions, that does not mean you are otherwise free to disclose it in any other manner.

### ▶§5.11(b) Helping Successor Counsel?

**I finally got rid of that pain of a client. He never tells me the truth, pays his bills late, calls at night and on weekends, comes up**

---

[42] RLGL §§82 and 93; *United States v. Chen*, 99 F.3d 1495 (9th cir. 1996), *cert. denied*, 520 U.S. 1167 (1997).

[43] RLGL §67.

with one scary proposal after another. I say good riddance. But this other lawyer called me. She's thinking about taking the guy on. Wants to know what I can tell her. On the one hand, I'd love to say nothing. That way he won't come back to haunt me. But I feel sorry for anyone who gets stuck with this bad actor client.

The good news is your self-interest and your ethical obligations coincide. Without your (you hope) former client's permission, you may disclose no confidential information. So your answer to the unsuspecting woman is that unless the client gives you authorization, you may not share anything with her.

This is as good a place as any to remind lawyers that the calls they receive from disgruntled clients are not unalloyed new business opportunities. The client who dislikes and disparages his present lawyer may be just as likely to dislike and disparage you after the honeymoon is over. Every law firm intake committee ought to pause an extra day before taking on a client midstream in a matter. Sometimes the disgruntled client is justified; just as often the disgruntled client is perpetually in that state.

### ▶§5.11(c) Defending Yourself

Perhaps the longest recognized confidentiality exception grants lawyers limited permission to use client confidences to defend themselves and to collect fees. Without such an exception, lawyers implicated in client wrongdoing would be powerless to extricate themselves from potential liability. The exception is triggered by an "assertion of such complicity," but does not require the commencement of a legal proceeding.[44] Lawyers also may use client confidences reasonably necessary to collect a justified fee on the theory that such evidence may be necessary to prove a meritorious claim.[45]

▶**Red Flag**▶ Whether defending yourself or collecting a fee, your interest conflicts with the client's, which means that the importance of "proportionate and restrained use or disclosure"[46] cannot be

---

[44] Model Rule 1.6(b)(5) and Comment [10]; RLGL §§64, 80, 92; *Meyerhofer v. Empire Fire & Marine Insurance Co.*, 497 F.2d 1190 (2d Cir.), *cert. denied*, 419 U.S. 998 (1974).

[45] Model Rule 1.6(b)(5) and Comment [11]; RLGL §§65, 80, 92.

[46] RLGL §65, comment d.

overemphasized. Seek fresh perspective from an uninvolved lawyer now, before you speak.

## ▶ §5.12 CONFIDENTIALITY EXCEPTIONS: SEEKING ADVICE
### ▶ §5.12(a) Help?

**Can I disclose confidential information to get advice from you?**

If your jurisdiction has adopted the new Model Rule 1.6 you would be permitted, without consulting the client, to disclose information to us in order to secure advice [§9.04]. The rule was changed to encourage lawyers to seek that advice, advice that a lawyer may not want the client to know she is seeking. Of course, before we pitch in, we would have to make sure we don't have a conflict of interest. It's terrible when an ethics advisor breaks the rules of professional conduct in providing ethics advice.

If your jurisdiction does not have this rule then you could justify your action—with no guarantee from us of success—by asserting that you come within the exception for defending a claim. In addition you can certainly seek advice outside your own firm if you are able to do so without disclosing any client confidential information. Through the use of carefully crafted hypotheticals, that can often be accomplished.

### ▶ §5.12(b) Getting Advice

Lawyers have long sought advice about client matters by using a hypothetical format that disguises the client's identity [§5.03(c)]. When client identity cannot be hidden, some consults intended to further the client's interest can be justified as impliedly authorized [§5.07]. But lawyers may most need advice when they must draw a line contrary to a client's expressed interests. Relatively new Model Rule 1.6(b)(5) creates an express exception for such disclosure to "secure legal advice about the lawyer's compliance with these rules." Such an exception facilitates ethics advice from other lawyers, bar counsel, and ethics hotlines. So, if you are unclear about what to do, especially if you suspect client wrongdoing, seek help [§10.02]. Rely on a hypothetical format as much as you can, and if you can't, hope that your jurisdiction has adopted this exception [§9.04]. If it hasn't, you either must wait until allegations surface against you to speak

[§5.11], or rely on implied authority (your client implicitly hired you to seek legal options, not to further an illegal act),[47] a far weaker argument especially when your interests and the client's diverge.

## ▶ §5.13 CONFIDENTIALITY EXCEPTIONS: LAW AND COURT ORDERS

### ▶ §5.13(a) The Deposition Lie?

**My client lied in a deposition. It was on a minor point, but she did contradict what she told me in prep. Maybe this is a good time to settle.**

Undoubtedly a good time to settle. Particularly if there is a new rather attractive offer on the table. The fly in the ointment is that you may not leave the lie—if it is material—in the deposition uncorrected. When your client lies you do not have to break your pencil or fall to the ground writhing in pain. You are free to and should counsel with your client about the least damaging way to correct the record. It can be done during the deposition. It can be done when the deposition transcript is submitted for signing. It can be done in a letter. But if the client refuses to make the correction, Model Rule 3.3 requires the lawyer to do so, even though the deposition did not take place before a tribunal and the lawyer has not offered or elicited the testimony. Since the whole purpose of discovery is to reveal the case to the lawyers and clients for evaluation, settling before the lie is corrected means that the process is being corrupted, even if you are prepared to argue that the lie was about a matter so "minor" that Model Rule 3.3 was not triggered. You also should steel yourself to respond to the argument that, though the lie may have been arguably immaterial, the fact of the lie itself is material. Although that reasoning would swallow the materiality standard, don't be surprised if opposing counsel advances it.

**What if I'm not aware it was a lie?**

If you don't know it was a lie you are not required to correct it. But you are free to do so if you reasonably believe that is the case. And remember "know" and "reasonably believe" are defined terms. The for-

---

[47] RLGL §21, comment e ("A lawyer's presumptive authority does not extend to retaining another lawyer outside the first lawyer's firm to represent the client…although a lawyer may consult confidentially about a client's case with another lawyer."); RLGL §79 comment c (subsequent unauthorized disclosure by a lawyer not in pursuit of a client's interests does not constitute waiver of the attorney-client privilege).

§5.13(c)                      CONFIDENTIALITY  •  123

mer means actual knowledge. But it also means the lawyer may not turn a blind eye to facts staring her in the face because knowledge may be inferred from the lawyer's circumstances. The latter means the lawyer believes the fact and that belief is reasonable. One thing this distinction forces the conscientious lawyer to do is consider carefully a decision not to disclose because the lawyer only has a belief; if the fact ever comes out someone may very well assert that you violated Model Rule 3.3 by turning a "blind eye" to your client's obvious lie.

### ➤ §5.13(b) The False Alibi?

**I have a criminal defendant client who insists on testifying (over my objection) and insists on providing a false alibi. What can I do? Don't tell me to resign. It's a court appointment, trial's next week and Judge Scrooge will never let me out.**

You cannot be a party to putting on false testimony. On the other hand your client probably has a right to present his defense and to learn if he will survive cross-examination. If remonstrating with the client doesn't solve that dilemma, some jurisdictions allow or require the lawyer to put the client on the stand and permit the client to tell his narrative without the aid of questions and answers [§§9.04, 9.06].[48] Even if the client testifies by narrative it would remain impermissible for the lawyer to argue from the client's "testimony" at closing.

### ➤ §5.13(c) Law and Court Orders That Require Disclosure

Other law that specifically requires disclosure may supersede a lawyer's fiduciary duty of confidentiality. Most common are court orders to disclose information in discovery, including those that find information unprivileged. As long as the lawyer has taken reasonable steps to protect the information, for example, by asserting an evidentiary or constitutional privilege, or properly appealing an adverse ruling, once the lawyer is ordered to disclose, the lawyer must do so or face contempt.[49] More controversial are other statutory legal require-

---

[48] *Commonwealth v. Mitchell*, 781 N.E. 2d 1237 (Mass.), *cert. denied*, 539 U.S. 907 (2003).

[49] Model Rule 1.6(b)(6); RLGL §63; *People v. Belge*, 372 N.Y.S.2d 798 (N.Y. County Ct. 1975), *aff'd*, 376 N.Y.S.2d 771 (N.Y. App. Div. 1975), *aff'd*, 359 N.E.2d 377 (N.Y. 1976)(client's Fifth Amendment rights supersede lawyer's obligation to disclose under "trivia of pseudo-criminal statute" that required report of a dead body).

ments, usually criminal, that require disclosure, such as child abuse reporting statutes and anti-money laundering provisions. In this situation, courts [§9.06] look to whether a legislature has determined that some other policy explicitly trumps client confidentiality. If so, courts [§9.06] usually will not apply an evidentiary privilege to prevent disclosure.[50] They may, however, rule that such a statute does not apply to lawyers for other reasons.[51]

## ►§5.14 JURISDICTION-SPECIFIC EXCEPTIONS AND CONFLICTS OF LAW

### ►§5.14(a) The Heavy Burden?

**My client uncovered some problems with its new drug. The folks I deal with thought the problem was serious but when the Board reviewed the matter, it concluded not to disclose the incident reports to the FDA. As I read the regs, the client must disclose this information even if no one has been seriously hurt. What can I do now?**

If you gave them your best advice and the client rejected it, you are not required to act further. If you think the failure to report is a crime or fraud likely to result in serious financial loss to third parties—banks, shareholders—you are free to disclose the confidential information outside the company if your jurisdiction has adopted an exception to permit disclosure to prevent a client future crime or fraud [§9.04]. If the client is a public company and you think the failure to report is a violation of law likely to result in injury to the issuer, you also may report out under the Sarbanes-Oxley regulations adopted by the SEC. Finally, if you live in one of the very few jurisdictions that have adopted a provision similar to Model Rule 1.13(c), and you know

---

[50] *Gerald B. Lefcourt, P.C. v. United States*, 125 F.3d 79 (2d Cir. 1997), *cert. denied*, 524 U.S. 937 (1998)(lawyer who claimed privilege not to provide client's name where required by IRS regulation did not have reasonable cause to violate reporting provision, rendering lawyer liable for statutory monetary penalty up to $25,000); *Henderson v. State*, 962 S.W.2d 544 (Tex. Crim. App. 1997), *cert. denied*, 525 U.S. 978 (1998)(attorney-client privilege required to yield to strong public policy of protecting children from serious harm).

[51] *N.Y. State Bar Ass'n v. F.T.C.*, 2004 U.S. Dist. Lexis 7698 (D.D.C. Apr. 30, 2004)(FTC overstepped statutory authority in subjecting lawyers to privacy provisions of Gramm-Leach-Bliley Act).

this failure to report will substantially injure the client, you also may breach confidentiality and report the information.

**That's a pretty heavy burden to put on the lawyer.**

It sure is. If the highest authority of the organization reaches one conclusion, and you reach another, you can trump the judgment of the client acting through its duly constituted authority. At least, so far, it is rare that this breach of confidentiality is required except in the precious few states that mandate disclosure.

➤ **§5.14(b) Guaranteed Confidentiality?**

**Can I put into my engagement letter that our firm would never exercise this discretion, so our clients don't have to worry about their lawyer turning on them?**

A great question, for which we do not yet have a definitive answer. Can a lawyer, in advance of knowing the circumstances that might give rise to an opportunity to disclose, agree not to do so? Or must discretion be exercised one matter at a time? The debate on this point rages. No one has yet been disciplined for writing such a clause into every engagement letter or running ads in the WSJ proclaiming "Hire Martyn & Fox: We promise confidentiality," so stay tuned.

➤ **§5.14(c) The Dizzying Diversity?**

**I am admitted in New Jersey; the matter is pending in Pennsylvania; my client is a California company. I just learned information that New Jersey would require me to disclose; Pennsylvania would permit me to disclose; and California would prohibit me to disclose. Whose rules apply?**

Conflicts of rules problems are as uncertain of confident resolution as conflicts of other law, perhaps even more so. The lawyer, generally, must abide by the rules of her state of admission. If the rules of the forum are different, often those must be followed. But here, since the confidentiality rule is designed to protect the client, you can reasonably argue that the client is entitled to the benefit of the rules of its home jurisdiction [§9.04]. You can see how difficult these conflict issues can be to resolve.

➤ **§5.14(d) Understanding Confidentiality Conflicts**

Although most jurisdictions recognize most of the exceptions discussed in the previous sections, each jurisdiction's definition of the exact scope of the exception may differ from the Model Rule or Restatement articulation [§9.04]. For example, Florida adds to the "court order" exception [§5.13(c)] the requirement that "a lawyer must first exhaust all appellate remedies,"[52] and Indiana provides that disclosures of client names to a Lawyer's Assistance Committee are "impliedly authorized."[53] Further, some jurisdictions have created unique exceptions not commonly seen elsewhere. For example, the District of Columbia lawyer code allows reasonable disclosure "to prevent the bribery or intimidation of witnesses, jurors, court officials, or other persons who are involved in proceedings before a tribunal,"[54] New York allows disclosures "implicit in withdrawing a written or oral opinion or representation previously given by the lawyer and believed by the lawyer still to be relied upon by a third persons where the lawyer has discovered that the opinion or representation was based on materially inaccurate information or is being used to further a crime or fraud."[55] Massachusetts adds disclosures "to prevent the wrongful execution or incarceration of another,"[56] Hawaii specifies that government lawyers may disclose "to prevent a public official or public agency from committing a criminal or illegal act that a government lawyer reasonably believes is likely to result in harm to the public good,"[57] Pennsylvania and Oregon allow disclosure of client names necessary to "effectuate the sale of a law practice,"[58] and Washington adds that lawyers may reveal to tribunals confidences "which disclose any breach of fiduciary responsibility by a client who is a guardian, personal representative, receiver or other court appointed fiduciary."[59]

Lawyers who practice in more than one jurisdiction can face contradictory obligations or allowances under these differing provisions [§9.04]. You should know that you are subject to the disciplinary authority of every jurisdiction where you are admitted to practice, but

---

[52] Fla. Rule 4-1.6(d).
[53] Ind. Rule 1.6(a).
[54] D.C. Rule 1.6(c)(2).
[55] N.Y. DR 4-101(C)(5).
[56] Mass. Rule 1.6(b)(1).
[57] Haw. Rule 1.6(c)(4).
[58] Pa. Rule 1.6(c)(6); Or. Rule DR 4-101 (C)(5).
[59] Wash. Rule 1.6(c).

§5.14(d)                      Confidentiality  •  127

in the case of a conflict, a tribunal will apply the rules of its jurisdiction, and for other conduct, the rules of the jurisdiction where the lawyer "principally practices" or where the conduct "clearly has its predominant effect"[60] are most likely to apply.

---

[60] Model Rule 8.5; RLGL §5.

# 6

# Conflicts of Interest: The Loyalty Obligation

- §6.01 The Loyalty Obligation
- §6.02 The Unexpected Conflict?
- §6.03 Identifying And Resolving Conflicts
- §6.04 Basic Steps To Identifying And Resolving Conflicts Of Interest
- §6.05 Law Firm Imputation
- §6.06 Conflicts Control Systems
- §6.07 Building And Using A Conflicts Control System
    - §6.07(a) Building A Database
        - §6.07(a)(1) Personal Conflicts: Law Firm Lawyers
        - §6.07(a)(2) Concurrent And Third-Person Conflicts: Current Clients
        - §6.07(a)(3) Former-Client Conflicts: Former Clients
    - §6.07(b) Using The Data Base
    - §6.07(c) Identifying And Responding To Conflicts
- §6.08 Recognizing Conflicts
- §6.09 Nonconsentable Conflicts
    - §6.09(a) The Friendly Divorce?
    - §6.09(b) When Client Consent Is Not Enough
- §6.10 Conflicts Of Interest: Lawyer Personal Interests

- §6.11 Business Deals With Clients
    - §6.11(a) A Share Of The Deal?
    - §6.11(b) Legal Regulation
    - §6.11(c) The Board Member?
- §6.12 Client Gifts
- §6.13 Literary Or Media Rights
    - §6.13(a) The Hollywood Story?
    - §6.13(b) Literary Or Media Rights
- §6.14 Proprietary Interests In The Subject Matter Of Litigation
- §6.15 Financial Assistance To Clients
    - §6.15(a) The Client In Need?
    - §6.15(b) Pending Litigation And Financial Assistance
- §6.16 Limitations On Lawyer Liability
- §6.17 Aggregate Settlements
    - §6.17(a) The Policy Limit Bonanza?
    - §6.17(b) Joint Decisions To Settle
- §6.18 Sexual Relationships With Clients
    - §6.18(a) Dating The CFO?
    - §6.18(b) Legal Implications Of Sexual Relationships With Clients
- §6.19 Personal Relationships
- §6.20 Imputation Of Personal Conflicts
- §6.21 Conflicts Of Interest: Joint Clients
- §6.22 Joint Client Confidentiality
    - §6.22(a) The Boiler-Plate Joint Defense Agreement?
    - §6.22(b) Handling Confidentiality In Joint Client Representations
- §6.23 Litigation Opponents
    - §6.23(a) Divorce And Dissolution
    - §6.23(b) The Family Accident?

- §6.24 Simultaneous Representation Of Adversaries In Unrelated Cases
- §6.25 Co-Parties: Civil Litigation
- §6.26 Joint Defendants In Criminal Cases
    - §6.26(a) Common Defense Among Friends?
    - §6.26(b) Co-Defendants: Criminal Defense
- §6.27 Joint Representation In Transactions
    - §6.27(a) The Simple Real Estate Transaction?
    - §6.27(b) The New Business Venture?
    - §6.27(c) Joint Wills?
    - §6.27(d) Co-Parties: Transactions
- §6.28 Positional Or Issue Conflicts
    - §6.28(a) Taking Different Legal Positions?
    - §6.28(b) Legal Regulation Of Issue Conflicts
- §6.29 Representing Entities
    - §6.29(a) The Corporate Transaction?
    - §6.29(b) The Employee Deposition?
    - §6.29(c) The Subsidiary Problem?
    - §6.29(d) The Homeowner's Association?
    - §6.29(e) Organizations And Employees
- §6.30 Imputation of Current-Client Conflicts
    - §6.30(a) Side-Switching?
    - §6.30(b) Law Firm Imputation
- §6.31 Conflicts Of Interest: Third-Person Direction
    - §6.31(a) Corporate Control?
    - §6.31(b) Relative Matters?
    - §6.31(c) Third-Person Payment
    - §6.31(d) Third-Person Influence
- §6.32 Insurance Defense
    - §6.32(a) Litigation Strategy?
    - §6.32(b) The Confidential Policy Defense?

▶ §6.32(c) Settlement?

▶ §6.32(d) Understanding The Tripartite Relationship

▶§6.33 Former-Client Conflicts Of Interest

▶ §6.33(a) The Hot Potato?

▶ §6.33(b) Firing A Client?

▶ §6.33(c) Keeping It In The Family?

▶ §6.33(d) The Substantial Relationship Test

▶ §6.33(e) The Substantially Related Transaction?

▶§6.34 Screens and Imputation For Former-Client Conflicts

▶ §6.34(a) Screens When?

▶ §6.34(b) The Joy of Screening

▶ §6.34(c) Chart: State Lawyer Code Rules That Allow Screens To Prevent Imputed Disqualification

▶§6.35 Former Clients And Peripheral Representation

▶ §6.35(a) The Lateral Hire?

▶ §6.35(b) The Peripheral Representation Exception

▶§6.36 Former Clients And Actual Receipt Of Confidential Information

▶§6.37 Conflicts Of Interest: Former Government Lawyers

▶ §6.37(a) A Typhoid Mary?

▶ §6.37(b) Legal Regulation Of Former Government Lawyers

▶§6.38 Conflicts Of Interest: Judges, Arbitrators, And Third-Party Neutrals

▶ §6.38(a) The Mediator Lawyer?

▶ §6.38(b) Subsequent Law Practice Of Adjudicative Officers And Mediators

## ▶§6.01 THE LOYALTY OBLIGATION

The fiduciary duty of loyalty, which can be traced back several hundred years in the law of agency, requires lawyers and other agents to identify, avoid, and resolve conflicts of interest. The law of agency has long recognized the legal right of a person or entity (the principal) to empower another (the agent) to act on the principal's behalf. Lawyers derive power from clients, but also have the ability to overpower client interests due to the lawyer's superior knowledge and skill. Loyalty imposes an obligation on lawyers to ensure effective client representation by providing the client with independent legal judgment, and to prevent client harm by recognizing and responding to any influences (conflicts of interest) that may interfere with the lawyer's obligation to act in the client's best interests, as defined by the client. Pursuing the best interests of a client requires lawyers to remain vigilant for conflicting interests that may arise or change throughout a representation.[1]

### ➤§6.02 THE UNEXPECTED CONFLICT?

**I don't know what to do. I told mother and daughter I would represent both of them in an automobile accident case. I figured between them their claims against the other driver were good for $500,000, and I thought the defendant employer would be on the hook for any judgment. We just received a terrible decision dismissing the employer on the ground the driver was not acting in the course of his employment. Driver has a $50,000 policy, and I have two very unhappy clients.**

You might have to make that two unhappy *former* clients. You now face a new, unexpected conflict that requires immediate response. Your clients now compete for a very limited resource, and they may not be able to agree to any allocation. Further, if one was a driver and one a passenger, it may now be in the latter's best interest to file a claim against the driver, creating a nonconsentable conflict [§6.09]. To make matters worse, you can't continue to represent the passenger without the former client-driver's consent. We hope you warned them this could happen in your initial conflicts waiver.

### ➤§6.03 IDENTIFYING AND RESOLVING CONFLICTS

Both the lawyer codes and the law governing lawyers recognize that conflicts can arise from the lawyer's own personal interests, the interests of other clients or third persons, and the interests of former clients. Once identified, a conflict must be disclosed to a client, unless doing

---

[1] ABA Model Rule of Professional Conduct 1.7, Comment [1] (2002)(hereinafter "Model Rules"); *Restatement of the Law Third, The Law Governing Lawyers*, §121 comment b (ALI 2000)(hereinafter "RLGL".)

so would violate another client's confidentiality, in which case, the lawyer cannot proceed in the matter. Once disclosed, the lawyer must initiate the informed consent process, because the client often (but not always) may waive the conflict. In some situations, the conflict is so pronounced that a lawyer may not seek waiver, and must turn down the prospective client, or withdraw from representing a current client. Failure to respond appropriately to a legally cognizable conflict creates a multitude of overlapping remedies for clients [§9.05], ranging from professional discipline to civil liability, disqualification, constructive trust, and fee forfeiture [Chapter 8].[2]

## ▶ §6.04 BASIC STEPS TO IDENTIFYING AND RESOLVING CONFLICTS OF INTEREST

To resolve conflicts of interest, you should engage in a five-step process [§6.04]:

1. Identify your client(s) [Chapter 1].

2. Determine whether a conflict of interest exists. The law recognizes six distinct categories of conflicts:

    A. Personal Interests Of A Lawyer

| | | |
|---|---|---|
| General Rule: | 1.7(b) | |
| Specific Rules: | 1.8(a) | Business transactions with clients |
| | 1.8(b) | Use of client information |
| | 1.8(c) | Client gifts to lawyer |
| | 1.8(d) | Literary rights |
| | 1.8(e) | Financial assistance to client |
| | 1.8(h) | Limitation of liability to client |
| | 1.8(i) | Proprietary interest in litigation |
| | 1.8(j) | Lawyer/client sexual relationship |
| | 3.7 | Lawyer as witness |

---

[2] Model Rule 1.7, Comment [21]; RLGL §122, comment f.

B. Interests of Another Current Client:
 General Rule:  1.7(a),(b)
 Specific Rule:  1.8(g), 1.13(g)

C. Interests Of A Third Person
 General Rule:  1.7(b)
 Specific Rules:  1.8(f), 5.4(c), 1.13(a)

D. Interests Of A Former Client:
 General Rule:  1.9

E. Government Lawyers:
 General Rule:  1.11
 Specific Rule:  1.12

F. Imputed Conflicts:
 General Rule:  1.10
 Specific Rules:  1.8(k), 1.11, 1.12

3. Decide whether the conflict is consentable.

4. If so, consult with affected clients and obtain informed consent. (Writing preferred or required.)

5. Remain vigilant for changes in circumstances that may create a new conflict or change the dimension of an already waived conflict. If this occurs, repeat the informed consent process or withdraw from the representation.

## ▶ §6.05 LAW FIRM IMPUTATION

Lawyers who practice in law firms [§1.30] owe the 4 C's, including the duty of loyalty, to all of the firm's clients. Both the lawyer codes and agency law impute the conflict of any lawyer to all other law firm lawyers. This means that your conflicts control system must reflect your own as well as every other lawyer's clients, former clients, third-party payors, and significant personal interests. In some limited circumstances, such as when former government lawyers and judges join a firm, the personally disqualified lawyer may be screened to prevent imputation to the rest of the lawyer's law firm. Some jurisdictions [§9.06] also allow nonconsensual screens for some former-client conflicts, but absent client consent, screens are not recognized as obviating any other imputed conflicts.

▶**Red Flag**▶ You will be in the best position to avoid harm to your clients and your firm if you assume that all conflicts are imputed, and respond by seeking client informed consent, which can include consent to screening the personally disqualified lawyer [§6.34]. If you cannot obtain client consent, do not assume you are free to set up some screen that you think will obviate the conflict without a careful check of your jurisdiction's specific rules [§ 9.04].

## ▶§6.06 CONFLICTS CONTROL SYSTEMS

Once you have identified your clients, you need to identify whether a conflict of interest exists. To do this, you need a conflicts control system, which will allow you to search for a potential adverse interest that may arise from either your own interests or the interests of others. When a prospective client arrives, you need to be sure you or your firm do not already represent the other parties to a matter, that third persons who are not clients will not interfere with your independent professional judgment, and that you do not have a conflicting personal interest.

Your conflicts control system should include two steps:

1. Searching a series of lists in a database that correspond to legally recognized conflicts, including current clients, former clients, third-party payors, and lawyer personal interests.

2. Sending an individual new client memorandum to all members of the firm that ferrets out any information omitted from the list database.

All conflicts detection and avoidance practices should be institutionalized by written policies and procedures that require compliance with these two steps by all law firm personnel. Law firms should establish a committee or designate a partner with responsibility to implement and supervise the conflicts control system. When potential conflicts are discovered, the partner or committee should have authority to decide how to respond. Law firm policy should include the requirement that any member of a law firm ethics committee potentially involved in any conflict be disqualified from considering its resolution. The partner or committee in charge of conflicts also should make clear that deviations from law firm policy are serious concerns that could result in appropriate penalties.

Following these procedures will not prevent conflicts, but it will put you in a position to know about them and respond appropriately.

If you have searched the database and found no matches, and no one in your firm has responded to your new client memo, you can proceed to take on an initially conflict-free representation, subject to your continuing duty of diligence.

➤**Red Flag**➤ Never rely on your memory for a conflicts check. Don't even rely on a computer database. Your innocent forgetfulness or less than full due diligence will be no defense to any of the myriad of remedies [§9.05] a client may seek, and some, such as fee forfeiture, constructive trust, and professional discipline, do not require that the client suffer any harm beyond the breach of loyalty.

### ➤ §6.07 BUILDING AND USING A CONFLICTS CONTROL SYSTEM

### ➤ §6.07(a) Building A Database

Current law regulates personal, concurrent, third-person, and former-client conflicts and requires precise identification of the client, nature of the matter, and the lawyers who will work on the case. Your firm needs a database that contains each category of information.

### ➤ §6.07(a)(1) Personal Conflicts: Law Firm Lawyers

A separate entry should be made in the law firm lawyers database for each lawyer in the law firm and should include:

1. The name of each lawyer;

2. A list of material interests (property, business, and financial) owned by that lawyer; and

3. Substantial property, business, or financial interests of persons in that lawyer's household.

### ➤ §6.07(a)(2) Concurrent And Third-Person Conflicts: Current Clients

Each entry for current clients should include at least four elements:

1. Identification of each current client, including subsidiaries, parents, or other affiliates, and control persons (key officers and employees) of entity clients as well as all changes or variations in corporate or personal name;[3]

---

[3] Commercial services make this information available to law firms.

2. A description of the subject matter of the client representation, including the identities (with changes when they occur) of actual and potential opposing parties;

3. Any third persons or entities, such as insurers, who are paying for or are direct beneficiaries of the representation; and

4. The names of all law firm lawyers working on the matter.

### ▶ §6.07(a)(3) Former-Client Conflicts: Former Clients

Each entry for former clients should include three elements:

1. Accurate identification of the client, including subsidiaries, parents, or other affiliates and control persons of entity clients as well as changes or variations in personal or corporate name;

2. Subject matter of the representation, including the identities (with changes when relevant) of related and opposing parties; and

3. The names of lawyers who worked on the matter.

Since former-client conflicts can be generated not only by past law firm representation but also by the past employment of law firm personnel, be sure to include the three elements listed above (client identification, subject matter, lawyers) for all of the following:

1. All former clients of the firm;

2. All former clients of lawyers joining the firm; and

3. All former clients of other firms on whose matters current law firm paralegals, secretaries, investigators, and related paraprofessionals worked.

### ▶ §6.07(b) Using The Data Base

Once the initial database has been established, new data should be added before any new client matter is opened by the firm, as well as at any time new personnel join the firm. Law firm lawyers also should be notified about new client matters through interoffice memoranda. This procedure both initiates and backs up centralized database searches and entries. Any information about changes in client identity, opposing parties, or lawyers working on the file should be entered on the day the change occurs or the firm becomes aware of it. Entries should be moved from the current-client to the former-client list whenever the firm concludes its representation in a client matter, whether by withdrawal, completion, or client firing.

§6.08 THE LOYALTY OBLIGATION • 139

A new client file should not be opened and no time should be billed to the client by the firm until at least four steps have been completed:

1. The prospective client's identifying information has been run through the law firm's database;

2. A written conflicts memo has been circulated throughout the firm;

3. The responsible lawyer has indicated in writing either that no matches were found, or if they were, that they indicate no conflict or a consentable conflict for which consent has been obtained; and

4. A neutral person has reviewed any information, matches, and explanatory memos.

### ►§6.07(c) Identifying And Responding To Conflicts

1. Search the law firm database for matches with the prospective clients, their probable opponents, and their lawyers.

2. If any matches occur, does the client's interest potentially differ from an interest of any of the matches?

3. If so, is the conflict consentable in your jurisdiction [§§9.04, 9.06]?

4. If so, are you free to disclose the requisite information consistent with your duties of confidentiality?

5. If so, seek informed consent of the client(s) in writing.

6. If not, you cannot represent both clients. However, if the conflict is a former-client conflict, does your jurisdiction [§§9.04, 9.06] recognize screens without the former client's consent?

7. If screens for former-client conflicts are available, establish an adequate screening mechanism, and seek consent from the prospective or current client as well.

8. If the firm withdraws from any representation, the entry for that client should be moved from the current-client list to the former-client list.

### ►§6.08 RECOGNIZING CONFLICTS

If your conflicts check indicates a potential personal, current- or former-client, or third-person conflict, you need to respond appropriately. A legally cognizable conflict exists if the representation of one client will be **directly adverse** to another current client, or if the interest of another client, former client, lawyer or third person creates a significant risk of **materially limiting** your responsibilities to the client.[4] Each client's interest must be separately analyzed with this standard in mind. Direct adversity and material limitation conflicts are identified by examining at least three factors:

1. The facts of the representation (who seeks what from whom, who owns what, who controls what);

2. The law governing the representation (who has legal rights or obligations to whom or what legal options are available to which client(s)); and

3. The personal relationships of the relevant persons and parties, including the lawyer and law firm.

Former-client conflicts are governed by the **substantial relationship** test, created to determine whether the lawyer's past receipt of confidential information should disqualify the lawyer in a subsequent substantially related matter [§6.33(d)]. Former government lawyer conflicts are governed by a less stringent standard: Whether the lawyer participated **personally and substantially** in the same **matter** while employed by the government [§6.37].

Once the conflict is identified, the lawyer may not proceed with the representation unless:

1. The lawyer reasonably believes that he or she will be able to provide competent and diligent representation to each affected client;

2. The representation is not prohibited by law;

3. The representation does not involve asserting a claim by one client against another client in the same litigation; and

4. Each affected client gives written informed consent [§3.05].

## ▶ §6.09 NONCONSENTABLE CONFLICTS

### ▶ §6.09(a) The Friendly Divorce?

Husband and wife showed up together the other day. I thought they wanted me to write their wills. It turns out they wanted me to preside over the death of their marriage. They told me they thought they could save some money by having me han-

---

[4] Model Rule 1.7(a); RLGL §121.

dle the whole matter. They think they have decided all of the important issues. Can I represent them both?

It is almost impossible to imagine this as an acceptable joint representation. All aspects of conflicts identification, legal rights, individual facts, and personal relationship of the parties potentially or actually conflict. They might think they have resolved all of the issues, but legally, their interests are directly adverse, at least insofar as one can always opt out of dissolution and into contested divorce. Further, what if they have not considered all of the relevant issues? If you identify a neglected issue it will be impossible to go forward because inevitably raising the issue will harm one spouse at the expense of the other. Many jurisdictions [§9.06] prohibit your doing this, and good practice suggests this is a minefield you want to avoid.

That having been said, it is possible under the rules for you to agree to mediate the dissolution of their marriage. In that situation neither of them will be your client. Your role will be limited to facilitating their getting to an agreement. You have to be very careful if you, in fact, agree to mediate this situation to make sure that neither is misled as to the nature of your role. Also you must think long and hard about whether these individuals are suitable candidates for pursuing the dissolution of their marriage unrepresented.

### ▶ §6.09(b) When Client Consent Is Not Enough

Some concurrent-client conflicts are nonconsentable, because one or more clients will not consent to disclosure of confidential information to others. Other concurrent-client conflicts are absolutely prohibited regardless of client consent. If the client consent will not adequately protect client interests burdened by a conflict, lawyer code provisions [§9.04] or decisional law [§9.06] may prohibit them. For example, all jurisdictions prohibit simultaneous representation of opposing parties in litigation, and nearly all prohibit negotiating for a share of a client's media rights [§6.13]. A few jurisdictions have declared some joint representation in transactions nonconsentable as well.[5] Other specific conflicts, such as business transactions with

---

[5] *Baldasarre v. Butler*, 625 A. 2d 458, 467 (N.J. 1993) (new "bright line rule" prohibits dual representation "in commercial real estate transactions where large sums of money are at stake, where contracts contain complex contingencies, or where options are numerous," even if both buyer and seller give informed consent).

clients, are heavily regulated, meaning that a lawyer may engage in a particular matter involving such a conflict only if very exacting disclosure and informed consent requirements have been met. All conflicts are governed by the key inquiry: Whether you "reasonably believe that you will be able to provide competent and diligent representation to each affected client," that is, would an objective lawyer agree that it was reasonable for you to seek a conflict waiver under these circumstances?[6]

➤**Red Flag**➤ Nearly every "ordinary" conflict listed below can morph into a nonconsentable conflict. Never assume that an initial conflicts waiver suffices to cover all subsequent circumstances. Whether addressing an initial potential or a realized actuality, do not forget to entertain the possibility that the conflict might be nonconsentable.

### ➤§6.10 CONFLICTS OF INTEREST: LAWYER PERSONAL INTERESTS

Personal conflicts are often the most difficult to identify and resolve, because of our human tendency to presume that we mean well. Understanding that the conflicts rules are written to protect and to prevent harm to your client-principal should help you remember that communication and written disclosure are essential, but not always sufficient, to vitiate such conflicts. If the conflict exists, a court will address whether, from the client's viewpoint, your interests (pecuniary, business, personal, or relational) created a significant risk of materially limiting your independent professional representation of the client's interests, including providing competent and diligent representation in the underlying matter. Some personal conflicts, such as acquiring literary rights [§6.13] and engaging in sexual relationships with clients [§6.18], present so much potential for adversity that they are absolutely prohibited, or are nonconsentable in many jurisdictions. Others, such as business deals with clients [§6.11], are allowed but subject to additional specific regulation. Failure to comply with the details of these requirements can mean both loss of your bargain as well as professional discipline [§9.05].

---

[6] Model Rule 1.7(b)(1); RLGL §122.

## ▶§6.11 BUSINESS DEALS WITH CLIENTS
### ▶§6.11(a) A Share Of The Deal?

**I can't tell you how excited I am. Instead of paying me in cash, my client wants to give me "friends and family" shares to help take the company public. I can retire five years early with this deal.**

Tread carefully, friend. It is okay to take stock for a fee; it's been done since time immemorial. But there are some pitfalls. First, you have to assure yourself that the fee is reasonable under the circumstances. The reasonableness of the fee will be judged on the basis of the value of the stock at the time of the transfer. But you should be prepared for a later challenge—when the stock soars—that the value of the stock at the time of the transfer was quite high in relation to the services provided.

Second, taking stock in lieu of cash usually is deemed a business transaction with a client under Model Rule 1.8(a). Given that conclusion, the transaction will be judged by its entire fairness and the client must be advised, in writing, to get other counsel who can provide independent legal advice with respect to this transaction. (Don't even think of paying *that* lawyer in stock). Finally, you must obtain your client's written informed consent to the terms of the deal (including your role).

Third, *you* should consider the added risk you are taking on if you receive these shares. Should things turn out badly you won't be surprised that disappointed investors turn to you and allege that your interest in freeing up your otherwise illiquid shares affected your legal advice and otherwise compromised your professional independence.

### ▶§6.11(b) Legal Regulation

Business deals with clients have always presented consentable conflicts of interest, but professional codes [§9.04] and cases [§9.06] have evolved to require specific and stringent written informed consent requirements, which make it nearly impossible to be certain that such an arrangement will pass ethical muster unless the client has the advice of independent counsel [§10.01].

▶**Red Flag**▶ Do not think that a business transaction must involve the exchange of money. Agreeing to accept any client property, including shares of stock in lieu of a fee, constitutes a "business transaction" as does a commission received, beyond legal fees, from the sale of investments.

To pass muster, the business transaction or acquisition of any ownership, possessory, security, or other pecuniary interest adverse to the client must include:

1. Fair and reasonable terms fully disclosed to the client in writing;

2. Written encouragement to the client on the advisability and desirability of seeking outside counsel, as well as reasonable opportunity to do so; and

3. Informed written consent of the client to the essential terms of the transaction and the lawyer's role in the transaction, including whether the lawyer is representing the client in the matter.[7]

These requirements are intended to prevent lawyers from intentionally or inadvertently overreaching in arranging the terms of a transaction with a client. To buttress them, the law of agency imposes a presumption of undue influence in any business transaction between client and lawyer, which you may overcome by demonstrating the fairness of the terms and the fact that you fully met the disclosure requirements of the rule. When a client seeks to void such a transaction, having some objective assessment of the value of the property or terms of the matter will prove necessary. Lawyers who have accepted shares in a client business start-up have more than occasionally lost their investment by neglecting these specifics.[8] If you want the benefit of a business transaction such as the sale of another business, tell the client or prospective client to retain another lawyer (outside your law firm).

▶**Ultimate Red Flag**▶ Do not think you can rely on your intuitive sense of right and wrong in a business transaction with a client. We explore further in §10.01 the rigors of the law and the lawyer's temptation to underidentify with the client in this situation.

---

[7] Model Rule 1.8(a); RLGL §126.

[8] *Passante v. McWilliam*, 62 Cal. Rptr. 2d 298 (Cal. App. 1997) (lawyer who "came through in the clutch" raising money for a client's company and was promised three percent of company stock unable to enforce oral promise because it did not comply with written disclosure and consent requirements and otherwise constituted a mere gratuitous promise); *Monco v. Janus*, 583 N.E.2d 575 (Ill. App. 1991) (lawyer failed to provide clear and convincing evidence of full and frank disclosure or of adequate consideration to support 50 percent business ownership interest in client business, despite spending hundreds of hours on the matter without other compensation).

### ▶ §6.11(c) The Board Member?

**More good news. I've been asked to go on the board of directors of one of our new clients, a start-up Internet antique shopping site. What a great chance to get in on the ground floor!**

That's one way of looking at it. But don't be so flattered. Maybe you are offering them far more than you will get in return—unless you add in the risk, that is.

**What do you mean?**

The real question is whether there is ever a reason for a lawyer to go on the board of a client. True, there is an ancient and hoary tradition of such service. Lawyers cannot resist the temptation to solidify the lawyer-client relationship and to become junior business people. The problems, however, are multiple. Is the lawyer-director giving legal advice? Will the privilege apply to what the board asks and how the lawyer responds? Is there a conflict between the advice the director would provide and the advice the lawyer would provide? Will the lawyer's judgment be second-guessed on the ground that this conflict in roles affected the result? Will the lawyer lose the ability to represent the client because of the lawyer's role as director just at the time the lawyer is most needed? Is the lawyer more likely to find herself a defendant if she served as a director? All of these serious issues [§9.02] suggest that if there is a desire to have a lawyer on the board (lawyers can make excellent directors), neither that lawyer nor that lawyer's firm should represent the company. And the lawyer for the company may sit in on board meetings, but should not serve as a member of the board.

### ▶ §6.12 CLIENT GIFTS

You may not solicit, but you may accept a client's gift, subject to the same presumption of undue influence that places the burden on lawyers in business transactions to prove the transaction was objectively fair and fully disclosed [§6.11]. Courts look for independent advice to clients, or at the very least clear and explicit disclosure from you and the opportunity to seek independent advice elsewhere. If the gift itself requires a writing, such as a testamentary gift, you may not draft the document at all unless you are a natural object of the client's generosity.[9] Outside of

---

[9] Model Rule 1.8(c); RLGL§127.

being that natural object, if you do the drafting, the gift is voidable and you will be subject to professional discipline [§§8.02, 8.09].

This rule does not prevent you from seeking to have a client designate you or your law firm as executor, trustee, or lawyer for a future estate, subject to the general conflicts rules, which require you to inform the client in writing of the availability of all other options for appointment of a fiduciary, and the nature and extent of your financial interest in the future position.[10]

➤**Red Flag**➤ If your client really wants to make you the beneficiary of his or her will or trust, tell him or her that you will not be allowed to receive the gift if you draft the document. Caving in to a client's insistence can cost you your license to practice as well.

## ➤§6.13 LITERARY OR MEDIA RIGHTS

### ➤§6.13(a) The Hollywood Story?

**I have a new idea. The CEO of Big Bank is in real trouble. What was he thinking, trading on inside information? Now his bank accounts have been frozen but he says he'll pay me by assigning the story rights to my firm. Talk about the perfect example of the excesses of the '90s. The movie'll make a fortune.**

Sorry. This one is prohibited. Until the matter is concluded, only Steven Spielberg can get the rights. Your career as the next Scott Turow will have to be put on hold.

**Can he assign me his house or his bank accounts?**

The house is a possibility, but not the bank accounts. The house qualifies as a business transaction with a client [§6.11] that will be judged by its entire fairness, whether you put everything in writing, and whether you advised your client that he should seek the advice of independent counsel as to the terms of the deal. And what's he going to pay that guy with? Not the movie rights. You also should be warned that if you take the house, the government may claim you're not entitled to it if it seeks civil forfeiture [§8.10]. Moreover, should your client go bankrupt, the assignment of the house might be challenged by other creditors.

The bank accounts are an entirely different matter, because they may well be the subject matter of the litigation, and lawyers cannot

---

[10] Model Rule 1.8, Comment [8].

acquire proprietary interests in litigation beyond the lawyer's interest in a reasonable contingent fee [§6.14].

### ▶ §6.13(b) Literary Or Media Rights

Lawyers may not negotiate or make an agreement to obtain future profits from a media or literary portrayal of any substantial part of a client representation before or during the time the lawyer provides legal services to the client.[11] Future media contracts give lawyers an incentive to favor the entertainment value of a client's matter (or the lawyer's ego) over the client's real interests, and also require disclosure of confidential information contrary to client interests, all at a time when the client will not be able to predict the harm that may occur. So long as you do not profit, this rule does not prohibit you from publishing beneficial information about your client, with the latter's consent. Nor does it prohibit such a contract with an informed former client after your services have been rendered, although such a contract is subject to the stringent requirements of the business transactions rule [§6.11].

### ▶ §6.14 PROPRIETARY INTERESTS IN THE SUBJECT MATTER OF LITIGATION

You cannot acquire a proprietary interest in a cause of action or subject matter of litigation, except that you may charge a contingent fee. Lawyers do not own claims; clients do. If lawyers could buy or subsidize lawsuits, they would have too great a stake in controlling the matter, including the determination of when to pursue, drop, or settle the case.[12] Although contingent fees provide opportunity for the same conflict, they present less threat to client interests and they are thought otherwise necessary to ensure access to the courts. The personal conflict of a lawyer inherent in settling a contingent fee matter is governed by the general conflicts provisions in Model Rule 1.7, which require that you inform the client about the settlement, alternatives to settlement, and your financial and personal interest in settling or trying the case to ensure adequate informed consent, both to the settlement [§2.08(d)] and to your personal conflict [§6.10].

---

[11] Model Rule 1.8(d); RLGL §36(3).
[12] Model Rule 1.8(i); RLGL §36(1).

## §6.15 FINANCIAL ASSISTANCE TO CLIENTS

### §6.15(a) The Client In Need?

**I've got a client with a great claim. But it will be next year until the case comes to court. And the defense refuses to make a reasonable offer. I think they are trying to capitalize on my client's impecunious circumstances. They may succeed. My client says I either loan him money for living expenses or she'll take the $75,000. This is a million dollar case.**

The situation is sad, but the rules are clear. You may take a case on a contingent fee. You may advance court costs and the expenses of litigation. But unless you practice in a select few jurisdictions [§9.04], such as California or the District of Columbia, no living expenses. Maybe you can help your client get a loan from someone else. Your client could assign to that third party a portion of the proceeds from the litigation as security.

### §6.15(b) Pending Litigation And Financial Assistance

The business transaction rule does not allow you to provide financial assistance to clients in connection with pending or contemplated litigation, except to finance litigation costs, such as filing fees and expert witness expenses. You may make your recovery of these litigation costs contingent on the outcome of the case. If you charge any interest or require any security, you become subject to the business transactions rule [§6.11].[13]

## §6.16 LIMITATIONS ON LAWYER LIABILITY

If your personal economic interest in a contingent fee can color your judgment about a settlement, your interest in avoiding malpractice liability creates an even stronger conflict. For this reason, lawyers are prohibited from limiting their liability for malpractice both prospectively and after a potential claim unless the client is independently represented. If you have missed a statute of limitations, you must tell the client [§4.07], and you cannot settle the potential claim unless you have notified the client, in writing, about the desirability of obtaining independent counsel and afforded the client an opportunity to seek

---

[13] Model Rule 1.8(e); RLGL §36(2).

that independent advice.[14] If you try to settle without meeting these requirements, you will be subject to professional discipline [§8.02] and your "settlement" is voidable at the client's sole option [§8.09].

## ▶ §6.17 AGGREGATE SETTLEMENTS

### ▶ §6.17(a) The Policy Limit Bonanza?

**I guess we were lucky on this one. Three clients were in the same auto accident, daughter, mom and grandma. After lots of discovery, the insurance company has finally offered policy limits to settle all claims. We accept the settlement and we've got a big payday.**

You like playing God? Do the policy limits cover all damages? And how are you going to decide who gets what? Maybe you want to get them separate counsel to help decide a fair allocation. If not, the aggregate settlement rule requires that you advise each of the total offer and your proposed allocation amounts, and make clear that they are free to seek separate advice with respect to that question. By the way, discipline [§8.02] isn't your only problem here. If you forget your fiduciary duty to each client, they can seek total fee forfeiture as well [§8.10].

### ▶ §6.17(b) Joint Decisions To Settle

Joint representation of tort plaintiffs or criminal defendants can result in an offer of an aggregate settlement or plea bargain. The opposing lawyer may not care how the money or even the jail time is distributed, but you must ensure that each client gives informed consent to each individualized outcome. To protect your fiduciary duty of loyalty to each client, and to protect each client's right to have the final say in settling a matter, the aggregate settlement rule requires specific disclosures and written informed consent. First, you must disclose the existence and nature of all the claims or pleas involved. Second, you must disclose the participation of each person in the settlement. Third, each client must give informed consent in a signed writing, which should repeat all of these disclosures.[15] This extensive regulation is required to prevent you from allowing your personal, economic, or

---

[14] Model Rule 1.8(h); RLGL §54.
[15] Model Rule 1.8(g); RLGL §128.

time interest to dominate a client's resolution of a matter. You have the obligation to work up each case individually, and to communicate each settlement offer in the same manner. If you represent a class of plaintiffs or defendants, you must provide the relevant information to class members through applicable notification rules, such as those found in FRCP 23.[16]

▶**Red Flag**▶ Failure to comply with the aggregate settlement rule constitutes a serious breach of fiduciary duty, which can result not only in professional discipline [§8.02], but also fee forfeiture, including your entire contingent fee [§8.10].

### ▶§6.18 SEXUAL RELATIONSHIPS WITH CLIENTS
### ▶§6.18(a) Dating The CFO?

**Get this. One of our associates is dating the CFO of Big Bank. As soon as I got done celebrating this new client development initiative, someone pointed out Sarah was actually violating the rules. Does this mean we might lose the business and have to turn Sarah in?**

It depends. First, does Sarah provide legal services to Big Bank? If so, what does her "dating" mean? If a sexual relationship between Sarah and CFO exists and does not predate the lawyer-client relationship, she is violating Model Rule 1.8(j). Some jurisdictions [§9.04] do not attempt to regulate truly benign conduct, and prohibit sexual relationships between lawyer and client only where coercion, intimidation, or undue influence is involved or incompetent representation may be the result. Others prohibit all sexual relationships with clients, including key personnel of organizational clients who supervise, direct, or regularly consult with the lawyer.

The good news is you don't have to lose your client, and probably don't have to report Sarah. First, this conflict is personal and not imputed to the rest of the firm. So if Sarah is engaged in a sexual relationship with CFO, she can continue her private life and other firm lawyers can continue to represent Big Bank's legal interests [§6.20]. Second, Model Rule 8.3 only requires reporting another lawyer if the conduct in question raises a substantial question as to Sarah's honesty, trustworthiness, or fitness as a lawyer. We agree that dating the CFO

---

[16] Model Rule 1.8, Comment [13].

§6.18(b)  THE LOYALTY OBLIGATION • 151

probably does not do that. Consider, however, how you might answer that inquiry if you learned that CFO was pressuring Sarah to approve nondisclosure of substantial off-balance sheet transactions, something your firm nearly always advises against.

**This is much more complex than I thought. The way we work poor Sarah it's a wonder she has a social life at all. Now I might have to worry about how her social life potentially might affect our malpractice liability.**

### ▶§6.18(b) Legal Implications Of Sexual Relationships With Clients

A growing number of cases [§9.06] impose professional discipline [§8.02] on lawyers who engage in sexual relationships with clients. Many of these cases involve coercion or use of client confidences by lawyers who (literally) overreach. Many also involve situations of clients rendered emotionally vulnerable by a personal situation with legal ramifications, such as a divorce, bankruptcy, or personal injury. Some of these cases involve clients who made the first move, but later complained of a betrayal of trust. Here, courts find lawyers have violated conflict of interest provisions by putting their own personal interest in a sexual relationship ahead of a client's interests.

To put it bluntly, you are a fool to respond to these overtures. Clients seeking relief from a difficult life situation depend on lawyers for relief, and may unconsciously project positive feelings or desires onto the lawyer who provides it. And a sexual relationship, even between "consenting" adults, carries with it the greatest risk of impairing human and professional judgment.

For these reasons, recently amended Model Rule 1.8(j) and a growing number of jurisdictions [§9.04] flatly prohibit sexual relationships with clients that do not predate the establishment of a client-lawyer relationship. For the purposes of this rule, "client" includes a constituent of an organizational client who "supervises, directs or regularly consults with" the lawyer.[17] Some jurisdictions [§9.04] prohibit sexual relationships with clients only if they involve coercion, intimidation, or undue influence.[18] Others prefer to rely on general conflicts

---

[17] Model Rule 1.8, Comment [19].
[18] Cal. Rule of Prof'l Conduct 3-120(B).

provisions, including the requirement that informed consent be obtained in writing.[19] Our advice: Decide whether you want to represent or engage in sexual relations with a client. Someone else in your firm can provide the legal services if you prefer the latter.

### ▶ §6.19 PERSONAL RELATIONSHIPS

We all live in a web of personal relationships that influence our thinking, loyalty, and judgment. Usually, we leave our clients at work, and our personal relationships at home. But we all recognize the spillover from one to another. When that occurs, for example, when your roommate represents the opposing party in litigation, the general conflicts provision in Model Rule 1.7 has been triggered. From the client's viewpoint, there probably exists a significant risk that the representation of one client will be materially limited by your personal relationship. This is a consentable conflict, but one you must disclose in writing. If you are married to, dating, or related to counsel on the other side of litigation or a transaction, disclose the relationship, promise complete confidentiality, and explain how your loyalty might be compromised before seeking to obtain informed consent. If your significant other accidentally answers your critical phone call about the case at home, you are into another round of informed consent [§3.05]. If the client matter is extremely sensitive and/or adversarial, it may be easier for you to get someone else in the firm to handle it. If you can stay away from the matter, your relationship conflict is not imputed to the rest of the firm [§6.20].

### ▶ §6.20 IMPUTATION OF PERSONAL CONFLICTS

Some personal conflicts are not imputed to the rest of your firm. Serious and specifically regulated personal conflicts are imputed, including all of those regulated by Model Rule 1.8, with the exception of sexual relationships with clients.[20] This includes business transactions, client gifts, media rights, financial assistance and proprietary interests in litigation, aggregate settlements, and limitations on liability, all of which apply to your entire firm. Other personal conflicts governed by Model Rule 1.7 are not imputed to your firm unless they "present a significant risk of materially limiting the representation of the client by

---

[19] *In re Halverson*, 998 P.2d 833 (Wash. 2000).

[20] Model Rule 1.8(k).

the remaining lawyers in the firm."[21] Some jurisdictions [§9.04], however, continue to impute all personal lawyer-client conflicts. In preparing your conflicts control system, it is far better to include all personal interests, because even a non-imputable personal interest becomes imputable if it creates a material risk to the representation.

### ▶§6.21 CONFLICTS OF INTEREST: JOINT CLIENTS

Resolving joint client [§1.15] conflicts requires that you engage in the five-step process outlined in §6.04:

1. Identify all of the clients you and your firm represent in a matter;

2. Determine whether either a directly adverse or a material limitation conflict exists [§6.08]; and if so

3. Determine whether the conflict is consentable [§6.09]; and if so

4. Obtain informed consent in writing [§3.05]; and

5. Continue to monitor the representation for material changes that may create a conflict.

Clients may seek a joint representation to save money or to avoid discord in a matter. Agency law [§9.06] protects the right of each client to independent judgment and effective representation. It is your job to figure out whether the facts and the law governing the matter, as well as the personal relationships of the parties, allow you to offer a joint representation [§6.08]. When you seek to represent more than one client in a matter, look at the facts, law, and relational situation from the vantage of each client to determine the state of potential conflict. In all joint client situations, you always must seek informed consent about how confidential information will be handled between your clients [§6.22]. Remember too that some joint representations are nonconsentable, and others can proceed, but only with extensive informed consent, and only if certain legal or factual developments do not materialize. The situations listed below are some of the most common joint client conflicts.

---

[21] Model Rule 1.10(a).

## ▶ §6.22 JOINT CLIENT CONFIDENTIALITY

### ▶ §6.22(a) The Boiler-Plate Joint Defense Agreement?

We signed one of those boiler-plate joint defense agreements. You know, so we can keep the privilege among this huge group of defendants that have been sued in this frivolous antitrust suit. That was two years ago. Now it turns out one of our group has just been disqualified. Seems his law firm had represented one of the plaintiffs—on this very topic. My question is: Will we be disqualified as well?

You recognize a serious problem. How far does imputation of confidential information run? It includes everyone within a practice setting. It might well include co-counsel for a client where one of the two law firms is disqualified. Whether it runs to counsel who are party to a joint defense agreement is a much less compelling proposition. Although it is conceivable that a court could order just such relief, one would expect that a draconian order disqualifying a bevy of counsel goes too far, unless the aggrieved client can make out a persuasive case that confidential information was in fact shared, a difficult burden but one justified by the harshness of the resulting remedy. The important matter is to be sure, before you recommend a client's agreeing to one of these joint defense agreements, that the client is fully aware of the risks, as well as the rewards, of signing on to such an arrangement.

### ▶ §6.22(b) Handling Confidentiality In Joint Client Representations

Every joint representation requires attention to the issue of client confidentiality. Your written waiver should include the clients' choice of confidentiality provisions. They can elect to have you disclose or not disclose to the other whatever either tells you in confidence. With respect to the attorney-client privilege, you must warn your clients that it attaches between commonly represented parties against opposing parties, but does not attach if litigation arises between these clients, including that initiated by a counterclaim.[22]

If you do not include a confidentiality provision in your conflicts waiver, and one joint client tells you some material fact in confidence, your duty of confidentiality to that client [§5.03] will directly collide

---

[22] RLGL §75.

§6.23(a)  THE LOYALTY OBLIGATION • 155

with your duty to keep the other client informed about material aspects of the matter [§3.02]. Your duties to one client now put you in a position of direct adversity to the other [§6.08], and unless they have instructed you what to do in advance, you now must withdraw from the representation of both.[23] Of course, withdrawal does not end the issue about disclosure. Here, absent a prior agreement between the parties, courts generally look to their own confidentiality exceptions to determine whether you may (or must) disclose.[24]

## ▶§6.23 LITIGATION OPPONENTS
### ▶§6.23(a) Divorce And Dissolution

The most obvious nonconsentable conflict occurs when one client asserts a claim in litigation against another.[25] Contested divorces are one clear example of this prohibition. But what about no-fault divorce or dissolution of marriage? The answer depends on whether applicable law aligns the interests of husband and wife against each other.[26] Since most jurisdictions treat dissolution, no matter how amicable, as a contested or contestable judicial proceeding, representing both parties constitutes a nonconsentable conflict. Recognizing the economic reality that many divorcing spouses face, some jurisdictions specify that a lawyer may represent one party, as long as the lawyer makes clear to the unrepresented spouse that the lawyer does not represent that person, and recommends that the unrepresented person have another lawyer look over the proposed settlement document [§§9.06, 9.07].[27]

Mediation of a divorce settlement presents a different situation. Lawyers who mediate a dispute do not "represent" the parties, and therefore may act as mediators (assuming the dispute is otherwise a candidate for mediation).[28] Can a lawyer combine these roles, first mediating the dispute, and then representing both spouses in drafting

---

[23] Model Rule 1.7, Comment [31].

[24] *A. v. B.*, 726 A.2d 924 (N.J. 1999) (law firm which provided estate planning services to husband and wife allowed to tell wife about husband's illegitimate child without husband's consent because state professional code recognized exception for disclosure to rectify the consequences of client's fraud using the lawyer's services).

[25] Model Rule 1.7(b)(3); RLGL §122, comment g(iii).

[26] RLGL §122, comment g(iii).

[27] Ill. State Bar Ass'n Adv. Op. 98-06 (Jan. 1999); Ohio State Bar Ethics Op. 30 (1975).

[28] Model Rule 2.4.

and filing appropriate papers with a court to effectuate their mediated result? Most jurisdictions say "no" to this, because regardless of the terms of the mediated settlement, many issues may remain to be worked out in the final document, and even if no factual issues remain, each spouse retains the legal right to contest the mediated settlement or seek other legal options to meet the client's goals. A few ethics opinions [§9.07] have reached a different result in the limited situation where the parties are firmly committed to the terms of the mediated settlement, the settlement is consistent with each spouse's objectives and legal rights, and no remaining points of contention exist.[29]

### ▶ §6.23(b) The Family Accident?

**Dad and son visited me the other day. They were involved in an automobile accident. Son was driving. The other driver was fined for speeding. Dad and son both suffered serious injuries. I can't wait to take on this double-barreled case.**

But wait you must. Though it seems at first blush that dad and son have identical interests, and that the other driver is solely liable, the interests of driver and passenger, even if they are relatives, often diverge. What if you learn that son had a couple of drinks that night? Or that son ran a red light? Dad may have a claim against son. Their interests also would diverge if the amount of money available for settlement or judgment were insufficient for both claims. Unless you can satisfy yourself that these potential conflicts can be avoided or get dad and son to waive the conflicts because it might make sense for them to be represented by the same lawyer, they need separate counsel. If not handled sensitively, this picture of family solidarity hides a real ethical minefield.

### ▶ §6.24 SIMULTANEOUS REPRESENTATION OF ADVERSARIES IN UNRELATED CASES

One issue [§9.02] sometimes occurs in litigation: Your firm represents a client against another party, whom your firm also represents in a separate and unrelated matter. Here, you do not represent both sides in the same litigation, but you owe loyalty obligations to each such that one client may feel betrayed by your simultaneous loyalty to the

---

[29] N.Y. State Bar Op. 736 (2001).

other. Most courts find this a consentable conflict, but readily disqualify a law firm [§8.08] or recommend professional discipline [§8.02] if either client objects.[30] In spite of these decisions, we find it highly problematic to seek a waiver from a client to sue it, and only in the most extraordinary circumstances should you make that call. Just think what the act of asking the question (may we sue you for X?) and preparing a written informed consent [§3.05] does to notions of client loyalty.

### ▶ §6.25 CO-PARTIES: CIVIL LITIGATION

Here, you should begin by identifying the conflict. First, examine the facts and the legal interests of the parties, which initially may seem aligned and not adversarial. With respect to facts, you have to examine whether your co-clients recall the same facts, and whether available settlement options will make them effective adversaries competing for limited resources (e.g., both are seriously injured and the defendant's liability limits will not cover the likely damages of either).[31] Second, with respect to law, consider how a counterclaim can realign the legal interests of even the closest family member co-plaintiffs. The wife-driver and husband-passenger you took on against the other driver (who seemed clearly at fault) suddenly have adverse interests when the defendant files a counterclaim alleging that your driver-client's speeding caused the accident. Third, be sure the clients' personal relationships can withstand these potential conflicts.

If you determine that the joint representation is possible, and obtain their written informed consent [§3.05], remember to address two key issues:

1. If the facts or legal rights of the parties change, you may have to withdraw from representing one or both; and

2. How your clients wish you to handle confidential information [§6.22].

---

[30] *In re Dresser Industries, Inc.*, 972 F.2d 540(5th Cir. 1992) (disqualification); *Universal City Studios, Inc. v. Reimerdes*, 98 F. Supp. 2d 449 (S.D.N.Y. 2000) (disqualification denied because professional discipline more appropriate).

[31] *Wolpaw v. General Accident Ins. Co.*, 639 A.2d 338 (N.J. Super. Ct. App. Div. 1994) (insurer required to provide independent counsel to each of three covered insureds where policy limits not sufficient to cover plaintiff's claim).

## §6.26 JOINT DEFENDANTS IN CRIMINAL CASES

### §6.26(a) Common Defense Among Friends?

Two guys showed up the other day. They both had been accused of insider trading. Criminal prosecutions, if you can believe that. They are old friends. They are not indigent and they want a common defense. I think they also want to save some money. They say their defenses are identical. I explained that a conflict might develop later. They're not worried. Can I represent both?

This may be no time for false economy. Representing two criminal defendants is problematic at best. Although these fellows might have a constitutional right to make this mistake, they don't have a constitutional right to you as their lawyer. The problem is that even if they are on the exact same page in terms of their defense, the clever prosecutor can instantly create an impossible and nonconsentable conflict of interest by seeking a plea bargain with one to go after the other. And no matter how many times they tell you that that would never occur as to them, there is something about the imminent empanelling of a jury that often changes loyalty to one's co-defendant into betrayal.

### §6.26(b) Co-Defendants: Criminal Defense

Co-defendants may seem legally aligned in interest, rather than adversaries. But a nodding glance at the facts and a recognition of each criminal defendant's legal rights quickly identify potential conflicts. One defendant may have a different view of the relative culpability of the codefendants. One may be asked to agree to a plea bargain in exchange for testimony against the other. Witnesses or physical evidence may inculpate one defendant more than others. One defendant may have more or less incentive or willingness to take the stand. Opening and closing statements must address facts and law in a manner consistent with each defendant's interests. Finally, even if all share a common defense, if all are convicted, sentencing may involve relative culpability and finger pointing between defendants. In short, the potential for conflict is so grave that ordinarily lawyers should not undertake such a joint representation.[32]

Yet, codefendants might consider joint representation advantageous to assure a common position. For that reason, most cases

---

[32] Model Rule 1.7, Comment [23]; RLGL §129, comment c.

[§9.06] hold that this conflict is consentable, but only in the "unusual situations when, after careful investigation, it is clear either that no conflict is likely to develop at trial, sentencing, or at any other time in the proceeding or that common representation will be advantageous to each of the codefendants represented."[33] Further, each of the codefendants must give written informed consent [§3.05], which should be made a matter of judicial record. Even then, if a prosecutor offers a plea bargain that includes testimony of one against the others, the conflict becomes unconsentable because that defendant needs independent advice about how to proceed.[34]

## ▶ §6.27 JOINT REPRESENTATION IN TRANSACTIONS

### ▶ §6.27(a) The Simple Real Estate Transaction?

**Buyer and seller have agreed on which property is to be sold at what price and on what date. Can I represent both of them?**

Think termites. If buyer and seller have not decided whether the agreement will include a termite clause, or a financing clause, or any other material issue that you reasonably believe you would have to raise with either buyer or seller if you were representing that party alone, then the joint representation will put you in an impossible conflict of interest situation, and you must decline to represent both parties.

### ▶ §6.27(b) The New Business Venture?

**Just got a visit from three nice guys. One's a long-time client of the firm. Quite wealthy. He's investing with the inventor and one of those MBA types in some nano-technology venture. Sounds exciting. They've got their act together, I think. They would like our firm to lawyer the deal. What do you think?**

Well, you certainly could become the lawyer for the company once it is up and running. But getting these three from here to there is a different story.

---

[33] *ABA Standards Relating to the Administration of Criminal Justice*, The Defense Function Standard 4-3.5.

[34] RLGL §129, comment c. 1; *Thomas v. State*, 551 S.E.2d 254 (S.C. 2001) (once prosecutor offers plea bargain, initial conflicts waiver not sufficient to continue joint representation).

**Look, I don't want to lose them. They'll never come back.**

We know, but the situation is fraught with peril. First, you've got a special relationship with your original client. And they are each playing a different role and therefore have different concerns.

**I tell you the last thing these guys need is three different lawyers.**

Well that may be true. But the fact is it's very hard to imagine how you can order their arrangements.

**Oh. They have already assigned shares.**

That's well and good, but what if our guy doesn't put up all the money, gets cold feet? What if the technology isn't all it's cracked up to be? Remember Sam Waksal? What if the CEO turns out to be a loser? Don't these fellows have to worry about the downside too?

**I hear you, but maybe I can mediate among them.**

Just remember what happens to the Good Samaritan who tries to break up a domestic dispute. And be clear whether you will actually "mediate," that is, act as a third-party neutral and not represent any of them,[35] or take on a common representation of all of them, relying on them to make all of the decisions and setting some ground rules for dealing with confidential information [§6.22].[36]

### ▶ §6.27(c) Joint Wills?

**Husband and wife ask whether I can draft a will for both of them. May I?**

There they sit. Figuratively (or literally) holding hands across your desk. You explain that the estate tax laws make it pay to leave all of each spouse's estate to the other. They agree and ask you to draft the wills. Not an hour after they leave, husband calls to disclose he has an illegitimate son, unknown to wife, for whom he must provide. "Don't tell my wife."

Of course, you can do this, so long as nothing in your conversations with the clients indicates any conflict. But one thing you had better do: Discuss with them together how you will handle confidential information [§6.22]. Do they agree you will share everything? Noth-

---

[35] Model Rule 2.4.
[36] Model Rule 1.7, Comments [29]-[33].

ing? That way when that phone call comes—and our friends in the trust and estate bar assure you that it will—you know what your obligation is as far as disclosure. Once that phone call comes, whether you may disclose or not, you must also determine whether the information you have received creates a conflict that requires you to withdraw from both representations (because, for example, of the legal, factual, and relational conflict created by the unknown son). As you can see, if disclosure is not permitted, the chances of being required to withdraw are much higher than if the other spouse can be informed of the new information that creates a conflict and, nonetheless, waive any conflict thereby created.

### ➤ §6.27(d) Co-Parties: Transactions

This situation presents the most likely candidate for joint representation, but the problems in this section demonstrate that you have some due diligence to perform before proceeding. First: Facts. Is one client a spendthrift that the other seeks to restrain? Will one be employed by the other in a new venture? Second: Law and legal rights of the parties. Will you be able to offer them all applicable legal options, leaving it to them to determine their own best interests? If you will avoid raising issues to avoid offending one or the other, they need separate counsel. Third: Personal relationships. Are the prospective clients relative strangers, friends, family? Do they trust each other? Once again, you must warn them about potential conflicts, and if they develop, withdraw.[37] And don't forget confidentiality [§6.22].

➤**Ultimate Red Flag**➤ Joint client transactional work invites both over- and under-identification with clients. We explore this dual professional difficulty for lawyers further in §10.05.

## ➤ §6.28 POSITIONAL OR ISSUE CONFLICTS

### ➤ §6.28(a) Taking Different Legal Positions?

**Our takeover practice is booming. We've been asked to challenge Colossus's poison pill. We're also defending Excelsior's. In fact, today we're the center of the M&A world.**

---

[37] *Matter of Wildermuth*, 416 N.W.2d 607 (Wis. 1987) (initial conflicts waiver of joint parties in the sale of a plaintiff's claim).

Let's hope you are successful in at least one of these. We need to know more, but if the matters are factually similar, involve the same state's corporate law and are in the same court, you had better watch out. You may have too much of a good thing. There is a potential conflict. The conflict of interest rules generally permit you to be on the opposite side of the same issue but not if there is a reasonable chance that your efforts on behalf of one of your clients will undermine another one. Lawyers argue for and against expansive discovery every day. But challenging the Pennsylvania anti-takeover statute as unconstitutional at the same time you are wielding it as a shield for a different client in the same court is definitely over the top.

You've identified this conflict issue [§9.02]. But the problem with issue or positional conflicts is that no one has figured out how to systematically review for them, particularly since these issues are not necessarily identifiable at the outset of a representation. This, of course, is why some lawyers, for example, only represent management, while others only represent labor. The best advice we can provide is to be alert to issue conflicts as a general matter, paying special attention to appellate or any other representation where you might be setting a precedent in one case that will materially harm another client in another pending matter.

### ▶§6.28(b) Legal Regulation Of Issue Conflicts

Lawyers are constantly called upon to advocate inconsistent legal positions on behalf of different clients, sometimes before the same judge. Ordinarily, advocating for different interpretations or applications of a legal rule causes no real conflict, because the result in one case creates no precedent and can be factually distinguished from the other. In a few situations, these premises no longer hold true. If a lawyer's legal argument will create a precedent that is likely to seriously weaken another client's position, a conflict arises. Generally such a conflict is consentable if both clients understand the nature of the problem.[38] In the rare but conceivable case where a precedent for one client would totally foreclose the other client's legal rights, the conflict becomes nonconsentable.

---

[38] Model Rule 1.7, Comment [24]; RLGL §128, comment f.

## ▶ §6.29 REPRESENTING ENTITIES

### ▶ §6.29(a) The Corporate Transaction?

**My client's CEO wants me to represent him in drafting a deed transferring some land from client to CEO. He is such a good guy. I want to help him.**

Proceed with caution, friend. When you represent an organization you do not thereby represent any of its constituents (a fancy word for employees, officers, directors, shareholders). And if you are going to represent a constituent, you must get the permission of someone at the organizational client other than the person you have been asked to represent if there is any possibility of a conflict of interest. In fact it is a good practice to let your organizational client know you are doing legal work for employees, officers, or directors even if there is no apparent conflict in the work you are doing. Your organizational client may be concerned that taking on these representations could compromise your loyalty to the organizational client.

In this case, because the proposed transfer brings with it a conflict of interest (client as seller; client as buyer), you must inform CEO that before you proceed you must get the consent of another officer of the organization. In seeking that permission, you also must determine that someone of authority (perhaps the CFO, perhaps the Board of Directors) shares the CEO's view that the land is of no value to the company and that it is in the best interests of the company to transfer this "liability" to CEO. We need no "son of Tyco" transactions in which you participate.

If CEO tells you not to pursue the request for permission ("don't bother; I'll handle it a different way") you may not be free to share CEO's request with anyone else at the company. Depending on how CEO approached you, CEO may have become a prospective client [§1.20], and would then be most assuredly entitled to the same level of confidentiality as any other prospective client. So even if you think mischief might be occurring on this land transfer, you should not share that view with anyone else at the corporate client unless you appropriately clarified that you represented the organization alone or one of the exceptions to your state's confidentiality rules applies. Of course the answer would be entirely different—you would be required to inform someone at the company of CEO's plans—if CEO had not approached you to represent him, but rather asked you as company counsel to arrange the transfer.

## ▶ §6.29(b) The Employee Deposition?

**I'm the company's litigation counsel. A legion of employees is about to be deposed. Should I tell them I represent them too?**

Sounds good, but it is really creating greater problems than it solves. First, taking on that many clients creates huge logistical problems. Then just contemplate for a moment the conflicts that lurk in this wholesale group of representations. Although these folks all work for the same organization, their interests are quite different. Some are management; some are labor. Some may be interested in "getting out." Others may harbor dreams of being the CEO. Some may hate the company and would be thrilled to do it in. Some may be involved in the matters; others are totally indifferent. You get the idea. Just representing a few organizational employees and the organization itself creates enough problems; representing everyone is an impossible ethical quagmire.

## ▶ §6.29(c) The Subsidiary Problem?

**I just received a call from Big Bank. They'd like me to sue Excelsior to collect a large debt. Problem is one of my partners is representing an Excelsior wholly owned subsidiary on a lease in a shopping center right now. Can I help Big Bank?**

This raises the interesting question of conflicts in the corporate family. Before you worry about the ethics of the matter, consider how Excelsior's subsidiary will react if you take the matter on. The likelihood is that even if you can undertake the matter under the rules, the subsidiary will be so offended that it will fire your firm. Can you live with that?

You also could ask for a waiver from the subsidiary. But before you pick up the telephone you had better inform Big Bank of your plans and get Big Bank's permission to seek a waiver. Big Bank is entitled to know of your predicament and to decide whether it is willing to have you seek a waiver, since seeking the waiver itself discloses confidential information of Big Bank.

If you decide you will run the risk of losing the subsidiary as a client and either don't want to or can't seek a waiver, then you must face the corporate family issue head on. By representing the subsidiary you do not thereby necessarily also represent the parent. Nonetheless, you have to ask these questions. If I sue Excelsior am I not really tak-

**Go to www.lawtechnews.com to request your FREE information on any of the products, systems, or services featured in this issue.**

Or, if you prefer, fill in the reader response card number of the products that interest you below:

## Do you wish to receive/continue receiving LawTechnologyNews FREE?  ☐ [14] YES  ☐ [15] No

NAME _____ TITLE _____

FIRM/COMPANY _____

ADDRESS _____

ADDRESS _____

CITY _____ STATE _____ ZIP _____

TELEPHONE _____

E-MAIL _____

☐ I do not wish to receive email from **Law Technology News (LTN)**
☐ I do not wish to receive email from business partners of LTN

150703

# BUSINESS REPLY MAIL
FIRST-CLASS MAIL    PERMIT NO. 9335    BUFFALO, NY

POSTAGE WILL BE PAID BY ADDRESSEE

www.lawtechnews.com

**LAW TECHNOLOGY NEWS**
**PO BOX 5179**
**BUFFALO, NY 14205-9879**

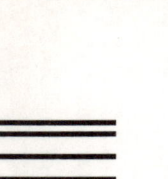

ing a position directly adverse to the subsidiary? Does the subsidiary depend on the parent for funding or services? Even if the representation adverse to Excelsior is not directly adverse to its subsidiary, will your services for Big Bank against Excelsior be materially limited by your loyalty to its subsidiary? Is there a real possibility that you will pull punches in your representation adverse to Excelsior because of your firm's relationship with its subsidiary?

If the subsidiary is really independent—in a product line, personnel and geographic sense—from Excelsior then there is respectable authority that you can take the matter on, despite the view of one of the authors that you can never take a position adverse to your client's wholly owned parent, sub, or sibling (does Ford care whether you get a $20 million judgment against the Mercury Division or the Jaguar subsidiary?). But you certainly should not do so if the same in-house lawyer you are dealing with at the subsidiary will also be handling this matter for Excelsior. Or if the CEOs of the two entities are identical. There is a narrow path here that would permit this representation, but as you can see it requires dexterity and finesse (and a little chutzpah) to get through it.

### ➤ §6.29(d) The Homeowner's Association?

**I hope you have a solution for this one. We've been representing this homeowner's association for years. Now it turns out we brought a lawsuit for a client against a member of the association. We ran a conflicts check but, of course, the association member's name did not come up. The association has over 100 members. Now she's moved to disqualify. Asserts we represent her. We do represent the association.**

Just as when you represent a corporation you don't necessarily represent its shareholders, when you represent an association you don't necessarily represent any of the members. There would have to be something special about this member of the association—you received confidential information from her in particular, she's the most important member of the association, whatever—before you would be required to treat her as a client for these purposes. Just think about representing the AARP. You'd never have another client! Or at least none over 50.

### ▶ §6.29(e) Organizations And Employees

Lawyers for organizations may be asked to represent employees or other constituents of the organization as well. This is perfectly permissible, but always subject to a clear-eyed conflicts analysis. Recognize first that your representation of an organization does not mean that you necessarily represent any constituent of the entity.[39] That said, the burden is on you to clarify whether you represent employees as well. If you don't disclaim representation, an employee's reasonable reliance on your legal advice can create a client-lawyer relationship where you and your employer-client do not want it [§1.18].

To analyze whether to take on the employee, look for direct adversity or material limitation conflicts by beginning with the facts: Are employee and employer aligned in interest? Are both named as parties in a matter, or is employee only a witness? Can or should one client defend conduct by blaming the other? Or did both do nothing "wrong"? Was the employee acting in the scope of employment? Next the law: Criminal responsibility for insider trading creates a different situation from a "routine" tort case. Finally, the relationship of the parties: Does the employer want to fire the employee for this conduct or because this case represents the last straw? Or is keeping this employee happy of vital concern? Has the employer agreed to provide representation as part of the employee's benefits or corporate by-laws?[40]

If you determine that you can proceed with a joint representation, obtain written informed consent [§3.05], paying careful attention to confidentiality [§6.22] and changes in facts or circumstances that will require a reassessment.

### ▶ §6.30 IMPUTATION OF CURRENT-CLIENT CONFLICTS
### ▶ §6.30(a) Side-Switching?

**The trial's next week. And my best associate just told me she's leaving this Friday to go to work for those blank blank lawyers on the other side. I've lost my right arm. My left, too. Help!!**

The rules of professional conduct apply to all lawyers. Even associates. And Model Rule 1.16 provides that, without cause, a lawyer

---

[39] Model Rule 1.7, Comment [34], 1.13(a)(f)(g).
[40] RLGL §131.

may only withdraw from a representation if it will not have an adverse effect on the client. Obviously, that is not the case here. Tell her she may only leave after the case is over.

**But who wants her now? If she's already lined up a job, that means she's been talking to the other side for a while. What a turncoat.**

You are right there. ABA Opinion 99-414 (Ethical Obligations When a Lawyer Changes Firms) concludes that you were entitled, as was the client, to know about these employment discussions well before now. In the words of the opinion, "no later than the commencement of serious discussions with the new firm." But that doesn't solve the present problem.

**Correct. What do I do now?**

In most states you may now move to disqualify [§8.08] the law firm on the other side.

**But my associate says she is being screened?**

That may be so but there is no authority for screening as a solution to side-switching, even in jurisdictions that otherwise recognize screens [§6.34]. Your associate's representation of your client and the confidential information she possesses is imputed to her entire new law firm. That imputation rule says that if one lawyer in a firm is disqualified then all lawyers are disqualified. So one thing seems reasonably certain. The trial may not be next week after all—that is, once your associate's new firm is barred from continuing the representation.

### ➤ §6.30(b) Law Firm Imputation

All concurrent joint-client conflicts are imputed to the lawyer's firm [§§1.30, 6.05].[41] If the conflict is consentable, the clients may include a screen of one or more firm lawyers as a condition of the consent. Otherwise, nonconsensual screens are not allowed to resolve imputed joint-client conflicts.

---

[41] Model Rule 1.10(a); RLGL §123.

### ▶§6.31 CONFLICTS OF INTEREST: THIRD-PARTY DIRECTION
### ▶§6.31(a) Corporate Control?

**I don't know what to do. I was retained by Big Bank to represent its CFO in a huge SEC investigation into insider trading. They've been paying my bills like clockwork. Now they tell me I have to tell them if I am negotiating a deal for CFO, or they will stop paying CFO's bills.**

You recognize how unethical that would be. Whenever a lawyer is paid by a third party the lawyer must, nonetheless, maintain the client's confidences and not let the third party interfere with the lawyer's professional judgment. Even when it is dad paying irresponsible son's legal bills, dad gets a cold shoulder from you as to confidential information regarding son.

Tell Big Bank there can be no conditions to your service. If that means they stop paying your fees, that is a result you and your client must live with. We don't have to tell you the by-laws or employment contract of Big Bank with CFO may require Big Bank to pay your client's fees, and, if they do, a condition of fulfilling that corporate obligation cannot be a requirement that you breach the confidentiality of the client.

### ▶§6.31(b) Relative Matters?

**This kid shows up the other day. Tells us his dad needs a new will. Seems dad is quite infirm. So son comes down to tell me what dad wants. Nice fellow. Dad wants to set up an education fund for the grandkids. I prepare the will; son will get dad to sign it.**

We think it's time to start making house calls. Remember dad is your client [§§1.13, 10.04]. You've got to make sure of two things. What are dad's wishes? And is dad fully capable of making decisions? When clients suffer from a disability, we are supposed to treat them as competent to the greatest extent possible. But if we conclude the client cannot order his affairs, we have to make sure we are taking directions from someone who has dad's best interest at heart. That may be true here. But you just don't know enough right now. Go visit dad or decline the engagement.

### ▶ §6.31(c) Third-Person Payment

Someone other than your client can pay for the representation, as long as the 4 C's you owe your client remains uncompromised. Three specific requirements are designed to make this happen:

1. The client must know about the payment and who makes it, and give informed consent;

2. You must make sure that there is no interference with your independent professional judgment, or the client-lawyer relationship; and

3. Confidences of your client remain sacrosanct, protected by your fiduciary duty to the client, not the third party.[42] In other words, the payor has no right to call the tune, whether it's an employer paying for the representation of an employee [§§1.18, 6.29(e)], one codefendant paying for the representation of all [§§1.15, 6.25, 6.26], parents paying for the representation of a child [§1.13], nondebtor third parties paying for the representation of debtor's counsel in bankruptcy, or a nonprofit organization that pays for the legal representation of its clients.

### ▶ §6.31(d) Third-Person Influence

Even when third parties do not pay for the representation of another, they nevertheless may seek to influence a client-lawyer relationship.

▶**Red Flag**▶ Do not assume that the person you talk to or the person who pays you is a client. Although this will often be the case, you have the obligation to clarify whom you represent and to make clear to third parties that they have no right to learn anything about the representation nor to influence it unless your client wants them to do so.

If you have been recommended, employed, or paid to provide legal services to another, you have the obligation to remember that your client is not the person who regularly or occasionally recommends you, or the person who perhaps speaks to you on behalf of another, say a family member. You must not allow that other per-

---

[42] Model Rule 1.8(f); RLGL §134.

son to direct or regulate your professional judgment on behalf of your client.[43]

▶**Ultimate Red Flag**▶ Triangular relationships create some of the most difficult professional responsibility issues. We explore these matters further in §10.06.

### ▶§6.32 INSURANCE DEFENSE

### ▶§6.32(a) Litigation Strategy?

**Can I take a representation in which the insurance company tells me how many depositions to take, whether and when to file dispositive motions and when to hire an expert?**

Who said anything about insurance companies? The first principle is that a lawyer may not permit the fact that the lawyer is being paid by a third party (an insurance company, a parent, an employer) to interfere with a lawyer's independent professional judgment. This does not mean that the lawyer necessarily follows every request for service by the nonpaying client. But it does mean that the lawyer must act in the best interests of the client and if the lawyer is of the view that the best interests of the client require the taking of 10 depositions or hiring an expert in the beginning of the case or filing a motion for summary judgment, the lawyer must assert her independence and insist on the lawyer's course of action, even if that means incurring the wrath of the third-party payor (that might be the source of lucrative repeat business). But one must be bold, strengthened in the knowledge that no insurance company wants to put itself in a position where it has not fulfilled its good faith obligation to provide a defense by rejecting the best judgment of the lawyer hired to represent its insured.

### ▶§6.32(b) The Confidential Policy Defense?

**Let's see if I understand how this works. I'm representing the insured. The insurance company, of course, issued a reservation of rights letter. The letter says, in its dense single-spaced three pages, inter alia, no coverage if conduct is deemed willful. I just found a memo to the file that suggests the conduct was willful. So I call the insurance company?**

---

[43] Model Rule 5.4(c); RLGL §134.

§6.32(d)  THE LOYALTY OBLIGATION • 171

Absolutely not. That's confidential information. And its disclosure will hurt your client, the insured. Even if you are in a jurisdiction [§9.06] in which the insurance company is considered a client, you will have to make it clear to the insurer that you do not represent it as to these issues and if the information is sufficiently volatile you will have to withdraw from the representation of the insurance company. Of course, you could never represent either if litigation ensues between the insurance company and the insured.

### ➤ §6.32(c) Settlement?

**What if the plaintiff is willing to settle for policy limits? So is the insurance company? But the insured says a settlement will ruin his reputation. Do I settle?**

Not if your client says not to. Your duty is to your client. Your client may not be entitled to any more coverage. Your client may not even be entitled to your continued services. That all goes to the terms of the insurance contract between the insured and the insurance company. But you cannot defy your insured client's wishes. You should explain, moreover, that should litigation ensue between the insured client and the insurance company you will represent neither.

**How about the reverse? The client wants to settle. There's a demand within policy limits. But the insurance company says the claim is frivolous.**

You should remonstrate with the insurance company. Remind them that if they defend and the judgment exceeds the policy limits the insured could claim the failure to settle is in bad faith. But you will not be able to handle that claim either.

### ➤ §6.32(d) Understanding The Tripartite Relationship

It isn't always clear whether you have one or two clients when an insurer hires you to represent insureds. All jurisdictions agree, however, that the insured is either your primary client or your only client [§1.17].

At least five results flow from this understanding:

1. You owe the insured the 4 C's, which means that the insured can sue you for malpractice. Some jurisdictions allow the insurer such relief as well, especially when harm occurs to the insurer, but not the insured, either because the insurer is deemed a joint client, or on an

equitable subrogation theory.[44] The prohibition against interference with your professional judgment [§6.31(d)] also means that the insurer probably will not be vicariously liable for your malpractice because it had no right to control the details of your work.[45]

2. The insured is entitled to confidentiality, meaning that you may not repeat what the insured has told you to the insurer.[46] With respect to the privilege, if the insurer is a co-client, then the co-client privilege protects matters of common interest against third persons. Some courts find that the insurer is not a client, but acts as an agent of the insured for purposes of preparing the defense.[47]

3. Some jurisdictions prohibit insurers from hiring inside counsel to defend insureds; others do not. Those who allow it heavily regulate the practice to prevent interference in the insured-lawyer relationship.[48]

4. Insurers have only limited control over fees and strategy. Lawyers can agree to direction that is "reasonable in scope" if the client-insured consents,[49] but insurers cannot require prior approval of billing or strategy.[50]

5. Insurers often assert control over settlement. Insurance law in many jurisdictions provides that an unreasonable refusal to accept an offer to settle within policy limits triggers a bad faith claim, which can result in liability for the entire amount of eventual damages, beyond

---

[44] *Pine Island Farmers Coop. v. Erstad & Riemer, P.A.*, 649 N.W.2d 444 (Minn. 2002).

[45] *State Farm Mut. Auto. Ins. Co. v. Traver*, 980 S.W.2d 625 (Tex. 1998).

[46] *Parsons v. Continental Nat'l Am. Group*, 550 P.2d 94 (Ariz. 1976) (insurer estopped from denying coverage where it learned of a policy defense from breach of confidentiality by lawyer for insured).

[47] *Paradigm Ins. Co. v. The Langerman Law Offices, P.A.*, 24 P.3d 593 (Ariz. 2001).

[48] *Am. Ins. Ass'n v. Ky. Bar Ass'n*, 917 S.W.2d 568 (Ky. 1996) (insurer's use of in-house lawyers and contracts for flat fees for insurance defense prohibited because these practices interfere with lawyer's independent professional judgment); *Petition of Youngblood*, 895 S.W.2d 322 (Tenn. 1995) (not a per se ethical violation for in-house lawyers to represent insureds but insurer cannot control the details of the lawyer's performance or dictate strategy).

[49] RLGL §134(2).

[50] *In re Rules of Professional Conduct*, 2 P.3d 806 (Mont. 2000); ABA Formal Op. 01-421.

original policy limits.[51] Even when the insurer wishes to settle but the insured does not, your primary client is the insured. You must relay the settlement offer and inform the insured of the option of releasing the insurer from its obligations, which would require the insured to defend the suit on his or her own.[52]

▶**Ultimate Red Flag**▶ Insurance defense creates a common triangular relationship that causes lawyers problems they would rather avoid. We explore these issues further in §10.06.

### ▶§6.33 FORMER-CLIENT CONFLICTS OF INTEREST

When you complete client representations [§1.24], whether because you finish the matter [§1.25], your client fires you [§2.11], you withdraw [§7.02], or a court disqualifies you [§8.08], your current clients become former clients, and you no longer owe them duties of communication or competence. Your confidentiality obligation, on the other hand, remains a firm commitment to former clients, even after a client's death.

### ▶§6.33(a) The Hot Potato?

We've been representing General Consolidated for years. But it's penny ante stuff. Collections. And it's almost dwindled to zero. Last year we billed GC $2,700. Now, we've been approached to bring an antitrust case against GC on behalf of some repair shops. This could be big. Real big. I figure we can return the last two files to GC. Tell 'em we won't even bill those files. That way they're a

---

[51] *Behn v. Legion Ins. Co.*, 173 F. Supp. 2d 105 (D. Mass. 2001) (insurer acted reasonably in refusing to settle when expert witness opined that insured physician had complied with standard of care, facts indicated comparative fault, and insured refused consent to settle); *Haddick ex rel. Griffith v. Valor Ins. Co.*, 763 N.E.2d 299 (Ill. 2001) (cause of action for bad faith found when liability conceded, medical expenses were in excess of policy limits, and insurer did not offer to settle for policy limits until one year after settlement demand initially made).

[52] *Saucedo v. Winger*, 915 P.2d 129 (Kan. App. 1996) (insurer had no right to settle without insured's consent in absence of clear policy language to the contrary); *Rogers v. Robson, Masters, Ryan, Brumund & Belom*, 392 N.E.2d 1365 (Ill. App. 1979) (lawyer liable for malpractice for failure to inform insured of settlement offer and option of defending suit on his own).

former client and, since the collections have nothing to do with this antitrust claim, we're okay ethics-wise. You agree?

It's a plan. But if GC chooses to challenge you, we're afraid you'll come up short. Rule 1.16 permits you to withdraw at any time for no reason at all so long as there's no material adverse effect on the client. But you cannot drop GC like a "hot potato" to take on a conflicting representation. That's where the courts have drawn a line.

**Well, maybe we can finish up those two matters real fast.**

So long as you don't compromise GC's rights in doing that, you can safely proceed.

**Maybe it would pay for us to pay GC the amount these guys owe.**

We're not going there.

### ➤ §6.33(b) Firing A Client?

**I'm beside myself. We had an estate client. Wrote a will; set up a trust; sent a final bill. That was four years ago. We filed a lawsuit three weeks ago against this former client's wholly owned company. It delivered some defective materials to one of our clients. Now we've got a motion to disqualify. Does this guy own us?**

You raise two issues [§9.02]. First, do you have to treat the wholly owned business of a present client as a client for conflict purposes [§6.29(c)]? Before answering the ethical question you should recognize the good lawyering point. Whether you are required to treat client's wholly owned company as a client or not, you can be sure your client would be very unhappy with that turn of events. Firing you from further representation of him would not be an unlikely result. And do you want to be known as a lawyer who sues his client's business?

As for the rules of professional conduct [§9.04], it would be hard to argue that when you sue an individual client's wholly owned business you are not taking a position directly adverse to your client. Whatever can be said about suing your large conglomerate client's parent, subsidiary or sibling does not apply here.

But that leaves the question whether your complaining individual is a present or former client. Although we all love to engage clients, we are rarely so enthusiastic about disengaging. After all, the largest source of new business is existing clients. Yet there are two good reasons for lawyers to be conscientious about disengaging

[§1.25]. The first concerns continuing competence and communication obligations. With that four-year-old trust sitting out there, do you want to be responsible for updating that individual on any changes in the law? Is this person relying on you for that? A polite letter terminating the arrangement can put that brooding issue to rest. The second issue concerns loyalty. Because you owe present clients duties of loyalty, the only way to end most of them is to end the representation. It's one thing to turn away juicy new business because you are serving and billing an active account. It is quite another to have a very stale file resurrect itself into a disabling conflict because you forgot to send the right communication.

**How do I do that?**

Firing a client while leaving the door open is an exercise that requires some finesse [§1.25]. What about, "It has been a pleasure being of service to you. We enclose our final invoice for professional services. If you should need our services in the future on a new matter, we hope you will keep us in mind."

**What if I did send such a letter?**

Then your estate client became a former client, making the substantial relationship test applicable. Read on.

### ▶§6.33(c) Keeping It In The Family?

**How's this for keeping it in the family? We used to do the tax returns for wife's business. Now husband gave us a ring. He wants us to represent him in a divorce proceeding.**

One big happy family. The question will be whether there is a substantial relationship between the work you did for wife and the divorce matter. That turns on a couple of questions. How long ago did you do the tax return? And could the confidential information you discovered about wife's business play some role in the divorce proceeding? Maybe the only issue between them is child custody. On the other hand if your work for wife's business was recent and the estranged couple is feuding about division of property, you should decline husband's invitation, because if you don't, wife can have you disqualified [§8.08].

### ▶§6.33(d) The Substantial Relationship Test

To implement your continuing duty of confidentiality, courts have created the "substantial relationship" test, which gauges whether it is likely you had access to facts that are substantially related to a matter you now wish to pursue against a former client.[53] Matters are substantially related if the current matter involves the same work you performed for the former client, or if there is a substantial risk that representing a current client will allow you to use confidential information from your former client.

To apply this standard, use a three-prong analysis:

1. Identify your former client(s) and the nature and scope of the prior representation(s).

2. Identify your current or prospective client and the nature and scope of the present matter.

3. Inquire whether, in the course of the prior representation, the client *might* have disclosed to you confidences which could be relevant to the present representation and detrimental to the former client.[54]

Note that this test creates an irrebuttable presumption that you received client confidences in the prior matter relevant to the scope and nature of that representation. The fact that you did not, or cannot remember anything is irrelevant. Otherwise, the former client would have to prove what you know (essentially giving up confidentiality) in order to protect his or her rights. If the current client's interests are materially adverse to the former client's and the matters are substantially related, you may not proceed with the current matter unless the former client consents. Some jurisdictions [§§9.04, 9.06] allow for nonconsensual screens [§6.34] to prevent imputation of a limited number of former-client conflicts in the case of firm-switching lawyers, but most allow the screen only if the former client consents to it.

▶ **§6.33(e) The Substantially Related Transaction?**

**I represented a guy who wanted to build a shopping center out by the interstate. We got him zoning two years ago. Now he's negotiating with Target to become a tenant. Guess who Target called? Can I do it?**

---

[53] Model Rule 1.9(a); RLGL §132.
[54] *Kanaga v. Gannett Co. Inc.*, 1993 Del. Super LEXIS 341 (Del. Super. Ct. Oct. 21, 1993).

We take it the shopping center guy is a former client?

**Well, I never terminated him but he paid his final bill more than a year ago.**

That raises a good point. Lawyers get most of their business from existing clients. So when one matter for a client is completed we hope there'll be another call. On the other hand, we don't want all our clients to remain present clients forever—that would create both possible ongoing duties and endless conflicts (without generating additional fees). So whether a client is now a former client is often an issue [§ 6.33(b)].

**Thanks for the advice. But in this case we can assume the shopping guy is a former client. Otherwise he might have called me on the Target lease.**

Right. So then the question is whether this matter is substantially related to what you did on the zoning. Superficially it would appear to be. It's the same shopping center. But the analysis is more nuanced than that. Since the substantial relationship test is a stalking horse for whether you have confidential information from the prior representation that could be used in this one, the question is whether the two representations deal with similar legal or factual issues.[55] Zoning deals with one set of issues. Leasing would appear to deal with a completely different set. Therefore, you have an excellent chance of successfully arguing there is no substantial relationship. This does not mean that the shopping center owner won't object, claiming you know important confidential information about his leasing strategy. He just shouldn't succeed, unless he can establish that you do.[56]

**What if we're asked to represent a competing shopping center across the street?**

Great question. Generally lawyers can represent competitors. Indeed some lawyers specialize in representations of a particular industry and use that expertise as an inducement to get retained. The question here will be whether the representation of the first shopping center developer brought to your attention confidential information that

---

[55] Model Rule 1.9(a).
[56] Model Rule 1.9(c).

could be used to the detriment of your former client in connection with this new opportunity. You can be sure if your first client is angry enough about your new foray, such an assertion will be made. Only you and ultimately a court can determine whether it has any validity. But if there is no substantial relationship between the two matters, the former client will have the burden to demonstrate that the lawyer has this specific information.

**There's an environmental group that claims our guy's shopping center will harm the local watershed. I can tell you when we handled the zoning matter the word environmental was never mentioned. So there's no substantial relationship if we want to handle the environmental group's claim, right?**

Well, the legal issues may be distinct. But what the hell are you doing taking money from a client to get him zoning, then sabotaging the whole enterprise on the basis of run-off from the parking lots? The applicable ethical doctrine is known colloquially as "fouling your own nest" and that's what you'd be doing if you took on this matter. Life's too short and you're too good a lawyer.

### ▶ §6.34 SCREENS AND IMPUTATION FOR FORMER-CLIENT CONFLICTS

### ▶ §6.34(a) Screens When?

**I've heard about screening. Is that just a made-up idea?**

Not at all. The rules of all jurisdictions [§9.04] permit the screening, without client consent, of government lawyers who leave public service.[57] Those lawyers are barred from being involved in any matter in which they were substantially and personally involved, but their new firms can handle such matters if they screen the former government lawyer from any participation in the matter. This special rule was adopted to encourage lawyers to undertake government service and not render these individuals unemployable by the very firms most likely to want to hire them because those firms deal regularly with those agencies.

---

[57] Model Rule 1.11; RLGL §124 (3).

§6.34(c)  THE LOYALTY OBLIGATION • 179

The other exception for screening—without client consent—involves judges, arbitrators, and mediators who join a firm.[58] The fact that the judge, arbitrator, or mediator presided over a matter does not prohibit the firm from taking a substantially related matter so long as the judge, arbitrator, or mediator is screened from the matter.

## ▶ §6.34(b) The Joy Of Screening

### What is a screen?

A great question. The word screen is used casually, but rarely are the requirements for an "effective" screen the subject of serious consideration. A screen should keep the individual with confidential information away from anyone on the other side of the screen. That really means the integrity of everyone involved is the only real safeguard for confidential information. Beyond that a screen might include memos reminding all lawyers of its existence, legending files to limit access, and establishing computer firewalls regarding these same matters. But those efforts are much more form than substance; substance comes from being able to trust everyone involved not to learn what the screened lawyers know.

### How come I hear people talk about screens so often?

Because oftentimes law firms, in order to induce a client or former client to consent to a conflicting representation, will offer to screen the lawyers working for the client from the lawyers working on the matter that created the conflict. These are voluntary screens. The client knows the nature of the matter and the identity of the lawyers involved and is totally free to make a case-by-case decision whether this screen is likely to be effective and whether its likelihood of effectiveness is enough incentive to cause the client to consent. Compare that with a situation, proposed at one time but firmly rejected by the ABA, that would simply inform the affected client that a conflict has arisen but that the problem has been solved by the institution of a screen.

## ▶ §6.34(c) Chart: State Lawyer Code Rules That Allow Screens To Prevent Imputed Disqualification[59]

---

[58] Model Rule 1.12.

[59] This chart compiles the Lawyer Code provisions in the named jurisdictions. It does *not* compile judicial decisions which may allow screens in some circumstances.

|  | Former Clients | Former Gov't Officers and Employees | Former Judge, (J), Arbitrator (A), Mediator, (M), or other Third-Party Neutral | Prospective Clients

Other |
|---|---|---|---|---|
| ABA Model Rules | Only with former client consent, 1.9(a), 1.10(a) | 1.11(b), (c); yes | 1.12 (c) J, A, and M, yes | 1.18(d) yes |
| Alabama | Only with former client consent, 1.9(a), 1.10(a) | 1.11(a), (b); yes | 1.12 (c) J, A; yes | None |
| Alaska | Only with former client consent, 1.9(a), 1.10(a) | 1.11(a), (b); yes | 1.12 (c) J, A; yes | None |
| Arizona | Only with former client consent, 1.9(a), 1.10(a) | 1.11 (a), (b); yes | 1.12 (c) J, A and M; yes | 1.18(d) yes |
| Arkansas | Only with former client consent, 1.9(a), 1.10(a) | 1.11(b), (c); yes | 1.12 (c), J, A and M; yes | None |
| California | Only with former client consent, 3-310(E) | None | None | None |
| Colorado | Only with former client consent, 1.9(a), 1.10(a) | 1.11(a), (b) | 1.12 (c) J, A; yes |  |
| Connecticut | Only with former client consent, 1.9(a), 1.10(a) | 1.11(a), (b) | 1.12 (c) J, A; yes | None |
| Delaware | 1.9(a), 1.10(a); yes | 1.11(b), (c) | 1.12 (c) J, A and M; yes | 1.18(d); yes |
| District of Columbia | Only with former client consent, 1.9, 1.10(a) | 1.11(d); yes | 1.11(c), J, yes; | 1.10(a)[60] |

---

[60] No imputed disqualification if lawyer consults with a potential client.

§6.34(c)      The Loyalty Obligation • 181

| | Former Clients | Former Gov't Officers and Employees | Former Judge, (J), Arbitrator (A), Mediator, (M), or other Third-Party Neutral | Prospective Clients<br><br>Other |
|---|---|---|---|---|
| **Florida** | Only with former client consent, 4-1.9(a), 4-1.10(a) | 4-1.11(a), (b); yes | 4-1.12 (c) J, A; yes | None |
| Georgia | Only with … | 1.11(a), (b); yes | 1.12 (c), J, A; yes | None |
| | | | 1.12 (c) J, A; yes | None |
| | | yes | 1.12(c), J, A, and M, yes | 1.18(d); yes |
| | | ; yes | 1.12(c); J, A; yes | None |
| | | ; yes | 1.12(c), J, A, and M; yes | 1.18(d); yes |
| | | (c); | 32:1.12 (c) J, A, and M, yes | 32:1.18(d) yes |
| | consent, 32:1.9(a), 32:1.10(a) | | | |
| **Kansas** | Only with former client consent, 1.9(a), 1.10(a) | 1.11(a), (b); yes | 1.12(c), J, A; yes | None |
| **Kentucky** | Only with former client consent, 1.9(a), 1.10(a) | 1.11(a), (b); yes | 1.12(c), J, A; yes | None |
| **Louisiana** | Only with former client consent, 1.9(a), 1.10(a) | 1.11(b), (c); yes | 1.12(c), J, A, and M; yes | None |

182 • Red Flags                                                              §6.34(c)

| | Former Clients | Former Gov't Officers and Employees | Former Judge, (J), Arbitrator (A), Mediator, (M), or other Third-Party Neutral | Prospective Clients<br><br>Other |
|---|---|---|---|---|
| **Maine** | Only with former client consent, 3.4(d)(1) | 3.4(d)(2); yes | 3.4(g)(2) J, A; yes<br>3.4(h)(7) M; yes | None<br><br>3.4(b)(3)(ii); yes (Law School Clinics) |
| **Maryland** | 1.9(a), 1.10(c); yes | 1.11(b), (c); yes | 1.12(c), J, A, M; yes | 1.18(d), yes |
| **Massachusetts** | 1.9(a), 1.10(a), 1.10(d); yes | 1.11(a), (b); yes | 1.12(c), J, A; yes | None |
| **Michigan** | 1.9(a), 1.10(a); yes | 1.11(a), (b); yes | 1.12(c), J, A; yes | None |
| **Minnesota** | 1.9(a), 1.10(a), 1.10(b); yes | 1.11(a), (b); yes | 1.12(c), J, A; yes | None |
| **Mississippi** | Only with former client consent, 1.9(a), 1.10(a) | 1.11(a), (b); yes | 1.12(c), J, A; yes | None |
| **Missouri** | Only with former client consent, 4-1.9(a); 4-1.10(a); 4-1.10(c) | 4-1.11(a), (b); yes | 4-1.12(c), J, A, yes | None |
| **Montana** | Only with former client consent, 1.9(a); 1.10(c); 1.10(d) | 1.11(b); 1.11(c); yes | 1.12(c) J, A, and M; yes | 1.20(d), yes |
| **Nebraska** | Only with former client consent, DR 5-108 | None | None | None<br><br>Support Personnel: Only with former client consent, DR 5-109 |
| **Nevada** | SCR 160; yes | SCR 161(1), (2); yes | SCR 162 (3) J, A; yes | SCR 156.1(4), 156.1(6); yes |

§6.34(c)            THE LOYALTY OBLIGATION • 183

| | Former Clients | Former Gov't Officers and Employees | Former Judge, (J), Arbitrator (A), Mediator, (M), or other Third-Party Neutral | Prospective Clients<br><br>Other |
|---|---|---|---|---|
| **New Hampshire** | Only with former client consent, 1.9(a); 1.10(a), (b), (c) | 1.11(a), (b); yes | 1.12 (c) J, A; yes | None |
| **New Jersey** | 1.9(a); 1.10(c); yes | 1.11(c); yes | 1.12(b); J, A, and M; yes | 1.18(c); yes |
| **New Mexico** | Only with former client consent, R 16-109(A); R 16-110(D) | R 16-111(A), (B); yes | R 16-112(C); J, A yes | None |
| **New York** | Only with former client consent, DR 5-108 [1200.27] | DR 9-101(B) [1200.45], yes | None | None |
| **North Carolina** | 1.9(a); 1.10(c); yes | 1.11(b); 1.11(c); yes | 1.12(b); J, A, and M; yes | 1.18(d); yes |
| **North Dakota** | Only with former client consent 1.9(a), (b); 1.10(d) | 1.11(a), (b); yes | 1.12(c); J, A; yes | None |
| **Ohio** | Only with former client consent, DR 5-105; DR 4-101(D) | None | None | None |
| **Oklahoma** | Only with former client consent, 1.9; 1.10 | 1.11(a); 1.11(b) | 1.12(c); J, A: | None |
| **Oregon** | 1.9(a); 1.10(c); yes | 1.11(b), (c); yes | 1.12(c); J, A, and M; yes | 1.18(d); yes |
| **Pennsylvania** | 1.9(a), 1.10 (b); yes | 1.11(b), (c); yes | 1.12(c); J, A, and M; yes | None |

|  | Former Clients | Former Gov't Officers and Employees | Former Judge, (J), Arbitrator (A), Mediator, (M), or other Third-Party Neutral | Prospective Clients<br><br>Other |
|---|---|---|---|---|
| Rhode Island | Only with former client consent, 1.9(a), 1.10(a) | 1.11(a); yes | 1.12 (c) J, A; yes | None |
| South Carolina | Only with former client consent, 1.9(a), 1.10(a) | 1.11(a), (b); yes | 1.12 (c) J, A; yes | None |
| South Dakota | Only with former client consent, 1.9(a), 1.10(a) | 1.11(b), (c); yes | 1.12 (c) J, A; yes | 1.18(d); yes |
| Tennessee | Only with former client consent, 1.9(a), 1.10(a) | 1.11(a), (b); yes | 1.12(b), (c)J, A; yes 2.4 (e)(2) M: no | None |
| Texas | Only with former client consent, 1.09(a), (b) | 1.10(b), (d); yes | 1.11(c) J; Yes | None |
| Utah | Only with former client consent, 1.9(a), 1.10(a), (b) | 1.11(a), (b); yes | 1.12 (c)J, A; yes | None |
| Vermont | Only with former client consent, 1.9(a), 1.10(c) | 1.11(a), (b); yes | 1.12 (c) J, A; yes | None |
| Virginia | Only with former client consent, 1.9(a), 1.10(a) | 1.11(b), (c); yes | 1.12 (c) J, A; yes 1.10(a), 2.10(e) M; no | None |
| Washington | 1.9(a), 1.10(e); yes | 1.11(b), (c); yes | 1.12 (c)J, A and M; yes | None |
| West Virginia | Only with former client consent, 1.9(a), 1.10(a) | 1.11(a), (b); yes | 1.12 (c)J, A; yes | None |

| | Former Clients | Former Gov't Officers and Employees | Former Judge, (J), Arbitrator (A), Mediator, (M), or other Third-Party Neutral | Prospective Clients<br><br>Other |
|---|---|---|---|---|
| Wisconsin | Only with former client consent, SCR 20:1.9(a), 20:1.10(a) | SCR 20:1.11(a), (b); yes | SCR 20:1.12 (d) J, A; yes | None |
| Wyoming | Only with former client consent, 1.9(a), 1.10 (c) | 1.11(a), (b); yes | 1.12 (c)J, A; yes | None |

## ▶ §6.35 FORMER CLIENTS AND PERIPHERAL REPRESENTATION

### ▶ §6.35(a) The Lateral Hire?

When we hire new lawyers we try so hard to be conscientious about conflicts. But this proves you can never be conscientious enough. We hired a third-year associate from a New York law firm. The associate told us everything she worked on. We're clear. So we hire her and, boom, a motion to disqualify us is filed in one of our really big cases. Seems, or so they claim, she worked on this case where we are on the other side. She'd forgotten the whole thing but now she vaguely recalls doing a research memo in her second week at the firm on—of all things—a motion to disqualify that was denied. She claims she spent less than two hours on the research, which was strictly related to the legal question of how long can you delay filing a motion to disqualify. On the basis of that, we are going to be disqualified?

We can understand your dismay; you were careful. You correctly recognized that the only conflicts the associate brought with her from her old firm are those arising from matters on which she worked and matters as to which she actually acquired "confidential information." The associate didn't remember the assignment, even though her work, whatever it was, was client confidential. Under these circumstances, you certainly can resist a motion to disqualify in good faith. There are a fair number of cases that label your associate's participation "peripheral" and refuse to disqualify a law firm in circumstances similar to these, on the grounds that the associate never "represented" the former client. This just goes to demonstrate that every time a technical violation of the professional rules occurs, the aggrieved party will not necessarily succeed in convincing a court to grant the ultimate sanction [§9.05].

### ▶§6.35(b) The Peripheral Representation Exception

There may be many situations where you did not actually "represent" a former client, but your law firm did, or you represented an organization and a constituent now claims he or she was your client. In these circumstances, as long as you are still at the same law firm, the conflict remains imputed. But if you have left the law firm, courts may view your prior representation as "peripheral" or "vicarious" and allow you to rebut the presumption that confidential information was received.[61] If, for example, you worked at a fairly large law firm and billed a few hours of research to a matter but did not otherwise have access to the client's file, once you leave the firm, you may be able to rebut the presumption, making it more likely your new firm will escape disqualification and keep its new client.[62] The same issue occasionally arises in joint defense agreements when separately represented parties agree to share some information [§6.22],[63] and when lawyers represent associations and members have supplied confidences to facilitate the representation [§6.29(d)].[64]

### ▶§6.36 FORMER CLIENTS AND ACTUAL RECEIPT OF CONFIDENTIAL INFORMATION

The peripheral representation rule won't help you if you actually received confidential client information even though you never worked

---

[61] Model Rule 1.9(b); RLGL §124(1).

[62] *Silver Chrysler Plymouth, Inc. v. Chrysler Motors Corp.*, 518 F.2d 751 (2d Cir. 1975).

[63] *Associated Wholesale Grocers, Inc. v. Americold Corp.*, 975 P.2d 231 (Kan. 1999) (lawyer who represented co-party under joint defense agreement not disqualified when agreement did not address sharing of confidential information and movant was unable to show that information was actually shared); *Analytica, Inc. v. NPD Research, Inc.*, 708 F.2d 1263 (7th Cir. 1983) (law firm disqualified because co-counsel relationship gave it access to potentially relevant confidential data).

[64] *Westinghouse Elec. Corp. v. Kerr-McGee Corp.*, 580 F.2d 1311 (7th Cir. 1978) (law firm disqualified at motion of members of a trade association former client when members provided confidential information to facilitate association's prior representation).

on the matter. For example, if your firm (but not you) represented a client, but you looked over the file or answered a phone call from that client, or shared office space with an associate working on the matter, you may have been privy to such information. If you leave the firm, that former client can have your new firm disqualified upon a showing that you were aware of such information.[65]

## ▶ §6.37 CONFLICTS OF INTEREST: FORMER GOVERNMENT LAWYERS

### ▶ §6.37(a) A Typhoid Mary?

**We've got a double-barreled problem. We've got a case with the FDA that's been going on for years. One of their top lawyers is looking to leave the agency. We're drooling to get her. But two years ago she gave a deposition *in our case*. If we hire her, does our client have to hire new counsel because of the ethics rules?**

Let's focus on hiring someone from the FDA, first. You are certainly free to hire her. The Ethics in Government Act, however, makes it a felony for her to appear or communicate with the FDA about the matter. The Model Rules mirror this requirement. If she was not personally and substantially involved in the pending matter, there are no conditions to the hire. If she was so involved, then your firm can continue to handle the matter as long as you notify the government and screen the new lawyer from the matter. Because we want to encourage lawyers to work in public service and not become so many Typhoid Marys when they look for post-government employment (employment which most likely would be with the firms that most often appear before the agency), the rules craft this exception to the normal treatment of the side-switching lawyer.

**What about the fact that she might be a witness?**

The Model Rule, unlike the old Model Code, provides for disqualification of the testifying lawyer, but not the firm, as long as the testimony does not materially and adversely affect the client. You must discuss with your client the possible detriment to the client's cause that might arise from calling a witness who is a lawyer at the client's law firm, something you had better do before you hire the FDA lawyer. But assuming the client consents to the arrangement, then there is no

---

[65] Model Rule 1.9(c); RLGL §132(2).

reason why the representation may not proceed. Cobbling together two exceptions will carry the day here [§7.15].

### ▶ §6.37(b) Legal Regulation Of Former Government Lawyers

Two bodies of law regulate the conduct of former government lawyers:

1. State and federal conflict of interest statutes, which govern the conduct of current and former government employees; and

2. Lawyer codes provisions [§9.04], which prohibit adverse representation against the former governmental agency in the same matter in which the lawyer participated "personally and substantially."[66] The former governmental unit can consent to this conflict, and the law firm can set up a nonconsensual screen of the tainted lawyer, which will allow the firm to take on the representation regardless of the former agency's wishes. Government lawyers also are prohibited from using confidential information acquired about private persons against those persons when they leave public employment.[67]

Some jurisdictions [§9.06] extend the substantial relationship test applied to former clients [§6.33(d)] in general to former government lawyers as well. The current version of Model Rule 1.11 restricts the application of this rule to actual receipt of confidential information while a government lawyer.[68]

### ▶ §6.38 CONFLICTS OF INTEREST: JUDGES, ARBITRATORS, AND THIRD-PARTY NEUTRALS

### ▶ §6.38(a) The Mediator Lawyer?

**If I mediated a dispute between A & B, can my firm take on a substantially related matter on behalf of A versus B?**

So long as you are screened, under new Model Rule 1.12 that is a permissible albeit surprising result.

---

[66] Model Rule 1.11(a); RLGL §133(1).

[67] Model Rule 1.11(c); RLGL §133(2)(a).

[68] Model Rule 1.11(a)(1); RLGL §133(2)(b).

### ▶ §6.38(b) Subsequent Law Practice Of Adjudicative Officers And Mediators

Model Rule 1.12 prohibits judges, arbitrators, and mediators from representing anyone in connection with a matter in which they personally and substantially participated without the consent of all parties, but like Model Rule 1.11, Model Rule 1.12 allows a law firm to screen the disqualified person and handle the matter.[69] This rule also prohibits judges, arbitrators, and mediators from negotiating for employment with any party to a matter over which they currently preside, but law clerks can do so if they notify their supervisors.[70] Some courts additionally [§9.06] apply the substantial relationship test [§6.33(d)] to former mediators, because of their access to confidential information.[71]

Extension of Rule 1.12's narrower scope of subsequent disqualification and its screening provisions to former mediators is somewhat controversial. Because mediators, unlike judges and arbitrators, have been privy to confidential information of the parties mediated, permitting a law firm to handle a matter (or a substantially related matter) formerly mediated by a law firm lawyer, so long as that lawyer-mediator is screened, still requires a significant leap of faith by the party adverse to the law firm whose confidences were shared with the mediator-lawyer at an earlier date. As a result, not all jurisdictions take as broad a view of the subsequent disqualifications of mediators as does Model Rule 1.12.

---

[69] Model Rule 1.12; RLGL §133.

[70] Model Rule 1.12(b).

[71] *Poly Software Int'l v. Su*, 880 F. Supp. 1487 (D. Utah 1995).

# Part Three

# Responding To ▶Red Flags▶: The Limits Of The Law

### THE LIMITS OF THE LAW

Once you understand your fiduciary duties to clients—the 4 C's—your life should be easier. You fulfill your professional obligation to clients by competently communicating with them, keeping their confidences, and remaining loyal to their interests. At the same time, every agency relationship is subject to one limitation: Neither the principal's power to control the representation nor the agent's duty to obey the principal allows either to violate the limits of the law. Agreeing to represent a client does not mean that you merge your personality with the client's. Agency law assumes that both of you remain responsible for the consequences of your conduct as autonomous legal persons.

Although it is obvious that killing a witness to prevent a client's conviction can get both of you thrown into jail and get you disbarred, many other legal limits which can result in similar consequences are much less clear [§7.01]. Our goal in this chapter is to alert you to these bodies of law, so that you understand both what it means to say "yes" to a client (the 4 C's) and when you must say "no" (to avoid incompetence and illegal conduct).

Every legal representation presents the need for you to know and communicate the limits of the law. If your client has used your services to stray outside these bounds, you must do something about it. In all of these situations, you should follow a four-step analysis:

1. Be competent. You must know the relevant law and facts that govern a client representation, including the law that limits your own and your client's behavior.

2. Communicate any relevant legal limits to your client. If you represent an organization, you have special obligations to disclose serious legal violations beyond your immediate supervisor.

3. If your client seeks to use or has used your services to effectuate illegal activity, withdraw from the representation.

4. Determine whether and when you also may or must disclose confidential information to prevent, mitigate, or rectify client harm.

# 7

# The Limits Of Zealous Representation: When You Must Say "No"

➤ §7.01 Chart: Legal Sources Of Some Common Limits Of The Law
➤ §7.02 Withdrawal: Voluntary And Involuntary
   ➤ §7.02(a) When You Really Want To Get Out?
   ➤ §7.02(b) Do I Have A Lien?
   ➤ §7.02(c) Legal Grounds For Withdrawal
   ➤ §7.02(d) Wrongful Termination?
➤ §7.03 Crime: Lawyer And Client
   ➤ §7.03(a) The Ponzi Scheme?
   ➤ §7.03(b) The Criminal Law And Professional Obligation
➤ §7.04 Fraud: Lawyer And Client
   ➤ §7.04(a) The Client Who (Most Likely) Won't Be Caught?
   ➤ §7.04(b) The Tester?
   ➤ §7.04(c) The Law Of Fraud And Professional Obligation
   ➤ §7.04(d) The Lying Tax Auditee?
➤ §7.05 Procedural Rules: Frivolous Lawsuits
   ➤ §7.05(a) The Last-Minute Lawsuit?
   ➤ §7.05(b) Legal Regulation Of Frivolous Advocacy
➤ §7.06 Procedural Rules: Discovery Abuse
   ➤ §7.06(a) The Damaging Documents?

➤ 7.06(b) Legal Regulation Of Discovery Abuse

➤ §7.07 Court Orders And Contempt

➤ §7.08 Candor To The Tribunal

➤ §7.08(a) The Undiscovered Case?

➤ §7.08(b) The Undiscovered Conviction?

➤ §7.08(c) The Undiscovered Witness?

➤ §7.09 Bias

➤ §7.09(a) The Sexist Opponent?

➤ §7.10 Contact With Represented And Unrepresented Persons

➤ §7.10(a) The Worthless Lawyer?

➤ §7.10(b) The Former CEO?

➤ §7.10(c) Employees?

➤ §7.10(d) The Justice Department Badges?

➤ §7.10(e) The Scared Defendant?

➤ §7.10(f) Legal Regulation Of Third-Person Contact

➤ §7.11 *Ex Parte* Communications With Judges And Jurors

➤ §7.11(a) Legal Regulation

➤ §7.11(b) The Misguided Expert?

➤ §7.12 Restrictions On Law Practice

➤ §7.12(a) Make That Lawyer Go Away?

➤ §7.12(b) Business Development?

➤ §7.13 Advertising And Solicitation

➤ §7.13(a) Chat Room Advertising?

➤ §7.13(b) Chart: Advertising, Solicitation, And The First Amendment

➤ §7.14 Trial Publicity

➤ §7.14(a) The Campaigning DA?

➤ §7.15 Lawyer As Witness

➤ §7.15(a) The Involuntary Witness?

➤ §7.16 Other Law: Federal And State Statutes And Regulations

➤ §7.16(a) The Curious IRS?

➤ §7.16(b) Sarbanes-Oxley Obligations Of Lawyers

## ▶ §7.01 CHART: LEGAL SOURCES OF SOME COMMON LIMITS OF THE LAW

| Law | Penalties | Corresponding Model Rule(s) |
|---|---|---|
| **Crime** (Approx. 4,000 Federal and 1,000 State provisions) | Fines, imprisonment [§8.03] | 1.2(d), 8.4(b) |
| **Tort** (e.g. fraud) | Damages, Loss of a Contractual Bargain [§§8.04, 8.05, 8.09] | 1.2(d), 3.3, 4.1, 8.4(c) |
| **Evidence** (privileges) | Contempt, Sanctions [§8.11] | 3.4 |
| **Court Orders** (inherent power of the court) | Disqualification, injunctive relief, court-ordered counsel [§8.08] | 3.4(c) |
| **Procedural Rules** (e.g., Fed. R. Civ. P. 11, 26, 37, 60) | Sanctions, injunctive relief [§§8.08, 8.11] | 3.1, 3.4 |
| **ADR Rules** (arbitration or mediation codes or procedures) | Disqualification [§8.08] | 1.12, 2.4 |
| **Administrative Regulations** (e.g., Sarbanes Oxley) | Agency Disbarment [§7.16] | 1.6(b)(6), 1.13 |
| **Federal and State Conflict of Interest Provisions** | Criminal penalties [§8.03] | 1.11, 1.12 |
| **Constitutional Law** | Professional Discipline (or not) [§8.02] | Advertising and Solicitation: Rules 7.1-7.5 |

## ▶ §7.02 WITHDRAWAL: VOLUNTARY AND INVOLUNTARY
## ▶ §7.02(a) When You Really Want To Get Out?

**My client stopped paying her bills. Can I withdraw?**

We hate involuntary pro bono, too. The question may turn on what your engagement letter says [§1.04]. If you made it clear that failure to pay could provide you with grounds to withdraw, then your right should be clear. No engagement letter or one that does not address the topic requires you to fall back on Model Rule 1.16, the withdrawal rule, which provides that failure of the client to fulfill an obligation to the lawyer regarding the lawyer's services is grounds for withdrawal. Does that cover the payment of fees? One cannot be certain without a clear retainer agreement. In any event, the case law [§9.06] makes it clear that the withdrawal can only come following an adequate warning to the client that withdrawal will be the consequence of a failure to pay.[1] Moreover, if the matter involves a court proceeding, grounds for withdrawal are not enough. The lawyer also must receive permission of the court to withdraw, permission that is not always granted, particularly if no substitute counsel is available or new counsel will substantially delay the case.

## ▶ §7.02(b) Do I Have A Lien?

**This guy already owes me quite a bit. If I withdraw, may I refuse to share my files with successor counsel until I get paid?**

That is not a question of ethics. Although the professional rules [§9.04] require that you cooperate with the client's securing of new counsel, and require that you surrender "papers and property to which the client is entitled,"[2] the rules punt on the question of whether you may retain the file as if you had a lien to secure your payment. For the answer to that question, you will have to consult the law of your jurisdiction. Some authorize it; others specifically prohibit the practice; and others distinguish between different kinds of liens, such as charging and retaining liens.[3] So be careful.

---

[1] *Gilles v. Wiley, Malehorn & Sirota*, 783 A.2d 756 (N.J. Super. Ct. App. Div. 2001).

[2] ABA Model Rule of Professional Conduct 1.16(d) (2002) (hereinafter "Model Rules").

[3] *Restatement of the Law Third, The Law Governing Lawyers*, §43 (ALI 2000) (hereinafter "RLGL"); Hazard & Hodes, §20.12.

### ▶ §7.02(c) Legal Grounds For Withdrawal

There are times you must get out (subject to the permission of a tribunal).[4] Three general circumstances require involuntary withdrawal from a client representation even if you wish or your client wants you to continue:

1. Your continued representation of a client would result in a violation of the rules of professional conduct [§9.04]. This could occur because you lack competence to complete the matter [Chapter 4], or because a conflict of interest [Chapter 6] becomes nonconsentable [§6.09] or you cannot secure the necessary consent to a consentable conflict [§3.05], or because your client insists that you engage in or assist the client in engaging in criminal or fraudulent conduct during the course of the representation [§§7.03, 7.04].

2. Your physical or mental condition materially impairs your representation of a client or clients.

3. Your client fires you. Clients have the absolute right to fire lawyers at any time for any or no reason.

Beyond involuntary withdrawal, you also have discretion to withdraw in a wide variety of circumstances (subject to the permission of a tribunal), including:

1. Any time withdrawal can be accomplished without adverse effect on a client's interests, e.g., for no reason.

2. Even if the withdrawal might adversely affect the client's interests, (a) when you reasonably believe (but do not yet "know") that your client persists in criminal or fraudulent conduct and your client has used your services to perpetrate a crime [§7.03] or fraud [§7.04]; (b) or your client insists upon action that you consider repugnant; (c) or the client has otherwise rendered the representation unreasonably difficult; (d) or your client substantially fails to fulfill a financial obligation after you have given a reasonable warning that you will withdraw unless the obligation is met; (e) or the representation imposes an unreasonable financial burden on you; (f) or when any other good cause for withdrawal exists. If you decide to withdraw, you must take steps to protect the client's interests by providing reasonable notice, time to employ substitute counsel, and any papers to which the client is enti-

---

[4] Model Rule 1.16; RLGL §32.

tled. You also need a disengagement letter [§1.25] to properly inform your client.

▶ **Red Flag** ▶ Courts do not construe all of the circumstances that appear to justify withdrawal at face value. For example, it is very difficult to show an "unreasonable financial burden" or "repugnance" in many jurisdictions. If you have more than one reason to withdraw, be sure you investigate cases [§9.06] in your jurisdiction to determine which ground will best support your instincts.

### ▶ §7.02(d) Wrongful Termination?

**One of my associates is so upset. We received a call from a lawyer who used to be at our firm and went in-house counsel to get himself the easy life. I think he got what he deserved. Turns out he thought his company was violating some serious environmental regulations. When he complained to the CEO about a plant superintendent's noncompliance, the response he received was a pink slip. Now he wants us to bring a wrongful termination suit. I thought, under our rules, clients were entitled to fire their lawyer at any time for any reason, and our guy's just going to have to look for other employment.**

You are right about the general proposition. Our rules give clients complete autonomy. But in the world of in-house counsel you have a clash between that principle and the protections that are afforded employee whistleblowers. Some jurisdictions have gone one way and adopted your understanding, even where they otherwise would recognize a cause of action for other corporate professional employees such as engineers.[5] Others have said that dismissed in-house counsel have all the rights of any other corporate whistleblower, stressing their dependence and the pressure to conform to corporate misconduct, and recognizing their right to reveal client confidences necessary to bring such a claim under the self-defense exception to confidentiality [§5.11].[6]

**I thought in-house counsel wanted to be treated like real lawyers.**

---

[5] *Balla v. Gambro, Inc.*, 584 N.E.2d 104 (Ill. 1991).
[6] *Crews v. Buckman Laboratories Int'l Inc.*, 78 S.W.3d 852 (Tenn. 2002).

Which lawyers? If you work for a law firm and are fired because you insist that they obey the Rules of Professional Conduct [§9.04], you may have a cause of action.[7] Of course, inside counsel situations involve a suit against a former client, not another lawyer or firm. Here, you're raising a good point but the fact that they are employees makes them seem to pick and choose. They don't want to get admitted in the state where they practice; they want to sue their clients for dismissing them; and, guess what, some courts agree.

### ▶§7.03 CRIME: LAWYER AND CLIENT

#### ▶§7.03(a) The Ponzi Scheme?

**The other lawyer's client. What a crook. I mean that literally. The guy is running a Ponzi scheme. All my client wants is his money back. Can we threaten that we'll report the crook to the U.S. Attorney unless we're paid in 10 days? Maybe that'll get their undivided attention.**

That you can do. The old Model Code prohibited it. But when the Model Rules were adopted, that provision was dropped. So long as the threat of criminal prosecution relates to the underlying civil claim, and does not constitute extortion, you are free to threaten away. Of course you had better have a good faith basis for the allegation. And make sure you direct publication of your complaint to the authorities. No courthouse press conferences. You don't want to buy a libel or slander counterclaim.

#### ▶§7.03(b) The Criminal Law And Professional Obligation

Lawyers have no special immunity from the criminal law, in representing clients or in their own personal conduct outside of law practice. You need to be aware of the contours of the vast scope of the criminal law (approaching 4,000 federal and about 1,000 state crimes) both to avoid committing crimes yourself and to provide competent counsel to clients. Courts typically impose severe disciplinary sanctions [§8.02] on lawyers convicted of serious crimes, including all felonies, and mis-

---

[7] *Wieder v. Skala*, 609 N.E.2d 105 (N.Y. 1992) (law firm associate had valid claim against firm for breach of contract when firm fired him after he insisted that the firm report another lawyer's professional misconduct to the bar).

demeanors that reflect adversely on the lawyer's fitness to practice, such as misrepresentation, fraud, deceit, bribery, extortion, theft and misappropriation, and crimes involving interference with the administration of justice.[8] The Model Rules also require that you refrain from knowingly counseling or assisting a client crime and if necessary, withdraw to prevent this from happening.[9]

You cannot avoid this obligation by stupidity or willful blindness. "Knowingly" means that you know of the client's activity, not that you "know" it constitutes a fraud or crime.[10] Further, your knowledge can be inferred from the circumstances.[11] If you fail to discover the crucial fact you hoped did not exist, you have disserved your client, who could have avoided the crime, and you may have set yourself up for a malpractice suit [§8.06] as well.

In short, you cannot commit a crime, and you cannot counsel or assist your client to do so. Remembering the four-step analysis we laid out in the beginning of Part Three can help you avoid both.

- First, be competent. Know the law and facts of a matter sufficiently to provide competent legal advice. Criminal law has reached into corners where you might not expect it, and a change in what your client does may push the conduct from legal into illegal territory (or vice versa).
- Second, communicate criminal law boundaries to your client and make clear that you do not counsel and cannot assist conduct that crosses those lines.
- Third, if your client's conduct is prospective or continuing, and after your heart-to-heart your client will not desist, you must withdraw to avoid assisting. If you have a reasonable belief but do not know that the conduct constitutes a crime or fraud, you may do so [§7.02(c)].
- Finally, if your client's future conduct threatens serious physical or financial harm, or if your client is an organization, check the excep-

---

[8] Model Rule 8.4(b); RLGL §5; ABA Model Rule for Lawyer Disciplinary Enforcement, Rule 19.

[9] Model Rule 1.2(d); RLGL §23.

[10] *In re Bloom*, 745 P.2d 61 (Cal. 1987) (lawyer could not defend disciplinary charge by arguing he did not know client's transport of plastic explosives to Libya was unlawful).

[11] Model Rule 1.0(f).

tions to confidentiality in your jurisdiction to determine whether you have discretion (or even an obligation) to disclose to prevent or rectify harm [§5.10].

▶**Red Flag**▶ Be especially careful about the criminal law when you represent a heavily regulated client, or when you represent a client in a matter where you have had little experience. Lawyers have been disciplined for helping clients commit crimes that the lawyer did not recognize as criminal.[12]

### ▶§7.04 FRAUD: LAWYER AND CLIENT

### ▶§7.04(a) The Client Who (Most Likely) Won't Be Caught?

My client stopped by for tax advice. As I questioned her closely she told me she had not been paying social security for her nanny. I warned her that the IRS did not look kindly on this kind of lapse. After she told me none of her friends pay it either, she asked what her chances were of getting caught. May I give her such advice?

So long as you don't file any papers that cover up the actual situation and urge the client to comply with the law with an appropriate warning regarding the serious consequences of noncompliance, you are free to provide your client with this information.[13]

### ▶§7.04(b) The Tester?

My client wants me to send one of my paralegals into the Burger Chef commissary posing as a food writer to see if they are using beef tallow to flavor the Freedom fries. What a great idea.

Not so fast. A lawyer may not engage in a misrepresentation. Nor may a lawyer do through the acts of another what the lawyer is prohibited from doing herself. As much as some claim that only good can come from such undercover inspections (somehow your view depends on whether you are the tester or the testee), lawyers run afoul of these

---

[12] *People v. Casey*, 948 P.2d 1014 (Colo. 1997) (lawyer who entered an appearance and got a case dismissed for a client who had given the police a false name assisted the client in committing the crime of criminal impersonation; lawyer suspended for 45 days, despite good faith but unsuccessful attempt to bring his ethical dilemma to a supervising lawyer's attention).

[13] RLGL §94 comment f.

rules if they send their paralegals into the plant.[14] The interesting question is whether the client is free to undertake such conduct. If it is not unlawful for the client, then the question arises whether and to what extent, beyond telling the client of the possibility, the lawyer may participate in the enterprise. It should be noted that there is nothing wrong with a lawyer engaging in surveillance in a public place.[15] It is the misrepresentation of the identity and purpose of the visit that runs afoul of Model Rule 4.1 and 8.4(c).

### ▶§7.04(c) The Law Of Fraud And Professional Obligation

The law of fraud limits the legally acceptable conduct of lawyers and clients. If you or your client commit fraud, civil or criminal consequences could result [§9.05]. If you do so, you also face a third possibility: professional discipline [§8.02]. The Model Rules contain four provisions that effectively incorporate all of the law of fraud, deceit, dishonesty, and misrepresentation into a professional obligation [§9.05]. Lawyers can be disciplined if they make any false statement of material fact to tribunals or third persons while representing clients, whether or not the statement is relied on, or causes harm.[16] Lawyers also can be disciplined for any conduct (representing a client or not) "involving dishonesty, fraud, deceit or misrepresentation."[17] Beyond your own conduct, you can be disciplined for knowingly counseling or assisting your client's fraudulent or criminal conduct.[18]

The vast scope of the modern law of fraud reflects its common occurrence and often-disastrous consequences. Liars are "free riders": Persons who hope to gain an advantage from everyone else's honesty while benefiting from their own deceit.[19] Deceitful practices can undercut competition, raise the price of goods, and cause loss of confidence in the market system by diminishing trust in its mechanisms. In some cases, fraud can chill faith in individual relationships and

---

[14] Model Rules 5.3, 8.4(a).

[15] *Gidatex v. Campaniello Imports, Ltd.*, 82 F.Supp.2d 119 (S.D.N.Y. 1999).

[16] Model Rules 3.3(a)(1) (making false statements of fact to a tribunal), 4.1(a) (making false statement of material fact to a third person).

[17] Model Rule 8.4(c).

[18] Model Rules 1.2(d), 3.3(a)(3) and (b), 4.1(b).

[19] Sissela Bok, *Lying: Moral Choice in Public and Private Life* 23 (Vintage Books, 2d. ed. 1999).

social ties. Your advice can play a central role in avoiding these massive personal and social costs.

The law of fraud includes hundreds of criminal provisions as well as extensive tort liability. Dishonest conduct also creates a defense to otherwise valid claims, and invalidates an otherwise lawful consent in tort, property, and contract law. In short, fraud vitiates everything, even court orders and judgments.[20]

To sum up: you cannot lie, and if your client does, you probably have to do something about it. Lies short of actual fraud or crime do not trigger a duty to remedy a client lie, but if you or your client are close to the line, remember the four steps to identifying and responding to the limits of the law:

1. Competence requires that you know just how close to which legal line the conduct or proposed conduct creeps.

2. Communication demands that you tell your client so, in clear terms.

3. If the conduct is over the line of crime or fraud, you must withdraw. If it makes you worry, and you have a reasonable belief it might constitute a crime or fraud, you may withdraw.

4. If your client will not desist from questionable conduct, you need to identify whether your withdrawal from the matter prevents your assistance in the matter. If it is not enough, check to determine whether your jurisdiction's confidentiality exceptions [§5.06(b)] allow or require disclosure to prevent, mitigate, or rectify the harm. If such an exception exists, you also may also have an obligation to disclose if reasonably necessary to prevent assisting the client's crime or fraud.[21]

►**Ultimate Red Flag**► Recognizing and responding to client fraud creates some of the worst lawyer headaches, and can tempt lawyers to overidentify with clients. We explore this problem further in §10.02.

►**§7.04(d) The Lying Tax Auditee?**

My client lied to an IRS agent during an audit. I couldn't believe it. Is this one of those candor to the tribunal deals?

---

[20] Sydney Edward Williams, *Kerr on Fraud and Mistake* 4 (Sweet & Maxwell, 5th ed. 1920); Fed. R. Civ. P. 60(b).

[21] Model Rule 4.1(b); RLGL §98.

Good question. The duty of candor is triggered when a lawyer appears before certain non-court bodies. Think of an administrative law proceeding or a hearing before City Council on a policy-determining issue. But when the lawyer is simply representing a client in a negotiation or other encounter with a government agency on the other side, that duty does not attach. Nor does it apply when you are representing a client in an investigation by one of these agencies.[22]

That having been said, Model Rule 4.1 does apply. If your client lied to the IRS agent, then you must determine whether the conduct of your client was criminal or fraudulent; if so, then you may be forced to disclose the lie if, but only if, disclosure is necessary to avoid your assisting a criminal or fraudulent act by your client.

The facts you have provided do not suggest that you have assisted your client in any way. Should you have prepared any documents that do reflect the lie, then you may be forced to disavow those. If your client insists on your preparing such documents, you may be forced to withdraw from the representation. Only as a last resort, if you have no alternative to avoid aiding and abetting your client, would you be required to disclose, and then only if the disclosure falls within a specific confidentiality exception in your jurisdiction.

## ▶ §7.05 PROCEDURAL RULES: FRIVOLOUS LAWSUITS
### ▶ §7.05(a) The Last-Minute Lawsuit?

**Client came to us at the last minute. The statute was about to run. Medical malpractice. If the client was correct, the damages were in the millions. Poor guy. So we filed a complaint without consulting an expert. Now we've been searching for someone to testify that the anesthesiologist breached the standard of care. No luck so far. And we've looked everywhere. We're beginning to think there is no claim. Problem is, if we withdraw the complaint now we're worried about a sanctions motion from the other side.**

It is time to cut your losses. You've got a great argument that what you did was correct. You didn't want the statute to run. So you are excused from a need to have consulted an expert pre-complaint. But now that the situation is so bleak, the best course is to withdraw the complaint. Now you know there's no good faith basis for the claim.

---

[22] Model Rule 3.9; RLGL §104.

Now you have a duty to discontinue the proceeding. And don't worry about sanctions. If you are dropping the suit as soon as you should have reasonably known the underlying facts, you're O.K. If, on the other hand, you wait until later, you may be facing sanctions.[23]

### ➤ §7.05(b) Legal Regulation Of Frivolous Advocacy

If you are competent, you won't file a frivolous lawsuit. If you aren't careful, you can be surprised by at least two well-defined bodies of law that govern frivolous court filings:

1. Procedural rules such as Fed. R. Civ. Pro. 11, federal and state statutes, and the inherent power of a court, which provide for monetary sanctions [§8.11] against errant lawyers or clients;[24] and

2. Several provisions of the Model Rules, which prohibit frivolous suits in parallel language and further prohibit lawyers from knowingly violating the rules of a tribunal.[25] This means that the imposition of sanctions can result in professional discipline, and vice versa [§9.05].[26] Claims and assertions must be supported by a good faith basis in law and in fact, including a good faith argument for an extension, reversal, or modification of existing law.[27] You should presume that fact and law investigation are required before you file. If you represent a criminal defendant, you certainly may passively defend the case so as to require that every element of the case is established beyond a reasonable doubt, even if your investigation otherwise leads you to believe that the defense is "frivolous."[28] In criminal appeals, *Anders* briefs require you to disclose "anything in the record that might arguably support the appeal."[29]

---

[23] *Jandrt ex rel. Brueggeman v. Jerome Foods, Inc.*, 597 N.W.2d 744 (Wis. 1999) (complaint filed close to time deadline was not frivolous when filed but became so when lawyer reasonably should have discovered the lack of causation by consulting an expert witness).

[24] Fed. R. Civ. P. 11.

[25] Model Rules 3.1 and 3.4(c); RLGL §§107, 110.

[26] *In re Blasi*, 660 N.Y.S.2d 151 (N.Y. App. Div. 1997) (lawyer was sanctioned for filing meritless lawsuits and suspended from practice five years).

[27] Model Rule 3.1; RLGL §110.

[28] Model Rule 3.1; RLGL §110(2).

[29] *Anders v. California*, 386 U.S. 738 (1967); Hazard & Hodes, §27.14.

▶Red Flag▶ Do not assume you are freed by notice pleading rules to allege a few facts and wait for discovery to find your cause of action. Doing so can result in sanctions [§8.11] and professional discipline [§8.02].[30]

### ▶ 7.06 PROCEDURAL RULES: DISCOVERY ABUSE

#### ▶ 7.06(a) The Damaging Documents?

**The bad news is my client unearthed some very damaging documents. They really will hurt my client's case. The good news is I think I've found the perfect defense to producing them. These documents came out of the warehouse of my client's subsidiary in Germany. We'll just respond that it's too burdensome for us to search for documents at any subsidiary and far too burdensome to search outside the mainland United States. No judge is going to let them go on such a fishing expedition.**

Well, you could get lucky and the other side could accept your objection. Or on motion practice the judge could rule your way. The problem is that you are misstating to the court and the other side the burden of producing *these* documents. You've already identified them. A similar ploy was tried on the *Fisons* case. Somehow the documents came out. And then the wrath of the court fell on the lawyers. Interposing such an objection was viewed harshly. And a very expensive sanction ($325,000) followed.[31]

When it comes to the discovery process, good lawyering often trumps clever objections. Even if you can assert some basis for delaying production of certain information, the question we lawyers must always ask is whether the approach is best for the client in the long run. How will the judge view the objection? What if the documents otherwise surface? Pyrrhic victories are rarely touted on law firm websites.

#### ▶ 7.06(b) Legal Regulation Of Discovery Abuse

Like frivolous lawsuits, discovery rules such as Fed. R. Civ. P. 26 and 37, combined with state and federal statutes and the inher-

---

[30] *Att'y Grievance Comm'n of Md. v. Zdravkovich*, 762 A.2d 950 (Md. 2000) (lawyer disciplined following a Rule 11 sanction for failing to read a federal statute that would have made it clear that removal was not allowed).

[31] *Wash. State Physicians Inc. Exch. & Ass'n v. Fisons Corp.*, 858 P.2d 1054 (Wash. 1993).

ent power of the court regulate how and when you must disclose information [§8.11]. Several provisions of the Model Rules incorporate these procedural rules [§9.05], subjecting you to professional discipline [§8.02] if you violate the procedural rule, or otherwise unlawfully obstruct another party's access to evidence or alter a document [§10.09(a)].[32]

### ▶§7.07 COURT ORDERS AND CONTEMPT

Courts have inherent power to control the conduct of matters before them, including the conduct of lawyers, parties, and witnesses. Your role as an advocate is subject not only to the limit of procedural rules, but also to specific orders of the court, such as judicial rulings about the admissibility of evidence and the application of an evidentiary privilege. Once the order is made, a lawyer must obey, appeal, or risk a contempt citation. A finding of civil contempt allows a judge to impose fines or imprisonment until a person complies with the court order [§8.08]. Criminal contempt punishes refusal to comply and requires elaborate procedural guarantees, similar to those in criminal trials. This power of court orders is recognized in several key provisions of the Model Rules, such as Model Rule 1.6(b)(6), which allows lawyers to disclose client information when "required by law or court order," and Model Rule 3.4(c), which requires lawyers to obey the rules of a tribunal, including court orders.[33]

Court orders also can be sought to assist your advocacy on behalf of a client. Model Rules 3.5(b) and (c) prohibit contact with jurors, unless authorized by law or court order, and Model Rule 4.2 recognizes that court orders can authorize contact with represented persons that might otherwise be prohibited by the rules.

### ▶§7.08 CANDOR TO THE TRIBUNAL

### ▶§7.08(a) The Undiscovered Case?

**You can solve this one for us. We're on appeal. The other side filed its brief. Fortunately they didn't find this key case. Can't imagine how they missed it. Since it's pure dicta, I don't think we should cite it. My colleague says we must.**

---

[32] Model Rule 3.4(a)-(c); RLGL §118-120.
[33] *See also*, RLGL §105.

It all depends. But before you address your obligation under the rules [§9.04] you might think about good lawyering. If the court discovers the case and you haven't told the court how the troubling part is dicta or why it was wrongly decided, the court might not reach those conclusions on its own. Moreover, the other side might cite it in its reply and allege you violated the applicable rule in not citing it yourself. So answer those lawyering questions first. Then if you decide you'd prefer not to cite it, you can consider your obligation under the rule. For that purpose you have to determine whether (a) this case is legal authority or it is, in fact, mere dicta; (b) this is a case in the controlling jurisdiction; and (c) this case is directly adverse to the position of your client. If in good faith you can wiggle out of any of these requirements, then you are not obliged to cite it.[34] Just don't be surprised if the other side takes a different view of the matter.

### ➤ §7.08(b) The Undiscovered Conviction?

**This candor stuff can go too far. When the judge sentenced my guy to probation today because he had no other convictions I stood silent. It's not my fault the records are so screwed up they didn't find his assault and battery conviction from two years ago.**

If you did not create the error, and your client did not either, you had no obligation to correct the judge. In fact, your duty of confidentiality undoubtedly prevented you from doing so. Even if you had been asked the question point blank, though you could not lie to the tribunal, you would have been permitted to avoid the question.[35] So the candor obligation does not go as far as you might think. Of course, if the judge later discovers the error—and discovers you knew of the error—you might incur the judge's wrath, but that goes with the territory. Any desire to ingratiate ourselves with the judiciary may not compromise our duties to our clients. Good practice, however, recommends that you discuss this dilemma with the client and what could happen if the information comes out later. But it's our bet it would be the rarest client who would urge correction now.

---

[34] Model Rule 3.3(a)(2); RLGL §111.
[35] Model Rule 3.3(a)(1); RLGL §120.

### ▶§7.08(c) The Undiscovered Witness?

**Next thing you know you'll tell me I have to tell the other side that the witness they've been trying to track down is sitting outside the courtroom.**

We don't go that far. Again, this is confidential information. And you have no obligation to help the other side. So long as you avoid any misrepresentation about mystery man's whereabouts, you may remain silent and start your prayers that the mystery man's identity remains your secret until the trial is over.

### ▶§7.09 BIAS

### ▶§7.09(a) The Sexist Opponent?

**She tells us that the lawyer on the other side was oppressive, kept referring to her as a "girl lawyer," and commented on her clothing, while the judge just seemed to enjoy this conduct, and certainly didn't do anything about it. What can we do? Our colleague is really upset.**

Bias in the courtroom is a lingering problem. Many courts have established task forces to identify and ameliorate such conduct and some have specifically amended their professional codes [§9.04] to prohibit various forms of discriminatory conduct.[36] There is no excuse for such behavior. It diminishes the system of justice to have lawyers disparage their colleagues, and it is up to the judge, if the conduct occurs in the courtroom, to correct the situation. You or your colleague can help the court by pointing out that lawyers have been sanctioned [§8.11], lost fees [§8.10], and been professionally disciplined [§8.02] for such conduct. We suggest that your colleague ask the court, on the record, to instruct such oppressive opponents to call her by her name, repeatedly if necessary. You might consider a phone call to the court as well, and perhaps it is time for this particular court to take a more institutional approach to the problem. You might be most helpful by citing the Code of Judicial Conduct, which explicitly prohibits judges

---

[36] Cal. Rule Prof'l Conduct 2-400; D.C. Rule of Prof'l Conduct 9.1; Mich. Rule of Prof'l Conduct 6.5; Ill. Rule of Prof'l Conduct 8.4(a)(9)(A); Minn. Rule of Prof'l Conduct Rule 8.4(g); N.Y. DR 1-102(A)(6); Tex. Disciplinary Rule of Prof'l Conduct 5.08; RLGL §106, comment d.

from manifesting bias or prejudice and requires them not to permit others subject to the judge's direction to do so.[37]

## ▶ §7.10 CONTACT WITH REPRESENTED AND UNREPRESENTED PERSONS

### ▶ §7.10(a) The Worthless Lawyer?

**The party on the other side of a matter just called me up. "My lawyer is expensive and worthless. Without him, I know you and I can settle this matter. My lawyer is the problem."**

Resist the temptation. No matter how many compliments the client on the other side heaps upon you, no matter how delicious the prospect of settling the matter might be to your client, you may not talk to the client or client representative on the other side without the permission of the other client's lawyer. This is so even if the client on the other side claims the lawyer has been fired. And you will want to observe this rule not just because you want to conform your conduct to the applicable standards of professional conduct [§9.04]. Here you have a lawyer who will quickly learn of your transgression and be only too delighted to speed you on your way to a date with disciplinary counsel [§8.02] or a motion to disqualify [§8.08].

### ▶ §7.10(b) The Former CEO?

**I've got a big case against X Corporation. Can I talk off the record to X Corporation's former CEO?**

It depends. Model Rule 4.2 tells us we cannot contact a represented person. When the represented party is an organization, we cannot contact certain employees of the organization. The text of the rule is silent about former employees, but a comment to the Model Rules exempts former employees of represented organizations from the ambit of the rule. Some states, however, have case law [§9.06] that concludes that Model Rule 4.2 covers former employees. So check before you contact. And when you contact you must make it clear to that person what your interest is in the matter because you are then dealing with an unrepresented person. Moreover, any time you contact present or former employees of a represented organization do not seek

---

[37] CJC Canon 3 B(5).

any information that in any way comes close to privileged information of the opposing party—or you might find yourself on the losing end of a disqualification motion in the matter.

### ▶ §7.10(c) Employees?

**My client wants me to contact an employee of the represented organization on the other side. How do I know if I can?**

Back to the minefield. Model Rule 4.2 tells us there are two categories of employees who may not be contacted. They are generally the individuals the organization's lawyer deals with in the representation (who's the lawyer taking instructions from?), and those employees whose conduct may be imputed to the organization (e.g., the truck driver who was at the wheel when the company truck backed into little old lady's SUV). The old Model Rule also included those employees whose admissions might bind the organization (e.g., the plant superintendent who admits the company could not afford to remediate the arsenic drums).

### ▶ §7.10(d) The Justice Department Badges?

**I can't believe it! I told the EPA that we were representing the oil company in its water pollution investigation. Yesterday—that was Sunday—three Justice Department lawyers interviewed the plant manager, the environmental officer, and the shift foreman at their homes. They flashed their badges and told them how much easier it would be if they cooperated! Damn government.**

Your outrage is understandable but may be unavailing. Model Rule 4.2 provides that a lawyer may not contact a represented person. Corporations are entitled to the protections of Model Rule 4.2, as we previously noted. And your calling the EPA should have been enough to assure that if any of these employees fit within the protected categories in your jurisdiction (as it sounds likely they did) then any contacts should have gone through you.

Alas, the federal government has resisted this rule. The civil disobedience has taken various forms. When Richard Thornburg was Attorney General he issued a memorandum seeking to exempt his lawyers from the restrictions of Model Rule 4.2. Attorney General Reno outdid him by issuing regulations to the same effect. The Eighth

Circuit in *McDonnell Douglas* struck down these regulations.[38] Then Congress got into the act, passing the so-called McDade Amendment (in honor of a former Congressman who was unsuccessfully prosecuted by the Justice Department), declaring that all government lawyers were required to comply with applicable state court rules of professional conduct [§9.04], including (or we should say especially) Model Rule 4.2.[39] Then came 9/11, the Patriot Act, and an aggressive Justice Department searching for new law enforcement powers, including its favorite unhappiness: limitations imposed by Model Rule 4.2.

Suffice it to say that in the current state of play the Justice Department maintains that Model Rule 4.2 should not apply pre-indictment, pre-complaint, that it even does not apply post-arrest, pre-indictment and that Model Rule 4.2 interferes with the legitimate needs (whatever they are) of law enforcement.[40] So you see your little question launches you far into controversial terrain. Your attempts to sanction or seek discipline for these Sabbath-violating lawyers will either strike down the indefensible Justice Department position or eviscerate the protections that Model Rule 4.2 provides when the government is on the other side. Good luck.

### ►§7.10(e) The Scared Defendant?

**One of my friends was representing a defendant and his employer in a criminal case. Apparently the defendant gets scared and calls the AUSA to cut a deal. AUSA offers 10 years for cooperation. My friend tells me that is no deal at all. Anything he can do?**

Model Rule 4.2 prevented the AUSA from talking to him at all.

**Oh we know that. But AUSA claims the guy wasn't really being represented because my friend has an impossible conflict of interest.**

Isn't it wonderful the way the government really cares about your friend's ethical obligations? Makes our hearts swell. The fact is

---

[38] *United States ex rel. O'Keefe v. McDonnell Douglas Corp.*, 132 F.3d 1252 (8th Cir. 1998).

[39] 28 U.S.C. §530B.

[40] *United States v. Grass*, 239 F. Supp. 2d 535 (M.D. Pa. 2003) (noncustodial preindictment communications by undercover agents with represented persons, which occur in the course of legitimate criminal investigations are "authorized by law").

that the AUSA should not be deciding these questions. The AUSA should have gone to the court and sought guidance: either the appointment of another lawyer or else an order from the court that the defendant was not represented because he voluntarily waived counsel. The last thing that should happen is for the adverse lawyer—especially one from the government—to decide what is in the best interests of your friend's client. In short, the Model Rule 4.2 violation should provide a sound basis for challenging the AUSA's conduct and reopening the negotiations.[41]

### ▶§7.10(f) Legal Regulation Of Third-Person Contact

These rules [§9.04] are simple, but not always intuitive. You may not contact a person represented by counsel in a matter about the subject of the representation without permission from his or her lawyer. Clients cannot waive this rule, which is designed to protect the relationship of that other client and lawyer and prevent you from interfering in it.[42] Courts can waive it or determine the scope of the responsibility, especially when the represented "person" is an entity.[43] When you deal with unrepresented non-clients, including witnesses, you may not mislead the non-client about your identity and the fact that you represent an opposing party; you must refrain from giving them legal advice except the advice to seek independent counsel; and if you reasonably should know that they misunderstand your role in the matter, you have an affirmative duty to correct the misunderstanding.[44] Of course, if procedural rules [§8.11] also limit your access to a witness, such as an expert, you must abide by those limitations.

---

[41] *United States v. Lopez*, 106 F.3d 309 (9th Cir. 1997) (government's improper *ex parte* contact with defendant created prejudice sufficient to take case out of the heartland of the sentencing guidelines); *In re Howes*, 940 P.2d 159 (N.M. 1997) (AUSA publicly censured for speaking to a represented defendant who initiated contact).

[42] Model Rule 4.2; RLGL §99.

[43] *Messing, Rudavsky & Weliky, P.C. v. President & Fellows of Harvard College*, 764 N.E.2d 825 (Mass. 2002).

[44] Model Rule 4.3; RLGL §103.

## ▶§7.11 *EX PARTE* COMMUNICATIONS WITH JUDGES AND JURORS

### ▶§7.11(a) Legal Regulation

This one is easy: Don't have *ex parte* contact with judges or jurors without specific legal authorization.[45] And don't be misled if either tries to initiate the contact with you.[46] Judges are prohibited from doing so, just as you are.[47] If such contact inadvertently occurs, it usually can be cured with appropriate notice to the other side. When *ex parte* motions are allowed by law, remember that you have enhanced disclosure obligations to compensate for the lack of advocacy on the other side, including the duty to disclose all material facts, whether adverse or not, that will enable the tribunal to make an informed decision.[48]

### ▶§7.11(b) The Misguided Expert?

**The other side is hiring a metallurgical expert whom I know quite well. He testified for me three years ago, and we got a very good result. I hate to see him testifying against my client. We belong to the same church, and the idea I had was to see him next Sunday and try to set up an appointment to persuade him of the error of his ways. My bet is the other side hasn't told him all the facts.**

We hope that is not the only reason you are going to church. Were we you, we would limit the conversations to the contents of the sermon or the quality of the choir. Although the other side's expert is not the client on the other side, too many courts in too many jurisdictions have concluded that contacts with the other side's expert are limited to those permitted by the applicable discovery rules. If the jurisdiction says you are entitled to answers to interrogatories, that is

---

[45] Model Rule 3.5; RLGL §113.

[46] *In re Ragatz*, 429 N.W.2d 488 (Wis. 1988) (lawyer disciplined for responding to ex parte communication of a judge).

[47] *Disciplinary Proceedings Against Aulik*, 429 N.W.2d 759 (Wis. 1988) (judge who initiated contact with lawyer in *In re Ragatz, supra* n. 46, suspended from the bench for 90 days for violating provision substantially the same as current CJC Canon 3 B(7)).

[48] Model Rule 3.3(d); RLGL §112.

what you get. If the jurisdiction permits you to review an expert report, that is what you get. And, if the jurisdiction permits depositions of experts, then that is what you get. Any informal discovery may get you disqualified [§8.08].[49]

## ➤§7.12 RESTRICTIONS ON LAW PRACTICE

### ➤§7.12(a) Make That Lawyer Go Away?

**My client is fed up. It faces one lawsuit after another from the same plaintiff's employment lawyer. And this lawyer is good. Can I make him go away? My client says I should offer the plaintiff an extra $100,000 if her lawyer agrees never to sue my client again.**

We don't think so. Model Rule 5.6 provides that lawyers may not offer or accept agreements that would restrict the right of a lawyer to practice law. That's what this is. Such arrangements are against public policy for a number of reasons. They deny to the public the services of what may be the best and the brightest and, in any event, lawyers of proven ability. They also create a conflict between lawyer and client. Here it is in the client's interest to receive the extra $100,000. It would even be in the client's interest to get an extra dollar. But the cost is no future business for the lawyer as to that defendant.

Things get no better if the money is offered to the lawyer, i.e. an offer to pay the lawyer not to sue the adverse party again. As soon as that "offer" ripens into real discussions, the lawyer and client are in a different but equally disabling conflict [§6.10]. Now the lawyer is negotiating with the adverse party for a payment to the lawyer at the same time the lawyer is supposed to be seeking the most advantageous result for the client at the expense of the adverse party.

Assuming this topic was never broached during the settlement negotiations, after the matter is completed the beleaguered company is free to hire the lawyer to represent it on any matter not substantially related to matters the lawyer handled against it. If the lawyer accepts, then so long as that new representation continues, the lawyer may not take a position directly adverse its new client.

---

[49] Model Rule 3.4(c) and (f); RLGL §116.

➤ **§7.12(b) Business Development?**

We've got this great business development idea. We're going to merge our firm with a local certified financial planning outfit. That way we can offer our clients soup to nuts. They come to us to write their wills. We offer them financial advice, life insurance, investment alternatives. Maybe we'll even add an investment advisor. One-stop shopping.

Multidisciplinary practice. You're not the first to think of this. Multidisciplinary practice. But our rules—for good reason—won't permit it. Model Rule 5.4 says that lawyers may not share fees with non-lawyers. Sounds like all we want to do is keep the money. In fact, it is designed to maintain lawyer independence; to make sure lawyers report to lawyers; to avoid inevitable conflicts of interest; and yes, to prevent American Express or Deloitte & Touche from entering the law business.

**What if we make the financial planners a subsidiary of the firm? That way there'll be no sharing of fees.**

Now you are talking about an ancillary business. Some firms have adopted these vehicles. It is permissible so long as there is no compromise of the protections we guarantee clients. Model Rule 5.7 provides a pretty good roadmap. The ancillary business must be operated in such a way that the clients are not confused about whether they are receiving legal services. They have to understand that the attorney-client privilege will not apply to these services. They have to understand how the ancillary business handles conflicts of interest. It can be done…with care. If you disregard care, clients of the firm may be confused and courts may side with them when they later claim that the lawyer codes [§9.04] provide the correct measure of the firm's responsibility.

➤**Ultimate Red Flag**➤ Ancillary businesses and multidisciplinary practices can create opportunity as well as trouble. We navigate this territory in greater depth in §10.08.

➤**§7.13 ADVERTISING AND SOLICITATION**

➤**§7.13(a) Chat Room Advertising?**

We're looking to expand our business. One of my partners thinks we should start cruising various chat rooms dedicated to

§7.13(b)                WHEN YOU MUST SAY "NO"  •  217

**health problems of the elderly. Maybe we'll pick up a few clients that have taken some of these dangerous drugs Big Pharma markets in the AARP Magazine.**

Slow down. The Supreme Court has held that targeted direct mail to likely clients in need of particular services is constitutionally permissible. But the states are free to ban in-person solicitation, including directed telephone calls. The recently revised Model Rules conclude that real-time electronic conversations are more akin to the latter than the former. So a broadside email is fine. But not what you suggest.

**How about telling everyone about our latest huge settlement in a Phen-Fen case? That'll get their attention.**

The general principal is that advertising may not be misleading. It is possible, we suppose, to think of a way of explaining the limitations that a prospective client must consider in hearing of your "victory," but the game may not be worth the candle. Past results don't assure future performance. The facts of each case are different. The settlement of that case may have been achieved because of many factors other than the ability of the law firm. You get the idea.

**Maybe we'll just say our firm has done better than any other firm in handling these cases?**

Comparisons are as dangerous as results. Better in which respect? Did those other firms really handle comparable cases? How do you know?

▶ **§7.13(b) Chart: Advertising, Solicitation, And The First Amendment**

In a series of cases [§9.06] over the past four decades, the Supreme Court has forced the rewriting of traditional lawyer code rules [§9.04] that prevented advertising and solicitation by applying the First Amendment to lawyer speech. In doing so, the Court has labeled some lawyer speech "political," some "commercial," and some as "unprotected." The following chart categorizes these cases and the current Model Rules [§9.04] that these cases have shaped.

| Level of Protection | Traditional First Amendment Protection (high level of scrutiny) | Commercial Speech (intermediate level scrutiny) | Unprotected Speech (no Const. protection) |
|---|---|---|---|
| Kind of speech | Political speech, speech that seeks access to the courts | Speech that proposes a commercial transaction | Speech that proposes an illegal activity; misleading commercial speech |
| Governmental interest necessary to justify regulation | Compelling Gov. Interest | Substantial Gov. Interest | Gov. Interest presumed |
| | Regulation must be the least restrictive means to promote governmental interest (no prior restraints) | Speech restriction must directly and materially advance gov. interest. Regulation must be narrowly drawn (prior restraints allowed). | Complete ban allowed |
| Cases | *NAACP v. Button*, 371 U. S. 415 (1963) | *Bates v. St. Bar. of Ariz.*, 433 U.S. 350 (1977) | *Ohralik v. Ohio St. Bar Ass'n*, 436 U.S. 447 (1978) |
| | *Bd. of R.R. Trainmen v. Va.*, 377 U. S. 1 (1964) | *In re R.M.J*, 455 U.S. 191 (1982) | |
| | *United Mine Workers v. Ill. St. Bar Ass'n*, 389 U. S. 217 (1967) | *Zauderer v. Disc. Counsel of S. Ct. of Ohio*, 471 U.S. 626 (1985) | |
| | *United Transp. Union v. St. Bar of Mich.*, 401 U. S. 576 (1971) | *Shapero v. Ky. Bar Ass'n*, 486 U.S. 466 (1988) | |
| | *In re Primus*, 436 U.S. 412 (1978) | *Peel v. Atty. Registration & Disc. Comm'n.*, 496 U. S. 91 (1990) | |
| | | *Fla. Bar v. Went For It*, 515 U.S. 618 (1995) | |
| Corresponding Model Rules | MR 7.3, DR 2-103, 2-104 | MR 7.1,7.2,7.4; DR 2-101,102,105 | MR 7.3(a) DR 2-103, 104 |

§7.13(b)  WHEN YOU MUST SAY "NO" • 219

The left column of the chart includes cases where the Supreme Court has afforded lawyer speech the highest level of First Amendment protection. Here, the Court allows an overbreadth analysis and requires a compelling interest to justify the restriction on speech. In addition, the regulation must be the least restrictive means to promote the governmental interest, and, to prevent chilling fragile First Amendment interests, no prior restraints are allowed.

In *Button,* for example, the court overturned a Virginia anti-solicitation regulation that had been applied to prohibit NAACP lawyers from general solicitation of persons to serve as plaintiffs in constitutional challenges by the NAACP to segregated education. The Court held that the regulation violated the NAACP's First and Fourteenth Amendment rights by "unduly inhibiting protected freedoms of expression and association." It characterized the NAACP's litigation activity as "political expression," which "may well be the sole practicable avenue open to a minority to petition for redress of grievances."[50]

In the next three cases, the court applied the same level of constitutional protection to the activities of labor unions that sought to provide low-cost legal services to their members. These decisions culminated with the statement in *United Transportation Union*: "the common thread running through our decisions in *NAACP v. Button, Trainmen,* and *United Mine Workers* is that collective activity undertaken to obtain meaningful access to the courts is a fundamental right within the protection of the First Amendment."[51]

In *Primus,* the Court returned to a distinction it had first made in *Button* to overturn an attempt by South Carolina to prohibit an ACLU lawyer from personally soliciting civil rights plaintiffs. The Court found that the ACLU, like the NAACP, used litigation as a "form of political expression," not as a means to resolve private differences. Responding to the state's argument that the ACLU's policy of requesting attorney's fees took the case outside of political expression, the Court found that such a possibility was not sufficient to equate the work of these lawyers "with that of a group that exists for the primary purpose of financial gain through the recovery of counsel fees."[52]

---

[50] *NAACP v. Button,* 371 U.S. 415, 429-430 (1963).

[51] *United Transp. Union v. St. Bar of Mich.,* 401 U.S. 576, 585 (1971).

[52] *In re Primus,* 436 U.S. 412, 428, 431 (1978).

The middle column of the chart lists a line of cases where commercial rather than political speech is at stake. Here, the speech proposes a purely commercial transaction, such as "I will sell you the X prescription drug at the Y price."[53] The First Amendment also protects commercial speech, but common sense differences between political and commercial speech justify a different level of constitutional scrutiny. Thus, a substantial rather than compelling governmental interest must be shown to uphold the regulation. Further, the regulation need not be the least restrictive means of promoting the governmental interest so long as it directly and materially advances the interest and is narrowly drawn. Prior restraints, such as requiring a bar ethics opinion [§9.07] before releasing an advertisement,[54] are allowed. To prevent fraud, the states can require that lawyers add disclaimers to their communication, such as "ADVERTISEMENT ONLY."[55] Finally, constitutional challenges to professional advertising can be made only as applied to the conduct of the person regulated. An overbreadth analysis is not available to challenge every conceivable application of the regulation because the commercial motive makes such speech likely to recur.[56]

This extensive line of cases means that states cannot completely prohibit advertising, but can regulate it to prevent false, fraudulent, or misleading statements. *RMJ* and *Shapero* made clear that "advertising" includes targeted mail as well as mass media communications. *Peel* addressed claims of certification in a letterhead, holding that states could not categorically ban lawyers from honestly advertising a certification granted by a national organization, but they were free to prevent potentially misleading certifications from private organizations by creating official state specialty designations.[57] In the context of a partial, time-based prohibition, *Went For It* added the protection of personal privacy and, when empirical evidence exists, the reputation of the profession as justifiable state interests.

---

[53] *Va. Pharm. Bd. v. Va. Consumer Council*, 425 U.S. 748, 761 (1976).

[54] *Central Hudson Gas & Elec. Corp. v. Pub. Serv. Comm'n of N.Y.*, 447 U.S. 557, 571(1980).

[55] *See, e.g.*, Ohio Code of Prof'l Responsibility DR 2-101(F)(2)(e) (2002).

[56] *Bates v. St. Bar of Ariz.*, 433 U.S. 350, 380-81 (1977).

[57] Model Rule 7.4 indicates the ABA response to *Peel*.

§7.13(b)  WHEN YOU MUST SAY "NO" • 221

Despite its extensive application of the First Amendment to lawyer speech, the Supreme Court has characterized one form of lawyer speech—in-person solicitation for pecuniary gain—as unprotected by the First Amendment. The right column of the chart summarizes these decisions. When lawyers attempt to speak face to face to potential clients, the state may presume harm in order to prevent it. In *Ohralik*, the court upheld a complete ban on in-person solicitation by lawyers, finding that speech was a subordinate part of a purely commercial transaction. Unlike media advertising, the pressure of in-person solicitation often demands an immediate response, not leaving the recipient free to evaluate the speech. The evils of fraud, undue influence, intimidation, and overreaching in such a circumstance can be presumed as so likely to occur that the state can prohibit all in-person solicitation to prevent them. No actual injury need be shown to justify a complete ban on speech in this circumstance.[58]

Although it is now clear that the First Amendment applies to lawyer advertising and solicitation, some issues, such as the line between "advertising" and "solicitation," remain unresolved. The Supreme Court has never addressed radio and television or email, but the Model Rules include them in the advertising category.[59] On the other hand, because it demands a more immediate response, real-time electronic contact is included in the ban on in-person solicitation in Model Rule 7.3.[60] When in-person contact may be combined with print material, not all jurisdictions draw the line in the same place.[61]

▶**Red Flag**▶ Be sure to check local rules [§9.04] when you advertise, and remember that a web site read by a person in a distant state may implicate that jurisdiction's rules as well, especially if any lawyer in your firm is licensed in the distant jurisdiction.[62] Bar ethics committees [§9.07] usually will be glad to offer you advice. And

---

[58] *Ohralik v. Ohio St. Bar Ass'n*, 436 U.S. 447, 466 (1978).

[59] Model Rule 7.2.

[60] Model Rule 7.3, Fla. St. Bar Ass'n, Op. A-00-1 (2000).

[61] *E.g.*, Ariz. Jud. Advisory Op. 02-08; Utah St. Bar Ethics Advisory Opinion 99-04 (lawyers at trade show booths).

[62] Cal. Formal Op. 2001-155 (citing opinions in Arizona and Iowa).

remember that constitutional challenges continue to be asserted as to rules that ban a category of otherwise truthful speech [§9.06].[63]

## ➤ §7.14 TRIAL PUBLICITY

### ➤ §7.14(a) The Campaigning DA?

**The damn DA just held a press conference on the courthouse steps that sounded like a campaign speech and a closing argument all at once. And he had all the networks there, catching "the jury" a week before trial.**

There are professional rules [§9.04] governing trial publicity by lawyers. Defining what is impermissible in the context of the First Amendment and enforcing violations of these trial publicity rules have always been difficult. Nonetheless, what you describe sounds like it went way beyond the safe harbor of accepted information and in fact was designed to prejudice the proceedings. Don't be surprised when those assertions are met with free speech rhetoric and the need to keep the public informed. But this conduct may provide grounds for postponement, a change of venue, and a disciplinary complaint against the DA.[64]

## ➤ §7.15 LAWYER AS WITNESS

### ➤ §7.15(a) The Involuntary Witness?

**Can you believe it? We've had this breach of contract case we've been handling for two years. Too many depositions. A zillion documents. Now the other side filed its pretrial order and they listed my partner, who negotiated the agreement, as a witness. Doesn't that mean we can't handle the case?**

---

[63] *Mason v. Fla. Bar*, 208 F.3d 952(11th Cir. 2000) (unconstitutional to require disclaimer explaining how Martindale-Hubbell compiled its ratings); *Walker v. Bd .of Prof'l Responsibility of the Sup. Ct. of Tenn.*, 38 S.W.3d 540 (2001) (regulation which required disclosure of whether a lawyer was certified as a specialist whenever lawyer advertised services in a particular area of law constitutional because reasonably related to promoting substantial interest of helping consumers to make informed judgments about which lawyer to entrust with a legal matter).

[64] Model Rule 3.6; RLGL §109; Hazard & Hodes, §32.5

Calm down. There is a lawyer-witness rule, which does prohibit a lawyer who is a necessary witness on a controverted matter from trying the case. So the first issue is whether your partner's testimony is "necessary" or merely duplicates other relevant evidence.[65] But in most states, even when "necessary," the rule only disqualifies the actual lawyer-witness.[66] That lawyer's colleagues may try the case. Simply because the lawyer-witness rule does not disqualify the lawyer's firm does not mean, however, you should plow ahead with the representation. This is a matter that must be reviewed with the client. First, what would be the nature of your partner's testimony? If it might be adverse to your client's interests, your client must understand this and consent to the firm's continued representation [§6.10]. If not adverse, there are still downsides to trying a case in which your partner is called to testify. How do you cross-examine your partner? How will the jury perceive it? How do you deal with that lawyer-witness's testimony in closing argument? In some cases there will be no effect. In others a slight effect, but the benefits of sticking with your firm may vastly outweigh any detriment. In still others, the lawyer-witness may create havoc.

Even in those states in which the lawyer-witness problem is imputed to the entire firm, it is not every lawyer-witness situation that will require the law firm to withdraw. If the lawyer is testifying about a non-controversial matter, the lawyer or her firm can still try the case. So too, if the lawye's testimony is about the value or nature of the legal services the law firm provided. And finally, to answer your question, when the lawyer-witness disqualification creates a hardship for the client, as it certainly could here, no disqualification is required.

### ➤ §7.16 OTHER LAW: FEDERAL AND STATE STATUTES AND REGULATIONS

### ➤ §7.16(a) The Curious IRS?

**We do a lot of tax planning for our clients. Advertise our innovative approach widely. It has gotten us a good clientele but**

---

[65] *Caplan v. Braverman,* 876 F. Supp. 710(E.D. Pa. 1995) (lawyer who was part of a conversation where party allegedly made an admission not "necessary" witness); *World Youth Day, Inc. v. Famous Artists Merchandising Exchange, Inc.,* 866 F. Supp. 1297 (D. Colo. 1994) (lawyer who was sole negotiator for party was a "necessary" witness).

[66] Model Rule 3.7; RLGL §108.

now it's gotten us a subpoena from the IRS. They want the names of our clients. Do you believe that?

Oh, we believe it all right. Those guys are getting very aggressive. Tax abuse and all that. The rule is that the identity of your clients, while confidential, is generally not privileged, unless disclosing the client's identity would disclose the substance of the underlying communication.[67] The fact that the information may incriminate the client is not enough. Either might be the case here. The client list is only sought because the IRS believes it will provide the agency with more than a list of names. So you can fight to protect the list in good faith. But we offer you no guarantees. Criminal justice lawyers who have sought exemption from IRS regulations that require disclosure of cash transactions of more than $10,000 have generally been unsuccessful.[68]

### ▶§7.16(b) Sarbanes-Oxley Obligations Of Lawyers

Lawyers who represent public companies are subject to special SEC regulations created by the Sarbanes-Oxley Act.[69] We outline these provisions below.

1. Lawyers who appear and practice before the SEC (transact any business with the SEC or communicate in any manner) who become aware of evidence of a **material violation** (violations of any federal or state securities law or material breaches of fiduciary duty under federal or state law) by the issuer or officers, directors, employees or agents of issuer **shall report evidence of the violation** to the CLO (Chief Legal Officer) or CLO and CEO of the issuer.

2. The CLO or CEO shall investigate whether a violation has occurred.

3. **Unless a lawyer reasonably believes that a CLO or CEO has made an appropriate response within a reasonable time, a lawyer shall report material violation to:**

---

[67] RLGL §69 comment g; *Dean v. Dean*, 607 So.2d 494 (Fla. App. 1992) (lawyer not required to disclose identity of client who retained him specifically to return stolen property and made it a condition precedent that client's identity not be disclosed).

[68] *Gerald B. Lefcourt, P.C. v. United States*, 124 F.3d 79 (2d Cir. 1997), *cert. denied*, 524 U.S. 937 (1998).

[69] 15 U.S.C. §7245; SEC Final Rule, 17 C.F.R. Part 205.

## §7.16(b)

- An audit committee of the board of directors; or
- A committee of outside directors; or
- The entire board of directors; or
- A qualified legal compliance committee of the board (QLCC).

4. Except when the lawyer has reported to a QLCC, the lawyer has an obligation to assess whether the issuer has appropriately responded. A lawyer who does not reasonably believe that the issuer has made an appropriate response within a reasonable time **shall explain his or her reasons therefor to the CLO, CEO, and the directors, and may disclose confidential information to the SEC** to the extent the lawyer reasonably believes necessary:

- To prevent material violations likely to cause substantial injury to the financial interest or property of the issuer or investors;
- To prevent the issuer from committing perjury or acts likely to perpetrate a fraud upon the Commission;
- To rectify the consequences of a material violation by the issuer that may cause substantial injury to the financial interest or property of the issuer or investors, in furtherance of which the lawyer's services were used.

5. **Subordinate lawyers** (those who appear or practice before the SEC under the direct supervision or direction of another lawyer) comply by reporting evidence of a material violation to their supervising lawyer, and may take the steps permitted or required above if the subordinate lawyer reasonably believes that the supervisory lawyer to whom he or she has reported has failed to comply with the regulatory requirements.

6. Violation of these regulations can result in discipline by the SEC, including disbarment. Lawyers who comply cannot be held civilly liable or disciplined under any inconsistent state rule.

7. Lawyers who are fired for complying with the regulations may report the firing to the Board of Directors.

8. The SEC has not yet decided whether lawyers should have mandated disclosure or noisy withdrawal obligations when they do not believe that the entity has made an appropriate response.

# Part Four

# ▶Red Flags▶ You Cannot Ignore: Remedies

### TEN REMEDIES YOU MUST UNDERSTAND

In this chapter we review ten legal remedies [§9.05] available for violations of the law governing lawyers:

1. Professional discipline;
2. Criminal accountability;
3. Misrepresentation;
4. Tort liability to nonclients;
5. Tort liability to clients: malpractice and breach of fiduciary duty;
6. Ineffective assistance of counsel;
7. Disqualification and other court orders;
8. Loss of contractual rights;
9. Fee forfeiture;
10. Procedural sanctions.

Some of these remedies, such as professional discipline, criminal accountability, the law of misrepresentation, and other intentional tort remedies, seek to protect the public interest in a competent and trustworthy system of legal representation. Many of these remedies, such as malpractice, ineffective assistance of counsel, loss of contractual rights, and fee forfeiture seek to protect individual clients, and provide a means to compensate them when fiduciary duties have been violated. Others, such as disqualification orders and procedural sanctions, seek to preserve and enforce the professional obligations of lawyers who appear before a tribunal.[1]

Each of these remedies has its own legal requirements, but multiple remedies [§9.05] may well exist for the same conduct.[2] For example, clients who can prove a breach of fiduciary duty that caused harm may be able to recover damages as well as fee forfeiture.[3] Similarly, a lawyer can be subject to disqualification as well as fee forfeiture and professional discipline for a conflict of interest.[4]

For many remedies, the breach of a fiduciary duty by one lawyer extends vicariously to the entire law firm. For example, in a case claiming fee forfeiture under RICO, the court disqualified the law firm because of the defendant's statement that he wanted to plead guilty, but could not, because such a plea would jeopardize the $103,000 fee he had paid his lawyer. Following disqualification, the court also ordered fee forfeiture, and upheld a common law conversion action to recover the fees the firm had already spent.[5]

---

[1] *Restatement of the Law Third, The Law Governing Lawyers*, §§5, 6 (ALI 2000).

[2] *See e.g., United States v. Bronston*, 658 F.2d 920 (2d Cir. 1981), *cert. denied*, 456 U.S. 915 (1982) (mail fraud conviction based on lawyer's conflict of interest).

[3] *Hendry v. Pelland*, 73 F.3d 397 (D.C. Cir. 1996); *Piro v. Sarofim*, 80 S.W.3d 717 (Tex. App. 2002).

[4] *Ennis v. Ennis*, 276 N.W.2d 341 (Wis. 1979). *See also, Image Tech. Serv. v. Eastman Kodak Co.*, 136 F.3d 1354 (9th Cir. 1998)(former client not entitled to attorney fees under Clayton Act for work done by lawyer who was later disqualified); *In re Conway*, 301 N.W.2d 253 (Wis. 1981)(public reprimand to lawyer in *Ennis*).

[5] *United States v. Moffitt, Zwerling & Kemler, P.C.*, 83 F.3d 660 (4th Cir. 1996), *cert. denied*, 519 U.S. 1101 (1997).

# 8

# So What Can Happen? Client And Third-Person Remedies

➤ §8.01 The Nervous Associate?
➤ §8.02 Professional Discipline
➤ §8.03 Criminal Accountability
    ➤ §8.03(a) The Client Fundraiser?
    ➤ §8.03(b) The Criminal Law
➤ §8.04 Misrepresentation
➤ §8.05 Lawyer Tort Liability To Non-Clients
    ➤ §8.05(a) The Estate Executor?
    ➤ §8.05(b) Legal Accountability To Non-Clients
➤ §8.06 Lawyer Tort Liability To Clients: Malpractice And Breach Of Fiduciary Duty
    ➤ §8.06(a) The Puny Settlement?
    ➤ §8.06(b) The Vast Scope Of Potential Liability
➤ §8.07 Ineffective Assistance Of Counsel
➤ §8.08 Disqualification And Other Court Orders
    ➤ §8.08(a) Dropping The Small Potato?
    ➤ §8.08(b) Losing A Client By Disqualification Or Injunction
➤ §8.09 Loss Of Contractual Rights

➤ §8.09(a) The Client Gift?

➤ §8.09(b) The Undue Influence Hurdle

➤ §8.10 Fee Forfeiture

➤ §8.10(a) The Lost Fee?

➤ §8.10(b) The Equity Of Fee Forfeiture

➤ §8.11 Procedural Sanctions

➤ §8.12 Avoiding Problems

## ➤ §8.01 THE NERVOUS ASSOCIATE?

**It's bugging me. I'm just an associate in my firm. The other day the partner on this case told me not to worry about this damaging document. "I'll take care of it," he said. I think it must be produced and I'm not sure what "taking care of it" means.**

Your concern is justified. Whether you are a partner or an associate, you are a lawyer. You must conform your conduct to the rules. If the boss's view reflects a reasonable resolution of an arguable question, then you may accept the partner's decision.[1] But if not, you must take further action. At a minimum you must learn what the partner meant and what he is doing. Then you have to re-examine the strength of your position. If you remain convinced that the duty is clear, you must take reasonable remedial action. First, remember client confidentiality and try to resolve the matter by seeing someone else in your firm. If that does not resolve the issue, it's probably time for you to retain your own counsel. You may have to withdraw from the firm. You may have to take steps to assure the document is produced. This is no time to act without a lawyer of your own. But something tells us you won't have to go that far. Every lawyer—young or old—should have a rabbi—inside the firm or out—with whom he or she consults when sensitive matters like this occur. The very best practice is for firms to institutionalize this role so that the reason the matter turns out badly is never the failure to consult with others regarding the knotty ethical question.

---

[1] ABA Model Rule of Professional Conduct 5.2 (2002) (hereinafter "Model Rules"); *Restatement of the Law Third, The Law Governing Lawyers*, §12 (ALI 2000) (hereinafter "RLGL").

## ▶ §8.02 PROFESSIONAL DISCIPLINE

Professional discipline forms the backbone of lawyer regulation and is designed to maintain public confidence in the profession. Over the past 30 years, state and federal courts have extensively clarified the content and scope of lawyer codes [§9.04], updated the procedures for disciplinary enforcement, and implemented guidelines to standardize disciplinary sanctions, resulting in more extensive discipline for a wider variety of lawyer misconduct. Model Rule 8.3 requires disclosure to the appropriate professional authority by lawyers who know of another lawyer's violation of the Rules of Professional Conduct "that raises a substantial question as to that lawyer's honesty, trustworthiness or fitness as a lawyer in other respects." This disclosure obligation is trumped by the lawyer's duty to uphold a client's confidentiality interest.[2]

▶**Red Flag**▶ Model Rule 8.4 makes six categories of conduct grounds for professional discipline:

1. Violating or attempting to violate any provision of the Model Rules.[3]

2. Committing any criminal act that adversely reflects on a lawyer's ability to practice[4] [§7.03].

3. Engaging in conduct involving dishonesty, fraud, deceit, or misrepresentation[5] [§7.04].

4. Engaging in conduct that is prejudicial to the administration of justice.[6]

5. Stating or implying an ability to improperly influence a government agency or official or achieve results by violating the Rules of Professional Conduct.[7]

6. Knowingly assisting a judge in violating the Judicial Conduct Rules.[8]

---

[2] Model Rule 8.3; RLGL §5.
[3] Model Rule 8.4(a); RLGL §5.
[4] Model Rule 8.4(b); RLGL §5.
[5] Model Rule 8.4(c); RLGL §§5, 16, 98.
[6] Model Rule 8.4(d); RLGL §5.
[7] Model Rule 8.4(e); RLGL §113.
[8] Model Rule 8.4(f); RLGL §113.

The fourth category, conduct prejudicial to the administration of justice, has been found in a variety of circumstances, from Bill Clinton's contempt of court for knowingly giving evasive and misleading answers, to lawyers who abandon law practice without notice to clients,[9] to prosecutors who seriously abuse their discretion,[10] and misconduct during litigation.[11] The last two categories further prohibit specific kinds of interference, including improper influence of judges or other public officials.[12] Some jurisdictions [§9.04] have added additional grounds for discipline, including various prohibitions against bias and discrimination [§7.09],[13] and nonpayment of child support.[14]

Disciplinary procedures are *sui generis,* neither civil nor criminal in nature. Clear and convincing evidence is required to impose disciplinary sanctions. The accused is afforded procedural due process guarantees such as notice of the charge, the right to invoke a Fifth Amendment privilege against self-incrimination, and a right to appeal. On the other hand, no right to a jury trial and no Fifth Amendment protection against double jeopardy exist. If you are disciplined in one jurisdiction, the National Lawyer Regulatory Data Bank will notify all jurisdictions where you are admitted to practice, often resulting in reciprocal discipline.[15] Typical disciplinary procedures begin with a triage that dismisses or refers minor complaints such as many fee disputes, failures to communicate, or isolated instances of incompetence to arbitration or mediation programs. Assuming adequate proof, the

---

[9] *In re Kendrick,* 710 So.2d 236 (La. 1998); *People v. Crist,* 948 P.2d 1020 (Colo. 1997).

[10] *In re Christoff,* 690 N.E.2d 1135 (Ind. 1997) (prosecutor who renewed a long dormant investigation against another lawyer who sought the prosecutor's job suspended for 30 days).

[11] *In re Jacques,* 972 F. Supp. 1070 (E.D. Tex. 1997) (lawyer assaulted person and verbally abused another lawyer during a deposition); *In re Wyllie,* 952 P.2d 550 (Or. 1998) (making court appearances while intoxicated); *In re Golden,* 496 S.E.2d 619 (S.C. 1998) (lawyer made threatening and degrading comments during deposition).

[12] *Disciplinary Counsel v. Cicero,* 678 N.E.2d 517 (Ohio 1997) (lawyer led prosecutor and client to believe that he was having a sexual relationship with judge after she recused herself); *Lisi v. Several Attorneys,* 596 A.2d 313 (R.I. 1991) (lawyers made loans to judges before whom they appeared).

[13] Model Rule 8.4 Comment [3].

[14] Cal. Bus. & Prof'l Code §490.5 (2005); Colo. R. Civ. P. §251.8.5(b); Fla. R. of Prof'l Conduct 4-8.4(h).

[15] ABA Model Rules for Lawyer Disciplinary Enforcement (2002).

§8.03(a)    CLIENT & THIRD-PARTY REMEDIES    •    233

disciplinary sanctions in more serious matters depend upon the nature of the offense, whether harm has occurred to the client or the public, and the lawyer's mental state.[16]

Lawyers in small firms are more at risk for professional discipline for a number of reasons. First, dissatisfied clients of large-firm lawyers tend to seek their own remedies by changing lawyers, negotiating reduced fees or litigating a malpractice suit, while the dissatisfied clients of smaller firm lawyers may be individuals who lack the experience or power to take advantage of these alternatives and therefore may be more likely to turn to the public disciplinary process. Lawyers in larger firms also have more peer assistance available to them, which may help them minimize substantial error. Small-firm lawyers may lack such support systems, and may face more severe financial pressures.[17] Moreover, the most effective defense to a disciplinary complaint is convincing the fact finder that bar counsel has failed to meet its burden of proof, and larger law firms may have the wherewithal to mount more successful defenses. This does not mean, however, that large-firm lawyers have not lapsed and with some very serious consequences.

▶**Red Flag**▶ If you receive a disciplinary complaint, do not overreact. You have a right to defend yourself, but you must be careful not to make things worse by covering up the truth, disclosing client confidences unnecessarily, or not responding to the matter at all. If serious allegations are made, you need counsel—now. If you aren't sure whether the matter is serious, you should contact a lawyer experienced in such matters to get an initial evaluation.

### ▶ §8.03 CRIMINAL ACCOUNTABILITY

#### ▶ §8.03(a) The Client Fundraiser?

Our client is a big real estate developer in a few towns in Exeter County. I can't tell you how many fundraisers he asks us to attend. You pay a thousand bucks, the food is lousy and you rub elbows with a bunch of politicians. Ugh! But now our client has gone over the top. He's trying to raise $50,000 for some guy run-

---

[16] ABA Standards for Imposing Lawyer Sanctions (1992).

[17] STATE BAR OF CAL., *Investigation and Prosecution of Disciplinary Complaints Against Attorneys in Solo Practice, Small Size Law Firms and Large Size Law Firms* (June 2001).

ning for County Executive. With our campaign finance laws his company's executives can only contribute $25,000. He wants our firm's lawyer to bundle the other $25,000. Tell the party Chairman it's "inspired" by our client. With all the new work we'll get from his company if this guy gets to be County Executive, developer says we'll earn the $25,000 back in no time. Can we do it?

It is perfectly legal to give political contributions. It is also perfectly legal to encourage others to do so. And so long as it's clear that your firm is not being reimbursed by the client for the contributions he is "encouraging" you to make, everything should be copasetic. But you must be very careful of two things. One, these must be your contributions. No extra charges to client for services to "earn" the contributions back. Two, you must assure yourself that your client is not engaged in bribery of public officials to receive either business on zoning approvals or leasing opportunities. The last thing your firm wants to confront is the charge that you aided and abetted illegal conduct by your client. That not only violates Model Rule 1.2(d); it could have you facing criminal charges.

### ➤ §8.03(b) The Criminal Law

We have already seen that criminal conduct constitutes a significant legal boundary that lawyers must understand, adhere to, and advise clients about [§7.03]. Failure to do so can result in malpractice suits from clients, and criminal accountability and professional discipline for lawyers. Lawyers who do not directly violate a criminal provision but advise clients who do so may be accountable as accomplices or co-conspirators. Further, lawyers who know that their clients are paying them with the fruits of the crime also risk statutory fee forfeiture [§8.10(b)], and other criminal accountability, such as a charge of aiding and abetting the crime or receiving stolen property.

Typical accomplice statutes prohibit the purposeful or intentional aiding, abetting, advising, assisting, counseling, or encouraging the criminal act of another.[18] The *mens rea* of these provisions roughly parallels the knowledge requirement of Model Rule 1.2(d), and the "counsels or assists" prohibition in the Model Rule roughly parallels the *actus reus* of these criminal statutes. Lawyers convicted of aiding

---

[18] Wayne R. LaFave, *Criminal Law* §13.1(e) (West, 4th ed. 2003); Model Penal Code §2.06.

and abetting usually face professional discipline [§8.02] for violating this provision and Model Rule 8.4(b).[19]

Lawyers who intend to commit a serious crime (*mens rea*) and agree to aid the client in committing it (*actus res*) also can become entangled in client crimes as co-conspirators.[20] Unlike accomplice liability, conspiracy to commit a crime constitutes a separate crime, even if the underlying crime is not completed. To be found guilty of conspiracy, a lawyer need not aid, abet, or assist the client's crime as long as she purposely promotes the criminal act and agrees with the client that one of them will commit it.[21] Like accomplices, lawyer co-conspirators often face professional discipline [§8.02] as well.[22]

### ▶ §8.04 MISREPRESENTATION

We have already seen that the law of fraud, deceit, and misrepresentation creates a definitive legal boundary to your own conduct and that of your clients, and is incorporated into your professional obligation by lawyer code provisions [§7.04] as well. Here, we address the tort of misrepresentation, which forms the basis for understanding the potential for liability far beyond a client-lawyer relationship. The *Restatement of Torts (Second)* §§525-552C lay out the basic elements of a cause of action for misrepresentation:

1. Making a false representation (by words or actions), or failing to speak when:

    a. a fiduciary obligation exists, or

    b. previous statements made have become untrue, misleading or material;

---

[19] *In re DeRose*, 55 P.3d 126 (Colo. 2002) (lawyer who pleaded guilty to aiding and abetting a client's illegal structure of financial transactions to evade reporting requirements disbarred).

[20] *In re Palmer*, 835 So.2d 410 (La. 2002) (lawyer who furthered entity client's sham transactions by backdating documents was convicted of conspiracy to defraud and disbarred, despite testimony of U.S. Attorney that convictions of principals would not have been possible without lawyer's cooperation).

[21] Model Penal Code §5.03; 18 U.S.C. §371.

[22] *In re Lee*, 755 A.2d 1034 (D.C. 2000) (lawyer convicted of conspiracy with client to launder money disbarred); *In re Petition of Anderson*, 851 S.W.2d 408 (Ark. 1993) (lawyer convicted of conspiracy with client to possess cocaine with intent to distribute failed to gain readmission to the bar).

2. Concerning a presently existing material fact;

3. Which the representor knows to be false or is made recklessly, knowing that there is insufficient knowledge upon which to base the representation, or which is made negligently;

4. For the purpose of inducing another to act;

5. The other party reasonably relies on the representation;

6. To his injury or damage.

In tort, "fraud" includes both intentional as well as reckless misstatements. To be liable, the defendant does not have to intend harm to the plaintiff, but only has to know he is lying or recklessly ignoring the truth.[23] This distinction is important, because the lawyer's liability for fraud extends to all foreseeable third persons who reasonably rely on the false information.[24] If the lawyer's material misrepresentation is merely negligent, liability usually extends to a more limited group of persons identified at the time the statements were made [§8.05].

Although the tort of misrepresentation usually requires an affirmative misrepresentation, there are a few occasions when failure to speak can generate liability as well. Fiduciary duties create obligations to disclose, which means that lawyers, who owe fiduciary duties to clients, have affirmative duties to disclose material information to them.[25] A duty to disclose also may arise when previous statements have become untrue, misleading, or material.[26] For example, a lawyer

---

[23] *Slotkin v. Citizens Cas. Co. of N.Y.*, 614 F.2d 301 (2d Cir. 1979), *cert. denied,* 449 U.S. 981 (1990) (insurance defense lawyer who settled medical malpractice case after stating that "to the best of my knowledge" there was no excess insurance coverage, when lawyer's file indicated otherwise, liable for fraud); *Fire Ins. Exch. v. Bell*, 643 N.E.2d 310 (Ind. 1994) (plaintiff's counsel had right to rely on insurance defense counsel's representation of policy limits even though plaintiff's lawyer could have used discovery to ascertain limits).

[24] RLGL §56 comment f; *Restatement (Second) of Torts*, §531 (1977); *Ultramares Corp. v. Touche, Niven & Co.*, 174 N.E. 441 (N.Y.1931).

[25] *E.g., Baker v. Dorfman*, 239 F.3d 415 (2d Cir. 2000) (lawyer who lied about the extent of his legal experience to a client liable for fraud, including compensatory, emotional distress, and punitive damages).

[26] *Restatement (Second) of Torts* §551. *E.g., In re Alcorn*, 41 P.3d 600 (Ariz. 2002) (trial lawyers who made a secret agreement with opposing counsel to dismiss action against their client fined and disciplined for failing to disclose agreement to trial judge who indicated he did not want any sweetheart deals or anything "crafted" that "would be

may have a duty to disclose tax liens to a prospective purchaser at a foreclosure sale if the buyer was induced to bid by the lawyer's incomplete prior representations.[27]

▶**Red Flag**▶ Whenever you state a fact orally or in writing that you expect another will rely on, do not depend solely on your client for determining the truth of the matter. Lawyers have been held liable for fraud and negligent misrepresentation to third parties when they believed their client's lie and innocently (they thought) repeated it.[28]

### ▶§8.05 LAWYER TORT LIABILITY TO NON-CLIENTS
### ▶§8.05(a) The Estate Executor?

**We've been representing the executor of an estate. Gave him tax advice. Now some of those spoiled brat kids of the decedent are claiming we made a mistake. They are threatening a malpractice suit. I say our only client was the executor and only she has a claim. She's a former partner here and I know she won't sue us.**

The law governing lawyers is evolving in this area. The case law [§9.06] now make it clear that when a client asks a lawyer to perform services on which the client expects third parties to rely, the lawyer owes certain duties—particularly the duties of competence and diligence—to these third parties. Here the client was the estate. Your question doesn't make it clear whether other estate beneficiaries benefited from the advice you provided while only these beneficiaries can claim "injury." If so, a successful claim may be unlikely. If not, it may be that these beneficiaries can seek recovery from you, even if the executor, in good faith, believes no claim should be brought.

---

misleading" to him); *People v. Rolfe*, 962 P.2d 981 (Colo. 1998) (lawyer who stated that a social worker had "begun" her investigation of the matter, but failed to inform the court about the existence of social worker's letter that concluded no abuse could be substantiated, censured for violating Model Rule 3.3(a)(1)).

[27] *Gerdin v. Princeton St. Bank*, 371 N.W.2d 5 (Minn. App 1985), *aff'd en banc*, 384 N.W. 2d 868 (Minn. 1968).

[28] *Greycas Inc. v. Proud*, 826 F.2d 1560 (7th Cir. 1987), *cert. denied*, 484 U.S. 1043 (1988) (lawyer who stated that he had "conducted a UCC, tax and judgment search" but instead relied on client's statements that no liens existed on farm property liable for fraud and negligent misrepresentation to lender when client defaulted on loan).

## §8.05(b) Legal Accountability To Non-Clients

Lawyers accustomed to the 4 C's easily can assume that their only responsibility is to their clients. Chapter 7, which traversed the limits of the law on client advocacy, should have disabused you of that notion. Here, we discuss your potential liability beyond your client.

For courts, the cases that have the easiest path to finding liability to non-clients involve intentional torts. Thus, lawyers who commit fraud,[29] abuse of process,[30] malicious prosecution,[31] conversion,[32] or the intentional infliction of emotional distress[33] do not escape liability simply because they did so in the act of providing services to a client. And do not forget that agreeing to assist a client's tortious act generally constitutes a concert of action or civil conspiracy.[34]

When negligence is alleged, courts generally recognize that antagonists do not have standing to seek enforcement of the lawyer

---

[29] *E.g., Hartford Accident & Indem. Co. v. Sullivan*, 846 F.2d 377 (7th Cir. 1988), *cert. denied*, 490 U.S. 1089 (1989) (lawyer liable for fraud in helping client obtain fraudulent bank loan); *Bonavire v. Wampler*, 779 F.2d 1011 (4th Cir. 1985) (lawyer who knowingly misrepresented client's honesty and experience liable for fraud); *Fire Ins. Exch. v. Bell*, 643 N.E.2d 310 (Ind. 1994) (lawyer who misrepresented policy limits liable for fraud).

[30] *E.g., Givens v. Mullikin*, 75 S.W.3d 383 (Tenn. 2002) (cause of action stated against lawyer for abuse of process (as well as insured client and insurer who directed the lawyer's conduct) for barraging opposing party with subpoenas, interrogatories, and a deposition seeking information that had already been turned over).

[31] *E.g., Raine v. Drasin*, 621 S.W.2d 895 (Ky. 1981) (lawyer liable for malicious prosecution for joining two physicians in malpractice case after reviewing records which clearly showed they had treated patient only after his injury had occurred).

[32] *E.g., ERA Realty Co. v. RBS Properties*, 586 N.Y.S.2d 831 (N.Y. App. Div. 1992) (lawyer who used void process to acquire funds liable for conversion).

[33] *E.g., Bevan v. Fix*, 42 P.3d 1013 (Wyo. 2002) (cause of action stated by child who witnessed lawyer physically abuse his mother/client); *Mack v. Soung*, 95 Cal. Rptr. 2d 830 (Cal. App. 2000).

[34] *Banco Popular N. Am. v. Gandi*, 823 A.2d 809 (N.J. Super. Ct. App. Div. 2003) (lawyer who handled transfers of assets from client to his wife that assisted client in obtaining bank loan made no actual misrepresentations to the bank and was not liable for common law fraud nor for negligence. Bank did state a claim, however for conspiracy to defraud a creditor as long as lawyer actively participated in the client's fraud); *but see, Central Bank of Denver N.A. v. First Interstate Bank of Denver, N.A.*, 511 U.S. 164 (1994) (no secondary liability or private action for aiding and abetting securities fraud; defendant must engage in a proscribed activity as a primary violator to be liable).

§8.05(b)      Client & Third-Party Remedies • 239

codes [§9.04] outside of a disciplinary context.[35] So, for example, non-clients probably should not be able to complain that you failed to warn them of client wrongdoing.[36] This limitation on duty dovetails with the general requirement in negligence that liability depends on a relationship to a foreseeable plaintiff, usually a client-lawyer relationship [Chapter 1, §8.06].

But if you or your client invites a third person to rely on your work, and if you negligently produce it causing harm to the third person, you can be held liable to both your client and the third person.[37] One example is an invitation to rely on your legal opinion (which may be required by the third person as part of a transaction) [§1.27].[38] You may avoid this reliance by making clear that your opinion or representation is intended for the client only, or by making clear that you are relying on the client's provision of facts without an independent investigation.[39] Similarly, if you invite a non-client to rely on your services [§1.12], for example by offering to record a deed at a real estate closing, and the opposing party suffers harm, that person will have a cause of action against you if you fail to follow through competently with the task you undertook.[40]

You also owe duties of competence to third-party beneficiaries of your client, such as intended beneficiaries of your client's will or trust[41] regardless of their reliance on your work. Here, everything depends on the clarity of your client's intent. When the parties are potential adversaries or incidental rather than intended beneficiaries, courts refuse to

---

[35] Model Rule Scope ¶20.

[36] RLGL §§66(3), 67(4); *Hawkins v. King County*, 602 P.2d 361 (Wash. App. 1979).

[37] RLGL §51.

[38] Model Rule 2.3; RLGL §95.

[39] RLGL §51, comment e.

[40] *Kremser v. Quarles & Brady, L.L.P.*, 36 P.3d 761 (Ariz. App. 2001) (corporation's lawyers undertook responsibility to perfect non-client creditor's security interest); *Nelson v. Nationwide Mortgage Corp.*, 659 F. Supp. 611 (D.D.C. 1987) (lawyer volunteered to answer questions and explain document).

[41] *In re Guardianship of Karan*, 38 P.3d 396 (Wash. App. 2002) (minor child has cause of action against mother's lawyer who set up child's trust to allow pilfering of the estate); *Lucas v. Hamm*, 364 P.2d 685 (Cal. 1961), *cert. denied*, 368 U.S. 987 (1962) (intended beneficiaries of a will could recover from lawyer whose negligence in drafting document caused them to lose their testamentary rights).

find a duty of care.[42] For example, courts have refused to impose a duty on the lawyer for a personal representative to the estate beneficiaries.[43] On the other hand, courts have imposed duties on a fiduciary's lawyer [§1.28] when the latter assisted his client in breaching a fiduciary duty.[44]

Beyond cases where your client intends to benefit a third party, most courts [§9.06] impose a duty to prevent economic harm only when liability for misrepresentation or its statutory equivalents, such as securities fraud, can be established.[45] This duty stems from the fact that once you have undertaken a duty to speak, you must do so with care. If you make the misrepresentation intentionally or recklessly, your liability extends to all persons who might foreseeably rely on it. Although a few jurisdictions extend liability for negligent misrepresentation this far as well,[46] most hold lawyers liable for negligent misrepresentation only to

---

[42] *Capitol Indem. Corp. v. Fleming*, 58 P.3d 965 (Ariz. App. 2002) (surety who posted bond for an estate's conservator incidental, not intended beneficiary of services provided by conservator's lawyer); *Bovee v. Gravel*, 811 A.2d 137 (Vt. 2002) (bank shareholders were not beneficiaries of law firm's representation of bank); *MacMillan v. Scheffy*, 787 A.2d 867 (N.H. 2001) (buyers in real estate transaction unable to prove that seller's lawyer, who drafted the deed, had the purpose to benefit them; mere fact they were grantees under the deed was not enough); *Kilpatrick v. Wiley, Rein & Fielding*, 37 P.3d 1130 (Utah 2001) (law firm's representation of a limited partnership does not create implied client-lawyer relationship with individual limited partners unless the latter reasonably believe the firm represents their discrete interests).

[43] *Jensen v. Crandall*, 1997 Me. Super. LEXIS 72 (Me. Super. Ct. Mar. 4, 1997); *Trask v. Butler*, 872 P.2d 1080 (Wash. 1994); *Neal v. Baker*, 551 N.E.2d 704 (Ill. App. 1990).

[44] *Chem-Age Indus. Inc. v. Glover*, 652 N.W.2d 756 (S.D. 2002) (lawyer can be liable for assisting a client in breaching a fiduciary duty to a third person if fiduciary was lawyer's client, lawyer knew fiduciary was breaching a fiduciary duty to plaintiff, and lawyer substantially assisted the breach causing damages).

[45] *Orshoski v. Krieger*, 2001 Ohio App. LEXIS 5018 (Ohio App. Nov. 9, 2001) (prospective buyers who relied on negligent misrepresentations of lawyer for developer concerning subdivision's restrictive covenants could sue for negligent misrepresentation, but not for legal malpractice); *Rubin v. Schottenstein, Zox & Dunn*, 143 F.3d 263 (6th Cir. 1998) (*en banc*) (lawyer who represented seller in a securities transaction assumes a duty to provide complete and nonmisleading information with respect to subjects on which he undertakes to speak under Rule 10b-5).

[46] *Molecular Tech. Corp. v. Valentine*, 925 F.2d 910 (6th Cir. 1991); *Mehaffy, Rider, Windholz & Wilson v. Central Bank Denver, N.A.*, 892 P.2d 230 (Colo. 1995) (lawyer who issued a legal opinion in connection with a municipal bond offering may be liable to third party investors under *Restatement (Second) Torts* §552 for negligent misrepresentation).

§8.06(a)    CLIENT & THIRD-PARTY REMEDIES  •  241

those in a limited class of persons for whose benefit and guidance the lawyer intends to supply the information or to those third persons to whom the lawyer knows the recipient intends to supply the information.[47]

▶**Ultimate Red Flag**▶ Lawyers who overidentify with clients can knowingly, recklessly, negligently, or innocently further a client's fraud. Special vigilance is required in transactional work for organizational clients. We discuss the need to avoid this instrumental role behavior in §10.02.

### ▶§8.06 LAWYER TORT LIABILITY TO CLIENTS: MALPRACTICE AND BREACH OF FIDUCIARY DUTY

### ▶§8.06(a) The Puny Settlement?

Clients! I can't believe them sometimes. This guy called us up to ask how the settlement proceeds from an employment discrimination suit would be treated for tax purposes. Guy was about to get $1 million, if you can believe that. Now he's threatening to sue us because one of his buddies, a guy with a similar claim, went to trial and won $3 million. Claims we should've warned him about the puny settlement!

Even the lawyer who handled the underlying claim should be all right. So long as the client was sufficiently informed of the risks and rewards of a settlement, the fact that a later case (even if identical) gained more by way of judgment does not mean the lawyer breached any duty to the client. However, if the client can prove [§9.08] that the lawyer's advice to settle was negligent, that lawyer may be in malpractice trouble.[48] And as for you, assuming the scope of your engagement was clear, what does a tax lawyer know about employment discrimination? The claim does highlight, however, the importance of defining the scope of the representation from the beginning. If you provided the client with an engagement letter that clearly limited your obligations to tax work, you will not have to worry [§1.04].[49]

---

[47] RLGL §51; *Restatement (Second) Torts*, §552(2).

[48] *Ziegelheim v. Apollo*, 607 A.2d 1298 (N.J. 1992) (lawyers who negotiate settlements are subject to the general rule that requires them to exercise reasonable knowledge, skill, and diligence possessed by the members of that profession in good standing in similar communities).

[49] *Kates v. Robinson*, 786 So.2d 61 (Fla. App. 2001) (lawyer hired to execute a judgment not responsible for failing to recognize other potential defendants).

## ▶ §8.06(b) The Vast Scope Of Potential Liability

Although professional discipline [§8.02] has become more common in the past three decades, it continues to reach only a small fraction of client complaints, usually ignoring those that allege neglect or incompetence. Other remedies, especially lawsuits for malpractice and breach of fiduciary duty, have expanded to fill this gap.

A malpractice case is a specialized negligence case with evidentiary rules that defer to professional custom. To establish a prima facie case, the plaintiff must prove four elements:

1. The existence of a client-lawyer relationship; that is, that the plaintiff is foreseeable or one to whom a duty of care is owed [Chapter 1].

2. Breach of the professional duty of care, usually established through expert testimony [§9.08], but subject to the common knowledge exception [§4.06].

3. Causation, actual and proximate.

4. Compensatory damages, which in some cases may include emotional distress damages.

Although some courts recognize breach of fiduciary duty as a subset of malpractice,[50] others characterize it as a separate cause of action (often with a separate statute of limitations) intended to remedy serious breaches of fiduciary duty.[51] Examples include a lawyer's failure to obey a client's instructions,[52] failure to communicate with a client about material aspects of the representation,[53] failure to keep client confidences,[54] misuse of client confidences,[55] or failure to avoid impermissi-

---

[50] *Kelly v. Foster*, 813 P.2d 598 (Wash. App. 1991).

[51] RLGL §49.

[52] *Vandermay v. Clayton*, 984 P.2d 272 (Or. 1999) (lawyer liable for failing to follow client's instructions about retaining a contract clause); *State v. Ali*, 407 S.E.2d 183 (N.C. 1991) (lawyer must comply with criminal defendant's wish not to strike a juror).

[53] *dePape v. Trinity Health Systems, Inc.*, 242 F. Supp. 2d 585 (N.D. Iowa 2003) (lawyers failed to provide any information to immigration client to enable client to comply with legal requirements, resulting in failed immigration attempt).

[54] *Perez v. Kirk & Carrigan*, 822 S.W.2d 261 (Tex. App. 1991) (lawyers turned over client's confidential statement about a serious accident to the prosecutor without his consent, resulting in multiple criminal indictments).

[55] *Tante v. Herring*, 453 S.E.2d 686 (Ga. 1994) (lawyer misused client's confidential information to coerce a sexual relationship with client).

ble conflicts of interest.[56] Many of these cases rest on the common knowledge exception to the expert testimony requirement in malpractice cases [§4.06], because the breach is obvious and can be understood by a jury. Others reach a similar result by allowing the plaintiff to establish the breach of fiduciary duty by showing a violation of a relevant professional code provision [§9.04].

In both malpractice and breach of fiduciary duty suits, courts generally hold that proof of a professional code violation [§9.04] constitutes evidence of breach of the standard of care but is not negligence per se.[57] They also require plaintiffs to prove both actual (but for) and proximate (foreseeable consequences or direct result) causation. Actual causation will often be difficult to show, because many errors lawyers make may not have made a difference in the outcome of a matter. In cases where a lawyer has missed a time deadline, courts [§9.06] require proof of the "case within a case," that is, that the plaintiff would have recovered if the suit had been timely filed. This burden requires the plaintiff to prove the merits of the underlying matter in the malpractice suit to establish that harm was caused, as well as to establish the extent of the damage.[58] A few courts are recognizing an alternative: Using expert testimony [§9.08] to prove what might have happened.[59] But most cling to the case-within-a-case-requirement.

Both malpractice and breach of fiduciary duty also require that compensatory damages be established. Usually, this involves financial loss caused by the lawyer's error. Courts also allow recovery for emotional distress to a client when a breach of duty is egregious and

---

[56] *Kilpatrick v. Wiley, Rein & Fielding*, 909 P.2d 1283 (Utah App. 1996) (law firm represented multiple clients interested in acquiring a television station).

[57] Model Rule Scope ¶20; RLGL §52(2).

[58] *Viner v. Sweet*, 70 P.3d 1046 (Cal. 2003) (case-within-a-case proof required for errors in transactions as well as litigation); *Winskunas v. Birnbaum*, 23 F.3d 1264 (7th Cir. 1994) (former client must prove that lawyer who failed to file timely appeal could have gotten his loss reversed on appeal).

[59] *Wolpaw v. General Accident Ins. Co.*, 639 A.2d 338 (N.J. Super. Ct. App. Div. 1994) (parties can use experts to prove whether and how non-conflicted counsel would have changed the outcome at trial).

directly causes severe emotional distress apart from other harm.[60] Punitive damages also are available for willful and wanton disregard of a client's rights.[61]

Defenses are difficult. Although statutes of limitation are often alleged against malpractice plaintiffs, many courts toll the statute during the time you continue to represent the client and further apply the discovery rule, which tolls the statute until the plaintiff reasonably should have discovered the elements of the cause of action. Similarly, lawyers cannot claim comparative fault when the client's failure to understand was caused by the lawyer's negligent explanation or the client's reasonable reliance.[62]

### ▶§8.07 INEFFECTIVE ASSISTANCE OF COUNSEL

Most criminal defense counsel function in an overworked and underfunded system where the stakes are exceedingly high. Although defendants in criminal cases have a Sixth Amendment right to effective assistance of counsel,[63] getting a conviction or sentence reversed on appeal has produced few incentives to cure the overworked, underfunded system. The Supreme Court has adopted a two-pronged legal standard to assess effectiveness, which comes very close to the malpractice standard of care. First, counsel's representation must fall below an objective standard of reasonableness, measured by prevailing norms of practice reflected in ABA standards (such as the Model Rules or the Criminal Justice Standards for the Defense Function), expert testimony (as in

---

[60] *dePape v. Trinity Health Systems, Inc.*, 242 F. Supp. 2d 585 (N.D. Iowa 2003) (lawyers who failed to provide immigration client with any information to make an informed decision about his immigration and attempted at last minute to convince him to perpetrate a fraud on the INS resulting in a failed entry to the U.S., liable for loss of client's income and emotional distress).

[61] RLGL §53 comment h; *Doe v. Roe*, 681 N.E.2d 640 (Ill. App. 1997) (lawyer abused his position to obtain sexual favors from divorce client); *Holliday v. Jones*, 264 Cal. Rptr. 448 (Cal. App. 1989) (criminal defendant who established that former lawyer's negligence caused his wrongful conviction liable for emotional distress damages due to incarceration).

[62] RLGL §54 comment d; *Olfe v. Gordon*, 286 N.W.2d 573 (Wis. 1980) (client who relied on lawyer to draft first mortgage not responsible for failure to discover that lawyer drafted second mortgage); *Clark v. Rowe*, 701 N.E.2d 624 (Mass. 1998) (upholding jury verdict that client was 70 percent at fault in refinancing a loan).

[63] *Strickland v. Washington*, 466 U.S. 668 (1984).

malpractice cases) [§9.08], or in a few situations, per se rules that presume error when lawyers breach basic fiduciary duties of obedience or loyalty. Second, to prove causation, counsel's deficient performance must have prejudiced the defendant. Most cases require proof of actual prejudice: but for counsel's unprofessional errors, the result of the proceeding would have been different, that is, this conduct was not harmless error. A few cases apply per se rules to presume prejudice, such as when counsel was denied during a critical stage of the proceeding.

As applied, these standards create an exceedingly difficult burden of proof for defendants, mostly because the Court presumes the validity of the underlying proceeding.[64] Yet despite these high hurdles, an amazing number of cases do result in relief. Using a per se standard, courts have reversed convictions when counsel failed to inform his client that he no longer represented him in an appeal, essentially depriving the accused of any lawyer at all.[65] Similarly, when counsel is present, but fails to test the prosecution's case, for example by conceding the defendant's guilt to the jury when the defendant consistently maintained his innocence,[66] or by a total lack of effort and explanation,[67] courts have no trouble finding a violation. Following a fact-specific inquiry, courts also have found counsel ineffective for failing to adequately investigate facts,[68] finding or understanding relevant law,[69]

---

[64] *McFarland v. Scott*, 512 U.S. 1256 (1994) (Blackmun, J., dissenting to the denial of *certiorari* and chronicling the denial of ineffective assistance claims in death penalty cases where defendants were executed).

[65] *Fields v. Bagley*, 275 F.3d 478 (6th Cir. 2001).

[66] E.g., *State v. Carter*, 14 P.3d 1138 (Kan. 2000); *Cf., Florida v. Nixon*, 125 S. Ct. 551(2004) (where lawyer advised defendant to concede guilt in light of overwhelming evidence against him and defendant gave no response, no presumption of prejudice).

[67] E.g., *People v. Bass*, 636 N.W.2d 781 (Mich. App. 2001) (defense counsel had no memory of trial, lost most of the file and offered no reason for failing to call witnesses); *Wenzy v. State*, 855 S.W.2d 47 (Tex. App. 1993) (when not allowed to withdraw, counsel refused to take an active role in defense).

[68] E.g., *Wiggins v. Smith*, 538 U.S. 510 (2003) (failure to expand investigation of mitigating evidence in death penalty case); *Wesley v. State*, 753 N.E.2d 686 (Ind. App. 2001) (failure to get psychiatric record of victim who had a history of false accusations); *In re K.J.O.*, 27 S.W.3d 340 (Tex. App. 2000) (failure to conduct investigation into juvenile's defense); *People v. Truly*, 595 N.E.2d 1230 (Ill. App. 1992) (failure to investigate and present alibi).

[69] E.g., *Stanford v. Stewart*, 554 S.E.2d 480 (Ga. 2001) (appellate counsel failed to recognize the significance of an error in jury instructions); *Pena-Mota v. State*, 986 S.W.2d

giving defective advice about whether to testify or accept a plea bargain,[70] and failing to object to improper evidence or procedures.[71]

A convicted defendant may succeed in establishing malpractice as well, but proof of actual causation requires either reversing the conviction or establishing actual innocence to prevail.[72] Even then, if the defense lawyer was a public defender, there may be sovereign immunity.[73] Assuming these hurdles can be leaped, the statute of limitations also can produce nasty problems.[74] When criminal convic-

---

341 (Tex. App. 1999) (failure to object to jury instruction resulted in a double jeopardy violation); *People v. Hayes*, 593 N.E.2d 739 (Ill. App. 1992) (mistake as to the burden of proof of insanity defense).

[70] *E.g., Crabbe v. State*, 546 S.E.2d 65 (Ga. App. 2001) (defense counsel did not advise defendant that guilty pleas would remove the possibility of parole); *State v. Donald*, 10 P.3d 1193 (Ariz. App. 2000), *cert. denied*, 534 U.S. 825 (2001) (receipt of a fair trial did not cure rejection of favorable plea bargain due to counsel's ineffective assistance); *Ross v. Kemp*, 393 S.E.2d 244 (Ga. 1990) ("fractured" defense by two lawyers who failed to effectively help defendant decide whether to testify).

[71] *Kimmelman v. Morrison*, 477 U.S. 365 (1986) (failure to move to suppress due to a total failure to conduct pre-trial discovery); *Dawkins v. State*, 551 S.E.2d 260 (S.C. 2001) (failure to object to hearsay statements of victim); *Evans v. State*, 28 P.3d 498 (Nev. 2001) (failure to challenge prosecutor's remarks during penalty phase of trial); *Ross v. State*, 726 So.2d 317 (Fla. App. 1998) (failure to object to improper remarks of prosecutor made during closing argument); *State v. Scott*, 602 N.W.2d 296 (Wis. App. 1999) (failure to object to prosecutor's breach of plea bargain); *Alaniz v. State*, 937 S.W.2d 593 (Tex. App. 1996) (failure to object to seating of a juror excused for cause); *State v. Crislip*, 785 P.2d 262 (N.M. App. 1989) (failure to protect defendant against unsworn, out-of-court accusation by co-defendant).

[72] RLGL §53 comment d; *Rodriguez v. Nielsen*, 650 N.W.2d 237 (Neb. 2002) (allegation that defendant acted in self-defense does not establish actual innocence); *Falkner v. Foshaug*, 29 P.3d 771 (Wash. App. 2001) (*Alford* plea, which allowed client to plead guilty without admitting guilt, did not preclude later proof of client's innocence in malpractice action against defense counsel).

[73] *Barner v. Leeds*, 13 P.3d 704 (Cal. 2000) (public defenders not protected by statutory immunity for discretionary acts); *Johnson v. Halloran*, 742 N.E.2d 741 (Ill. 2000) (public defenders not protected by sovereign immunity). *But see*, Public and Appellate Defender Immunity Act, 745 Ill. Comp. Stat. 19/1 (2004); *Wooton v. Vogele*, 769 N.E.2d 889 (Ohio App. 2001) (Ohio Tort Immunity Statute protects public defenders from suit); *Dziubak v. Mott*, 503 N.W.2d 771 (Minn. 1993) (public defenders protected from suit by judicial immunity).

[74] *Schreiber v. Rowe*, 814 So.2d 396 (Fla. 2002) (statute begins to run when conviction reversed); *Gebhardt v. O'Rourke*, 510 N.W.2d 900 (Mich. 1994) (statute begins to run on date of conviction, unless lawyer handles appeal).

tions are reversed for ineffective assistance of counsel, a few courts [§9.06] also have imposed discipline [§8.02], even against experienced defense counsel.[75]

### ➤§8.08 DISQUALIFICATION AND OTHER COURT ORDERS
### ➤§8.08(a) Dropping The Small Potato?

We've got a chance to bring a claim against Ajax Corporation. Problem is we do work for an Ajax subsidiary. But the present work is small potatoes and this claim could be really big. In an area we've been trying to break into. I say we should just fire away. Worse that can happen is we will get disqualified. We could join a long line of distinguished lawyers who have been so honored.

That could be the result. You are correct. On the other hand, the consequences [§9.05] could be worse. First, don't take this flyer without telling your prospective client. That client is entitled to decide whether it wants to run this risk [§3.05]. You don't want to be disqualified and suffer a malpractice claim [§8.04] from this new client as well. And you had better reach an understanding with the client as to who is going to shoulder the financial burden of the motion to disqualify, to avoid fee forfeiture [§8.10]. Second, although the only sanction typically meted out for conflicts of interest is disqualification, a violation of the lawyer codes [§9.04] can result in discipline as well [§8.02]. Although your bar counsel is spending most of her time chasing lawyers who steal from clients, she would be free to commence a proceeding against your lawyers. Third, you really have to decide what kind of lawyers you want to be. When some of us catalog prestigious firms that went way over the line, we don't mention that as a way of enhancing their prestige. Violating the rules of professional conduct is no badge of honor.

### ➤§8.08(b) Losing A Client By Disqualification Or Injunction

The last problem identifies multiple remedies [§9.05] that the law of agency has made available to clients whose lawyers breach fiduciary duties of loyalty or confidentiality. In the past half-century, however, courts have examined most conflicts of interest in the context of motions

---

[75] *In re Wolfram*, 847 P.2d 94 (Ariz.1993).

to disqualify lawyers.[76] Often these cases present circumstances where harm is threatened but has not yet occurred. Clients, former clients, and other litigation participants can seek to prevent harm by using a disqualification motion in a matter pending before a court. Outside of court, clients and former clients can seek injunctive relief to prevent the representation of other clients in transactional representations.

Disqualification motions originated over a century ago as requests for court orders addressed to the inherent power of a court.[77] The motion to disqualify may be made by the lawyer's client, former client, or any other party to the litigation, and judges are also empowered to raise such an issue [§9.02] *sua sponte*.[78] Although a few courts initially thought they had no such power, litigation over the past 50 years has left no doubt that courts can, and should, disqualify lawyers when their conduct threatens the fairness of a judicial proceeding.[79] Disqualifica-

---

[76] *Franklin v. Callum*, 782 A.2d 884 (N. H. 2001) (both parties granted disqualification of the other side's lawyer on different legal theories).

[77] *Id.*; *Williams v. State of Del.*, 805 A.2d 880 (Del. 2002) (appellate counsel disqualified for positional conflict of interest). Appellate courts review disqualification decisions of trial courts using an abuse of discretion standard. *See, e.g. People ex rel. Dept. of Corporations v. Speedee Oil Change Sys., Inc.*, 980 P.2d 371, 378 (Cal. 1999).

[78] This may be especially likely to occur in criminal cases, where judges assume special responsibility for the fairness of the proceeding. *E.g.,* Fed. R. Crim. P. 44(c) (federal district courts required to inquire into any proposed joint representation); *Cuyler v. Sullivan*, 446 U.S. 335 (1980) (trial judge has important role in assuring fairness of trial of joint defendants).

[79] *Ennis v. Ennis*, 276 N.W.2d 341, 348 (Wis. App. 1979). Administrative law judges also exercise this power in appropriate circumstances. *See, e.g., Prof'l Reactor Operator Soc'y v. United States NRC*, 939 F.2d 1047 (D.C. Cir. 1991) (Administrative Procedure Act's right to counsel guarantee requires concrete evidence that counsel's presence would impede the investigation in order to exclude a lawyer from representing a subpoenaed witness); *SEC v. Csapo*, 533 F.2d 7 (D.C. Cir. 1976) (same standard required for similar SEC rule granting agency authority to disqualify lawyers); *In re Scioto Broadcaster*, 5 FCC Rcd. 5158 (1990) (FCC review board and Commission will intervene only in cases of clear conflicts of interest). Arbitrators also consider motions to disqualify, *See, e.g., Pour Le Bebe, Inc. v. Guess? Inc.*, 5 Cal. Rptr. 3d 442 (Cal. App. 2003)(court will not overrule denial of disqualification motion by arbitration panel unless party to arbitration can show clear and convincing evidence that a conflict existed and that it had substantial impact on the panel's decision), although some courts disagree, *Biderman Industries Licensing Inc. v. Avmar N.V.,* 570 N.Y.S. 2d 33 (N.Y. App. Div. 1991)(application to disqualify counsel in arbitration proceeding is within exclusive jurisdiction of the courts).

tion is sought to prevent a lawyer or former lawyer (and that lawyer's current law firm) from representing another client. When granted, disqualification can ensure that the case will be presented without conflicting loyalties or that confidential information of a former client will not be used against that client in the current matter.[80]

Injunctive relief provides a similar equitable remedy for breaches of statute or common law fiduciary duty. Injunctive relief is a remedy that should only be granted when there is an urgent necessity to avoid injury and no adequate legal remedy exists, such as harm threatened by a law firm's use of a former client's business secrets to benefit its current client's direct competitors. If injunctive relief were not available in such a case, the former client would be forced to wait until it lost all or part of the company's business before claiming a remedy.[81]

Although disqualification and injunctions provide relief from real or serious threats to client loyalty or confidentiality, unlike other remedies, they can impose costs on other parties to a proceeding. When the motion to disqualify comes from the opposing party or the court, a client can be deprived of a chosen lawyer, and that client must be afforded additional time to retain new counsel.

Courts recognize that motions to disqualify can be used by opposing parties in litigation to tactical advantage and have responded in three ways to this potential for misuse of the court's power. First, courts are careful to scrutinize the facts and law offered in support of disqualification motions. Second, courts increasingly use the doctrine of laches, estoppel, or waiver to deny motions to disqualify when they have not been timely made.[82] Third, orders granting or denying disqualification usually are not appealable until a final judgment on the merits.[83] This means that when disqualification is denied, the targeted lawyer may continue the representation, but the other side can raise

---

[80] RLGL §6, comment i.

[81] *Maritrans GP Inc. v. Pepper, Hamilton & Scheetz*, 602 A.2d 1277 (Pa. 1992).

[82] *Universal City Studios, Inc. v. Reimerdes*, 98 F. Supp. 2d 449 (S.D.N.Y. 2000).

[83] In the federal courts, an order granting or denying disqualification cannot be appealed until a final judgment on the merits has been reached. *Richardson-Merrell Inc. v. Koller*, 472 U.S. 424 (1985); *Flanagan v. United States*, 465 U.S. 259 (1984); *Firestone Tire & Rubber v. Risjord*, 449 U.S. 368 (1981). State courts are split on this issue. *See,* David B. Harrison, *Appealability of State Court's Order Granting or Denying Motion to Disqualify Attorney*, 5 A.L.R. 4th 1251 (1981).

the issue on appeal. On the other hand, if the motion is granted, the client represented by the now-disqualified lawyer is forced to find new counsel.[84] If that client settles or wins the case, the disqualified lawyer has no independent right to appeal. Only if the client loses the case can the issue be raised on appeal.

In assessing whether a lawyer should be disqualified, courts begin with the conflict of interest rules in the relevant professional code [§9.04], statute, or case law.[85] The moving party has the burden of proving the violation. If professional code provisions [§9.04] have been violated, disqualification commonly follows. A few courts require more: that the violation would "taint" the court proceeding.[86] More typical are courts that explicitly reject this "hands-off approach," finding motions to disqualify counsel to be "the proper method for a party-litigant to bring the issues of conflict of interest or breach of ethical duties to the attention of the court."[87]

One issue [§9.02] that commonly arises is whether a law firm that defends a disqualification motion can charge its current client for the defense. Some clients in this position may agree to fight the motion. Others may agree but only at the firm's own expense.[88] Others may not be willing to defend at all, especially if the issue is close, and the client faces a real risk of losing your services.

▶**Red Flag**▶ Whenever you or your firm is subject to a disqualification motion, remember that a court order of disqualification means you have breached a fiduciary duty, thereby setting up a client's partial or complete defense to the payment of legal fees [§8.10].[89] If

---

[84] Successor counsel will usually be allowed to use the disqualified lawyer's work product if it does not contain impermissible client confidential information. RLGL §6, comment i.

[85] *In re Leslie Fay Companies*, 175 B.R. 525 (Bankr. S.D.N.Y. 1994).

[86] *The European Community v. RJR Nabisco, Inc.*, 134 F. Supp. 2d 297 (E.D.N.Y. 2001) (reviewing Second Circuit decisions).

[87] *In re American Airlines, Inc.*, 972 F.2d 605, 611 (5th Cir. 1992), *cert. denied*, 507 U.S. 912 (1993).

[88] *Padco v. Kinney & Lange*, 444 N.W.2d 889 (Minn. App. 1989).

[89] *In re Bonneville Pacific Corp.*, 196 B.R. 868 (Bankr. D. Utah 1996), *aff'd in part, rev'd in part sub nom. Hansen, Jones & Leta, P.C. v. Segal*, 220 B.R. 434 (D.Utah 1998); *Goldstein v. Lees*, 120 Cal. Rptr. 253 (Cal. App. 1975).

the conflict has affected the representation from an earlier date, your now former client also may seek disgorgement of fees already paid.[90]

## §8.09 LOSS OF CONTRACTUAL RIGHTS

### §8.09(a) The Client Gift?

**I've got this client. Loves me. How rare is that? Now he wants to remember me in his will. I'm talking a real gift. Course I have to outlive him but....**

Client gifts are suspect. If they are large they are presumptively void because of the law of undue influence. If he *really* wants to do this and you think he is capable of making that judgment, then the last thing you want is for you or anyone in your firm to draft the will. Send him to another lawyer.

**Then maybe that lawyer will end up with the gift.**

That could be, but if your firm drafts it you have no chance of getting the gift.

### §8.09(b) The Undue Influence Hurdle

Lawyer-agents who breach duties of obedience, loyalty, or confidentiality lose their entitlement to contractual rights because they have violated a basic fiduciary obligation essential to rendering the contract enforceable. Courts [§9.06] begin by applying relevant lawyer code [§9.04] or agency objections to determine whether a breach of fiduciary duty occurred. Once that is established, they apply the agency presumption of undue influence, both to protect individual clients and to create an incentive for lawyers to fulfill fiduciary duties. In many cases, the lawyer is unable to rebut the presumption and loses the benefit.[91]

---

[90] *In re Fountain*, 141 Cal. Rptr. 654 (Cal. App. 1977).

[91] *Petit-Clair v. Nelson*, 782 A.2d 960 (N.J. Super. Ct. App. Div. 2001) (lawyer who secured payment of legal fees with mortgage on client's house unable to foreclose on mortgage); *Passante v. McWilliam*, 62 Cal. Rptr. 2d 298 (Cal. App. 1997) (lawyer who "came through in the clutch" by raising money for client's business not able to enforce client's promise to pay him three percent of the company's stock); *Monco v. Janus*, 583 N.E.2d 575 (Ill. App. 1991) (lawyer who provided hundreds of hours of legal services to business startup unable to rebut presumption of undue influence when he sought to dissolve the corporation).

Lawyers can lose a contractual benefit when they sue a client to enforce the contract's terms, or when they sue to collect a fee and the client alleges breach of fiduciary duty in a counterclaim. If the contractual benefit has already been received, the client can seek return of the benefit through other equitable remedies [§9.05], such as a constructive trust or fee forfeiture. Lawyers have been forced to account for, return, or hold in constructive trust specific property acquired because of the improper use of confidential information.[92] Another example denies the lawyer's entitlement to client gifts of property when the lawyer has breached fiduciary duty by drafting the document of gift.[93]

### ►§8.10 FEE FORFEITURE

### ►§8.10(a) The Lost Fee?

**I can't believe it. We did a great job for the client. The contract is the best they could have gotten. Our only transgression was we forgot to tell the client, before we undertook the representation, that someone else in our firm was doing work for the other side on a completely unrelated matter. I did the work and I had no idea. So this so-called conflict could not possibly have affected my loyalty. But now the client has written us a nasty letter. Seems someone from the other side told our client what good lawyers we were because they used us too. The client claims we should refund our entire fee. Or else they will report our technical rule violation to the disciplinary folks. Is that fair?**

It hardly seems fair. As you say, the client got great services. But it could happen. Cases of forced fee disgorgement for, as you say, "technical" violations of the ethics rules are out there. Even if the client cannot recover for malpractice, the client who can persuade a court you breached a fiduciary duty might get an order to return all or part of the fee.

---

[92] RLGL §6, comments d and e.

[93] *Comm. on Prof'l Ethics v. Randall*, 285 N.W.2d 161 (Iowa 1979), *cert. denied*, 446 U.S. 946 (1980) (lawyer made himself sole beneficiary of client's will); *In re Putnam*, 177 N.E. 399 (N.Y. 1931) (gift to lawyer in document lawyer drafted presumed to be the product of undue influence).

### ▶§8.10(b) The Equity Of Fee Forfeiture

The remedy of fee forfeiture can be traced back three centuries.[94] Unlike legal remedies, such as malpractice, it does not require proof of causation or damages, but only that the client or former client shows breach of a clear and serious fiduciary duty.[95] The more serious the breach, the greater the fee forfeited to the former clients.

Breaches of the core agency duties of obedience, disclosure, confidentiality, and loyalty usually qualify as clear and serious breaches, although the source of the duty can be civil law (for example, legal malpractice) or criminal law (for example, fraud) as well.[96] Most common are conflicts of interest, such as representing a client's wife in a divorce,[97] failing to disclose that the law firm employed the opposing party's adjuster,[98] or pressuring a client to change a fee contract,[99] all of which evidence clear disloyalty. Settling a client's case without consent also qualifies.[100]

The first factor, whether the violation was "clear," is determined by an objective standard: whether "a reasonable lawyer, knowing the relevant facts and law reasonably accessible to the lawyer, would have known that the conduct was wrongful."[101] For example, the lawyers in one recent case were not able to claim they had no idea Model Rule 1.8(g) prohibited aggregate settlements.[102] The second factor, whether the violation was "serious," often is established when multiple breaches of fiduciary duty occur in the same case.[103] Inadvertent isolated

---

[94] *Silbiger v. Prudence Bonds Corp.*, 180 F.2d 917, 920 (2d Cir. 1950), *cert. denied,* 340 U.S. 813 (1950) (citing cases). *See also, Woods v. City Nat'l Bank and Trust Co. of Chicago,* 312 U.S. 262 (1941).

[95] RLGL §49.

[96] RLGL §37, comment c.

[97] *Jeffry v. Pounds,* 136 Cal. Rptr. 373 (Cal. App. 1977).

[98] *Rice v. Perl,* 320 N.W.2d 407 (Minn. 1982).

[99] *Searcy, Denney, Scarola, Barnhart & Shipley, P.A. v. Scheller,* 629 So.2d 947 (Fla. App. 1993).

[100] *Francisco v. Foret,* 2002 Tex. App. LEXIS 2610 (Tex. Ct. App. Apr. 11, 2002).

[101] RLGL §37 comment d. *See, e.g., Hardison v. Weinshel,* 450 F. Supp. 721 (E.D. Wis. 1978) (lawyer who withdrew from case shortly before trial because he mistakenly believed client would not prevail forfeits all fee).

[102] *Burrow v. Arce,* 997 S.W.2d 229 (Tex. 1999).

[103] *Piro v. Sarofim,* 80 S.W.3d 717 (Tex. App. 2002).

breaches, such as the failure to fully explain the terms of a settlement when the trial judge explained them to the client, do not rise to the level of a clear and serious breach.[104]

Once a clear and serious breach of fiduciary duty has been shown, fee forfeiture initially is presumed to be total.[105] Most courts recognize that partial fee forfeiture may be more appropriate when the misconduct can be separated in time from other valuable services the lawyer has performed. Factors such as the willfulness of the violation, its effect on the client, and the adequacy of other remedies [§9.05], as well as "the public interest in maintaining the integrity of attorney-client relationships" all are relevant.

Thus, when the breach of fiduciary duty permeates the entire relationship, the grounds for total fee forfeiture are found. This explains why so many of the full fee forfeiture cases involve a conflict of interest that tainted the entire representation. On the other hand, when the conflict materializes during the representation, the lawyer may be reimbursed for services provided before she was obliged to respond to the conflict.[106]

Finally, note that liability insurance usually will pay a damage award, but rarely will be available to cover a fee forfeiture claim. One court has analogized fee forfeiture to punitive damages and concluded that insurance covering a lawyer's individual breach of fiduciary duty was contrary to public policy, but coverage for a law firm's vicarious responsibility was not.[107]

Fee forfeiture also can occur pursuant to statute. Most prominent are statutes that provide for forfeiture of the fruits of criminal activity, including lawyer's fees.[108] Forfeiture statutes provide for civil forfeiture of the client's funds traceable to criminal activity, on the theory that they passed to the government at the time of the crime.[109] The government can seize all assets of a defendant at the point of indict-

---

[104] *Hoover v. Larkin*, 2001 Tex. App. LEXIS 6313 (Tex. Ct. App. Sept. 13, 2001).

[105] RLGL §37, comment e.

[106] *E.g., Hill v. Douglass*, 271 So.2d 1 (Fla. 1972) (lawyer did not forfeit fee until he should have known he would be a witness).

[107] *Perl v. St. Paul Fire & Marine Inc. Co.*, 345 N.W.2d 209 (Minn. 1984).

[108] *E.g.*, 21 U.S.C. §§848, 853 (2000).

[109] *See*, Hazard & Hodes, §9.32 (2005).

§8.11 CLIENT & THIRD-PARTY REMEDIES • 255

ment on a showing of probable cause to believe that the assets will ultimately be found to be subject to forfeiture.[110] If the criminal case determines that the assets are the proceeds of the crime, they are forfeited permanently to the government.

The Supreme Court has held that these statutes are intended to reach lawyer's fees, as well as other assets of the defendant, and that using this statutory power to freeze cash paid to a lawyer does not violate a client's rights.[111] The practical reality created by these cases [§9.06] is that a lawyer retained by a defendant where such a statute applies takes a risk of nonpayment. Further, because the statute exempts a "bona fide purchaser for value" of property otherwise subject to forfeiture, lawyers essentially must audit the source of the client's money in order to assure themselves of payment.[112]

Together, the common law agency remedies [§9.05] of fee forfeiture and other loss of contractual benefits, as well as statutes that accomplish the same result, create minefields for unwary lawyers. You can avoid these client remedies by honoring your fiduciary duties, including the duties of obedience, disclosure, confidentiality, and loyalty. Avoiding statutory fee forfeiture requires understanding of case law and careful investigation of facts.

## ▶ §8.11 PROCEDURAL SANCTIONS

Courts use a variety of procedural rules, statutes, and inherent powers to impose monetary sanctions on lawyers, clients, and law firms who file frivolous lawsuits or evade applicable discovery obligations. Procedural rules like Fed. R. Civ. P. 11 require lawyers to perform due diligence, that is, a reasonable inquiry into both facts and law before filing a pleading, written motion, or other paper. No finding of delay or

---

[110] *United States v. Monsanto*, 924 F.2d 1186 (2d Cir. 1991) (*en banc*), *cert. denied*, 502 U.S. 943 (1991).

[111] *Caplin & Drysdale v. United States*, 491 U.S. 617 (1989); *United States v. Monsanto*, 491 U.S. 600 (1989).

[112] A "bona fide purchaser for value" is a person who "was reasonably without cause to believe that the property was subject to forfeiture" when he took the property. 21 U.S.C. §853(c). *See, e.g., United States v. McCorkle*, 321 F.3d 1292 (11th Cir. 2003) (burden of proof on lawyer F. Lee Bailey to identify the portion of the fee collected while he was a bona fide purchaser for value).

significant expense is required.[113] If the complaint is legally or factually baseless from an objective perspective and the lawyer has not conducted a reasonable inquiry into the law or facts, sanctions can follow. Sanctions may include court directives of a nonmonetary nature, orders to pay a penalty into the court, and orders directing payment of reasonable attorney's fees to the movant for expenses incurred as a direct result of the violation. In federal court, current Rule 11 provides for a 21-day safe harbor to withdraw the offending pleading or document after a sanctions motion has been made. Earlier versions still in effect in some states have no such safe harbor.

With respect to discovery abuse, Fed. R. Civ. P. 26(g) requires discovery requests to be signed with a certification similar to Fed. R. Civ. P. 11, and Fed. R. Civ. P. 37 provides for sanctions that parallel those in Fed. R. Civ. P. 11 for certifications made without substantial justification. Rules of appellate procedure include similar provisions.[114]

Each of these provisions extends to specific conduct. For example, Fed. R. Civ. P. 11 and similar state provisions do not extend to conduct beyond written documents, such as oral deposition abuses or oral misstatements to a court. But beyond these procedural rules, courts have inherent power to control such conduct as long as they make explicit findings that the conduct is the equivalent of bad faith.[115] Inherent power sanctions can include fines, disqualification, discipline, and claim or defense preclusion. They do not include the "wielding of legislative power" such as the power to order parties to pay fines outside of the litigation.[116]

Federal courts also can rely on 28 U.S.C. §1927, which authorizes them to impose "excess costs, expenses, and attorneys' fees" on a lawyer who "multiplies the proceedings unreasonably and vexatiously," a standard that essentially also requires a finding of bad faith. If bad faith is found, other remedies [§9.05] such as state tort law actions for malicious prosecution might follow, at least when the plaintiff can

---

[113] *Christian v. Mattel, Inc.*, 286 F.3d 1118 (9th Cir. 2002).

[114] *Matter of Hendrix*, 986 F.2d 195 (7th Cir. 1993) (Federal Rules of Appellate Procedure allow for imposition of sanctions and discipline for failing to cite relevant law).

[115] *Chambers v. NASCO, Inc.*, 501 U.S. 32 (1991).

[116] *In re Tutu Wells Contamination Litigation*, 120 F.3d 368 (3d Cir. 1997).

§8.12

show the institution of an action without probable cause, malice (which can be inferred by lack of probable cause), and termination of the action in favor of the plaintiff.[117] Of course, any finding of a procedural rule violation also can result in professional discipline [§8.02] for violating Model Rules 3.1 or 3.4.

### ▶ §8.12 AVOIDING PROBLEMS

You can avoid the adverse consequences [§9.05] of the law governing lawyers by doing three things:

1. Know who your clients are [Chapter 1];

2. Mind your 4 C fiduciary duties [Chapters 3-6], which are embedded in the professional codes [§9.04] and the basis of all client remedies [§9.05]; and

3. Know the limits of the law [Chapter 7], which create legal boundaries and concomitant remedies to both clients and others. For most lawyers most of the time, this is common sense and intuitive. As we have tried to demonstrate throughout this book, however, many of these issues [§9.02] are not clear at the moment you face them.

In the next two chapters we target ways to avoid these adverse consequences, by focusing on problems that illustrate the ultimate red flags you cannot ignore. We begin in Chapter 9 by examining when and how to help yourself by researching the law governing lawyers. We conclude in Chapter 10 by offering you the tools to recognize those occasions when you must seek further advice and perspective.

---

[117] *See, e.g., Mattel, Inc. v. Luce, Forward, Hamilton & Scripps*, 121 Cal. Rptr. 2d 794 (Cal. App. 2002), which upheld a cause of action for malicious prosecution following sanctions for the same conduct in *Christian, supra* n. 113.

# Part Five

# ►Red Flags►:
# How To Get The Help You Really Need

# 9

# How To Help Yourself: Researching The Law Governing Lawyers

➤ §9.01 Why Research?
    ➤ §9.01(a) The Imposition?
    ➤ §9.01(b) Researching The Law Governing Lawyers
➤ §9.02 Issue Spotting
    ➤ §9.02(a) Which Issues?
    ➤ §9.02(b) Spotting All Of The Red Flags
➤ §9.03 Basic Resources
    ➤ §9.03(a) Lawyer Codes
    ➤ §9.03(b) The Restatement
    ➤ §9.03(c) Treatises
    ➤ §9.03(d) On-Line Resources
➤ §9.04 Finding Lawyer Code Provisions
    ➤ §9.04(a) Which Rules?
    ➤ §9.04(b) Finding All Relevant Rules
➤ §9.05 Recognizing Overlapping Remedies
    ➤ §9.05(a) Which Remedies?
    ➤ §9.05(b) Identifying All Of The Consequences
➤ §9.06 Judicial Opinions
    ➤ §9.06(a) Which Cases?

➤ §9.06(b) Uncovering All Of The Law
➤ §9.07 Ethics Opinions
➤ §9.07(a) Which Ethics Opinions?
➤ §9.07(b) Discovering Additional Guidance
➤ §9.08 Using Experts
➤ §9.08(a) Do We Need An Expert?
➤ §9.08(b) Which Expert?
➤ §9.08(c) Relying On Expert Testimony

### ➤ §9.01 WHY RESEARCH?

#### ➤ §9.01(a) The Imposition?

I've been in this large law firm only a year. Trying to learn business planning. Then a big shot partner informs me that he met with an important client; seems client's daughter is in "a bit of trouble" and he wants me to handle the case, "as a favor." Turns out our important client's teenage daughter was at a party and got busted for underage drinking, and she gave the police her friend's name and driver's license. I researched the law about underage drinking, appeared at a pretrial conference and got the city attorney to agree to dismiss the matter. I even met with the daughter's "friend," explained everything was taken care of, but told her—correctly—that she would have to petition on her own to get the criminal record in her name sealed. Now the friend has reported me to the city attorney and the bar. Didn't I do everything right? I even consulted with my senior partner about the case.

Well, . . . no. You missed four important issues, and three of them concern legal ethics. First, when your client persisted in using her friend's identity, she committed another crime: criminal impersonation. Second, when you entered an appearance in her friend's name, you assisted that criminal activity in violation of Model Rule 1.2(d). Third, when you told the city attorney and the court that you represented the person whose name appeared on the driver's license, you lied, violating Model Rules 3.3, 4.1(a) and 8.4(c). Finally, Model Rule 5.2 provides that you cannot rely on your senior partner unless he gave you a "reasonable resolution of an arguable question of professional duty." If he knew what you knew and told you all was okay, you got very bad advice. In short, you researched what you thought was the law governing the client's case, and forgot about your professional obligations to heed the limits of the law in your own and your client's conduct. If you or your senior partner had recognized the need to research the professional rules and criminal code in your jurisdiction, rather than just the law about underage drinking, you might not now be facing professional discipline.[1]

▶**Ultimate Red Flag**▶ Knowing when you can rely on another lawyer's judgment requires more than trust. We explore this topic further in §10.09.

### ▶§9.01(b) Researching The Law Governing Lawyers

Lawyers searching for a concrete resolution of any legal issue need to find jurisdiction-specific law. If you presume you are a good person and don't need to inquire about the ethical implications of your representation, you may miss an important opportunity both to provide your client with competent representation and to avoid negative consequences yourself.

This chapter will help you find the relevant sources you need to provide reliable answers to issues about lawyer conduct. To do this, you will need to identify issues, understand the basic resources that can provide you with the knowledge you need, employ some specialized research techniques, and evaluate the materials you discover to know whether to pursue additional research in other jurisdictions.

We have relied on national standards (the ABA Model Rules and the ALI's *Restatement of the Law Governing Lawyers*) in writing this book. Although these models provide the template for most state law, the answer to the issue that you face may differ in any given jurisdiction. This is why you must know how to locate your jurisdiction's

---

[1] In *People v. Casey*, 948 P.2d 1014(Colo. 1997), the lawyer engaging in such conduct was suspended from practice for 45 days and ordered to take the Multi-State Professional Responsibility Exam.

lawyer code [§9.04], case law [§9.06], and ethics opinions [§9.07], as well as the range of remedies that may exist for the conduct you propose or have engaged in [§9.05]. If your jurisdiction has not yet addressed an issue, you will need to find relevant analogs in other jurisdictions, and recognize when it is time to find an expert [§9.08].

## ▶ §9.02 ISSUE SPOTTING

### ▶ §9.02(a) Which Issues?

Got a call from an employee of the opposing company in this case. I know right away I have to worry about whether I can meet him. I establish he's not in the control group, he wasn't involved in the underlying events, and he couldn't possibly bind the company. So we meet. I get some juicy documents. My case is going great. Last week I used some of the documents in the deposition of CFO. You should have seen the look on my opposing counsel's face. Warmed my heart. But now they have moved to disqualify me. And have reported me to the bar. How can I be in so much trouble when I was so careful?

Well, you were careful about Rule 4.2 and professional discipline [§8.02]. You were free to talk to this individual. What we assume has happened—or at least what the other side must be asserting—is that you learned privileged information. That usually is juicy. The problem is if you learn privileged information from someone not authorized to waive the organization's privilege, you can be disqualified [§8.08]. And you may have also run afoul of Rule 4.4, which makes it a disciplinary rule violation to invade the other side's privilege. You must spot all of the issues in a problem before you can proceed with confidence.

### ▶ §9.02(b) Spotting All Of The Red Flags

If we've done our job, this book should help you identify legal ethics issues. It also should familiarize you with sections of the lawyer codes that speak to general obligations of lawyers, such as communication [Chapter 3] competence [Chapter 4], confidentiality [Chapter 5], conflicts of interest [Chapter 6], and the limits of the law [Chapter 7]. When a problem involving the conduct of lawyers arises, the first step in solving it is to define these issues. You may immediately dis-

§9.03(a)   RESEARCHING THE LAW GOVERNING LAWYERS • 265

cover some, such as confidentiality or loyalty, and you may immediately recognize the relevance of specific professional rules, such as Model Rule 1.6 or 1.7. Whether or not this occurs, be open to the possibility that additional lawyer code provisions [§9.04] or other legal remedies [§9.05] also may be relevant to your inquiry.

## ►§9.03 BASIC RESOURCES

### ►§9.03(a) Lawyer Codes

Lawyer codes are easy to find online. For a link to the most recent version of your jurisdiction's rules, go to www.abanet.org/cpr/links.html or www.law.cornell.edu/ethics/. On LEXIS or Westlaw, go to your state's court rules file ("XXRule" on LEXIS, "XXRules" on Westlaw).[2] Westlaw additionally provides a topical database in "Legal Ethics and Professional Responsibility" that contains files which include "state rules of professional conduct" and leads you directly to the "XXRules" menu. In the federal courts, district courts usually provide for reciprocal discipline and discipline following a felony conviction, and further impose the state court rules of the jurisdiction in which they sit.[3] Each court has added some distinctive nuances, however, which makes finding and reviewing local rules imperative.[4] To search the relevant circuit rules file, use a search such as "discipline."[5] Each circuit's rules impose slightly different standards, but they usually defer to some extent to individual state rules.[6] Federal district court local trial rules also can be searched online.

---

[2] "XX" standing for the state's two-letter postal abbreviation.

[3] *E.g.,* N. D. Cal. Civ. Local R. 11-7 (2005); C.D. Cal. Local Civil L.R. 83-3.1.2 (2005); N.D. Tex. Local Crim. R. 57.8 (2004).

[4] *E.g.,* N.D. Cal. Civ. L.R. 11-6(b) (2005) ("attorney" includes law corporations and partnerships); N.D. N.Y. Local R. 83.4(j) (2005) (ABA Code of Professional Responsibility applies to lawyer conduct).

[5] *E.g.,* U.S. Tax Ct. R. 201 (2005) (ABA Model Rules govern lawyer conduct).

[6] *E.g.,* 4th Cir. Rule 46(g) (2005) (rules of professional conduct where lawyer maintains principal office); 11th Cir. Addendum Eight R.1 (2004) (ABA Model Rules and rules of professional conduct where lawyer is licensed to practice if not inconsistent with ABA Model Rules).

Once you have found your jurisdiction's current lawyer code, recall that most jurisdictions have adopted some version of the Model Rules of Professional Conduct during the past 20 years. If you wish to find all of the relevant law on point, you will therefore need to be aware of equivalent Model Code of Professional Responsibility provisions in effect before the current rules were adopted. Although very little case law [§9.06] developed before the Model Code, to find all relevant law, you also may need to travel back to your jurisdiction's version of the Canons of Professional Ethics, in effect before 1970. The chart below lists this general historical development.

### Professional Rules Governing Lawyer Conduct

**I. LAWYERS**

    A. Disciplinary Rules

        1. ABA Canons of Professional Ethics (1908-1969).

        2. ABA Model Code of Professional Responsibility (1969-1983). (Superseded in most jurisdictions by the Model Rules of Professional Conduct.)

        3. ABA Model Rules of Professional Conduct (1983-2003). Adopted by nearly all jurisdictions. Exceptions include: California, Iowa, Maine, Nebraska, and Ohio. (New York has retained the Model Code format, but has adopted the substance of many of the Model Rules.)

        4. Ethics 2000 Commission (1997-2002). www.abanet.org/cpr/ethics2k.html. In February 2002 and August 2003, the ABA House of Delegates adopted nearly all of the revisions recommended by the Ethics 2000 Commission. The current revised ABA Model Rules are published in The Center for Professional Responsibility's Edition of the Model Rule of Professional Conduct, or can be found at www.abanet.org/cpr/mrpc/mrpc_toc.html.

**II. JUDGES**

    A. ABA Code of Judicial Conduct (1972)

    B. ABA Model Code of Judicial Conduct (1990-2003)

    C. Proposed revisions to the 1990 Code should be presented to the ABA House of Delegates in 2006.

### ▶ §9.03(b) The Restatement

Published in 2000 after 13 years of development, the *Restatement of the Law Third, The Law Governing Lawyers* restates nearly all the law governing lawyer conduct, including lawyer codes [§9.04], common law [§9.06], and statutes. It is organized by topic, and covers most issues addressed by lawyer codes, with the exception of advertising and solicitation [§7.13]. It addresses in depth issues of civil liability [§§8.04-8.06], the attorney-client privilege [§5.04], and work-product doctrine [§5.05]. If your jurisdiction lacks authority or the result in your jurisdiction strikes you as odd or wrong, the Restatement may be especially helpful in putting an issue in perspective. Many courts also rely on the Restatement when addressing a new issue or application of their previous common law principles to lawyer conduct.

The Restatement includes extensive comments and illustrations as well as Reporter's Notes, which add citations to relevant primary and secondary authority, following each Restatement section. A Table of Codes, Rules, and Standards at the end of Volume II includes Restatement citations to Model Rule sections, individual state lawyer code provisions, other Restatements, and the Model Penal Code.

You should be aware that while the Restatement was being developed between 1988-1999, a number of courts, articles, and books cited and relied on the tentative drafts. The final Restatement renumbered the sections consecutively, changing some of the earlier cited section numbers. The chart nearby indicates these changes in numbers. If you decide to research by Restatement section number, be aware that you should include both the old and new numbers in your search. If you search for a Restatement provision in a case law database, try "law governing lawyers" and the section numbers, or "law governing lawyers" and the general topic for which you are looking. You can also search the text of the Restatement on Westlaw, under the topical heading of "Restatements" or "Legal Ethics and Professional Responsibility". Be careful to select the final version, not the archive database, which contains the numerous tentative drafts.

## *Restatement of the Law, Third The Law Governing Lawyers*
### Conversion Table

OLD = tentative and final drafts (1988-1999)

### NEW = final restatement sections (2000)

| OLD # | NEW # | OLD # | NEW # | OLD # | NEW # | OLD # | NEW # |
|---|---|---|---|---|---|---|---|
| 1-8 | **1-8** | 53 | **41** | 124 | **74** | 167 | **107** |
| 10 | **9** | 54 | **42** | 125 | **75** | 168 | **108** |
| 11 | **10** | 55 | **43** | 126 | **76** | 169 | **109** |
| 12 | **11** | 56 | **44** | 127 | **77** | 170 | **110** |
| 13 | **12** | 57 | **45** | 128 | **78** | 171 | **111** |
| 14 | **13** | 58 | **46** | 129 | **79** | 172 | **112** |
| 26 | **14** | 59 | **47** | 130 | **80** | 173 | **113** |
| 27 | **15** | 70 (71) | **48** | 131 | **81** | 174 | **114** |
| 28 | **16** | 71 | **49** | 132 | **82** | 175 | **115** |
| 29 | **17** | 72 | **50** | 133 | **83** | 176 | **116** |
| 29A | **18** | 73 | **51** | 134A | **84** | 177 | **117** |
| 30 | **19** | 74 | **52** | 134B | **85** | 178 | **118** |
| 31 | **20** | 75 | **53** | 135 | **86** | 179 | **119** |
| 32 | **21** | 76 | **54** | 136 | **87** | 180 | **120** |
| 33 | **22** | 76A | **55** | 137 | **88** | 201 | **121** |
| 34 | **23** | 77 | **56** | 138 | **89** | 202 | **122** |
| 35 | **24** | 78 | **57** | 139 | **90** | 203 | **123** |
| 37 | **25** | 79 | **58** | 140 | **91** | 204 | **124** |
| 38 | **26** | 111 | **59** | 141 | **92** | 206 | **125** |
| 39 | **27** | 112 | **60** | 142 | **93** | 207 | **126** |
| 40 | **28** | 113 | **61** | 151 | **94** | 208 | **127** |
| 41 | **29** | 114 | **62** | 152 | **95** | 209 | **128** |
| 42 | **30** | 115 | **63** | 155 | **96** | 210 | **129** |
| 43 | **31** | 116 | **64** | 156 | **97** | 211 | **130** |
| 44 | **32** | 117 | **65** | 157 | **98** | 212 | **131** |
| 45 | **33** | 117A | **66** | 158 | **99** | 213 | **132** |
| 46 | **34** | 117B | **67** | 159 | **100** | 214 | **133** |
| 47 | **35** | 118 | **68** | 161 | **101** | 215 | **134** |
| 48 | **36** | 119 | **69** | 162 | **102** | 216 | **135** |
| 49 | **37** | 120 | **70** | 163 | **103** | | |
| 50 | **38** | 121 | **71** | 164 | **104** | | |
| 51 | **39** | 122 | **72** | 165 | **105** | | |
| 52 | **40** | 123 | **73** | 166 | **106** | | |

## ▶ §9.03(c) Treatises

Treatises can help you identify issues, find law, and understand the history as well as current status of the law governing lawyers. We hope this volume has already helped you with these tasks and we list additional resources below in alphabetical order. Be careful to note the date of the volume you consult, because recent changes in lawyer code provisions [§9.04] or common law [§9.06] may affect the outcome of the matter you are researching.

If you have no idea where to begin your research, check the table of contents or index of this book or one of these resources. Hornbooks or treatises about the law of professional responsibility in a specific jurisdiction also may assist you. Increasing numbers of law review articles and ALR annotations also address a wide variety of issues about lawyer conduct. You may find one or several directly on point.

ABA, *Annotated Model Rules of Professional Conduct* (5th Ed. 2003; 1,003pp.)

> Content and Organization: Organized by Model Rule Sections, this series of case annotations provides helpful examples of representative court and ethics opinions as well as selected citations to secondary authorities. New editions are published every few years.
>
> Special Features: Two tables at the end of the volume provide parallel tables between the ABA Model Code and the ABA Model Rule provisions.

*ABA/BNA Lawyers' Manual on Professional Conduct* (2004; 3 loose-leaf volumes, monthly updates)

> Content and Organization: This resource is divided into three different volumes. The first, called the "Manual," is organized by topics that generally follow the order of the Model Rules. Each topic begins with a short "practice guide," followed by "background" and "application" sections. Bibliographies follow each topic. The Manual covers the scope of the entire law governing lawyers, and adds special sections that focus on specialized practices and malpractice. The second series of volumes includes the full text of ABA and some state ethics opinions. Other state opinions are described in annotations. The third loose-leaf volume contains "Current Reports," and an index to these reports, which are both published every two weeks.

> Special Features: The Current Reports are the most complete recent updates to case law, rules changes, and ethics opinions. Each issue includes cites to Internet sources and ABA contacts that can assist your research. The Manual includes both a topical and a case index.

Geoffrey C. Hazard and W. William Hodes, *The Law of Lawyering* (Aspen, 3d ed., 2005; 2 loose-leaf volumes, yearly updates)

> Content and Organization: This loose-leaf service is organized topically, following the order of the Model Rules of Professional Conduct. The treatise reflects latest developments in the law of lawyering, including citations to the Restatement, ethics opinions and case law. The authors discuss multiple remedies, including malpractice, disqualification, discipline, and fee forfeiture.
>
> Special Features: Each section includes illustrations that apply the law governing lawyers to concrete situations. The Appendix in Vol. II includes the text of the ABA Model Rules and the black letter of the Restatement.

Ronald D. Rotunda, *Legal Ethics: The Lawyer's Deskbook on Professional Responsibility* (ABA 2002; 1,373 pp.)

> Content and Organization: This treatise follows the organization and logic of the Model Rules. It includes footnotes with citations to some cases and Restatement sections. It also mentions topics such as the attorney-client privilege and remedies beyond professional discipline, such as fee forfeiture or disqualification.
>
> Special Features: Footnotes include citations to relevant portions of the predecessor Model Code of Professional Responsibility and to ABA Ethics Opinions. Appendices include the text of 12 ABA Model Rules or Standards for Regulating Lawyers, such as Trust Account Overdraft Notification, Fee Arbitration, Lawyer Disciplinary Enforcement and Aspirational Goals for Lawyer Advertising.

Charles W. Wolfram, *Modern Legal Ethics* (West, 1986; 1,363 pp.)

> Content and Organization: This hornbook is organized by topic and covers all the issues. It is especially helpful for understanding the historical development of the professional code provisions and case law.
>
> Special Features: Each section includes pre-formulated computer searches to locate case law. Appendices include parallel

tables among the ABA Canons, ABA Model Code, and ABA Model Rules.

### ▶ §9.03(d) On-Line Resources

- To view the current version of the ABA Model Rules, go to http://www.abanet.org/cpr/mrpc/mrpc_toc.html.
- To find the most recent version of a particular jurisdiction's lawyer code, go to http://www.abanet.org/cpr/links.html or http://www.law.cornell.edu/ethics/.
- ABA and state ethics opinions are available on Westlaw and Lexis and at most local state bar or state supreme court websites.
- The Restatement and the *ABA/BNA Lawyers' Manual* are available on Westlaw, under the topical heading "Legal Ethics and Professional Responsibility."

### ▶ §9.04 FINDING LAWYER CODE PROVISIONS

### ▶ §9.04(a) Which Rules?

**I was representing this company. Then a conflict came up. I called the client and I distinctly remember getting a conflicts waiver. I even remember the client saying "no problem." It's two months later and now client has filed a motion to disqualify. Claims there is a conflict. Of course that is correct, but I got a waiver!**

Even if you have a tape recording of that telephone conversation, we fear that might not be enough. The new model rules adopted in more and more states reflect a recent change to the ABA Model Rule that requires a conflicts waiver be "confirmed in writing."[7] That rule was designed to protect clients. But it was also designed to protect lawyers whose clients might be forgetful. So if you were relying on the old model rules book you picked up in law school, you probably didn't know of this requirement, but we bet your state is one that has changed its rules. That is why your (former?) client feels confident about its motion to disqualify [§8.08], and why you should have looked up the current rule in your jurisdiction before proceeding.

---

[7] Model Rule 1.7(b)(4).

### ▶§9.04(b) Finding All Relevant Rules

Once you identify ethics issues, you should consider whether any professional rules address them. Of course, if the issue is professional discipline [§8.02], the lawyer codes directly apply. If the issue involves other law, such as disqualification or malpractice [Chapter 8], we have seen that the lawyer codes also speak to the underlying legal ethics issue, and often guide court decisions concerning agency remedies [§9.05]. For this reason, once you have targeted the relevant issues, you will need to identify the relevant lawyer code provisions in your jurisdiction. Of course, some issues, such as the attorney-client privilege or work-product doctrine [§§5.04-5.05], might be resolved without citations to lawyer code provisions. Be careful, however, because the privilege issue may overlap with the professional rules governing confidentiality.

To find your jurisdiction's lawyer code, remember that the judicial branch of government regulates lawyers, so you will be searching for a state or federal court rule in most jurisdictions. These court rules often may be found in a separate volume in a set of annotated statutes. A few jurisdictions such as California regulate the bar through both statutes and court rules.

Once you find the court rules volume or file, search by rule number or text of a rule. If you do not know the relevant rules, go back and identify issues first. You may be surprised to find that your jurisdiction's rule contains distinctive language or provisions not found in the ABA Model Rules. This occurs with some frequency, so never rely on the Model Rules (or Model Code) provisions alone.

▶**Red Flag**▶ Nearly every jurisdiction has just completed or is in the process of reviewing its lawyer code. Be careful to identify the most recent version of your jurisdiction's rules. Use links at the two websites listed above [§9.03(d)] or check on your state bar or state supreme court website.

### ▶§9.05 RECOGNIZING OVERLAPPING REMEDIES
### ▶§9.05(a) Which Remedies?

I can't believe it! Our firm thought we had a great argument, that we shouldn't be disqualified from suing Magna Corporation just because we were doing work for one of its multiple subsidiaries. But Magna moved to disqualify and the court bought their stupid arguments. We thought that was the end of it. But last week the client we were representing against Magna sued us. The client wants its fees back, and it claims damages because we failed to warn it about the conflicts problem, and that delayed its lawsuit by six months. As if that wasn't bad enough, one of my partners got an inquiry from the state disciplinary board. This is piling on.

You are right about the piling on. Everyone is attacking you guys. First, it was the motion by Magna; then the assault by your former client; now someone is trying to lift your partner's ticket. But the truth is that lawyers are subject to multiple remedies, and the fact that one remedy is imposed does not mean that others might not also be sought and received. Lawyers are answerable to clients, former clients, the courts, and disciplinary authorities for various forms of relief [Chapter 8] and all of lawyers' conduct should be considered in light of those possibilities.

### ➤§9.05(b) Identifying All Of The Consequences

Remedies may be identified in your research, but often will require a specific search by remedy, such as disqualification, fee forfeiture, or the like [Chapter 8].[8] Begin by identifying potential remedy issues. For example, conflicts of interest are governed by lawyer codes [§9.04], so discipline could follow for their violation [§8.02]. Tribunals also regulate conflicts by using their inherent power to disqualify errant lawyers [§8.08]. Lawyers who breach a clear fiduciary duty such as loyalty also are subject to fee forfeiture [§8.10] and civil liability [§8.06].

Treatises may assist you in understanding your jurisdiction's view of these and other remedies. For some topics, a hornbook in a related area of law may come in handy. For example, a text on criminal procedure would help in understanding ineffective assistance of counsel [§8.07], just as a treatise on evidence can assist you in understanding the finer points of the attorney-client privilege or work-product doctrine [§§5.04-5.05].

---

[8] Recall that a list of these remedies can be found in *Restatement of the Law Third, The Law Governing Lawyers*, §6 (2000).

## ▶ §9.06 JUDICIAL OPINIONS

### ▶ §9.06(a) Which Cases?

We have this little problem. We got this call from Acme Corporation to bring a RICO claim against Colossus. When we circulated a conflicts memo, one of our partners told us we were about to close a loan for Big Bank to Colossus. So we didn't take the RICO claim. Now it turns out our partner who represents Big Bank told the bank about the RICO claim. And we've been sued by Acme for breach of Rule 1.18, the prospective client confidentiality rule. When we confronted our partner, he was contrite but he cannot understand how they can sue. Before he disclosed he read the Scope section of the Rules that says: "Violation of a rule should not give rise to a cause of action ...."

We are sorry to report that your predicament is one that was addressed in the recent changes to the Model Rules, too late for your partner and your firm, but maybe in time for everyone else. Now the revised Scope section of the Model Rules adds: "Nevertheless, since the Rules do establish standards of conduct by lawyers, a lawyer's violation of a Rule may be evidence of breach of the applicable standard of conduct," a clear warning that although the rules are rules of discipline their violation can get a lawyer in trouble with more people than the bar authorities.

But there is another object lesson in your partner's transgression: You should never rely solely on the lawyer codes in researching a question about lawyer conduct. A simple search of the case law in you jurisdiction probably would have disclosed a sentiment similar to the new Model Rule Scope section.[9] These cases, *Maritrans* being the most important example, remind lawyers that a violation of the lawyer codes (which after all stem from agency roots) not only can result in disci-

---

[9] *E.g., dePape v. Trinity Health Systems, Inc.,* 242 F. Supp.2d 585, 609 (N.D. Iowa 2003)("Although the Iowa Code of Professional Responsibility for Lawyers does not undertake to define standards of civil liability, it constitutes some evidence of negligence."); *Welsh v. Case,* 43 P.3d 445, 452 (Or. App. 2002)("Disciplinary rules, together with statutes and common law principles relating to fiduciary relationships, all help define the duty component of the fiduciary duty owed by a lawyer to his or her client."); *Fishman v. Brooks,* 487 N.E.2d 1377, 1382 (Mass. 1986)(expert "properly could base his opinion on an attorney's failure to conform to a disciplinary rule.")

pline but also can give rise to civil actions for breach of fiduciary duty or other untoward results.[10]

### ►§9.06(b) Uncovering All Of The Law

Once you have identified the relevant professional rules [§9.04], you can begin to search for cases that apply, construe, or provide remedies [§9.05] for violations of these provisions. Or, you might choose to begin your search with cases you have discovered in a secondary source. Most instances of professional discipline [§8.02] result in written court opinions, which are easily found in annotated volumes of court rules or online by searching with a rule cite or text. At this point, be sure to search for cases construing parallel provisions from earlier professional codes, such as the Code of Professional Responsibility. You also might want to check Shepard's *Professional and Judicial Conduct Citations*, which collects citations to Code of Professional Responsibility and Model Rules provisions, Code of Judicial Conduct provisions, and ethics opinions.[11]

Research resources such as those listed in §9.03 will help you put your jurisdiction's rules and cases in perspective. Many courts have found the Restatement especially helpful when no prior authority exists in a given jurisdiction, and in identifying majority and minority rules. Before you decide to cite a treatise, Restatement, or case from another jurisdiction, be sure that that authority construes lawyer code provisions similar to the ones in your jurisdiction. If the authority addresses a remedy [Chapter 8] such as fee forfeiture or disqualification, check to determine what your jurisdiction has to say about the substantive and procedural requirements for the same remedy [§9.05].

### ►§9.07 ETHICS OPINIONS

### ►§9.07(a) Which Ethics Opinions?

**I got this fax. I was fairly sure it wasn't for me just from the cover sheet. It said "All Defense Counsel," and I am plaintiff's counsel. I wasn't sure what to do, so I found an ABA ethics opinion. It said I should call the sender and abide that lawyer's instruc-**

---

[10] *Maritrans GP Inc. v. Pepper, Hamilton & Scheetz*, 602 A.2d 1277 (Pa. 1992).

[11] *See*, Shepard's *Professional and Judicial Conduct Citations*.

tions. She asked me to return and I did. Now my client has sued me for failing to tell him I got the fax and for failing to claim privilege waiver to his advantage during the trial. Client's right about one thing. Using that fax would have been really helpful.

You certainly were correct in researching the ABA opinions. They can provide helpful analyses on the Model Rules. But they are only useful to the extent they construe the same rule in your jurisdiction. Further, they bind no one. Thus one can never limit one's research just to those opinions. In fact, the opinion you relied on warned you about jurisdictional differences in implied waiver doctrines.[12] If you had looked farther, you would have discovered that some state and local bar committees have a different view.[13] Some of these state and local committees have official standing; others offer purely advisory opinions, as the ABA does. But in any event, these local groups have the advantage of construing your jurisdiction's professional rules. For this reason, never limit your research to one set of these opinions and think the recommended course is one that can be pursued with impunity.

### ▶§9.07(b) Discovering Additional Guidance

If you find no authority in your jurisdiction, or want to inquire whether the authority you have found may be distinguishable from the situation your firm or you face, you should consider asking a local or state bar for an ethics opinion.[14] Both the American Bar Association and state and local bars have ethics committees that answer individual questions about the application of their rules to a proposed course of conduct. These committees address many issues [§9.02] before they ever reach a court. Many organizations, including disciplinary counsel in many states, also offer ethics hotlines to answer your questions or get you started on finding an answer. Remember that Model Rule 1.6(b)(4), if adopted in your jurisdiction, also allows use of client confidences reasonably necessary "to secure legal advice about the lawyer's compliance with these Rules." With these resources, you should be

---

[12] ABA Formal Op. 93-372 (1993).

[13] *E.g.,* Maryland Op. 00-04; Mass. Op. 1999-4; Ohio Op. 93-11, Utah St. Bar Op. 99-01.

[14] *See, e.g., In re Request for Instructions from Disciplinary Counsel,* 610 A.2d 115 (R.I. 1992).

§9.08(a)    RESEARCHING THE LAW GOVERNING LAWYERS  •  277

able to identify ethics issues [§9.02] and find the answers you need to practice responsibly.

For these reasons, you should check your jurisdiction's ethics opinions for useful insight. Although these opinions are not binding, courts are very reluctant to discipline a lawyer who complies with an ethics committee's advice. At the same time, if you find an ethics opinion, be sure to search your jurisdiction's cases to see whether it has been addressed, approved, or disapproved by the court.

Ethics opinions are most easily accessed online. Most state bar associations have websites for their members, which often include full text of at least recent ethics opinions.[15] Many states also publish these opinions in state or local bar journals. Both LEXIS and Westlaw have ethics opinions online, but neither service covers all jurisdictions. Your state will be on one or the other, but probably not both. ABA ethics opinions can be found in both places, however. Here, the topical approach works well. For LEXIS, click on "Ethics," for Westlaw, "Legal Ethics and Professional Responsibility." The menus that follow list the jurisdictions included in that service.

### ➤ §9.08 USING EXPERTS

### ➤ §9.08(a) Do We Need An Expert Witness?

**We've got this legal malpractice claim on a contingency. We have already spent a fortune on depositions. Do we really need an expert witness? The defendant law firm's conduct seems so egregious.**

If the conduct is not only egregious but obviously in error, you might save the money. Just as you don't need an expert physician to tell a jury that the surgeon should not have left a sponge in the patient, you don't need an expert to demonstrate that the lawyer was obliged to follow the direction of the client or make a timely filing [§4.06]. But if the alleged breach of the standard of care is any less obvious than that, you are going to need expert testimony. It is not enough to assert there is a rule of professional conduct [§9.04] that requires some particular action, and failure to take that action violates the standard of care. Rather, you need an expert to testify that the requirement in your juris-

---

[15] Access to many of these cites can be obtained through FindLaw, www.findlaw.com, using the topic "ethics and professional responsibility".

diction's lawyer code [§9.04] does provide the standard of care, which you can then prove was violated by this law firm.

### ▶ §9.08(b) Which Expert?

**We've been accused of malpractice. The plaintiff has hired some fancy university professor to explain what we did was wrong. Where might this lead?**

Now may not be the time to call in a chit with one of your practicing law buddies, asking that lawyer to opine on the propriety of your conduct. All experts, of course, are hired guns. But you want your expert to be as untainted as the payment of some high fee will permit. You also want to assure that the person you choose can qualify as an expert. Although it doesn't take 25 years of teaching and writing on the topic to reach that threshold, you certainly want someone a jury will view as sufficiently credentialed, even if the most important credential is not spending time in some ivory tower, but practicing law in the trenches.

### ▶ §9.08(c) Relying On Expert Testimony

The use of lawyer experts is a curious topic. On the one hand, perhaps because lawyers are required to testify about the standard of care in many cases of legal malpractice [§8.06] or because the professional responsibility obligations of lawyers seem particularly opaque (unless you've read this book), courts regularly entertain expert testimony from lawyers in disciplinary matters [§8.02], disqualification motions [§8.08], fee forfeiture claims [§8.10], client/lawyer fee disputes [§§2.13, 10.07], and other matters that range far beyond legal malpractice. On the other hand, in some of these cases, a lawyer expert really asserts what the law is or should be, which is something the lawyers in the case should be able to present to the court, and the court should be able to decide without expert testimony. Most of those hired to be experts (including one of the authors) regularly warn clients that there is no certainty that someone won't object to the expert's testimony on the ground that the expert is merely opining on the law. And it is true that every once in a while such expert testimony is barred. But in the great majority of cases concerning lawyer conduct, courts receive the expert testimony from lawyer experts on both sides, in many different contexts, with respect to all aspects of lawyer conduct under applicable lawyer code obligations.

▶**Red Flag**▶ You should distinguish your need to rely on an expert witness from your need to consult other lawyers for advice and perspective. In Chapter 10, we conclude by exploring critical circumstances that should prod you to seek the advice of others before you act.

# 10

# When You Need To Seek Additional Advice And Perspective

### Part One: Representing Clients

➤ §10.01 Investing In A Client Business

    ➤ §10.01(a) The Business Opportunity?

    ➤ §10.01(b) The Directive Lawyer And Fiduciary Duty

➤ §10.02 The Expanding Enterprise

    ➤ §10.02(a) Too Good To Be True?

    ➤ §10.02(b) The Instrumental Lawyer And The Limits Of The Law

➤ §10.03 Successor Counsel

    ➤ §10.03(a) The New Client?

    ➤ §10.03(b) The Collaborative Lawyer Alternative

➤ §10.04 Clients With Diminished Capacity

    ➤ §10.04(a) The Misguided Will?

    ➤ §10.04(b) Understanding The Autonomy And Best Interests Of Impaired Clients

➤ §10.05 Joint Clients

    ➤ §10.05(a) The Cooperative Venture?

    ➤ §10.05(b) Dual Professional Difficulties

➤ §10.06 Triangular Relationships

- §10.06(a) Music To Your Ears?
- §10.06(b) Dual Difficulties Revisited
    - Part Two: Operating Your Law Practice
- §10.07 Unpaid Fees
    - §10.07(a) Pure Ingrates?
    - §10.07(b) Collecting Fees
- §10.08 Expanding Beyond Law Practice
    - §10.08(a) Doing Fine?
    - §10.08(b) Whose Rules?
    - §10.08(c) Ancillary Businesses And Multidisciplinary Practice
- §10.09 Supervisory And Subordinate Lawyers
    - §10.09(a) Supervising Discovery?
    - §10.09(b) When To Defer To Another Lawyer's Judgment
- §10.10 Helping Colleagues
    - §10.10(a) The Disconnect?
    - §10.10(b) Law And Life

## PART ONE: REPRESENTING CLIENTS

### §10.01 INVESTING IN A CLIENT BUSINESS

#### §10.01(a) The Business Opportunity?

How often I envy my clients. While I am slogging away simply being paid by the hour, my income limited by my ability to push my colleagues to give up sleep for billable endeavors, my clients often seem to be earning income even while they are on vacation. And sometimes I know all too well how much they make and I am more than slightly green with envy. So when an "opportunity" arises for me to invest with my clients I am tempted. The idea of investing with my clients is a way of reflecting my loyalty to them. I also like the feeling that I am an insider getting a special ticket for admission to a great payday.

If the foregoing sounds like an invitation for suspension of disbelief, that is certainly the case. So many vectors line up in the same direction, recommending to even the most conscientious lawyer investing some of the lawyer's money in this way. Our tendency to be their advocates renders us even less objective than we otherwise might be about such an investment. Our happiness on stumbling across a great opportunity further clouds judgment.

This is why the road to investment with our clients is one that has to be very carefully traversed. First, there is the question of our special rules that govern doing business with clients, designed to protect the 4 C's [§6.11]. These rules invite anyone to second-guess your investment decision, particularly at a time when the investment is about to bestow its greatest rewards. The "entire fairness" of the transaction may look completely different years after the fact. In addition, those same rules provide some strict notice and informed consent requirements with which we must comply.

Far beyond concerns about Model Rule 1.8's admonitions regarding doing business with clients, there are concerns relating to liability. If you are providing legal services in a context in which you are also an investor, the way in which you handle the matter will always be subject to special scrutiny because it will be said that you lacked objectivity as a lawyer because of your business interest.

Yet, lawyers do invest with their clients. It can be done and it can be done without negative consequences. The lesson here, however, is to approach such a matter with great circumspection, asking yourself whether, among the opportunities available to you, it really makes sense to invest in this opportunity which comes to you with so much baggage. Your consultation with another lawyer to explore the contours of your investment may be a very wise decision indeed. And your client's consultation with a disinterested other lawyer creates a safe harbor for your investment. At the very least, if your client chooses to rely on you alone, you should have an objective third party evaluate the fairness of the transaction from your client's point of view.

### ▶ §10.01(b) The Directive Lawyer And Fiduciary Duty

Agency law long has recognized the problem of generalized expertise: the tendency of experts to assume that their professional competence equates with the ability to know best what the client should do, and direct the client to do it.

Fiduciary duty is the legal remedy for this tendency to direct client behavior. The 4 C's [Part Two] exist to assure that the client's moral values, as defined by the client, control the agency relationship, by steering lawyers away from benefiting someone other than the client. These duties also protect clients from lawyers who might take advantage of the trust and power reposed in them for personal gain.

Directive behavior is most endemic and least justified when lawyers represent individual clients unfamiliar with the law. These clients may be financially strapped and may face litigation concerning past actions or may be seeking advice about a business opportunity. Here, where clients are most vulnerable, lawyers need to be most diligent in guarding against preempting their clients' personal judgments by concentrating on zealous advocacy of their clients' articulated interests.

Judge John Noonan labels directive behavior "underidentification with a client."[1] Lawyers who underidentify with their clients misconstrue their role, acting as directors who can intentionally or inadvertently impose their own private judgment about the matter on a trusting, unsuspecting client. If you perceive yourself as a professional authority or legal expert who should handle a legal matter with little or no client consultation, you risk underidentification and liability for breach of fiduciary duty [§8.06]. Why? Because underidentification allows you to be influenced by interests potentially contrary to your client's, such as your own financial gain [§6.11], the interest of another client [§10.05], or a third-party payor [§10.06].

This is why the need for zealous advocacy of the client's interests becomes doubly necessary when a lawyer stands to gain from a transaction with a client. When you intend to do business with a client, the 4 C's stand ready to counter your subconscious tendency to direct the transaction. The 4 C's are buttressed by the law of undue influence, which presumes that lawyers will favor their own interests over a client's and makes lawyers liable regardless of their intent for tort damages and subject to professional discipline when they breach fiduciary

---

[1] John T. Noonan Jr., *The Lawyer Who Overidentifies with his Client*, 76 Notre Dame L. Rev. 827, 833 (2001). Other commentators identify this defect as "paternalism" or "parentalism." *See, e.g.*, Richard A. Wasserstrom, *Lawyers as Professionals: Some Moral Issues*, 5 Human Rights 1, 19 (1975). We would prefer, with Professors Shaffer and Cochran, not to see parenthood as a morally objectionable image. Parents are supposed to limit a child's freedom for the child's benefit. The problem is that lawyers should not act like parents, because they should not assume that they know what is best for the client. Thomas L. Shaffer & Robert F. Cochran, Jr., *Lawyers, Clients and Moral Responsibility* 6 (West 1994).

§ 10.02(b)   ADDITIONAL ADVICE AND PERSPECTIVE • 285

duties. Lawyers who understand that special scrutiny of business transactions is designed to offset their natural instincts will follow these heightened requirements to implement the 4 C's. They also will not fall prey to professional discipline [§8.02] or subject themselves to the civil relief afforded to clients whose lawyers betray them [§8.06]. Even better, they will move toward respecting client interests, rather than acting as authorities or judges who know best.

## ▶§ 10.02 THE EXPANDING ENTERPRISE

### ▶§ 10.02(a) Too Good To Be True?

**I wonder if something is askew. My client's business plan seems too good to be true. My client's employees leave me uncomfortable. I am just not sure everything is on the up and up. Yet it is nothing I can put my finger on. And the fellow is paying my bills promptly and they have been marching steadily upward as my client's mini-empire begins to expand. Now I'm doing estate planning. Someone mentioned an IPO. And I am flattered by the idea that I might go on the client's board.**

This is a time to pause. We all want to provide top-notch, enthusiastic service for an ever-growing list of expanding enterprises. We all want to be cheerleaders for our client's endeavor. And pausing seems so disloyal and counterproductive. But pause we must and act just a little bit like the accountants, not by compromising our loyalty or undertaking duties to the public, but by adopting an attitude of healthy skepticism. Maybe everything is totally legitimate. Maybe your client is the next Microsoft. And, even if not, there may be nothing of concern. The plea here is simply not to get caught up in the wave of enthusiasm without stepping back and placing your own work for this client in a larger context so that you do not find yourself a participant (and some may say later an aider and abettor) in a fraudulent scheme. The simple process of sharing with another lawyer what you know and why you feel uneasy could serve as a great reality check.

### ▶§ 10.02(b) The Instrumental Lawyer And The Limits Of The Law

We have seen that the agency relationship between client and lawyer requires the 4 C fiduciary duties to assure that a lawyer acts subject to the client's control [Chapters 3-6]. At the same time, every agency relationship is subject to one limitation: neither the principal's power nor the agent's duty to obey allows either to violate the limits of the law [Chapter 7].[2] When an agent agrees to act subject to the control of a principal, the law does not assume that the principal merges her legal personality into the agent's. Both principal and agent remain responsible for the consequences of their own conduct. Agency law recognizes principal and agent as distinct, autonomous legal persons, and anticipates that they will behave accordingly.[3]

When fraud or other legal misconduct occurs, it usually is viewed from a public perspective after its massive costs are known. From this vantage point, lawyers may appear to have misconstrued their role in the representation. In one example, Judge Stanley Sporkin upheld the federal receivership of Lincoln Savings and Loan, concluding his opinion with these observations:

> There are other unanswered questions presented by this case. Keating testified that he was so bent on doing the "right thing" that he surrounded himself with literally scores of accountants and lawyers to make sure all the transactions were legal. The questions that must be asked are:
>
> Where were these professionals, a number of whom are now asserting their rights under the Fifth Amendment, when these clearly improper transactions were being consummated?
>
> Why didn't any of them speak up or disassociate themselves from the transactions?
>
> Where also were the outside accountants and attorneys when these transactions were effectuated?[4]

Judge John Noonan warns us that some lawyers can overidentify with a client. These lawyers often act instrumentally, continuing to advocate for such a client after red flags have been raised. He describes the transformation of an influential lawyer, Hoyt Moore, whose representation of Bethlehem Steel led him to bribe a federal judge to secure this client's goals.[5] Lawyers who overidentify with clients can negli-

---

[2] *Restatement of the Law Third, The Law Governing Lawyers*, §23 (ALI 2000). (hereinafter "RLGL"); *Restatement (Third) of Agency* §1.01, comment f (1) (ALI, Tentative Draft No. 2 2001).

[3] *Id*. at comment c.

[4] *Lincoln Savings and Loan Assn. v. Wall*, 743 F. Supp. 901, 919-920 (D.D.C. 1990).

[5] Noonan, *supra* note 1 at 840-41.

gently or knowingly become instruments of client wrongdoing or accessories to corrupt and dishonorable conduct [§8.05]. Further, no lawyer or law firm is invulnerable to serious allegations of complicity in client misconduct [§7.04].[6]

If you identify yourself as a hired gun, if you assume that most clients do not want to be fair, or if you see your job as assisting clients in getting away with what they can, you risk overidentification with your client and entanglement in your client's potentially illegal activities. Why? Because overidentification with a client or a client's goals can tempt you to suppress your own moral judgment and view law as a malleable means to pursue a client's objectives, rather than a set of rules with some definitive limits that should have shaped both your client's behavior as well as your own. In some circumstances, relevant law imposes clear legal boundaries on a client's intended conduct. In these situations, lawyers should expect to inform a client that certain actions cannot be taken or even that certain goals cannot be realized. If you do not competently discover these provisions and are not clear about them with your clients, you can be characterized as allowing yourself, wittingly or unwittingly, to be used as an instrument or technician of inappropriate conduct by a client.

It is important to realize that lawyers can be subjected to allegations of assisting client misconduct in at least three different circumstances. In the first, lawyers unwittingly or innocently participate in the client's fraud by providing legal advice to a client who, unbeknownst to the lawyer, is using that advice to break the law. In the second, lawyers act negligently by failing to identify or act upon legal red flags, which with the benefit of 20-20 hindsight, will be characterized

---

[6] *In re American Continental Corporation/ Lincoln Savings & Loan Securities Litigation,* 794 F. Supp. 1424 (D. Ariz. 1992) (upholding securities fraud and common law breach of fiduciary duty causes of action against accountants and lawyers who represented Lincoln Savings & Loan). The law firm of Jones, Day, Reavis & Pogue eventually settled the private claims of the stockholders against the firm for $24 million and the government claims for an additional $51 million. They were able to bill ACC about $1.2 million for their services. Rita Henley Jensen, *Lawyers Share the Blame for the Savings and Loan Scandal,* 95 Bus. & Soc'y. Rev. 54, 57-59 (Sept. 1995). The law firm that represented Lincoln on regulatory matters after Jones, Day, Kaye, Scholer, Fierman Hays & Handler, also settled with both private investors ($21 M) and the government ($41 M). Stephen Labaton, *Law Firm Will Pay a $41 Million Fine in Savings Lawsuit,* N. Y. Times, Mar. 9, 1992 at A1.

as clear warnings that the client was engaged in wrongful conduct. In the third, and most serious, lawyers act recklessly or intentionally by blindly ignoring clear warning signs or, worse, purposefully assisting a client to violate the law. Everyone recognizes the last as a clear example of lawyer misconduct. But the middle example can get lawyers in almost as much trouble, and the first, unwitting involvement, requires immediate response at the point the lawyer discovers the client's unlawful activity. In all of these circumstances, the lawyer who fails to keep the proper distance and overidentifies with the client is the lawyer who is most likely to ignore the warning signs that will seem much clearer after the fact.

Special vigilance is called for in representing entity clients, because while your marching orders come from certain constituents of the client, other constituents, after the fact and with benefit of perfect hindsight, may assert that not just those other constituents, but you, following their orders, engaged in actionable conduct. Shareholders, receivers, or trustees in bankruptcy may bring claims against corporate officials, who may have violated legal regulations, and who, in turn, may blame the professionals they say they relied on. These officials may waive the attorney-client privilege so that all documents and conversations the lawyer thought would never see the light of day may appear on page one of the Wall Street Journal. The lawyer who acted instrumentally may in fact have agreed to the course of action, knowing it was risky, but believing all along that the corporate official would prevail on behalf of the entity. When that fails, the legal advice will be very carefully scrutinized by a successor in interest to the now failed enterprise.

Recent specific amendments to Model Rule 1.13 and the Sarbanes-Oxley Act of 2002 [§7.16] also become relevant at this point.[7] Lawyers who believe that constituents of entity clients are acting against its best interests should seek outside opinions and refer the matter to a higher authority within the organization. If that does not stop the wrongdoing, the lawyer should resign.[8] Model Rule 1.13 as recently revised further allows lawyers who reasonably believe it neces-

---

[7] 15 U.S.C. §7201 *et seq.*(2003); 17 C.F.R. Part 205, 68 Fed. Reg. 6296 (Feb. 6, 2003).

[8] ABA Model Rule of Professional Conduct 1.13 Comment [4] (2002). (Hereinafter "Model Rules"). Comment [6] provides that a lawyer in such a situation also "may" resign. Of course, Model Rule 1.2(d) makes withdrawal mandatory when the ongoing conduct is criminal or fraudulent and the lawyer knows about it.

sary to prevent substantial injury to the organization to disclose information to prevent, stop, or rectify the wrongdoing.[9]

So if you find yourself tending toward instrumental behavior, be careful to know and communicate the limits of the law to your clients, and be ready to withdraw when they step over the line. Keeping a clear understanding of the legal limits to your clients' behavior will allow you to serve your clients well, and also will provide you with a necessary opportunity to prevent entangling yourself in your client's behavior when it crosses the legal limit.

## ▶ §10.03 SUCCESSOR COUNSEL

### ▶ §10.03(a) The New Client?

**The call elicits instant chest swelling. It's a prospective client who has been treated very badly by one of my professional rivals at another firm. "I should have gone with my instincts and picked you in the first place," the caller intones. What a great opportunity! Snatching a lucrative client from a rival. All the more sweet.**

Or is it? Sure you are in a rivalry with the other lawyer. You do think you are better. But you know, if you'll let yourself admit it, that this other lawyer is a pretty fine professional herself. Maybe not up to your lofty standards, but certainly a worthy rival. And one not likely to leave clients disgruntled.

So you may proceed to take on the new matter. But instead of making the reason for the opportunity generate extra enthusiasm for the engagement, exactly the opposite should occur. If possible, secure client permission to talk to predecessor counsel. If that permission is denied, your guard should be raised even more. In either event, a full explanation of the reason for the change, the history of the engagement, and the nature of what remains to be done plus a demand for a very large retainer should all precede every agreement to take on the matter.

This is because although many clients do switch lawyers for totally legitimate reasons, some may be involved in questionable conduct. Even if this is not the case, far too many who switch can never be satisfied, will become disgruntled with you after a while, and will put you on the end of a call from *your* successor counsel long before the matter is concluded.

---

[9] Model Rule 1.13(c)(2).

## ▶ §10.03(b) The Collaborative Lawyer Alternative

Each client-lawyer relationship brings with it the potential for a directive, instrumental, or a collaborative client-lawyer relationship. When a client fires a lawyer [§§1.24 and 2.11], or a lawyer "fires" a client by withdrawing from a representation [§7.02], successor counsel gains a new opportunity to establish such a relationship. The prospective client could have ended the past client-lawyer relationship because the client believed that the lawyer underidentified with the client and perhaps even breached some or all of the 4 C's, for example by failing to offer competent service [Chapter 4] or communicate with the client [Chapter 3]. Or, the lawyer may have ended the relationship to avoid overidentification with a client who refused to conform to the limits of the law [Chapter 7].

Lawyers who create collaborative client-lawyer relationships are most able to avoid the extremes and risks of both under- and overidentification that can lead to directive or instrumental behavior. Lawyers who act as collaborators with their clients do not control or manipulate their clients and observe all of the fiduciary duties the law demands. They act competently and loyally, communicate with their clients (thus enabling their clients to make decisions about the matter), and they keep their client's confidences. At the same time, they do not shrink from clear explanations to clients when the latter's conduct approaches legally unacceptable boundaries. When necessary, these lawyers refuse to act instrumentally, and tell their clients why. They are empathetic, but offer objective advice. They identify enough with their clients to do a good job, but do not become tools of their client's wrongdoing. When collaborative lawyers disagree with a client's proposed conduct, they respect the client enough to remonstrate with the client about the propriety of the client's conduct. When legal and ethical competence demands that they draw a line between their clients' and their own behavior, they do so.

In order to achieve this balance, collaborative lawyers realize that their clients have a story to tell, one that the lawyer will have to translate into legally recognized language. They need to be educated by their clients about the client's predicament, and the client's need for legal services.[10] To do this well, lawyers must respect each client's moral

---

[10] A rich clinical literature explores the art of interviewing and counseling clients. *See, e.g.*, Robert F. Cochran, Jr., John M. A. DiPippa & Martha M. Peters, *The Counselor-*

autonomy, but also need to assist each client in understanding the moral values and public policy choices embedded in the law itself.

Collaborative lawyers also recognize that law blends clear boundaries with less-determinate general obligations that require application to client matters. In each case, they are not only translating the client's desires to the legal system and legal norms back to the client, but they are also acting as private lawmakers, who both influence and are influenced by the law and legal system they function in. Therefore, they are prepared to see occasions where they disagree with clients as opportunities to educate clients about the limits of the law, and if clients do not listen, to extricate themselves from facilitating the client's unlawful behavior [7.02].

In other words, lawyers learn from and advocate for the client, but also teach and advocate to the client about competing moral values or public policy choices the law has embodied to protect the interests of others. In most cases, lawyers can help a client achieve a legal goal. When a clear legal boundary directs the client's behavior, collaborative lawyers draw the line. That is, collaborative lawyers are continually informed by their responsibilities to clients and the limits of the law to assure them that the action they take will be well within the scope of professional discretion.

## ▶ §10.04 CLIENTS WITH DIMINISHED CAPACITY

### ▶ §10.04(a) The Misguided Will?

**The client asks me to meet with him at his house. Doesn't get around well anymore, he complains. He wants estate planning advice. The estate is sizeable and he tells me how disgusted he is with his children. He'd rather give his money to the government. Or maybe leave all his money to the nice nurse who is taking care of him, now that the kids have abandoned him. A familiar scenario. Entirely plausible. It is his money and now that he is wid-**

---

*At-Law: A Collaborative Approach to Client Interviewing and Counseling* (Lexis 1999); David A. Binder and Susan C. Price, *Lawyers as Counselors: A Client-Centered Approach* (Thomson/West, 2d ed. 2004); Robert M. Bastress and Joseph D. Harbaugh, *Interviewing, Counseling and Negotiating: Skills for Effective Representation* (Little Brown 1990). *See also,* Marcus T. Boccaccini, Jennifer L. Boothby & Stanley L. Brodsky, *Client-Relations Skills in Effective Lawyering: Attitudes of Criminal Defense Attorneys and Experienced Clients,* 26 Law & Psychol. Rev. 97 (2002).

owed, these are choices he is totally free to make. The client seems to have all his faculties. He was smart enough to call me. But there is something about his affect that bothers me. Sometimes he searches a long time for the right word. And the discussion has been anything but linear.

The professional rules [§9.04] tell us to treat all clients as autonomous to the greatest extent possible. We also have a virtually absolute duty of confidentiality to our clients. You can tell any suggestion that this client is operating at less than full capacity will be rejected out of hand. As a result you find yourself in one of the most ethically sensitive areas our profession must face.

You must take direction from your client. You must act in the best interests of the client. The client has defined the client's view of best interest. And the last place you can run is to the client's children. But if you are dealing in an area where you do not have the expertise to make a further determination, you may seek advice, most suitably from a health professional, to determine whether you may accept your client's directions at face value or whether your client, in fact, lacks the capacity to make these important decisions. Then, and only then, may you breach client confidentiality to take whatever steps are required to act in the client's best interests.

### ►§10.04(b) Understanding The Autonomy And Best Interests Of Impaired Clients

When should the lawyer stay her hand in the name of her client's autonomy? On the one hand, lawyers are admonished by fiduciary duty to do everything they can to help fulfill the client's goals of the representation, goals that are to be determined by the client. On the other, clients often make decisions that the lawyer believes reflect bad judgment or, worst of all, risk substantial harm to the client. When lawyers place too much weight on the former proposition—simply being instruments unquestioningly abiding their client's instructions—they can disserve their clients' true autonomy by failing to share their independent view of the merits of the course of action. If the client has legal obligations to others, accepting a client's decision at face value also can open such a client (and perhaps the lawyer as well) to potential liability [§1.28].

Model Rule 1.14 creates the best opportunity for a collaborative relationship with a client who suffers from diminished capacity. It par-

§10.04(b)  ADDITIONAL ADVICE AND PERSPECTIVE • 293

allels mental health law by envisioning autonomous capacity as a spectrum, and it recognizes several causes of diminished capacity, such as minority, old age, mental retardation, dementia, chemical dependency, or depression. Following the logic and dictates of this rule can help you determine whether your conduct risks underidentification and directive behavior or overidentification and instrumental behavior that disregards your client's real interests.

Model Rule 1.14 begins by admonishing lawyers to maintain a normal client-lawyer relationship to the extent reasonably possible. When a client proposes to act within legal bounds, lawyers ordinarily can and should rely on the client's decisions. When the decision seems idiosyncratic or contrary to what most clients would believe in their best interests, the lawyer instinctively may pause to consider whether the client suffers from some compromise in judgment that disserves the client's autonomous self or true interests. But whenever a lawyer does this, the lawyer should do so within the goal of maintaining a normal client-lawyer relationship by remembering the 4 C's.

You can start by recognizing that communicating with an impaired client should require more rather than less explanation, and may require the assistance of others who know the client well. The client may elect to have family members, trusted friends, or clinicians participate as the client's agents in discussions to help articulate the client's interests. If you secure the client's consent to the help of these third persons, they become agents for the purpose of the attorney-client privilege. If you fail to obtain that consent, communication with third persons present may destroy the privilege [§5.04].

With respect to decisionmaking, the lawyer should rely on informed consent, explaining the matter to the extent necessary to enable the client to understand the risks of the behavior or decision as well as the alternative choices to enable the client to determine his or her own best interests. Such an explanation should include the lawyer's experience with similar clients or situations in the past and the reasons most people might find the client's articulated choice unrealistic. Further, because capacity can fluctuate, the lawyer should expect to give the client additional time to consider the matter, as long as a delay does not prejudice the client's interests. A lawyer who has known a client for some time should consider whether the client has ever spoken of similar matters in the past, and if so, should remind the client about former expressions of belief that may inform the current decision.[11] Once again, a client's decision within the bounds of the law, even if idiosyncratic, must be upheld.

As lawyer and client elect to expand the decisionmaking process, the lawyer must remember confidentiality and loyalty. Disclosures to family members or others without the client's consent are not in order. If someone other than the client (such as family members) retains the lawyer, your remembering that the payor is not the principal in such a triangular relationship [§10.06], will help keep your eye on the articulated interests of your client.

If the client suffers from significantly diminished capacity [§1.22], which prevents the client from recognizing his or her own interest, maintaining such a normal relationship may involve seeking the advice or assistance of others. If the client's decision or inaction risks substantial physical, financial, or other harm to the client unless action is taken, the lawyer may make disclosures to outsiders such as clinicians to seek assistance without the client's consent. Shifting from an autonomy orientation to a best interests mode is justified to protect the client from harm (such as suicide) [§5.08], on the theory that the same client with full capacity would recognize the danger and respond accordingly.[12] If no one else can protect the client, protective action may even include seeking the appointment of a guardian or conservator over the client's stated or unstated objections. Here, disclosures to

---

[11] RLGL §24, comment d.

[12] *Estate of Robinson ex rel. Robinson v. Randolph County Comm'n,* 549 S.E.2d 699, 706-07 (W. Va. 2001) (Starcher, J., concurring) (defense lawyer who allegedly knew his incarcerated client was suicidal should have intervened to seek adequate care to prevent suicide); *People v. Fentress,* 425 N.Y.S.2d 485, 497 (N.Y. County Ct. 1980) (court found client waived confidentiality and commented that lawyer-friend of criminal defendant "would have blindly and unpardonably converted a valued ethical duty into a caricature, a mockery of justice and life itself" had the lawyer not warned the police about the client's suicide threat); Mass. Ethics Op. 01-2 (a lawyer may notify family members, adult protective service agencies, the police, or the client's doctors to prevent the threatened suicide of a client if the lawyer reasonably believes that the suicide threat is real and that the client is suffering from some mental disorder or disability that prevents him from making a rational decision about whether to continue living). At the same time, courts have refused to find criminal defense lawyers liable for failing to prevent a client's suicide. *See, e.g., Snyder v. Baumecker,* 708 F. Supp. 1451 (D.N.J. 1989) (lawyer who allegedly delayed the prosecution of decedent's criminal defense not liable for client's suicide because suicide is not a foreseeable risk of legal malpractice).

protect the client's best interests may be "impliedly authorized" under Model Rule 1.14(c), but only if reasonably necessary to protect the client. Model Rule 1.13(c)(2) allows similar disclosures on a similar theory in representing organizations, in the name of the best interests of the organization [§5.07(f)].

## ➤ §10.05 JOINT CLIENTS

### ➤ §10.05(a) The Cooperative Venture?

It's so counterintuitive. We, as human beings, want and need to work together. So many more endeavors are possible with cooperation. Family solidarity. Successful business partnerships. Innovative joint ventures. All are models of people working together. Yet we lawyers atomize things. Our paradigm is one lawyer/one client. Undivided loyalty. We are also expensive. The costs for the legal fees associated with any endeavor present an impediment to securing the necessary legal services. To compound that expense by requiring each prospective client to hire his, her, or its own lawyer only makes matters worse.

With that tension palpable, the temptation for the lawyer confronted with multiple clients to help them economize is quite high. And it can be done with ethical impunity. But it must be done very carefully from the very beginning of the joint relationship. The initial interview of the prospective clients becomes a critical event. The correct information must be elicited. And the proper warnings must be delivered, preferably in writing. Then, if the lawyer reaches the conclusion that the lawyer can thread the professional responsibility needle, based on what the lawyer then understands the circumstances to be, the lawyer may proceed.

But if that is the decision two things must occur. First, the lawyer must set out carefully the ground rules for the joint representation. What will the lawyer do with one client's confidential information [§§3.05, 6.22]? What will occur if the lawyer identifies a conflict of interest [§6.21]? May the lawyer agree now to represent only one of the co-clients, subject obviously to potential challenge later by the others? Second, the lawyer must remain ever vigilant for the development of conflicts during the representation and immediately notify the clients and address the matter—it would be hoped based on prior understandings.

There is a reason the ABA Ethics 2000 Commission jettisoned former Model Rule 2.2, "Lawyer as Intermediary." The concern was that lawyers seeing a rule labeled as such might be misled into thinking that being "lawyer for the situation" was an easy assignment. Now the comments of former Model Rule 2.2 governing that situation have been rightfully moved to the general conflict of interest rule governing concurrent client conflicts of interest, thus raising the appropriate red flags.[13]

So if there are two or more people sitting across from your desk seeking legal services (even husband and wife), we want all of your ethical antennae to be poised, and if you have any doubts whether the representation can go forward on these terms, consult another lawyer for advice.

### ▶§10.05(b) Dual Professional Difficulties

Lawyers can find themselves in situations where they are tempted toward the excesses of both directive and instrumental role behavior at the same time. For example, a lawyer can act instrumentally toward one potential client, and inappropriately direct the other client, who is equally entitled to representation complete with a full array of fiduciary duties. In serving the one, the lawyer may be tempted to breach duties to the other.

Judge Noonan points out that these dual professional difficulties can infect the behavior of even the most able and well-meaning lawyers. He recalls a famous incident that became the focus of future Justice Louis Brandeis's Senate confirmation hearings. Brandeis recommended that a client assign his business assets for the benefit of creditors. He did not tell the client that this assignment constituted an act of bankruptcy, or that Brandeis's law firm represented one of the creditors. Five days later, Brandeis, representing the creditor, instituted involuntary bankruptcy proceedings against the client who had assigned his business assets. Brandeis later claimed that he had been "counsel to the situation," not counsel to each of his individual clients. Here is Judge Noonan's characterization of Brandeis' conduct:[14]

> Underidentification is here, no doubt, carried to the point of caricature. The lawyer does not remember that he

---

[13] Model Rule 1.7, Comments [29]-[33].

[14] Judge Noonan points out that this episode was far from typical, but was the "most damaging episode" that Brandeis's enemies could cull from a distinguished 30-year career in law practice. Noonan, *supra* note 1 at 829.

took the client as a client. The lawyer does not give the client the most elementary advice about the consequences of the act the lawyer is advising him to perform. The lawyer represents another client and, acting for that client, puts his unremembered client into bankruptcy. At the heart of the situation is the lawyer's desire to abstract himself from the needs and pressures of a particular individual in order to go on and straighten out a mess. In some other world, law could be practiced in that fashion. It is not the way law has been generally practiced in ours.[15]

Lawyers like this, who abstract themselves from clients, risk ignoring fiduciary duty to one client because they favor another client's interest. In doing so, they can assume the role of an authority who knows best and directs one client-lawyer relationship for the benefit of the other client. In intentionally or inadvertently favoring one client over another, the lawyer chooses to act as an instrumental lawyer willing to do the favored client's bidding, perhaps presuming that that client seeks the maximum financial reward, liberty, or security from the other client. At the same time, the lawyer chooses to act as a directive lawyer for the other client, perhaps assuming that the favored client's best interest requires the lawyer to direct a particular result.

The law governing lawyers responds to both of these extremes with concrete incentives that steer lawyers away from the dangers of violating fiduciary duty and exceeding the bounds of legitimate advocacy. If you favor or tend toward an instrumental role with some or all of your clients, you need to be especially alert to the limits of the law [Chapter 7] that apply to your own conduct as well as those of your clients. The lawyers who evade those limits suffer liability for fraud and malpractice [§§8.04- 8.06], sanctions for violations of procedural rules [§8.11], criminal liability [§8.03], disqualification [§8.08], and professional discipline [§8.02]. If you favor or tend toward a directive role in some or all of your client-lawyer relationships, you would be wise to recall client remedies [§9.05] for breach of fiduciary duty, such as malpractice liability [§8.06], disqualification [§8.08], loss of a fee [§8.10] and professional discipline [§8.02].

Fortunately, most lawyers avoid both of these extremes most of the time by acting as collaborators with their clients. They do not favor

---

[15] *Id.* at 833.

one client over another, or, if they worry about whether they might, they refuse to take on a joint representation. They realize that the rules of professional conduct [§9.04] allow them a great deal of professional discretion to do the right thing.

When considering whether to represent joint clients, this means that your advocacy role must be tamed to allow the joint clients to take over greater responsibility for the representation. You provide all of the legal options and they make the decisions. If they are unable or unwilling to do so, you must refuse to serve both (because you will not be able to do so) or withdraw from representing both of them. They won't be surprised at this result if you have warned them about it at the outset, including memorializing the confidentiality agreement they chose in your engagement letter [§1.04].

### ►§10.06 TRIANGULAR RELATIONSHIPS

### ►§10.06(a) Music To Your Ears?

**It's music to my ears. A client calls me up. Can you represent me? My legal fees are going to be paid by a) my Dad, b) my employer, c) my insurance company. What a deal: A client who won't complain about your hourly rate or the number of hours.**

But then you wake up from the dream and realize that while you represent A and you are being paid by B, B, surprise, surprise, does not take a totally passive view toward your bills or even how you are handling the matter.

B wants regular reports. B wants to keep the cost down. B asks for detailed billing. B does not want you to take certain steps in the matter without prior approval.

The tension is real. Your understanding of the ethics rules [§9.04] reminds you that you must remain independent of the third-party payor, that you owe primary or sole loyalty to the client, that you are to exercise independent professional judgment. You also know it is in your client's best interests to have your representation paid for by another, that the person who is paying the bills has some rights, that a happier third-party payor is better than a disgruntled one.

So enforcing absolute principles may be counterproductive to the best interests of the client. Nonetheless, if you share confidential information without client consent that redounds to the detriment of your client, your excuse that you only shared the information with someone who was paying you will fall on deaf ears. And if you compromise your independent professional judgment (don't hire an expert or defer two depositions), your liability will not be diminished by the third-party payor excuse.

When these triangular relationships cause your collar to tighten, it is time to remember the 4 C's, the limits of the law, and to seek advice from others before you proceed.

### ➤ §10.06(b) Dual Difficulties Revisited

If you can't favor one client's interest over another, you certainly can't allow yourself to be directed by a non-client third person. Yet some allegiance to the person or entity that pays you seems natural, especially if you hope for or become accustomed to repeat business. Once again, you face dual difficulties. An insurer can cause you to act instrumentally on its behalf, because your financial instinct is to further the insurer's business and approval of your services in order to keep the business coming. But doing so opens you to directive behavior with your other primary client, the insured. In serving the interests of the insurer, you may be tempted to breach duties to the insured or even aid the insurer in neglecting its contractual obligations to the insured.

If you translate the least bit of third-person allegiance into influence or advocacy, you mistake the payor for the true principal—your client. And, if the third-person influence is carried just a bit too far, you risk breaching some or all of the 4 C fiduciary duties you owe your clients. You can violate your client's confidentiality by disclosing your client's confidences without your client's consent. You can disregard loyalty by favoring the third person's interests over your client's. You can act incompetently by failing to recognize or implement viable legal options for your client. You can ignore basic obligations to communicate by failing to obtain your client's (not the third person's) informed consent about key issues that surface during the representation. All of this can cause incalculable damage to clients.[16]

---

[16] In *Perez v. Kirk & Carrigan,* 822 S.W. 2d 261 (Tex. App. 1991), the court upheld a cause of action for breach of fiduciary duty against lawyers who represented both employer and employee following a truck accident where 21 children died. The

The remedy: Remember your client, to whom you owe the 4 C's, and expect to explain these fiduciary obligations to the third person. You cannot permit the third person to regulate or to interfere with your independence of judgment on behalf of your client.[17] You may accept third-person direction only if your client consents to it. Even when this occurs, you must remain vigilant that it never compromises the 4 C's.[18]

Of course, the power and influence of some third-person payors, such as insurers, makes it difficult to resist their attempts to interfere. Fortunately, other law, such as insurance bad faith, helps you because it imposes penalties on the third party when it seeks to interfere, say by refusing to settle within policy limits or by insisting that you help it establish a policy defense.[19] Courts also help by imposing obligations on third parties to provide separate counsel where conflicts arise between the third-party payor and the clients.[20] And don't forget collaboration. Your client may want to consent to disclosures to Dad or involvement by daughter in estate planning. Your job is to clarify your client's interests apart from third-person influence.

---

lawyers promised the employee truck driver confidentiality and took his sworn statement about the accident. Without his consent, they then gave his statement to the prosecutor, who indicted the driver for 21 counts of involuntary manslaughter. The employee waited over three years for trial and was acquitted on all counts. Maggie Rivas, *Truck Driver Says He Spent Years After Bus Crash Doing Penance; He Went Into Self-Imposed Exile At Home As Punishment*, The Dallas Morning News, May 7, 1993 at 1A, Maggie Rivas, *Trucker Absolved of Bus Deaths; '89 Alton Tragedy Killed 21 Students*, The Dallas Morning News, May 6, 1993 at 1A.

[17] Model Rules 1.8(f) and 5.4(c).

[18] RLGL §134; *In re Rules of Professional Conduct*, 2 P.3d 806 (Mont. 2000) (Montana lawyers may not abide by an insurer's billing and practice rules which impose conditions limiting or directing the scope and extent of the representation of insureds and may not submit detailed descriptions of professional services to outside persons or entities without first obtaining the informed consent of the insured).

[19] For a case involving sexual misconduct by a physician where the court found that the lawyer offered a "splendid" defense under a reservation of rights, *see, St. Paul Fire and Marine Ins. Co. v. Engelmann*, 639 N.W.2d 192 (S.D. 2002). For a case where the lawyer failed to get it right, *see, Beckwith Mach. Co. v. Travelers Indem. Co.*, 638 F. Supp. 1179 (W.D. Pa. 1986), where the failure to send a reservation of rights letter or file a declaratory judgment action estopped the insurer from denying coverage and created liability for bad faith and breach of contract.

[20] *Wolpaw v. General Accident Ins. Co.*, 639 A. 2d 338 (N.J. Super. Ct. App. Div. 1994).

## PART TWO: OPERATING YOUR LAW PRACTICE

### ▶ §10.07 UNPAID FEES

▶ **§10.07(a) Pure Ingrates?**

**Damn clients! They ask us to jump and we say "how high?" Nights, weekends, we know no limits to the dedication we will show to the cause. And then how often do they turn out to be pure ingrates? If they are satisfied with the result, it demonstrates they did not need us in the first place. If they are dissatisfied with the result, it is our fault. Only we know how much we brought to the table in terms of added value and extra effort.**

Your immediate reaction is to sue the ingrates. Your recollection of missed dinners and Little League games only reinforces your anger. You turned a sow's ear into a silk purse and get stiffed on the bill as your reward. But before you sue that client, take one figurative deep breath. Think long and hard about the cost of such a proceeding. Think long and hard about whether the judgment you secure, if any, can be collected. Think long and hard about how long it will be until you get a successful result. Think long and hard about how much of your time will be dedicated to pursuing the matter and, finally, most unpleasantly of all, think long and hard about whether your collection lawsuit will generate a malpractice counterclaim.

We know you think you handled the matter perfectly. We know you think no one could have done any better. But that does not mean that your now former client will not conjure up a hundred reasons how you treated him or her badly, deciding that the best defense is a vigorous offense.

In other words, what we want you to do is give yourself the same tough advice you would give any client who feels aggrieved and wants to bring a lawsuit. You would remind that person of the expense, aggravation, and the possibility of counterclaim before you would ever let such a lawsuit be launched. Now you are not just the lawyer but a client as well, and you are just as likely to take an unobjective view of the matter as any other client.

This does not mean all ingrate clients should be let off scot-free. It only means that if these claims are to be pursued, they must be pursued only after the most careful and reflective contemplation.

## ▶ §10.07(b) Collecting Fees

Lawyers must not only provide clients with clear fee agreements, but also abide by their provisions in charging and collecting their fees, and provide clarifications where necessary.[21] Lawyers who amend fee contracts after the representation has commenced are subject to the law of undue influence designed to enforce their fiduciary obligations to clients [§§6.11, 6.12]. This means that changes to initial agreements are subject to general personal conflict of interest rules [§6.10] and are voidable by the client [8.09].[22]

Lawyers who execute otherwise valid fee contracts may also engage in what ABA Opinion 93-379 called "problematic billing practices." Unfortunately, some of these practices include fraud.[23] Surveys of lawyer billing practices find that more subtle deception, ranging from performing unnecessary work and "estimating" billable hours to deliberately padding bills or expenses, occurs more than occasionally.[24] Of course, if deliberate, these practices constitute

---

[21] *Cox's Case*, 813 A. 2d 429(N.H. 2002) (lawyer who failed to respond to client's request for accounting data reprimanded for violating Model Rules 1.4 and 1.15(b)).

[22] *Brown & Sturm v. Frederick Road Ltd. P'ship*, 768 A.2d 62 (Md. Ct. Spec. App. 2001); 2 Ronald E. Mallen & Jeffrey M. Smith, *Legal Malpractice* §15.9 (West 5th ed. 2000).

[23] Lisa G. Lerman, *Blue-Chip Bilking: Regulation of Billing and Expense Fraud by Lawyers*, 12 Geo. J. Legal Ethics 205 (1999). For example, one judge described the practices of one of these lawyers as "almost fictional," because he included nearly $100,000 billed for services that were never performed, nearly $500,000 for work done by paralegals that was actually performed by secretaries and a receptionist, and $66,000 for legal research that cost the firm $395. His partners helped cover up the fraud when complaints were made. *Id.* at 238. *See also, Dresser Indus. v. Digges*, 1989 U.S. Dist. LEXIS 17396 (D. Md. Aug. 30, 1989). Because the conduct was fraudulent, a later case determined that the law firm's insurer had no contractual obligation to pay the judgment the client obtained against the firm. *St. Paul Fire & Marine Ins. Co. v. Dresser Indus.*, 1992 U.S. App. LEXIS 18561 (4th Cir. Aug. 10, 1992) The lawyer pleaded guilty to one count of mail fraud and was sentenced to 30 months in prison, and ordered to pay $1 million in restitution to the client and a $30,000 fine. Lerman, *supra,* at 264.

[24] *See,* William G. Ross, *The Honest Hour: The Ethics of Time-Based Billing by Attorneys* 23-38 (Carolina Academic Press 1996); Lisa G. Lerman, *Lying to Clients*, 138 U. Pa. L. Rev. 659, 705 (1990). The bill padding was accomplished by billing for hours not actually worked, or by "premium billing," which adds lump sums to a bill based on the lawyer's subjective determination of its value. *Id.* at 709-715.

§10.07(b)    ADDITIONAL ADVICE AND PERSPECTIVE  •  303

fraud,[25] and if done repeatedly, mail or wire fraud under state and federal criminal statutes.[26] When such a breach constitutes a clear and serious violation of a lawyer's duty to a client, it also becomes grounds for total or partial fee forfeiture [§8.10]. Further, sloppy or negligent billing that does not accurately reflect the agreement or the time spent may be grounds for a breach of contract, malpractice, or breach of fiduciary duty claim [§8.06].[27]

Lawyers and law firms must monitor the accuracy of fee billings to prevent both intentional and inadvertent wrongdoing. The power of clients to fire lawyers at any time [§7.02] means that regardless of the nature of the fee agreement, every lawyer must keep records of time actually spent on each matter to be able to establish the alternative basis for quantum meruit recovery. Billing systems should include efficient and nearly simultaneous recording of time. Good record keeping also serves to document adherence to contractual terms, and provides the basis for lawyers to recover fees against clients who refuse to honor their own obligations. In law firms, no lawyer should have carte blanche to send out any bill he or she wishes.[28] Lawyers who lose their fees or are subject to damages in civil actions usually bind their law firms as well. Model Rule 5.1 also makes supervisory lawyers responsible for violations by other lawyers in their firms over whom they have supervisory authority.

To sum up: You have every right to be compensated for your work, as long as the compensation is reasonable. To protect yourself, and increase your chances of avoiding or winning a fee dispute, you should reduce fee agreements to a writing or include them in written retainer agreements [§1.04], and you should keep accurate records of the time you spend on each client matter [§2.07]. The time these tasks

---

[25] *See, e.g., Ratcliff v. Boydell*, 674 So.2d 272 (La. App. 1996) (lawyer who misrepresented amount of client's annuity at settlement to increase his contingent fee and later sued client for defamation and malicious prosecution liable for fraud, intentional infliction of emotional distress, and abuse of process); *Cantu v. Butron*, 921 S.W.2d 344 (Tex. App. 1996) (lawyers who increased fee from 40 to 45 percent liable for fraud and breach of fiduciary duty, including punitive damages).

[26] Lerman, *supra* note n.23 at 263-271 (detailing criminal prosecutions of nine lawyers for billing fraud).

[27] *Cripe v. Leiter*, 703 N.E. 2d 100 (Ill. 1998) (citing cases).

[28] William G. Ross, *The Honest Hour: The Ethics of Time-Based Billing by Attorneys*, 249-260 (Carolina Academic Press 1996).

take will more than repay you in client goodwill and will undergird your action against the ungrateful client if you decide to seek legal recovery of unpaid compensation.

## ➤ §10.08 EXPANDING BEYOND LAW PRACTICE

### ➤ §10.08(a) Doing Fine?

Our firm is doing fine, plenty of clients, lots of good work, but some of my colleagues never seem to be happy. Revenues go up five percent; they wish they went up ten. Everyone gets nice Christmas bonuses. Some of my colleagues think the bonuses at other firms are larger. Ideas about expanding the business change from vague ramblings to a business plan. Why don't we set up an exclusive referral arrangement with a stockbroker? Why don't we offer our clients investment advisory services? Or business consulting? Or computer advice?

The urge to expand beyond the practice of law is not a new one. Lawyers have often offered other services, particularly in some jurisdictions. The incentive to do this, however, seems to have increased many fold in the last decade. But the path to multidisciplinary services is not only fraught with multiple ethical impediments, it is also a potential source for lawyer liability.

Lawyers regularly refer business to other ventures and, of course, lawyers regularly receive business referrals back. But making such arrangements exclusive raises all kinds of questions about whether the lawyers are sacrificing independent professional judgment and whether the lawyers are in effect paying referral fees for business. At a minimum, any referral agreement requires significant disclosure to the clients. Beyond that, the lawyer who goes that route must worry whether the arrangement will create liability to the lawyer for simply making the referral.

Offering services other than legal services in-house raises still more questions. First, lawyers have to ensure that none of their arrangements can be viewed as the sharing of legal fees with non-lawyers and also have to ensure that no non-lawyers end up being viewed as partners of the law firm. Equally important, the offering of non-legal services raises all kinds of questions as to the scope of the client protections provided by the rules of professional conduct [§9.04]. Those who receive non-legal services must recognize that they are not receiving these protections. And even if there is no confusion among the customers for non-legal services, how does the firm deal with its law clients, vis-à-vis these non-legal customers? Are not the law firm's clients entitled to know to what extent, if at all, the law firm is offering non-legal services to the client's adversaries? And certainly no lawyer wants to be challenged by a client who claims the client was misled into thinking it would receive the benefit of attorney-client privilege when, in fact, it will not.

Again, law firms can offer non-legal services but the path to providing these services is filled with potholes. So before you embark on a brave new venture into reciprocal back scratching or one-stop shopping, make sure you think through exactly how you plan to approach the matter.

### ➤ §10.08(b) Whose Rules?

**Our firm has an ancillary business. We sell life insurance. To large employers. Now one of our customers has moved to disqualify us from representing a debtor in bankruptcy, claiming they are a major creditor of that debtor. Can you believe that?**

There is no surprise there. You are a law firm. Unless your engagement to sell insurance made it absolutely clear that the "customer" would receive none of the protections of being your client, the customer may be able to conflict you out. And that's only half the problem!

**What do you mean?**

Well, did you disclose to debtor that one of its biggest creditors was a customer of your firm? Debtor may well claim that your relationship with the life insurance customer creates a material limitation on your ability to represent debtor vis-à-vis this large creditor [§6.08].

### ➤ §10.08(c) Ancillary Businesses And Multidisciplinary Practice

Multidisciplinary practice (MDP) occurs when lawyers and non-lawyers collaborate to provide clients legal and non-legal services. Under current lawyer code rules [§9.04], this is perfectly acceptable so long as lawyers and non-lawyers do not share legal fees or work in an organization in which lawyers and non-lawyers share managerial control. In other words, lawyers can hire non-lawyers but cannot be hired by for-profit organizations controlled by non-lawyers. Lawyers also can refer clients to non-lawyers pursuant to a reciprocal agreement, but only if the agreement is not exclusive and the client is informed of the existence and nature of the agreement.[29]

In 1998, the ABA established a Multidisciplinary Practice Commission that recommended allowing some fee sharing, but the ABA House of Delegates soundly defeated these proposals. Nevertheless, some states are still considering rule changes to allow some form of MDPs. Current proposals include some combination of the following changes:[30]

- Shared ownership or equity interest in the firm with non-lawyers;
- Ancillary business ownership by lawyers;
- Strategic alliances (formal affiliations of law firms and other service providers);
- Specifications that MDP clients be governed by the legal profession's confidentiality and conflict of interest rules;
- Requirements that non-lawyers in MDPs be members of another licensed profession;
- Disclosure to clients that reveals the extent of shared ownership or contractual agreement to provide non-legal services;
- Permission from the relevant court to establish an MDP.

New York, for example, has amended its lawyer code, but has also declared: "Multi-disciplinary practice between lawyers and non-lawyers is incompatible with the core values of the legal profession" and therefore requires "strict division between services provided by lawyers and those provided by non-lawyers."[31] The new rule does allow nonexclusive referral arrangements between lawyers and non-lawyers in professions approved by court rule. Mandatory disclosures to clients also are required.[32]

States considering MDP reform must face a number of issues [§9.02]. First, empirically, do clients want diversified professional services? Second, if client demand is present, will clients benefit from MDPs? Third, if demand occurs and clients seem happy, what will

---

[29] Model Rule 7.2(b)(4).

[30] For an account of proposals, *see,* Robert A. Esperti, *et al., Latest Developments on the State of Multidisciplinary Practice,* 29 Est. Plan. 267 (2002).

[31] N.Y. Code of Prof'l Responsibility, DR 1-107(2002).

[32] N.Y. Comp. Codes R. & Regs tit. 22, pt. 1205 (2005).

happen when a client who receives MDP services claims competence, confidentiality, or loyalty obligations from such an integrated firm? Will courts impose lawyers' fiduciary duties if lawyers are members of the firm even if other professionals offer a large part of the service?

As you might expect, lawyers differ tremendously over the answers to these questions. Those who favor change dream of "an unregulated marketplace," where "clients would have the choice of hiring a single firm that provided all of these services or multiple firms that specialized in some subset."[33] These proponents for change also argue that self-interested economic behavior furthers social welfare in a market economy, and they are willing to dilute or destroy both confidentiality and loyalty. With respect to confidentiality, they maintain that clients can decide when the attorney-client privilege is important enough not to risk an MDP.[34] With respect to loyalty, MDPs could represent clients with adverse interests as well as those who interests are adverse to former clients of the firm in the same or substantially related matters. Screens "may not work perfectly" but, along with "structural separations," would for the most part protect clients from information sharing.[35]

Those who oppose MDPs or exclusive referral arrangements could not disagree more.[36] The social welfare is promoted by the entire law governing lawyers that imposes fiduciary duties on lawyers [Chapters 3-6] to assure that client interests curb lawyer economic advantage. Loyalty rules including imputed disqualification [§§1.30, 6.05] mean that lawyers must say "no" to some clients in order to protect the interests of others.[37] Association with other service providers easily could compromise the confidentiality obligations of lawyers [Chapter 5], because MDPs need shared information among professionals to thrive. Worst of all, MDPs could come to compromise the independent judgment of lawyers [§§6.31, 10.06] in the same way HMOs have come to compromise the independent medical judgment of some physicians. Lawyers may be tempted to cheat on competence

---

[33] Daniel R. Fischel, *Multidisciplinary Practice*, 55 Bus. Law. 951 (2000).

[34] *Id.* at 964.

[35] *Id.* at 966.

[36] Lawrence J. Fox, *Dan's World: A Free Enterprise Dream; An Ethics Nightmare*, 55 Bus. Law. 1533 (2000).

[37] *Id.* at 1557-1559.

if their part of the package is the loss leader that brings in the business but needs to be subordinated to some other service such as the sale of securities or insurance in order to maximize profit.[38]

If MDPs and reciprocal referral agreements grow and multiply, eventually an aggrieved client will seek legal relief, such as malpractice [§8.06], disqualification [§8.08], or fee forfeiture [§8.10]. At that point, courts will have to decide first, whether the law governing lawyers applies [§9.02], and if so, whether it also creates remedies [§9.05] against the entire MDP. In truly integrated entities, ordinary agency principles of vicarious liability easily could mean that the entire firm is subject to the law governing lawyers, and that lawyers in the firm also are subject to legal provisions that govern other professionals with whom they are associated, such as Sarbanes-Oxley requirements for accountants.

For example, in a British case, an accounting firm hired lawyers to offer pre-litigation services in teams with other professionals. They later took on an audit of a matter adverse to the former pre-litigation services client in a substantially related matter. The House of Lords applied the substantial relationship test applicable to lawyers [§6.33] in deciding the dispute, even though the accounting firm argued that such a standard was not required by accounting profession rules for audit matters.[39] The reasonable expectations of the client, who understood that lawyers were part of the pre-litigation services team, trumped the accounting firm's assumption that it could define loyalty and confidentiality obligations by the standards of another profession.

Professionals in MDPs probably will have to face the prospect that the legal standards governing all professionals in the group provide a wide range of remedies [§9.05] to their clients. If you are planning some form of MDP or referral arrangement, we recommend you include in your deliberations whether the expanded liability [§8.06] and range of remedies [§9.05] opened to clients of the firm is worth the prospect of increased profits.

---

[38] *Id.* at 1546-1547.

[39] *Prince Jefri Bolkiah v. KPMG*, 2 A.C. 222, 2 W.L.R. 215 (H. L. 1998).

## ▶§10.09 SUPERVISORY AND SUBORDINATE LAWYERS
### ▶§10.09(a) Supervising Discovery?

It just does not seem right. I was asked to supervise a document production. The search yielded a few unfortunate e-mails to say nothing of a memorandum written by the CFO. I brought the offending documents to the attention of the partner in charge. He tells me that I'll have to produce the e-mails but I can withhold the memo on the ground of privilege. I agreed but as I started thinking about it I wondered how could that memo be privileged? I got up enough nerve to ask and the partner replied that responsibility for making such determinations is why he is paid the big bucks. No reasoning, but he did take responsibility.

Can you simply leave the decision to the partner? Let us hope not. You are a lawyer, albeit one of lower rank in your firm. But that does not absolve you of responsibility. You may accept a decision with which you disagree from a supervising lawyer if it is a reasonable resolution of an arguable question. For example, you might think it is not privileged because a copy was sent to a third party; but the partner might assert that the client can claim the third party was an agent for the purpose of the representation and therefore sending the copy to that individual did not break the privilege. But here it sounds like there is no arguable point. And if that is your view, then this is one of those occasions when you must seek further consultation. It could be you should consult someone in your practice setting. Perhaps your firm has a designated ombudsman with whom you could chat. Whatever the possibilities, this is no time to resolve the question yourself, even if it means going outside your firm to counsel with a former professor or a lawyer who specializes in advising lawyers [§5.12].

Partners, it is true, are more experienced. They also might have a different perspective. But pressures from the client may distract that perspective. Even the most objective of lawyers sometimes succumb to these forces. And partners don't have a monopoly on wisdom. So as difficult as it may be, you must now take responsibility.

### ▶§10.09(b) When To Defer To Another Lawyer's Judgment

Life would be simplified if we could rely on the judgment of an identified sage. But because even the wisest lawyer can miss an issue [§9.02], a nuance in fact, or the meaning of a legal doctrine [§9.06], you may find that you occasionally differ with another lawyer whose judgment you trust (or know nothing about). If so, the first step is to figure out why. It may be because one of you knows more about the facts, the law, or the application of the law to the facts. When you discover why, you need to identify whether the issues [§9.02] include a question of legal ethics as well as a question about the application of "other" law. We have seen, for example, that the lawyer codes [§9.04] read several bodies of law into their provisions, including criminal law [§7.03], the law of fraud [§7.04], and procedural rules [§7.06]. If your disagreement touches on any of these areas of law, more is at stake than just your client's conduct. You need to be clear about the legal limits to your own conduct as well.

Once you identify the reason you disagree and the law governing lawyers implications, you need to ask yourself whether the answer to your question is arguable. If it is not, you may not rely on another lawyer's judgment. One way to make this clear to yourself and others is to write a memo that explains the law governing the matter and why the proper response is or is not arguable. Offer your work product to the lawyer with whom you disagree or ask another experienced lawyer to consider it. Do the same for the law governing lawyers issues [§9.02] and implications of the matter. Be sure to mention relevant and potentially overlapping penalties [§9.05] that conceivably could occur, such as professional discipline, malpractice, disqualification, fee forfeiture, or litigation sanctions [Chapter 8] and ask another experienced lawyer for advice. Many grievance authorities and bar associations can assist you in understanding local lawyer codes [§9.04] if you call a bar hotline, or find a relevant ethics opinion, or request an opinion from an ethics opinion service [§9.07].

If you are not in a position to make what you believe to be the only correct decision and are still uncomfortable with another lawyer's resolution of the issue [§9.01], decide whether you must do something about it (tell the client, a court, the bar, or withdraw from a representation). Ultimately, such a choice might also include a hard look at whether you want to or are able to continue to practice law at that law firm.[40] Remember, criminal activity isn't justified by relying on your

---

[40] *Kelly v. Hunton & Williams,* 1999 U.S. Dist. Lexis 9139 (E.D.N.Y. June 17, 1999) (lawyer who reported partner's billing fraud several times within the firm entitled to cause of action for wrongful discharge where firm conditioned a favorable job reference on his silence if the firm placed him in a position of choosing between continued employment and the consequences of failing to report the partner's conduct to the bar).

§10.10(a)   ADDITIONAL ADVICE AND PERSPECTIVE • 311

supervisor.[41] Nor is failing to correct your senior partner's lie to a court during an ex parte hearing.[42] If you are the supervisory lawyer, failing to properly supervise your associate to be sure the work is done in a timely and competent manner also constitutes an independent breach of the professional rules [§9.04].[43]

## ▶ §10.10 HELPING COLLEAGUES

### ▶ §10.10(a) The Disconnect?

**What a disconnect there is between the statistics we know and the conduct we observe. We know high percentages of the population and even higher percentages of lawyers are alcoholics, suffer from depression, and have other serious behavioral disorders. Yet we look around our practice setting and we see nothing but conscientious professionals working way too hard to deliver excellent services to very demanding clients. And we know that the reality is not in what we observe, but in the statistics. So it is our obligation to be particularly observant and to do our level best to identify those who either are, or might become, troubled lawyers. We do so for our own selfish interests since, by definition, we are responsible for the misdeeds of our colleagues, but also because these are our colleagues and we should be doing everything we can to assist them with their personal problems.**

---

[41] *People v. Casey*, 948 P.2d 1014 (Colo. 1997) (lawyer who assisted his client in committing the crime of criminal impersonation was not relieved of responsibility because he was assigned to the matter by his senior partner and consulted with his senior partner about the case).

[42] *Daniels v. Alander*, 844 A. 2d 182 (Conn. 2004) [(associate who failed to correct partner's false statement to a court witnessed by associate during an emergency custody hearing violated Rule of Professional Conduct 3.3)].

[43] *In re Myers*, 584 S.E.2d 357 (S.C. 2003) (supervising prosecutor who failed to supervise deputy prosecutors privately reprimanded for violating Model Rule 5.1); *In re Wilkinson*, 805 So. 2d 142 (La. 2002) (lawyer who failed to supervise law school graduate not admitted to the bar suspended for 60 days); *In re Sheridan's Case*, 781 A.2d 7 (N.H. 2001) (lawyer whose associate was handling a probate estate had duty to see that work was done properly and, because his misconduct occurred mainly before injuries that might have been protected by the ADA, public censure was proper); *Att'y Grievance Comm'n v. Ficker*, 706 A.2d 1045 (Md. 1998) (lawyer who conducted high volume practice failed to properly supervise inexperienced and overburdened associates so as to avoid incompetent representation; lawyer was suspended for 120 days).

The first problem is recognition. The second problem is what do we do if, in fact, we recognize that one of our colleagues, or even one of our adversaries, is laboring under the handicap of substance abuse or related problems. One's first reaction is undoubtedly denial, and the second reaction, equally predictable, is to let someone else take care of it. But the truth is it is our responsibility, and the further truth is that this is not a responsibility we should undertake without professional help.

It is not for untrained lawyers to engage in interventions or to recommend treatment. Rather, it is for lawyers to counsel with other lawyers who can identify healthcare service providers experienced in these matters and follow their guidance on how to address the problem.[44] It may be that lawyers can play a direct role in assisting the individual, but this is no time for amateur assistance. Many bar associations have committees that help lawyers address these matters. Many hospitals and clinics will provide guidance.[45] Many law firms have employee assistance programs that can be extremely valuable resource tools. Whatever the course, it is a course you must pursue, and pursue with experienced guidance so that your clients don't suffer and your colleagues receive the very best opportunities for addressing their problems.

### ▶ §10.10(b) Law And Life

Lawyers who represent clients zealously within the bounds of the law act as collaborators who translate or mediate between the private

---

[44] ABA Formal Op. 03-429 (2003) (If a lawyer's mental impairment is known to partners in a law firm or to a lawyer having direct supervisory authority over the impaired lawyer, steps must be taken that are designed to give reasonable assurance that such impairment will not result in breaches of the Model Rules. If violations have already occurred, an obligation may exist to report the violation to the appropriate professional authority. If the impaired lawyer resigns or is removed from the firm, the firm may have an obligation to discuss with the client the circumstances surrounding the change of responsibility. The obligation to report a violation of the Model Rules by an impaired lawyer is not eliminated by departure of the impaired lawyer.)

[45] For more facts about addiction and the professions, we suggest Robert Coombs' book *Drug Impaired Professionals*, (Harvard 1997), and an abridged version of one chapter entitled *Addiction's Defining Nature*, 64 Tex. B. J. 166 (Feb. 2001). Additional clinical data can be found in Jordi Camí and Magí Farré, *Drug Addiction*, 349 N. Eng. J. Med. 975 (Sept. 4, 2003).

world of clients and the public world of law. We do the same thing for ourselves, mediating between our own personal values and the law that governs our own conduct. Most people and most lawyers want to reconcile their personal values with their professional life. To do so requires continuing dialogue between your personal beliefs and your professional practice.[46]

Helping colleagues as well as helping clients is an unavoidable and often rewarding part of the collaborative practice of law. In representing clients as well as in assisting colleagues, collaborative lawyers consider both their personal values and the values embodied in the law. They learn from the law governing lawyers to avoid the extremes of both instrumental and directive behavior and to recognize them in other lawyers. They avoid instrumental thinking by being aware of the limits of the law [Chapter 7] and by refusing to "exclude [their own] personal values from all professional decisionmaking."[47] At the same time, they avoid directive thinking by recalling the dictates of fiduciary duty [Chapters 3-6], and by checking their personal beliefs against their professional obligations to represent clients zealously within the bounds of the law. They also recognize that impaired colleagues can lose the ability to recognize these issues. When this occurs, the impaired person who ignores either fiduciary duty or a limit of the law (or both) will put you and your firm at risk of suffering a myriad of client and third-party remedies [Chapter 8].[48] Yet, most impaired lawyers can recover and return to practice.[49]

---

[46] *See*, George W. Kaufman, *The Lawyer's Guide to Balancing Life and Work: Taking the Stress Out of Success,* (ABA 1999).

[47] Bruce A. Green, *The Role of Personal Values in Professional Decisionmaking,* 11 Geo. J. Legal Ethics 19, 56 (1997).

[48] *In re Matson,* 56 P.3d 160 (Kan. 2002) (depression and attention deficit disorder mitigating factors in disciplinary hearing concerning lawyer's incompetence); *State ex rel. Okla. Bar Ass'n v. Schraeder,* 51 P.3d 570 (Okla. 2002) (lawyer may use professional burnout diagnosed by his physician as a mitigating factor in discipline if there is a causal relationship between the medical condition and professional misconduct); S.C. Ethics Ad. Op. 02-13 (2002) (lawyer who refers a client to another lawyer and knows that that the referee-lawyer has developed a medical condition that renders him unable to practice law competently must inform referred client and, subject to client's consent, inform disciplinary authorities).

[49] *Mullison v. People,* 61 P. 3d 504 (Colo. O.P.D.J. 2002) (lawyer who was disbarred from law practice for forging documents, neglecting client matters and diverting client

Ultimately, the law governing lawyers prods us to consider how we ought to respond to those we choose to serve. Fiduciary duty [Chapter 3-6] and the limits of the law [Chapter 7] require concrete action, not just intent or thought. They also prod us to realistically assess risk. Doing this for clients as well as colleagues offers us an opportunity for the blessing of a life that integrates our personal and professional selves. The lawyers able to discover this connection will be most capable of practicing what they advise their clients and colleagues: moving on with their lives, perhaps with a renewed sense of vision, influenced both by the ordinary world and the lessons of law that support it.

---

funds to support his cocaine addiction readmitted ten years later following successful treatment for his drug addiction, full restitution to all affected persons, retaking the bar exam, and candidly acknowledging that his conduct justified disbarment).

# Index Of Subjects

## A

Abandonment of law practice, 8.02
Abuse of process, 8.05(b)
Accommodation clients
　chief financial officers, 1.29(a)
　third-party beneficiary, 1.29(b)
Accomplice statutes, 8.03(a)
Administration of justice, conduct prejudicial to, 8.02
Administration of justice, interference with, 7.03(b)
Administrative regulations, 7.01
ADR rules, 7.01
Adverse ruling, properly appealing, 5.13(c)
Advertising and solicitation
　chat room advertising, 7.13(a)
　disclaimers, 1.07
　do not lie or falsely suggest rules, 1.07
　First Amendment applied to lawyer speech, 7.13(b)
　targeted mailings and e-mail, 1.08(b)
　website advertising, 1.08(a)
Advice from other lawyers, bar counsel, and ethics hotlines, 5.12(a), 5.12(b), 10.02(a), 10.09(b)
Agreement never to sue entity again, 1.23(a)
Aiding and abetting client misconduct, 8.03(a), 10.02(b)
Alibi, false, 5.13(b)
Ancillary businesses, 7.12(b), 10.08(b), 10.08(c)
Anti-money laundering statutes, 5.13(c)
Appeal, right to, 8.02
Appeals
　communication of client choices in, 3.03(c)
　in criminal cases, 7.05(b)
Arbitration
　of fee disputes, 2.13
　of lawyer misconduct disputes, 8.02
Arbitrators, 6.38(b)
Attorney-client privilege, 5.01(b), 5.01(c), 9.04(b)
　ancillary business, 7.12(b)
　exceptions, 5.06(a), 5.06(b)
　express and implied authorization, 5.07(f)
　organizations and employees, 5.04(f), 5.04(g)
　scope of, 5.04(b), 5.04(e)
Audits of trust accounts, 2.14
AUSA, 7.10(e)

## B

Back pay awards, 2.05(b)

Bank accounts of client,
    assignment of, 6.13(a)
Bankrupt entity, 1.21(b)
Beneficiaries, duties owed to,
    8.05(a), 8.05(b)
Bias, 7.09(a)
Billable hours, 2.02(b), 10.07(b)
    actual time spent on matter,
        2.07(a), 2.07(b)
    and fee collection, 2.13
    multiple clients, 2.07(b)
    and quantum meruit, 2.11
Board of directors of client, serving
    on, 6.11(c)
Breach of fiduciary duty, generally,
    1.01
Bribery by lawyer, 7.03(b)
Business deals with client, 6.04
Business deals with clients, 6.10,
    10.01(a), 10.01(b)
    assignment of house, 6.13(a)
    serving as board member,
        6.11(c)
    stock given in lieu of cash,
        6.11(a), 6.11(b)
    written informed consent
        requirement, 6.11(b)
Buyer and seller in real estate
    transaction, 6.27(a)

## C

Candor to the tribunal, 7.08
Chief financial officers as
    accommodation clients,
    1.29(a)
Child abuse reporting statutes,
    5.13(c)
Child support, and contingent
    fees, 2.08(d)
Civil liability, 9.05(b)
Civil rights laws, and fee shifting,
    2.05(c)
Class actions, 1.23(a), 1.23(b)

Client protection fund, 2.14
Client trust accounts. *See* Trust
    accounts
Collaborative client-lawyer
    relationship, 10.03(b),
    10.10(b)
Common knowledge exception to
    expert testimony
    requirement, 8.06(b)
Communication, 1.01, 4.06(c),
    7.03(b), 7.04(c)
    appeals, 3.03(c)
    and attorney-client privilege,
        5.04(b)
    conversation, 3.01
    criminal cases, client choices in,
        3.03(c)
    disclosure, 3.01
    failure to communicate material
        facts, 2.11
    general duty to communicate,
        3.02
    material aspect of case, 6.22(b),
        8.06(b)
    of material information, 8.04
    plea bargains, 3.03(a), 3.03(b)
    settlement offers, 3.03(a),
        3.03(d)
    and waivers of confidentiality
        or conflicts, 3.04, 3.05(a) *et
        seq.*
Competence, 1.01, 7.03(b),
    7.04(c)
    care and diligence, 4.01, 4.05
    common knowledge, 4.06
    not competent to undertake
        matter, 1.02(a)
    obvious errors, 4.06
    and prospective clients, 1.05(d)
    skill and knowledge, 4.02
    third parties, duty owed to,
        8.05(a)
Competitors, representation of,
    6.33(e)

INDEX OF SUBJECTS • 317

Complicity in client misconduct, 7.04, 10.02(b)
Conduct limitations, 3.02
Confidentiality, 1.01, 4.06(c), 8.09(b), 9.04(b)
  authorization to waive, 5.07
  boilerplate warning, 5.04(d)
  client fraud exception, 5.10
  clients with diminished capacity, 1.22, 10.04(b)
  conflict of laws, 5.14(c)
  consent to disclosure, 3.04, 5.03(c)
  and consulting lawyers, 1.10
  continuation of duty after representation, 5.02(b)
  and death of client, 1.24, 5.02(b)
  and engagement letter, 5.14(b)
  exceptions, 5.06(a), 5.06(b)
  express and implied authorization, 5.07(f)
  failure to keep confidences, 8.06(b)
  forfeiture of fee, 2.11
  former clients, 6.36
  future crime exception, 5.09(a), 5.09(b)
  and helpful opponents, 5.07(e)
  identity of client, 5.04(c)
  insurance defense, 1.17(a), 6.32(b), 6.32(d)
  joint clients, 1.15, 6.21, 6.22(a), 6.22(b)
  law and court orders, 5.13
  misuse of confidences, 8.06(b)
  practice in multiple jurisdictions, 5.14(d)
  and privileged information, 5.03(c)
  prospective clients, 1.05(c), 1.05(d), 5.02(a), 5.02(b)
  prospective waivers, 3.05(a)
  and public information, 5.03(a), 5.03(c), 5.04(c)
  and refusal to testify, 5.04(a)
  scope of, 5.01(a), 5.01(b), 5.01(c), 5.03(c)
  seeking advice, 5.12(a), 5.12(b)
  selective waiver, 5.07(b)
  settlement authority, 3.03(d)
  and successor counsel, 5.02(b), 5.11(b)
  third parties present during communications, 5.07(c)
  third-party beneficiary, 1.27(b)
  threatened serious bodily harm exceptions, 5.08
  use of confidential information, 5.03(b)
  waivers of, 3.04, 3.05(b)
Conflict of laws, and confidentiality issues, 5.14(c)
Conflicts check, 1.08(a), 1.10
  consentable conflicts, 1.15
  joint clients, 1.15
  nonconsentable conflicts, 1.15
  pro bono services, 1.14(b)
Conflicts control system, 6.06, 6.07
Conflicts database, 1.11, 1.19, 1.21(b), 1.24, 6.06, 6.07(b)
Conflicts of interest. *See also* specific actions, e.g., Business deals with clients
  arbitrators, 6.38(b)
  buyer and seller in real estate transaction, 6.27(a)
  codefendants in criminal cases, 6.26(a), 6.26(b)
  consentable conflicts, 6.04
  contingent fees, 2.08(d)
  co-parties in civil litigation, 6.25
  corporate buyouts, 1.20(a)
  corporate transactions, 6.29(a)

direct adversity conflicts, 6.08
disqualification, 8.08(b)
divorce and dissolution,
    6.09(a), 6.23(a)
employee deposition, 6.29(b)
errors and mistakes, 4.07(a),
    4.07(b)
failure to avoid impermissible
    conflicts, 8.06(b)
family accident, 6.23(b)
federal and state provisions,
    7.01
fiduciary-client, 1.28
forfeiture of fee, 2.11
former clients (*See* Former
    clients)
government lawyers, 6.37(a),
    6.37(b)
homeowner's association,
    6.29(d)
identifying conflicts, 6.03, 6.04
imputed conflicts, 6.04, 6.05,
    6.20, 6.30(a), 6.30(b)
insurance defense (*See*
    Insurance defense)
issue or positional conflicts,
    6.28(a), 6.28(b)
joint clients, 1.13, 3.05(d),
    6.07(a)(2), 6.09(a), 6.09(b),
    6.21, 6.22(a), 6.22(b), 6.25,
    6.27(d)
joint wills, 6.27(c)
judges, 6.38(b)
law firm imputation of conflict,
    6.05, 6.30(b)
material limitation conflicts,
    6.08
mediator lawyer, 6.38(a),
    6.38(b)
new business ventures, 6.27(b)
nonconsentable, 6.09(a),
    6.09(b)
nonwaivable conflicts, 3.05(b)

organizations and employees,
    1.18(a), 1.18(b), 6.29(e)
personal interests of lawyer,
    6.04, 6.07(a)(1), 6.10
prospective waivers, 3.05(a)
recognizing, 6.08
and referral fees, 1.11
resolving, 1.01, 6.03, 6.04
simultaneous representation of
    adversaries in unrelated
    cases, 6.24
subsidiary transactions, 6.29(c)
third-party beneficiary, 1.27(b)
third-party direction, 6.31(a),
    6.31(b)
third-person influence, 6.31(d)
third-person payment, 6.31(c)
thrust upon conflict, 1.20(a)
unexpected conflicts, 6.02
waiver of, 3.05(b), 3.05(c)
writing requirement for waiver,
    9.04(a)
written disclosures or waivers,
    3.05(c), 3.05(d)
Consensual client-lawyer
    relationship, 1.03(b)
Conspiracy to commit a crime,
    8.03(a)
Constitutionality of advertising
    and solicitation rules,
    7.13(b)
Constitutional law, 7.01
Consulting lawyers as prospective
    clients, 1.10
Consumer protection laws, 2.05(c)
Contact with represented and
    unrepresented persons, 7.10
Contempt, 7.07
Contingent fees, 1.03(a)
    child support, 2.08(d)
    collecting, 2.08(d)
    conflicts of interest, 2.08(d)
    dissolution, 2.08(d)
    divorce, 2.08(d)

INDEX OF SUBJECTS • 319

forfeiture of, 6.17(b)
modification of agreement,
 2.04(a)
reasonableness of, 2.02(b),
 2.08(b)
reverse contingent fees, 2.08(c),
 2.08(d)
statutory fee shifting, 2.05(b)
statutory limitations on, 2.05(a)
windfalls, 2.05(b), 2.08(a)
written agreements, 3.06
Contract law in determining
 establishment of
 relationship, 1.03(b)
Conversion, 8.05(b)
Corporate buyout, 1.20(a)
Corporate whistle blowers, 7.02(d)
Corporations and employees
 and conflicts control,
  6.07(a)(2)
 conflicts in transactions, 6.29(a)
 contact with represented and
  unrepresented persons,
  7.10(d)
 as joint clients, 1.18(a), 1.18(b)
Court appointments
 duty to accept, 1.02(a)
 involuntary appointment,
  1.02(a)
 mandated lawyer-client
  relationship, 1.02(b)
 public policy underlying,
  1.02(b)
Court orders, 7.01, 7.07
Criminal action requested by
 client, 4.04(b)
Criminal actions by client, 7.02(c),
 7.03(b)
Criminal actions by lawyer,
 7.03(b), 8.02, 8.03(a)
Criminal actions by other lawyer's
 client, 7.03(a)
Criminal cases, 7.01
 appeals, 7.05(b)

 communication of client
  choices in, 3.03(c)
 conflicts with representing
  codefendants, 6.26(a),
  6.26(b)
 future crimes, 5.09
 ineffective assistance of counsel,
  4.06(b), 8.07
 pleading in, 4.04(b)
 prevention of future crime,
  5.14(a)
 separate counsel for defendants,
  3.05(b)
Criminal contempt, 7.07
Current clients, and conflicts
 control, 6.04, 6.07(a)(2)

**D**

Damages, 8.06(b), 8.10(b), 8.11,
 9.05(b)
Death of a client
 and confidentiality, 1.24
 confidentiality after, 5.02(b)
 settling case following, 1.21(a)
 survivor statutes, 1.21(b)
 wrongful death statutes, 1.21(b)
Deceit by lawyer, 8.02, 8.04
Deceit practiced by lawyer, 7.03(b)
Defenses to malpractice actions,
 8.06(b)
Deposition abuse, 8.11
Depositions, lying in, 5.13(a)
Depositions of employees, 6.29(b)
Derivative clients, 1.28
Diligence and promptness, 4.05,
 4.06, 8.05(a)
Diminished capacity, clients with,
 1.22, 5.07(f), 5.08(a),
 10.04(b)
 wills, 10.04(a)
Disagreement with partners in
 firm, 8.01
Disclosure, 3.01

Discovery abuse, 7.06(a), 7.06(b), 8.11
Disengagement letter, 1.25, 4.07(b)
Dishonesty by lawyer, 8.02
Disqualification, 1.01, 8.08(a), 8.08(b), 9.05(b)
Divorce and dissolution, 1.21(b)
　conflicts of interest, 6.09(a), 6.23(a)
　conflict with former client, 6.33(c)
　contingent fees, 2.08(d)
　fees and expenses, 2.02(b)
　joint representation, 6.09(a)
　mediation, 6.23(a)
　no-fault divorce, 6.23(a)
　statement of client's rights and responsibilities, 3.06
Double jeopardy, 8.02

## E

Emotional distress, 8.05(b), 8.06(b)
Employees. *See* Corporations and employees; Organizations and employees
Ending a representation, 1.24
Engagement letter, 1.03(a), 1.04
　communication regarding, 3.02
　confidentiality, 5.14(b)
Environmental statutes, and fee shifting, 2.05(c)
Ethics opinions, 9.07(a), 9.07(b)
Executor, appointment as, 6.12
Ex parte communication with judges and jurors, 7.11(a), 7.11(b)
Expenses. *See* Fees and expenses
Expertise or experience, 1.02(b)
Expert testimony in malpractice cases, 8.06(b), 8.07, 9.08(a), 9.08(b), 9.08(c)

Extortion by lawyer, 7.03(b)

## F

Factual research, 4.06, 4.06(b), 5.04(e), 8.07
False or misleading statements in advertising, 7.13(b)
Family businesses as clients, 1.20(b)
Family members
　accident involving, 6.23(b)
　joint wills, 6.27(c)
　prospective clients, 1.13
　third-party direction, 6.31(b)
Fee awards, 2.05(b)
Fees and expenses
　advance payment of, 2.14
　advice about collecting, 1.10
　arbitration of disputes, 2.13
　collecting, 2.02(b), 2.13, 5.11(c), 10.07(a), 10.07(b)
　communication regarding, 3.02
　contingent fees (*See* Contingent fees)
　contracts, 2.01
　defense to payment, 8.08(b)
　disclosure statement of expenses, 2.02(a)
　dissolution cases, 2.02(b)
　divorce, 2.02(b)
　engagement letter, 7.02(a)
　failure to pay, 7.02(a), 7.02(b)
　fees and expenses, 2.02(a), 2.02(b), 2.03
　fee sharing, 3.06
　fee splitting, 2.12(a), 2.12(b)
　and fiduciary duty, 2.02(b)
　and firing by client, 2.07(b)
　and firing of lawyer, 2.11
　fixed or flat fee, 2.09(a), 2.09(b)

INDEX OF SUBJECTS • 321

forfeiture of, 1.01, 2.02(b),
   2.11, 6.17(b), 8.03(a),
   8.10(a), 8.10(b), 9.05(b),
   10.07(b)
hourly fees, 2.07(a), 2.07(b)
   (*See also* Billable hours)
insurance defense, 2.02(b),
   2.09(b)
and joint representation, 1.13
judicial power to limit, 2.06
lien to secure payment, 7.02(b)
modification of, 2.04(a),
   2.04(b)
quantum meruit, 2.02(b),
   2.04(a), 2.07(b), 2.11,
   10.07(b)
reasonableness of, 2.02(a),
   2.02(b), 2.07(b), 2.09(b),
   2.12(b)
referral fees (*See* Referral fees)
retainers (*See* Retainers)
scope of representation, 4.03(a)
sharing with non-lawyers,
   7.12(b)
statutory fee shifting, 2.05(c)
statutory limitations on, 2.05(a)
statutory windfall, 2.05(b)
stock in lieu of cash, 6.11(a),
   6.11(b)
third-party payment, 1.16,
   1.17(a), 1.17(b), 6.31(c),
   10.06(a), 10.06(b)
unanticipated bad case, 2.04(a)
and undue influence, 2.04(b)
upon firing by client, 2.02(b)
on withdrawal from case, 2.11
written agreements, 2.02(a),
   2.02(b), 2.03, 2.12(b), 2.13
Fee shifting statutes, 2.05(c)
Fiduciary-client, 1.28
   conflict of interest, 1.28
   malpractice actions, 1.28

Fiduciary duty, 1.01. *See also*
   specific duty, e.g.,
   Communication
breach of, 4.06(c)
claims for breach of, 2.13
fees and expenses, 2.02(b)
and fee splitting, 2.12(b)
loss of contractual rights,
   8.09(b)
and objectives of representation,
   4.04(b)
obvious errors and common
   knowledge, 4.06(c)
quasi-fiduciary duty, 1.26
remedies for breach of, 8.06(b)
Financial assistance to client, 6.04,
   6.15(a), 6.15(b)
Financial hardship resulting from
   taking case, 1.02(a)
Financial harm threatened by
   client, 7.03(b)
Firing a lawyer, 7.02(c), 10.03(b)
   fees, 2.11
   and fees, 2.07(b)
   fees and expenses, 2.02(b)
Former clients
   and divorce proceedings,
     6.33(c)
   firing a client, 6.33(b)
   interests of, 6.04, 6.07(a)(2)
   peripheral representation,
     6.35(a), 6.35(b)
   receipt of confidential
     information, 6.36
   screening, 6.34
   substantially related
     transactions, 6.33(e)
   substantial relationship test,
     6.33(d)
   withdrawal from case, 6.33(a)
Fraud, 7.01
   in advertising, 7.13(b)
   asserting that dead client is
     actually alive, 1.21(b)

and attorney-client privilege, 5.01(c)
and billable hours, 2.07(b)
by client, 5.10, 7.04, 7.04(c)
and confidentiality, 5.01(c)
by lawyer, 7.03(b), 7.04(c), 8.02, 8.04, 8.05(b), 10.02(b), 10.07(b)
prevention of future fraud, 5.14(a)
Fraudulent action requested by client, 4.04(b)
Frivolous lawsuit
sanctions against, 7.05(b)
withdrawal of complaint, 7.05(a)
Fundraisers held by client, 8.03(a)

## G

Gifts from client, 6.04, 6.12, 8.09(a)
Government agency or official, attempting to influence, 8.02
Government entities, and conflicts, 3.05(b)
Government lawyers, 6.04, 6.05, 6.37(a), 6.37(b)
screening, 6.34

## H

Historical development of professional conduct rules, 9.03(a)
Homeowner's association, 6.29(d)
House belonging to client, assignment of, 6.13(a)

## I

Identifying clients, 1.01 *et seq.*
Identity of client, 5.03(c), 5.04(c), 7.16(a)

Impaired client. *See* Diminished capacity, clients with
Impaired lawyers, 10.10(a), 10.10(b)
Imputed clients, 1.30
Inculpatory statements or acts, 5.07(f)
Ineffective assistance of counsel, 8.07
Information requests by client, 3.02
In-house counsel, termination of, 7.02(d)
Injunctive relief, 8.08(b)
Insider information, 6.04
Insider trading, 5.03(b), 5.07(f), 6.26
Instructions, failure to obey, 8.06(b)
Insurance defense
confidentiality, 6.32(d)
confidential policy defense, 6.32(b)
duty to primary client, 6.32(d)
fees and expenses, 2.02(b)
fixed or flat fee, 2.09(b)
inside counsel to defend insureds, 6.32(d)
joint clients, 1.17(a), 1.17(b)
litigation strategy directed by insurer, 6.32(a)
privileged communications, 1.17(a)
settlements, 6.32(c), 6.32(d)
statement of insured client's rights, 3.06
and third-person payment conflicts, 1.16
Intentional infliction of emotional distress, 8.05(b)
Interest on Lawyer Trust Account (IOLTA), 2.14
Intimidation, 7.13(b)

INDEX OF SUBJECTS • 323

IRS regulations
    disclosure of cash transactions of more than $10,000, 7.16(a)
Issue spotting, 9.02(a), 9.02(b), 9.04(a)

## J

Joint and several liability for representation as a whole, 1.11
Joint clients, 1.15, 10.05(a), 10.05(b)
    boilerplate joint defense agreement, 6.22(a)
    confidentiality, 1.15, 6.21, 6.22(a)
    conflicts checks, 1.15
    conflicts of interest (*See* Conflicts of interest)
    engagement agreements, 1.13
    family accident, 6.23(b), 6.25
    family members, 1.13
    insurance defense, 1.17(a), 1.17(b)
    organizations and employees, 1.18(a), 1.18(b)
    plea bargains, 6.17(b)
    settlements, 6.17(a), 6.17(b)
Joint ventures as clients, 1.20(b)
Joint wills, 6.27(c)
Judges, 6.38(b), 9.03(a)
    ex parte communication with, 7.11(b)
    improper influence of, 8.02
Judicial Conduct Rules, judge violating, 8.02
Judicial opinions, 9.06(a), 9.06(b)
Jurors, ex parte communication with, 7.11(b)
Jury trial
    right to, 8.02
    waiver of, 3.03(c), 4.04(b)

## L

Law firm imputation of conflict, 6.05, 6.30(b)
Lawyer code provisions, 9.04(a), 9.04(b)
Lawyer self-defense, 5.01(c), 5.06(b), 5.11
Legal research, 4.06, 4.06(b), 8.07, 9.01 *et seq.*
Legal services hotline, 1.14(a), 1.14(b), 4.03(b), 5.12(b)
Legal treatises, 9.03(c), 9.05(b)
Liability insurance coverage, 3.06, 8.10(b)
Libel counterclaim, 7.03(a)
Limitation of liability to client, 6.04, 6.16
Limited term pro bono services. *See* Pro bono services
Literary rights, 6.04, 6.10, 6.13
Loyalty, 1.15, 6.01, 8.09(b). *See also* Conflicts of interest
    clients with diminished capacity, 10.04(b)

## M

Malicious prosecution, 8.05(b), 8.11
Malpractice, 1.01, 1.10, 8.03(a), 8.06(a), 8.06(b)
    counterclaim of, 2.13
    counterclaims for, 2.06
    diligence and promptness, 4.06(a)
    fiduciary-client, 1.28
    skill and knowledge, 4.02
    third-party beneficiary, 1.27(b)
    waiver of liability, 4.03(a)
McDade Amendment, 7.10(d)
Mediation
    of divorce settlement, 6.23(a)
    of lawyer misconduct disputes, 8.02

Mediators, 6.38(a), 6.38(b)
Medical information, disclosure of, 5.08(b)
Mental condition impairing ability to represent client, 7.02(c)
Mentoring, 8.01
Minors, lawyers representing fee arrangements, 2.05(a)
Misappropriation by lawyer, 7.03(b)
Misconduct during litigation, 8.02
Misrepresentation, 7.03(b), 7.04(b), 8.02, 8.04
   innocent misrepresentation by client, 5.10(b)
   third-party beneficiary, 1.27(b)
Misstatements to a court, 8.11
Mistake by lawyer, 4.06, 4.07
Mistake made in legal matter, 3.02
Model Rules, violations of, 8.02.
*See also* specific rules
Multidisciplinary practice, 7.12(b), 10.08(a), 10.08(c)

## N

National Lawyer Regulatory Data Bank, 8.02
Negligent misrepresentation, 1.05(b)
New business ventures, 6.27(b)
New client file, 6.07(b)
New client memorandum, 6.06
Non-engagement letter, 1.05(b)

## O

Obedience, 4.04(a), 4.04(b), 4.06(c), 8.09(b)
Objecting to improper evidence or procedures, 8.07
Objectives and means, 4.04(b)
Objectives of representation, 4.04(a)
   communication regarding, 3.02

Officer of the legal system, lawyer as, 1.01
Opinion letters, and third-party beneficiaries, 1.27(a)
Opposing interests in litigation, one firm representing, 3.05(b)
Organizations and employees
   attorney-client privilege, 5.04(f), 5.04(g)
   conflicts of interest (*See* Conflicts of interest)
   contact with represented and unrepresented persons, 7.10(b), 7.10(c)
   as joint clients, 1.18(a), 1.18(b)
   work-product privilege, 5.04(f)

## P

Personal interests of lawyer, 6.04, 6.07(a)(1), 6.10
Personal relationships, and conflicts, 6.19
Physical condition impairing ability to represent client, 7.02(c)
Physical harm, threat of, 5.08(c), 7.03(b)
Plea bargains
   advice about whether to accept, 8.07
   communication regarding, 3.03(a), 3.03(c)
   joint clients, 6.17(b)
Political contributions, 8.03(a)
Prepared witnesses, 5.10(d)
Private attorneys general provisions, 2.05(c)
Privilege, 5.01(a), 9.04(b). *See also* Attorney-client privilege; Work-product privilege
Privileged communications
   insurance defense, 1.17(a)

INDEX OF SUBJECTS • 325

Privileged information, 5.01(a), 5.04(a), 9.02(a)
    boilerplate warning, 5.04(d)
    and confidentiality, 5.03(c)
Privileged persons, 5.04(b)
Probate codes, 2.05(a)
Pro bono services
    conflicts check, 1.14(b)
    legal services hotline, 1.14(a), 1.14(b)
    for nonprofit programs, 1.14(b)
Procedural rules, 7.01
Professional discipline, 1.01, 6.10, 6.17(b), 6.18(b), 7.04(c), 7.06(b), 8.02, 9.05(b)
Promising a particular result, 1.02(b)
Proprietary interest in litigation, 6.04
Proprietary interest litigation, 6.14
Prosecutorial discretion, 8.02
Prospective clients
    advertising, 1.07
    competence owed to, 1.05(d)
    confidentiality, 1.05(c), 1.05(d), 5.02(a), 5.02(b)
    consulting lawyers, 1.10
    family members, 1.13
    in-person solicitation of, 7.13(b)
    non-engagement letter, 1.05(b)
    pro bono services (*See* Pro bono services)
    prospective waivers, 1.05(c)
    public speeches, 1.06
    referral fees, 1.11
    rejection of, 1.05(a)
    social gatherings, 1.09
    unrepresented parties, 1.12
Public information, and confidentiality, 5.03(a), 5.03(c), 5.04(c)
Publicity, trial, 7.14(a)
Public offerings, 1.27(b)
Public speeches, 1.06
Puffing, 5.10(a)

## Q

Quasi-clients, 1.26

## R

Reciprocal referral agreements, 10.08(c)
Referral fees, 2.12(a), 10.08(a)
    and conflict of interest, 1.11
    prospective clients, 1.11
Reliance by unrepresented third parties who may be beneficiaries of client, 1.05(b)
Remedies, choice of, 9.05
Reorganizations, 1.21(b)
Repugnant actions taken by client, 1.02(a)
Restatement, 9.03(b)
Restricting right of lawyer to practice law, 7.12(a)
Restriction on right to practice law, 1.23(a)
Retainer agreement, 1.03(a), 7.02(a)
Retainers
    advanced payment retainer, 2.10(b)
    advance payment of, 2.14
    client trust accounts, 2.10(b)
    general or availability, 2.10(b)
    nonrefundable, 2.10(a), 2.10(b)
    special or specific, 2.10(b)

## S

Sanctions against lawyer, 8.11
Sarbanes-Oxley obligations, 7.16(b), 10.02(b)
Scope of representation, 3.02, 4.03(a), 4.03(b)

Screening
    defined, 6.34(b)
    state lawyer codes permitting, 6.34(c)
    without client consent, 6.34(a)
SEC, practice before, 7.16(b)
Securities fraud, 8.05(b)
Securities laws, and fee shifting, 2.05(c)
Self-incrimination, privilege against, 8.02
Settlements
    aggregate settlements, 6.17(a), 6.17(b)
    communication regarding, 3.03(a), 3.03(b), 3.03(c), 3.03(d)
    confidentiality, 3.03(d)
    following death of client, 1.21(a)
    instructions from client, 4.04(b)
    insurance defense, 6.32(c), 6.32(d)
    and limitations on liability, 6.16
    negligent advice to settle, 8.06(a)
    opinion about proposed settlement, 4.03(b)
    with represented persons absent their lawyer, 7.10(a)
    ridiculous offers, 3.03(a)
    and uncertified class, 1.23(a)
    unreasonable clients, 3.03(b)
Sexism, 7.09(a)
Sexual relationship with client, 6.04, 6.10, 6.18(a), 6.18(b)
Shared office space, 1.30
Shareholders, actions by, 10.02(b)
Side-switching, 6.30(a)
Slander counterclaim, 7.03(a)
Social gatherings, and prospective clients, 1.09

Social security disability claims, 2.05(a)
Solicitation. *See* Advertising and solicitation
Sovereign immunity, 8.07
Specialized area of practice, 4.02, 4.03(b)
Standard of care, 1.02(b)
Status of legal matter, 3.02, 4.07(b)
Statutes of limitations, 4.06(a), 4.07(a)
    case-within-a-case requirement for malpractice action, 8.06(b)
    and limitations on liability, 6.16
    malpractice actions, 8.07
Stolen property received by lawyer, 8.03(a)
Subsidiaries as client, 1.20(b), 6.29(c)
Substance abuse by lawyers, 10.10(a), 10.10(b)
Successor counsel, 10.03(a), 10.03(b)
    confidentiality, 5.11(b)
    and confidentiality, 5.02(b)
Suicidal client, 5.08(a), 10.04(b)
Suing one's own client, 3.05(b)
Supervisory lawyers, 10.09(a), 10.09(b)
Survivor statutes, 1.21(b)

**T**

Targeted mailings and e-mail, 1.08(b)
Tax audits, and lying by client, 7.04(d)
Tax avoidance by client, 7.04(a)
Tax compliance matters, 5.10(c)
Testamentary gifts, 6.12, 8.09(a)

Testimony by client, 3.03(c), 4.04(b)
Theft by lawyer, 7.03(b)
Third parties, duties owed to, 8.05
Third-party beneficiaries
    accommodation clients, 1.29(b)
    confidentiality, 1.27(b)
    conflict of interest, 1.27(b)
    duty to intended beneficiaries, 1.27(b)
    malpractice actions, 1.27(b)
    misrepresentation action, 1.27(b)
    and opinion letters, 1.27(a)
Third-party direction, 10.06(a), 10.06(b)
Third person, interests of, 6.04, 6.07(a)(2), 6.31(a), 6.31(b)
Third-person influence, 6.31(d)
Title VII cases, 2.05(b)
Tort cases, 7.01
Torts analysis of client-lawyer relationship, 1.03(b), 1.05(a)
Trial publicity by lawyers, 7.14(a)
Trust accounts, 2.13
    rules governing, 2.14
    and special retainers, 2.10(b)
Trustee, appointment as, 6.12

## U

Unbundled legal services, 4.03(a), 4.03(b)
Undiscovered case, 7.08(a)
Undiscovered conviction, 7.08(b)
Undiscovered witness, 7.08(c)
Undue influence, 4.07(b), 7.13(b), 8.09(b), 10.01(b), 10.07(b)
    and fee modification, 2.13
    and fee modifications, 2.04(b)
Unrepresented parties: prospective clients, 1.12

## W

Websites
    advertising, 1.08(a)
    broadside e-mail, 7.13(a)
    legal research, 9.03(a), 9.03(b), 9.03(d), 9.07(b)
    targeted e-mail, 1.08(b)
Wills
    clients with diminished capacity, 10.04(a)
    joint, 6.27(c)
    third-party direction, 6.31(b)
Withdrawal, 1.10, 4.04(b), 10.03(b)
    errors and mistakes, 4.07(b)
    fees, 2.11
    former clients, 6.33(a)
    involuntary withdrawal, 7.02(c)
    legal grounds for, 7.02(c)
    when client is committing crime, 7.03(b), 7.04(c)
Withdrawal of complaint, 7.05(a)
Witness
    lawyer as, 6.04, 7.15(a), 7.16(b)
    limitation on access to, 7.10(f)
Witnesses' statements, and work-product privilege, 5.05(b)
Worker's compensation cases, 2.05(a)
Work-product privilege, 5.01(b), 9.04(b)
    exceptions, 5.06(a), 5.06(b)
    express and implied authorization, 5.07(f)
    inadvertent disclosure, 5.07(d)
    notes, memoranda, and other materials, 5.05(c)
    organizations and employees, 5.04(f)
    scope of, 5.04(e), 5.05(a)
    witnesses' statements, 5.05(b)
Wrongful termination of in-house counsel, 7.02(d)